Get a FREE eBook

To register this book, scan the code or go to
www.manning.com/freebook/saikali

By registering you get

- **FREE eBook copy**
  download in PDF and ePub

- **FREE online access**
  to Manning's liveBook platform

- **FREE audio**
  read and listen online in liveBook

- **FREE AI Assistant**
  it knows the book and what you are reading when it answers

- **FREE in-book testing**
  fun tests to lock in your knowledge

In Manning's liveBook platform you can share discussions and comments with other readers, add your own bookmarks and highlights, insert personal notes anywhere on the page, see color versions of all the book's graphics, download source code and other resources, and more!

To register, scan the code or go to www.manning.com/freebook/saikali

 MANNING

Software Security for Developers

i

Software Security for Developers

WITH EXAMPLES IN JAVA AND SPRING

ADIB SAIKALI
LAURENŢIU SPILCĂ

MANNING
SHELTER ISLAND

Manning Publications Co.	Development editor: Dustin Archibald
20 Baldwin Road	Technical development editor: John Guthrie
PO Box 761	Review editor: Angelina Lazukić
Shelter Island, NY 11964	Production editor: Keri Hales
	Copy editor: Keir Simpson
	Proofreader: Jason Everett
	Typesetter and cover designer: Marija Tudor

ISBN 9781617298585
Printed in the United States of America

brief contents

v

contents

preface

What does security mean in the daily life of a software developer? Many would answer with words like *encryption, authentication,* and *compliance.* Others might think of security as something handled by a separate team, reviewed late in the process, or added through configuration and checklists. In practice, security is none of these things alone. It's a property that emerges from thousands of small decisions made while designing, implementing, and operating software.

As developers, we spend most of our time building systems that communicate, store data, and make decisions on behalf of users. Every one of these activities carries implicit trust assumptions. Which data can be trusted? Which systems are allowed to talk to each other? Who is allowed to perform an action, and under what conditions? These questions are rarely labeled "security work," yet they define how secure a system actually is.

Security problems often arise not because developers ignore security but because they don't completely understand the underlying mechanisms. Encryption is enabled, but it's used incorrectly. Authentication works, but authorization is too coarse or too permissive. Certificates are configured, but their trust model is unclear. In many cases, the system appears to function correctly until it fails in subtle ways, so we must understand both what a mechanism does and what it doesn't do.

This book was written to help developers build that understanding. Rather than present security as a collection of rules or defensive tricks, it explains the building blocks of modern application security—cryptography, identity, secure communication, and authorization—and shows how they fit together in real systems. The focus is on clarity, practical reasoning, and avoiding common misconceptions that lead to fragile or insecure designs.

All examples in this book were written in Java simply because a concrete language is necessary to explain ideas precisely. The concepts themselves, however, aren't tied to Java or the Java virtual machine (JVM). The security principles discussed here apply regardless of language, framework, or platform.

Our goal is not to turn you into a security specialist but to make you a more effective and confident developer—one who can reason about security, recognize risky patterns, and make informed tradeoffs. In modern software systems, security isn't a separate concern; it's part of professional software development. We hope that this book helps you treat it that way.

acknowledgments

This book wouldn't be possible without the large number of smart, professional, and friendly people who helped us throughout its development process.

We'd like to thank the entire Manning team for their huge help in making this book a valuable resource. We especially want to call out Dustin Archibald for being incredibly supportive and professional. His advice brought great value to this book.

Thank you also to our friend Ioana Göz for the drawings she created for the book. She easily turned our thoughts into the cartoons you'll discover here and there.

Further, we'd like to thank everyone who reviewed the manuscript and provided useful feedback that helped us improve the content of this book: Adrian Rossi, Alain Lompo, Anirudh Murali, Antonio Bruno, Bobby Lin, Christoph Schubert, Clifford Thurber, Conor Redmond, Diego Lapiduz, Dima Knivets, Dror Helper, Emilio Grande, Gitanjali Vohra, Grant Lennon, Greg MacLean, Jakob Mayr, Jeremiah Griswold, Joe Ivans, Joel Caplin, Jose Lecaros Cisterna, Matthew Todd, Miguel Montalvo, Mladen Knežić, Nicholas Selpa, Özay Duman, Patricia Ray, Radhakrishna MV, Renato Gentile, Richard Meinsen, Ryan Sharif, Sam De Coster, Sani Sudhakaran Subhadra, Sanjeev Jaiswal, Snahil Singh, and Travis Hoyt.

about this book

Because you've opened this book, we assume that you're a software developer or are closely involved in building software systems that run in production and handle real users, real data, and real risks. You might work primarily with Java and the JVM, but the principles in this book apply equally if you use Kotlin, Scala, or any other modern platform. Security isn't tied to a single language; it's tied to how systems are designed, built, and operated.

As a developer, you already make security-related decisions every day, often without realizing it. How you store passwords, how services talk to one another, how keys and certificates are managed, how data is serialized, logged, or cached—all these choices have security implications. Yet many security concepts are taught at a highly theoretical level or from the perspective of attackers, leaving developers unsure how to apply them in real systems.

This book takes a different approach. It focuses on security from a developer's point of view. It explains how systems fail, how security mechanisms actually work, and how to use them correctly. The goal isn't to turn you into a cryptographer or a security specialist; we want to give you enough understanding to make good decisions, recognize dangerous patterns, and ask the right questions.

Throughout the book, we focus on practical scenarios drawn from real-world systems: microservices, APIs, cloud deployments, and enterprise environments. We emphasize why things exist, not simply how to configure them. When something goes wrong, you should understand what broke, why it broke, and how to fix it safely. By the end of the book, you should feel more confident discussing security topics with colleagues, reviewing security-related code, and designing systems that are secure by default rather than secure by accident. We discuss topics such as the following and illustrate them with examples:

- Core security principles every developer should know
- How cryptography works in practice (and where it's often misused)
- Secure communication using Transport Layer Security (TLS) and mutual TLS (mTLS)
- Authentication, authorization, and identity in distributed systems
- How to protect secrets, keys, and certificates
- Common security pitfalls in application and system design

Who should read this book

This book is for software developers who want to understand security and build systems that are safe by design. Regardless of the programming language you use, security concepts such as authentication, encryption, identity, and secure communication apply everywhere. If you write code that runs in production, handles user data, or communicates over a network, security isn't optional; it's part of your job.

The book is especially valuable for developers who feel that security is often presented as too abstract or specialized. It explains why security mechanisms exist, what problems they solve, and how they fail when they're misunderstood or misused. The goal is to give you the knowledge you need to make informed decisions and avoid common and costly mistakes.

All examples in this book were written in Java. We made that choice for consistency and clarity, not because the material is Java-specific. The principles, patterns, and pitfalls discussed here apply equally to any modern programming language or platform.

The only prerequisite is a basic understanding of programming concepts. No security knowledge is required.

How this book is organized: A road map

This book is divided into five parts, each addressing a distinct aspect of application security. The progression is intentional because security is best understood by starting with the big picture and then gradually moving toward concrete mechanisms, protocols, and real-world service-to-service interactions. You can read the parts independently, but following them in order will give you a coherent mental model of how modern application security fits together:

- *Part 1—Application security: The big picture*

    We begin by looking at application security as a whole. This part explains what application security means, why it matters, and how it fits into modern software systems. We introduce key concepts such as trust boundaries, threat models, and security responsibilities, and we discuss common standards used for authentication and service-to-service communication. The goal is to establish context and align expectations before diving into specific technologies.

- *Part 2—Cryptography foundations*

    Cryptography underpins almost every security mechanism used today but is often misunderstood or misapplied. In this part, we focus on the fundamentals of cryptography as used in real systems: message integrity, authentication, symmetric encryption, and public key cryptography. We explore both RSA and elliptic-curve–based approaches, emphasizing practical use cases, guarantees, and common mistakes rather than mathematical detail.

- *Part 3—Securing communication channels*

    When cryptographic foundations are in place, we turn to secure communication. This part covers public key infrastructure (PKI), X.509 certificates, and TLS. You'll learn how certificates are issued and managed, how trust is established between systems, and how TLS protects data in transit. The focus is on understanding what these mechanisms guarantee—and what they don't—so you can reason about secure communication with confidence.

- *Part 4—Modern authentication and identity*

    Modern applications rarely rely on simple username-and-password authentication. In this part, we explore contemporary identity and authentication mechanisms, including JSON Object Signing and Encryption (JOSE), OAuth 2.0, OpenID Connect (OIDC), and single sign-on (SSO). We also examine passwordless approaches such as magic links, one-time passwords, and WebAuthn. This section explains how identity flows work end to end and where they commonly fail in practice.

- *Part 5—Securing service-to-service call chains*

    Finally, we focus on securing communication between services in distributed systems. This part addresses service identity and authorization across call chains, including role-based, attribute-based, and relationship-based access control models. The emphasis is on designing authorization that scales with system complexity, avoids implicit trust, and remains understandable as systems evolve.

Each chapter is designed to stand on its own, allowing you to jump directly to topics that are relevant to your current work. But following the road map in order will help you develop a complete understanding of application security, from high-level concepts to concrete mechanisms used in modern distributed systems.

About the code

The book comes with about 30 projects designed to show particular applications of the discussed security topics. Even if the Java technologies we use are less relevant for the techniques we teach, we chose to use the latest long-term-supported Java version (Java 21) and Spring, one of the most-used Java application frameworks today.

Each project is built with Maven, making it easy to import it into any IDE. We used IntelliJ IDEA to write the projects, but you can choose to run them in Eclipse, Apache NetBeans, or any other tool of your choice. The appendix gives you an overview of installation and setup.

This book contains many examples of source code both in numbered listings and inline with normal text. In both cases, source code is formatted in a `fixed-width font` `like this` to separate it from ordinary text. Sometimes, code is also **`in bold`** to highlight code that has changed from previous steps in the chapter, such as when a new feature adds to an existing line of code.

In many cases, the original source code has been reformatted; we've added line breaks and reworked indentation to accommodate the available page space in the book. In rare cases, even this was not enough, and listings include line-continuation markers ( ). Additionally, comments in the source code were removed from the listings when the code is described in the text. Code annotations accompany many listings, highlighting important concepts.

You can get executable snippets of code from the liveBook (online) version of this book at https://livebook.manning.com/booksoftware-security-for-developers. The complete code for the examples in the book is available for download from the Manning website at https://www.manning.com/books/software-security-for-developers and from GitHub at https://github.com/Software-Security-For-Developers/software-security-for-developers.

liveBook discussion forum

Purchase of *Software Security for Developers* includes free access to a private web forum run by Manning Publications where you can make comments about the book, ask technical questions, and receive help from the authors and other users. To access the forum and to subscribe to it, go to https://livebook.manning.com/#!/book/software-security-for-developers/discussion.

Manning's commitment to our readers is to provide a venue where meaningful dialogue between individual readers and between readers and authors can take place. It isn't a commitment to any specific amount of participation on the part of authors, whose contributions to the forum remain voluntary (and unpaid). We suggest that you try asking the authors some challenging questions lest their interest stray! The forum and the archives of previous discussions will be accessible on the publisher's website as long as the book is in print.

about the authors

ADIB SAIKALI is a software engineer and architect with extensive experience designing and building secure, large-scale distributed systems. He has worked on numerous projects across various industries, helping teams adopt modern security standards and best practices in real-world environments. Adib is passionate about application security and believes that developers play a critical role in building secure systems, which drives his work in mentoring, sharing knowledge, and advocating for practical, developer-friendly security approaches. He can be reached at X (Twitter) handle @asaikali.

LAURENȚIU SPILCĂ is a dedicated development lead and trainer at Endava and a Java Champion. He has experience with dozens of projects that used various technologies of the Java ecosystem. Laurențiu believes that it's important not only to deliver high-quality software but also to share knowledge and help others upskill. This belief drives him to design and teach courses related to Java technologies and deliver presentations and workshops. You can reach him at X (Twitter) handle @laurspilca or on YouTube at handle @laurspilca.

about the cover illustration

The figure on the cover of *Software Security for Developers* is "Armenien de perse," or "Armenian of Persia," taken from a collection by Jacques Grasset de Saint-Sauveur, published in 1788. Each illustration is finely drawn and colored by hand.

In those days, it was easy to identify where people lived and what their trade or station in life was by their dress alone. Manning celebrates the inventiveness and initiative of the computer business with book covers based on the rich diversity of regional culture centuries ago, brought back to life by pictures from collections such as this one.

Part 1

Application security: The big picture

Computer security is a vast field with many technologies that must be learned independently and then combined correctly in an application. Application developers and architects typically learn security technologies on the job when they first encounter them, under pressure to deliver product features and bug fixes. Reading blog posts, copying and pasting configuration settings, and searching Stack Overflow (or, more recently, using AI tools) for help can leave developers feeling that they don't understand security and don't have the time and resources to learn it properly.

Part 1 aims to provide a step-by-step plan that breaks security technologies into easily digestible chunks that a developer or architect can learn quickly and independently on the job. The plan starts by building a mental model of cloud-native application security. The model allows you to answer the following questions with confidence:

- What security technologies do you need to know to implement security on the application you're currently working on?
- What is the best order in which to learn security technologies so you don't get stuck because you're missing a prerequisite for what you're learning?
- What level of depth should you aim for when learning a security technology?
- What is the division of roles and responsibilities between application developers, architects, cloud automation engineers, infrastructure providers, and security engineers?

Part 1 will help you grasp the big picture and connect the dots between the security standards and technologies widely used for cloud-native applications. It will also help you zoom in on the parts of the book most relevant to your needs.

Making sense of
application security

This chapter covers

- Why learning security is important
- The consequences of poor security practices
- What are the roles in the information security field
- Identifying the security skills you should possess as an application developer

Every week we are treated to a headline about some security vulnerability in a widely used piece of software or a data breach at a mega-corporation affecting millions of users (figure 1.1). My bank replaced my credit card twice in a five-year period due to data breaches at large retailers where I shopped.

We used to think that security vulnerabilities are primarily a software issue. Hardware security vulnerabilities have been common in recent years, though. The Meltdown and Spectre vulnerabilities, disclosed in January 2018, allowed attackers to bypass CPU hardware protections and gain unauthorized memory access (https://meltdownattack.com/). In a cloud or multi-tenant environment, Meltdown and

Spectre made it possible for one cloud tenant to see the memory of another tenant. The hardware walls we depend on to isolate workloads were suddenly full of holes for attackers to sneak through.

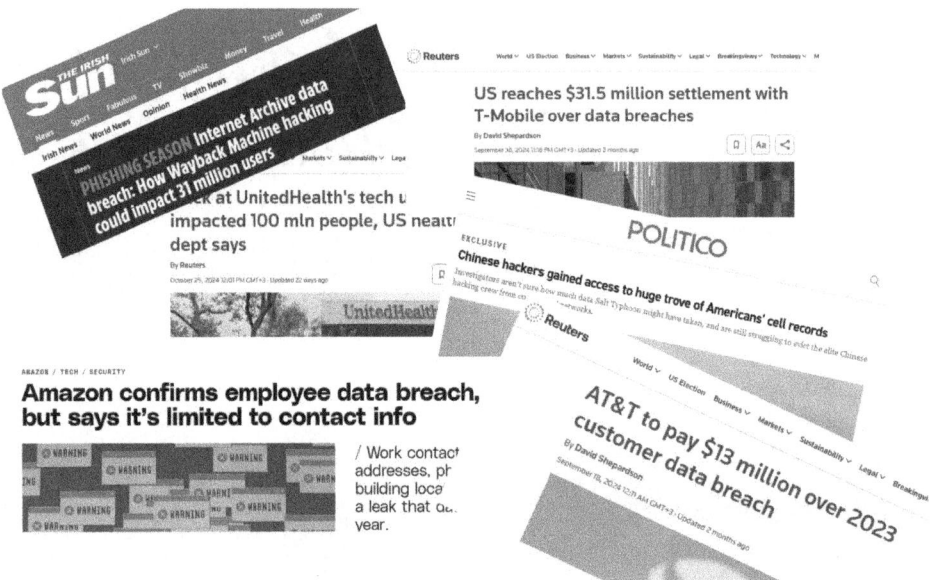

Figure 1.1   Headlines showcasing major recent data breaches and security vulnerabilities, emphasizing the widespread impact on millions of users and the persistent threat to digital security

The past few years have taught us that every layer of the stack, from hardware all the way to JavaScript in a web browser, can have security vulnerabilities. Security is everyone's collective responsibility to build and run IT systems, from hardware engineers who design the processors in our phones to application developers who build the e-commerce applications that keep our kitchens stocked with food. Regardless of your role in the IT world, security is your responsibility.

1.1   *Developers' responsibility in software security*

This book helps software developers understand security in a practical, realistic way. It explains why modern systems are hard to protect and what tradeoffs we face between speed, cost, and safety. You'll learn the core ideas behind cryptography, authentication, and secure communication, and how they show up in everyday tools like TLS, certificates, and cloud platforms. If some of these terms are new, they won't stay that way for long.

This isn't a book about becoming a hacker or a cryptography professor. It's a guide to building software that doesn't become tomorrow's headline. A serious security incident can end a company.

1.1.1 *What does secure development actually look like?*

To make this concrete, let's look at a simple example. Suppose you build a web application that allows users to search for a product by name. The application receives input from a web form and queries a database. A naive implementation might look like this:

```
String query = "SELECT * FROM products WHERE name = '" + userInput + "'";
Statement stmt = connection.createStatement();
ResultSet rs = stmt.executeQuery(query);
```

At first glance, this looks harmless. The developer simply takes the user's input and builds a SQL query. But this common approach opens the door to a class of attacks known as SQL injection. If an attacker enters the following input:

```
' OR '1'='1
```

The query becomes

```
SELECT * FROM products WHERE name = '' OR '1'='1'
```

Now the database returns all products instead of one. With more malicious input, an attacker could delete data, modify records, or extract sensitive information. This vulnerability exists not because the developer intended harm, but because the developer did not understand how untrusted input interacts with the database. Secure development means recognizing these risks and writing code that prevents them. In this case, the secure solution would use parameterized queries or prepared statements.

This example is a classic one, and you may have already heard of SQL injection. It serves as a simple illustration of what a security flaw looks like and why we must adopt a security-first mindset. Throughout this book, we won't focus only on SQL injection–type issues, but on a wide range of scenarios—some simple, some more complex—that can lead to incorrect application behavior and negatively impact users and organizations.

As a developer, security shows up in your daily work in several stages:

- *Design*—Choosing authentication mechanisms, deciding how services communicate, defining trust boundaries
- *Implementation*—Writing code that validates input, uses encryption correctly, and avoids insecure patterns
- *Dependency Management*—Selecting and updating third-party libraries
- *Configuration*—Enabling TLS, configuring identity providers, setting secure defaults
- *Deployment and Maintenance*—Responding to vulnerabilities, patching dependencies, rotating secrets

This book walks through these responsibilities step by step. You will learn not only what the standards and protocols are, but how they influence your decisions at each stage of the development lifecycle.

1.1.2   *How security expectations shape the developer's role*

The heightened focus on security by senior business leaders affects application developers in the following ways:

- Use all product security features: executives expect developers to use every security feature available in products to secure an application. Do you know how to configure and use the security features in the application server, database, object store, message broker, API gateway, service mesh, cloud services, programming language, and development frameworks being used on a project you are working on? It is no longer enough to know how to use a product, you must know how to use it securely.
- Follow corporate security standards: executives expect applications to pass strict corporate security assessments and audits. As a developer, you must explain to assessors and auditors how your application meets corporate security standards. This means you need to be able to speak the security language used by information security professionals so you can avoid costly remediation work to fix security issues late in the development cycle.
- Design and implement secure applications: executives expect architects and developers to design and implement secure applications. This means that you must be familiar with many security protocols and technologies required to design and implement secure applications.
- Enable DevSecOps Transformation: executives are investing heavily in breaking down the silos between the development, operations, and security teams. We call this set of practices DevSecOps. As a developer you need to become familiar with new tools, processes, and practices used to implement DevSecOps.

Figure 1.2 provides a map of the broad areas of application security. As a developer, you spend your time in the middle layer of the pyramid. The top of the diagram above represents the goals of senior business leaders to build secure applications that can stand up to attacks. The higher layers of the diagram depend on the layers below them. To secure an application, you need to use security libraries; for example, a Java web application might use Spring Security to authorize user access.

But security libraries are not enough to provide security. You must design, code, and maintain the application in a secure way by following the corporate security practices for application development, for example, performing a security code review or setting code analyzers that detect common security coding mistakes.

Security libraries and frameworks provide implementations of industry-standard protocols and patterns in specific programming languages. For instance, the Java Standard Libraries include support for *Transport Layer Security* (TLS), which we'll explore in chapter 11, while Spring Security offers robust support for *OpenID Connect* (OIDC), discussed in chapters 12 and 13. Developers often invest significant effort into mastering these security libraries, which are critical to building secure applications, though many developers find these libraries challenging to learn and cumbersome to use effectively (figure 1.3).

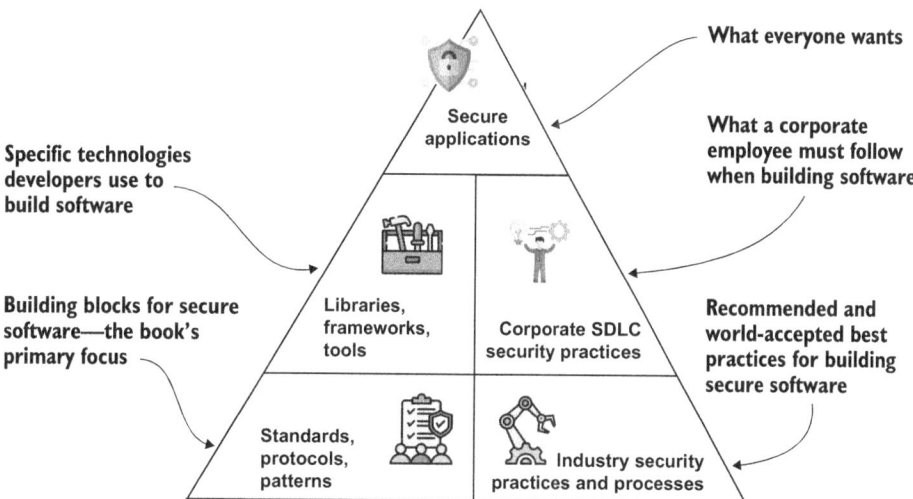

Figure 1.2   Layers at the top depend on the layers below them. All the layers are required to produce secure application. The standards, protocols, and patterns used to secure applications are the primary focus of this book; they are the foundation that you need to use security libraries in your application effectively.

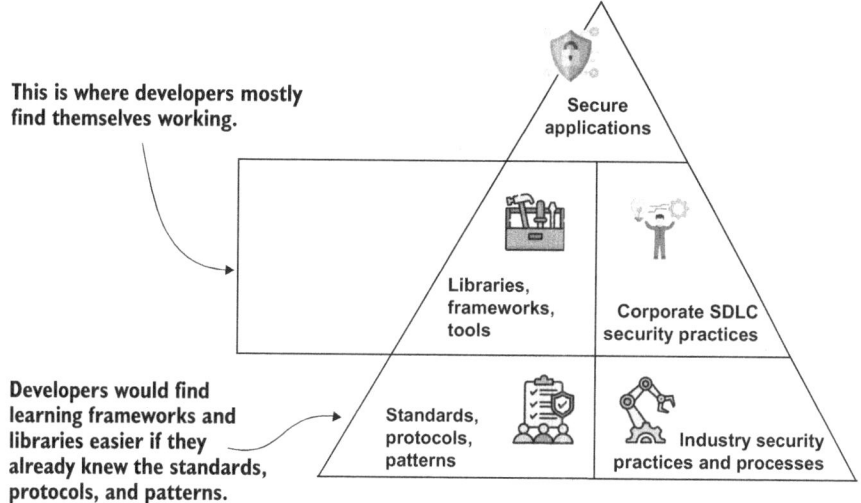

Figure 1.3   While developers often focus on libraries, frameworks, and tools at the mid-level, true security stems from foundational knowledge of standards, protocols, and patterns, as well as adherence to corporate and industry security practices. Bridging the gap between these layers leads to more effective and secure development.

The root cause of developer difficulties using security libraries is a lack of knowledge about the underlying standards, protocols, and patterns the libraries implement. If you understand the underlying security standards, protocols, and best practices, you will find security libraries and frameworks much easier to learn and use. For example, if you understand the OpenID Connect standard, you will find configuring *Single Sign On* (SSO) authentication with Spring Security easy to configure and debug.

> **TIP** If you are familiar with the standards, protocols, and patterns, using security libraries and frameworks becomes much easier. Investing time to understand these underlying principles will significantly enhance your ability to work effectively with security tools.

We focus on teaching you the standards, protocols, and patterns implemented by the majority of application security libraries and frameworks through understanding the use case sample applications. The sample applications are implemented in Java using plain Java but also open-source frameworks such as Google Tink, Nimbus, Spring Security and others.

1.2   *Securing the supply chain risk*

Applications are built on top of hundreds of open-source libraries and propriety software components. For example, today I am working on a Spring Boot application that depends on 106 open-source third-party libraries. I have seen some enterprise applications with 250+ library dependencies. Reusing software components across applications is a huge time and cost saver. It also introduces the possibility of catastrophic security failures.

In 2017, the American credit reporting agency Equifax was hacked, exposing the credit histories of 150 million American citizens. As of May 2019, Equifax has spent over 1.4 billion dollars on cleanup costs (https://www.bankinfosecurity.com/equifaxs -data-breach-costs-hit-14-billion-a-12473). The hack was caused by a known vulnerability (CVE-2017-5638) in the Apache Struts library that Equifax failed to patch even though the vulnerability was known for months (https://www.zdnet.com/article/equi fax-confirms-apache-struts-flaw-it-failed-to-patch-was-to-blame-for-data-breach/). The Equifax hack illustrates the importance of keeping all components in an application's software supply chain updated.

In 2018, a backdoor for stealing Bitcoin was added to a popular JavaScript library called Event-Stream, which averages 2 million weekly downloads from the NPM repository (https://www.zdnet.com/article/hacker-backdoors-popular-javascript-library-to -steal-bitcoin-funds/). The backdoor successfully attacked the Copay Bitcoin wallet versions 5.0.2 to 5.1 (https://arstechnica.com/information-technology/2018/11/hacker -backdoors-widely-used-open-source-software-to-steal-bitcoin/). The attack occurred after the original author of the Event-Stream package got tired of working on it and transferred control of the project to a new developer who added the backdoor.

The Event-Stream attack is not an isolated incident. Many other attacks like it have been reported over the past few years. The Event-Stream attack illustrates the importance of vigilance against software supply chain attacks. Attacks against the software supply chain are increasing because they are highly effective and devastating.

To secure an application, all direct and indirect dependencies must be validated because every library becomes part of the final executable, even if its code is not explicitly used. Supply chain security is an industry-wide challenge since software depends on long chains of external providers. New tools and processes are required to manage this risk.

Automated vulnerability scanners can identify insecure dependencies by analyzing source code, build files, and artifacts, and comparing versions against known vulnerability databases. These scanners should run on every commit as part of the Continuous Integration (CI) pipeline and fail builds that introduce vulnerable libraries.

Scanners must also rescan applications when vulnerability databases are updated, since new flaws can be discovered after deployment. Modern scanners can even upgrade dependencies automatically, making it possible—when combined with automated testing and delivery pipelines—to patch production systems within hours of a newly disclosed Common Vulnerabilities and Exposures (CVEs).

I recently encountered a mission-critical system still using a 12-year-old Java library because developers had written over 100,000 lines of code against internal APIs that were later removed. The high cost of refactoring delayed upgrades for more than a decade.

> **NOTE** Always use publicly documented APIs so upgrades remain possible. This protects your future self and other developers and is the correct and secure practice.

GitHub's Dependabot provides free vulnerability scanning, and many other mature commercial tools exist in a rapidly evolving ecosystem. Modern Continuous Integration and Deployment (CI/CD) pipelines now also include automated code scanning and AI-assisted code review, which can detect security risks such as unsafe APIs, injection flaws, and insecure patterns. Tools like CodeRabbit and investments from major vendors, including Google, reflect this shift.

Developers must recognize the seriousness of software supply chain security, stay current with new solutions, and encourage their organizations to adopt them. While this book cannot cover every tool, it explains the cryptographic foundations on which they are built. Part 2 of the book covers the foundational security technologies and standards used in all security areas, so make sure to read part 2 so you can more easily stay up to date with progress and developments in securing the software supply chain.

1.3   Roles and responsibilities in security

Computer security is a massive topic with many different subfields and specializations. It can take a lifetime to master computer security. As a developer, you must focus on the subset of computer security subjects most relevant to your needs for writing secure applications. Figure 1.4 shows a continuum of security-related skills that can help you understand what you need to know and where to focus your efforts to learn security.

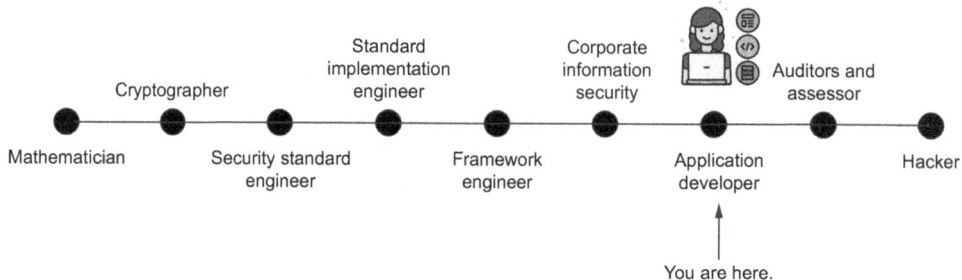

Figure 1.4   The spectrum of technical roles involved in computer security roles and responsibilities

Mathematicians produce the foundations upon which computer security rests. For example, elliptic curves are used to implement public key cryptography, frequently used in the TLS. Advances in mathematics can make new security algorithms possible or break existing ones. As a developer, you do not need to be familiar with the mathematics underlying computer security since you'll not work directly with these equations. However, you must understand what cryptographic mechanisms are designed to protect, where they should be applied, and what risks arise when they are misused.

Cryptographers use specific areas of mathematics to design foundational algorithms for encryption, secure key (password) exchange, hashing, random number generation, digital signatures, and secure combinations between systems. Cryptographers also analyze security algorithms and protocols for weaknesses. As a developer, you don't need to understand how cryptographic algorithms work, but you need to understand what the algorithms do, when to use them, and how to configure them. Part 2 of the book covers foundational algorithms that you should be familiar with as a developer.

Security standard engineers define security standards that allow applications to interoperate across network boundaries, operating systems, and programming languages. Transport Layer Protocol (TLS) and OpenID Connect are standards you will frequently encounter as a developer. It is essential to be familiar with the security standards so you can

- Write secure applications that pass corporate security audits
- Quickly configure libraries and frameworks that implement the standards without spending hours searching blogs and online resources such as stackoverflow.com
- Debug security issues and configurations quickly

Standard implementation engineers implement security standards as reusable libraries in a variety of programming languages. For example, OpenJDK engineers implement a large number of security standards as part of the Java standard libraries. As an application developer, you need to learn how to use libraries that implement security standards correctly. The book provides Java-based implementations for the standards we will study.

Framework engineers implement libraries to accelerate application development in a specific programming language. Framework developers focus on common use cases that applications need to implement and provide out-of-the-box code to implement the functionality. As an application developer, you need to master these frameworks to build applications effectively. The book uses the Spring Framework ecosystem to demonstrate how to implement a variety of common security use cases.

Corporate information security is the team responsible for the security of all applications deployed in a company. They write the corporate security standards that applications must adhere to and consult with development teams to help them secure their applications and comply with corporate standards. As a developer, you need to become familiar with your employer's security standards; this book provides you with the technical background to quickly understand corporate security standards. A key goal of the book is to help you become a better partner to your InfoSec team.

Auditors and assessors evaluate the design and implementation of applications to ensure that that they comply with security best practices and corporate standards. Information Security audit/assessment is a prerequisite for getting an application to production. Failing the security audit means a delay in releasing to production. A key goal of this book is to teach you security skills so that your applications pass security audits and assessments without costly length rework.

Hackers break into systems either (if they are bad intentioned) to steal data, money, and products, or to find the vulnerabilities before the bad intentioned ones do (we'll also refer throughout the book to the bad intentioned hackers as attackers or hostile actors). This book does not cover the numerous techniques that hackers use to break into applications. You can find more about these in books such as *The Web Application Hacker's Handbook: Finding and Exploiting Security Flaws, Second Edition,* by Dafydd Stuttard and Marcus Pinto.

As you can see, computer security brings together many roles, each with its own responsibilities and expertise. You don't need to become a mathematician, a cryptographer, or an auditor to write secure code. But you do need to understand enough of their work to use it wisely. This book focuses on the developer's part of the spectrum: learning how to apply standards, use libraries, and build applications that meet both technical and corporate security expectations. With this foundation, you'll be better equipped to collaborate with security teams, pass audits with confidence, and most importantly, create software that users can trust.

1.4 *What you will learn in this book*

We'll begin with a clear, big-picture view of what security means in real software projects, so you understand why it matters. Step by step, we'll then dive into the basics of cryptography and explore the protocols and standards that bring those ideas to life.

By the end, you'll not only know how these pieces fit together but also feel confident applying them to build safer and more reliable applications.

The book's examples are provided with Java and Java-related libraries, but the skills you learn from the book are invaluable regardless of the language and platform you use. You're invited to read the book even if you don't declare yourself a Java developer as long as you understand standard OOP language instructions.

When you finish the book, you will have learned the following skills:

- Understanding what security means in real-world software development
- Recognizing common risks and how attackers might exploit them
- Applying the basics of cryptography to protect data
- Using protocols and standards (like TLS and OAuth) in practice
- Designing applications with identity, authentication, and authorization in mind
- Building secure communication between services
- Knowing how to spot and fix common security mistakes in code
- Gaining confidence to make design choices that keep applications safe

Summary

- Security vulnerabilities can exist at every layer of the stack, from hardware (e.g., Meltdown, Spectre) to application code.
- Security is everyone's responsibility, not just InfoSec teams—developers play a central role.
- The business impact of breaches is massive (e.g., Marriott, Equifax), often costing millions or even billions.
- Security libraries (like Spring Security) are essential but hard to use unless you understand the underlying standards and protocols.
- Supply chain attacks (e.g., Equifax Apache Struts, Event-Stream Bitcoin theft) highlight the need for vigilance in managing dependencies.
- Automated vulnerability scanning in CI/CD pipelines is a best practice to detect and fix issues quickly.
- Stick to published APIs in libraries to ensure maintainability and security over time.
- Different roles contribute to security: mathematicians, cryptographers, standards engineers, framework engineers, InfoSec teams, auditors, and developers.
- Developers don't need deep expertise in all these roles, but they must understand enough to apply standards and use libraries correctly.
- This book teaches developers the foundations (cryptography, protocols, standards) so they can confidently build secure, reliable applications.

Standards for implementing authentication

This chapter covers

- Analyzing customer, employee, and partner preferences for authentication
- Discussing standards to enable secure user authentication
- Identifying the technologies for securing sensitive application credentials

All applications, whether they're million-line monoliths or thousand-line microservices, must solve various security problems. Here are four:

- Securing communication channels
- Authenticating and authorizing users
- Handling sensitive credentials such as API keys required to access external services
- Running the application securely in a cloud environment or on-premises

In chapter 10, we'll explore how Transport Layer Security (TLS) secures communication channels, locking the door to your data so no one can sneak in. But what good is a locked door if you're handing out keys to anyone? That's where authentication comes in.

Clearly, if you're securing an application, you need to first make sure that the person knocking at your app's front door isn't an attacker in disguise (or, worse, your ex trying to get into your Netflix account). Let's dive into the tools and methods for implementing authentication.

Think of authentication as a club bouncer. You wouldn't want the bouncer to let everyone in without checking IDs, would you? By understanding the authentication landscape, you'll learn how to be a bouncer who knows who belongs, who doesn't, and what to do with those using a fake ID.

Mastering these tools is essential. If you don't know how to authenticate users properly, you're effectively leaving the door open. Let's make sure your app is secure and smarter than your average bouncer. Are you ready to level up?

2.1 Logging users in

Applications accessed over the network require users to log in so the application can ensure that users can access only the data and functionality they're authorized to use. Most commonly, logging in to an application means entering a username-and-password combination (figure 2.1).

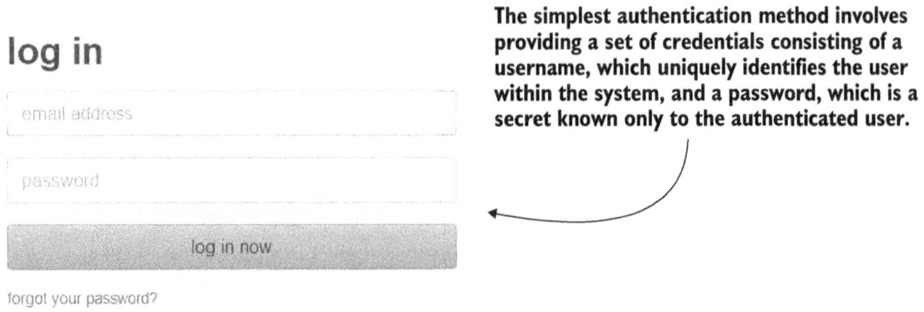

log in

email address

password

log in now

forgot your password?

The simplest authentication method involves providing a set of credentials consisting of a username, which uniquely identifies the user within the system, and a password, which is a secret known only to the authenticated user.

Figure 2.1 An authentication form (commonly referred to as a login form) is the primary interface through which users enter their credentials to log in to and access the system.

Passwords are easy to implement in an application, but they provide poor security and a poor user experience for the following reasons:

- *Weak passwords*—Humans have a hard time remembering long, complex passwords, so many people use weak passwords that are easy to remember.
- *Password reuse*—I have 308 online services that have asked me for a username and password. I can't remember more than 300 unique username-and-password combinations, so I use a password manager to generate complex, unique passwords for each site. Most users don't use a password manager, so they reuse the

same username and password across many online services. When a password leak occurs on a service, hackers use the leaked passwords to compromise user accounts in unrelated services.

- *Storing passwords is hard and expensive*—Storing passwords securely on the server side is a complex problem that requires deep security expertise to implement correctly. Even well-funded Silicon Valley companies get password storage wrong. LinkedIn for example, leaked 6.5 million passwords in 2012; worse, the leak wasn't noticed until 2016 (https://www.csoonline.com/article/534628/the-big gest-data-breaches-of-the-21st-century.html). It's not enough to implement password storage securely by using today's best practices; you must also keep up to date on advances in attack techniques. If you're storing passwords on the server side, you must be ready to invest time and money to keep those passwords secure.

You can easily avoid storing passwords in your application by using a single sign-on (SSO) service through an industry-standard protocol such as OpenID Connect (OIDC). SSO services solve many problems beyond password storage, as we'll discuss in chapter 12.

Consider a shoe retailer with 1,000 physical stores in multiple countries and an online shopping application. Customers can buy shoes from the stores or online using a web application or native iPhone and Android mobile apps. Call this retailer ACME Inc. We'll use this example in the following sections and chapters to demonstrate the subjects we discuss. ACME has three categories of users that need access to its systems: customers, employees, and partners. Each user type has different authentication preferences and needs, which we'll examine to understand what capabilities an SSO service must provide.

2.1.1 Customer authentication

Like all online stores, ACME wants to minimize friction in the checkout process to maximize sales. Returning customers should be able to log in quickly to place an order. They should also be able to use the comfortable authentication method of their choice (figure 2.2). New customers should be able to create a new account quickly so that checkout is fast when they return to buy more shoes.

We'll discuss three main approaches that you can use to implement on-demand account provisioning and login for customers:

- *Use a third-party account via OAuth2 or OIDC.* Many customers have accounts with popular online services such as Google, Microsoft, Facebook, X, and GitHub, which they can reuse with ACME. Reusing existing accounts saves the user from having to create a new username-and-password combination, and it shifts the responsibility for protecting the user's account to large organizations with more resources and expertise. OAuth2 and OIDC are industry-standard, widely supported protocols that enable users to use existing accounts across online services. Chapters 12 and 13 show you how to use OAuth2 and OIDC to log users into apps.

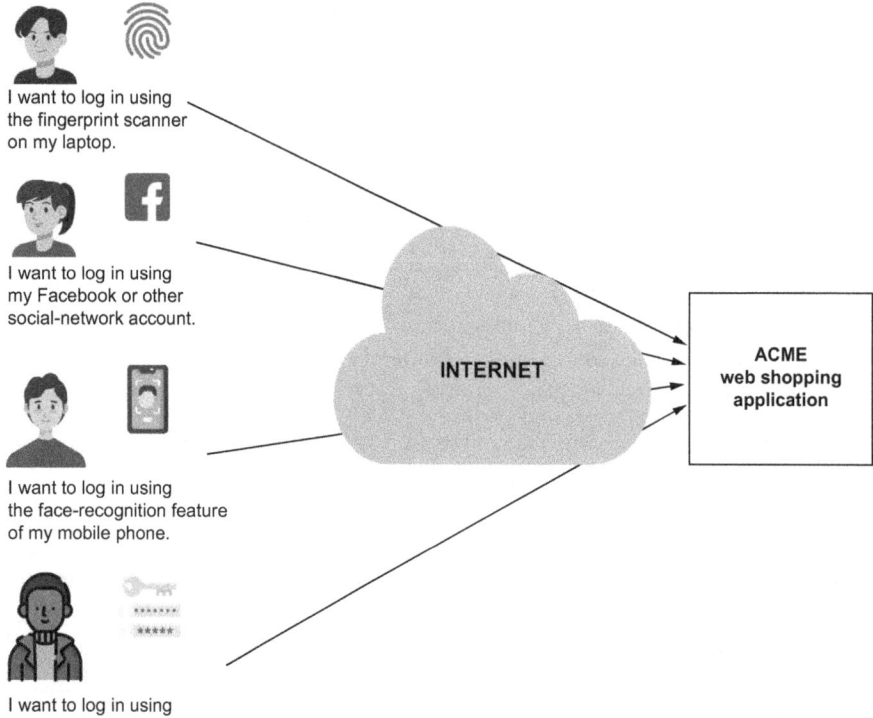

Figure 2.2 Customer authentication preferences. Some customers want to use biometric authentication features, such as fingerprint scanners and face recognition, on their phones and other devices. Others want to log in using existing accounts with large online service providers such as Google and Facebook. Still others want to log in using a traditional username-and-password combination. SSO services can accommodate all these authentication preferences and more.

- *Perform a passwordless biometric login with WebAuthn.* Modern smartphones and laptops allow users to unlock them using facial recognition or a fingerprint scan. Logging in to a personal device with a biometric scan is convenient and popular. ACME's customers want to create an account and log in using the biometric capabilities of their devices to access the online shopping site. WebAuthn is a new industry standard for web authentication via device biometrics. It's widely supported across the Apple and Android ecosystems and desktop web browsers. You can try the WebAuthn user experience at https://webauthn.io. Use the WebAuthn protocol to eliminate passwords from the login process. We cover WebAuthn in chapter 15.

- *Use username-and-password-based multifactor authentication.* If users don't have a device that supports WebAuthn or an account on a social network that they want to reuse, you can provide a fallback to username-and-password-based authentication. As a best practice, you should give users the option of multifactor authentication (using authenticator apps or SMS codes) with password-based multifactor authentication. We cover multifactor authentication technologies in part 5 of the book.

It's possible to implement social login using OIDC, biometric login using WebAuthn, and password-based multifactor login in a monolithic application using popular libraries and frameworks. A Spring Boot application, for example, can use Spring Security to implement authentication in the application itself.

But most companies have multiple monolithic applications. Implementing security in each application is expensive and time-consuming, and it leads to interoperability problems. It's a best practice to externalize authentication to an SSO service, as we'll discuss in chapters 12 and 13.

Figure 2.3 shows how Alfred (a regular user) uses multiple applications for work and leisure. These applications integrate with an SSO service, enabling Alfred to authenticate easily using various login options.

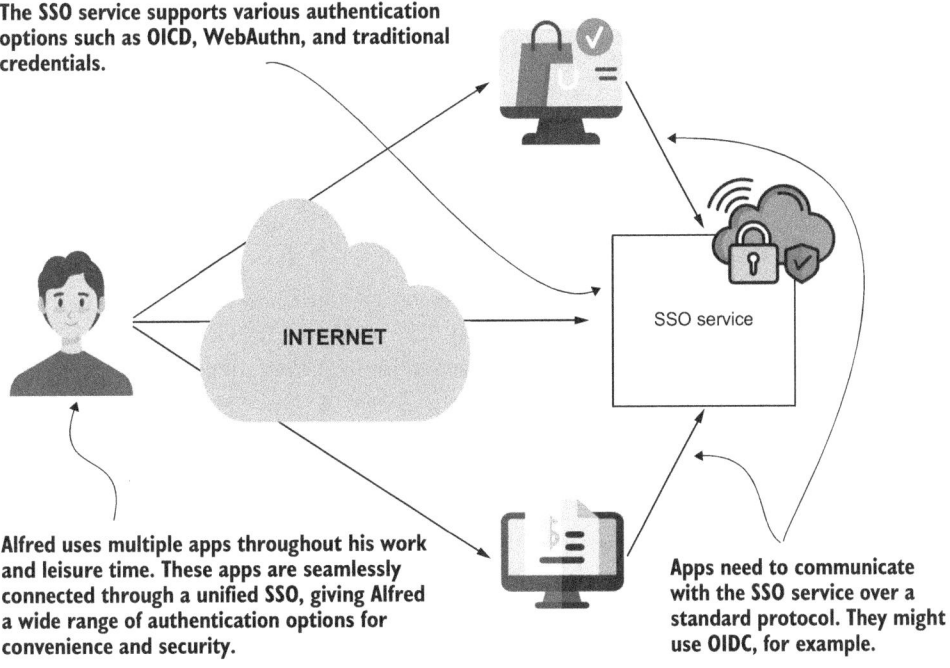

The SSO service supports various authentication options such as OICD, WebAuthn, and traditional credentials.

INTERNET

SSO service

Alfred uses multiple apps throughout his work and leisure time. These apps are seamlessly connected through a unified SSO, giving Alfred a wide range of authentication options for convenience and security.

Apps need to communicate with the SSO service over a standard protocol. They might use OIDC, for example.

Figure 2.3   An SSO service handles user account creation and authentication. Multiple applications can use the same SSO service, simplifying security for application developers. The SSO service supports authentication using OAuth2, OIDC, WebAuthn, and password-based multifactor authentication.

Applications delegate user-account creation and authentication to the SSO service. Applications can interact with the service using industry-standard protocols. OIDC is the most popular modern protocol, but other protocols, such as Security Assertion Markup Language (SAML), also work. There are three ways to access an SSO service:

- *Fully managed Software as a Service (SaaS) SSO service*—Many companies offer fully managed, cloud-based SSO services. Okta, VMware, Amazon, Google, and Microsoft are among the leading providers of SaaS-based SSO services.
- *Self-run off-the-shelf SSO service*—If you want to run your own SSO service, you can use commercial products such as Workspace ONE, PingFederate, CA SiteMinder, and ForgeRock or an open source project such as Keycloak or Dex IdP.
- *Self-built and self-run SSO service*—If you have business and technical needs that an SaaS solution or off-the-shelf packaged solution can't meet, you can build and run your own SSO service on top of popular open source libraries.

The choice among a fully managed SaaS, an off-the-shelf solution, and a custom SSO service is based on a variety of technical and business requirements. Ideally, you want to avoid building your own service, which can be quite complex. For most organizations, using an SaaS, commercial, or open source solution is the best path forward.

For developers who are getting comfortable with OAuth 2.0, OIDC, WebAuthn, and the technologies behind password-based multifactor authentication, these tools provide a complete toolbox for their authentication needs today.

Part 5 of the book shows you how to build a custom SSO service example that implements OAuth2, OIDC, WebAuthn, and password-based multifactor authentication, using the Spring Security authorization server. This example will deepen your understanding of SSO technologies

2.1.2 *Employee authentication*

Let's get back to the ACME scenario, in which you're in charge of setting up and managing security for the organization. ACME operates 1,000 retail stores across five countries; each store has two Windows desktop computers that employees use to manage the store location.

ACME's corporate headquarters has 250 employees who use corporate phones, tablets, and laptops (Windows and macOS). Like many enterprises, ACME uses Microsoft Active Directory (AD) to authenticate employees when they log in to desktops, laptops, and other corporate systems. Employees need to access the following types of applications:

- *Internally deployed commercial off-the-shelf applications*—These apps are built by vendors who have added AD to their products, allowing ACME's system administrator to configure AD as the authentication mechanism for these internal applications. AD is a central directory that stores user accounts and passwords and decides who is allowed to log in to and access company systems.
- *External cloud-based SaaS applications*—ACME employees use many SaaS services, such as Jira for project management and Slack for chat. Employees want to be able to log in to these remote SaaS applications using their corporate-issued AD credentials. Most SaaS applications bill ACME on a per-user basis, so ACME

wants to control which employees have access to these external services based on how they're set up in AD. When an employee leaves ACME, their external SaaS accounts should be deprovisioned automatically.

- *Internal-only employee-facing custom-built applications*—ACME has several custom-built internal, employee-facing applications. Employees want to access these applications using their existing AD credentials.
- *Employee-only interfaces on customer-facing applications*—The online shopping application that customers use includes several screens that only employees can access. How can the application allow customers to sign in with customer accounts and employees to sign in with their AD accounts?

The Single Sign On (SSO) service we introduced in the previous section (figure 2.4) can be used to allow employees to access internally deployed commercial off-the-shelf applications, external SaaS based applications, internal custom-built applications, and the employee-facing interfaces on customer-facing applications.

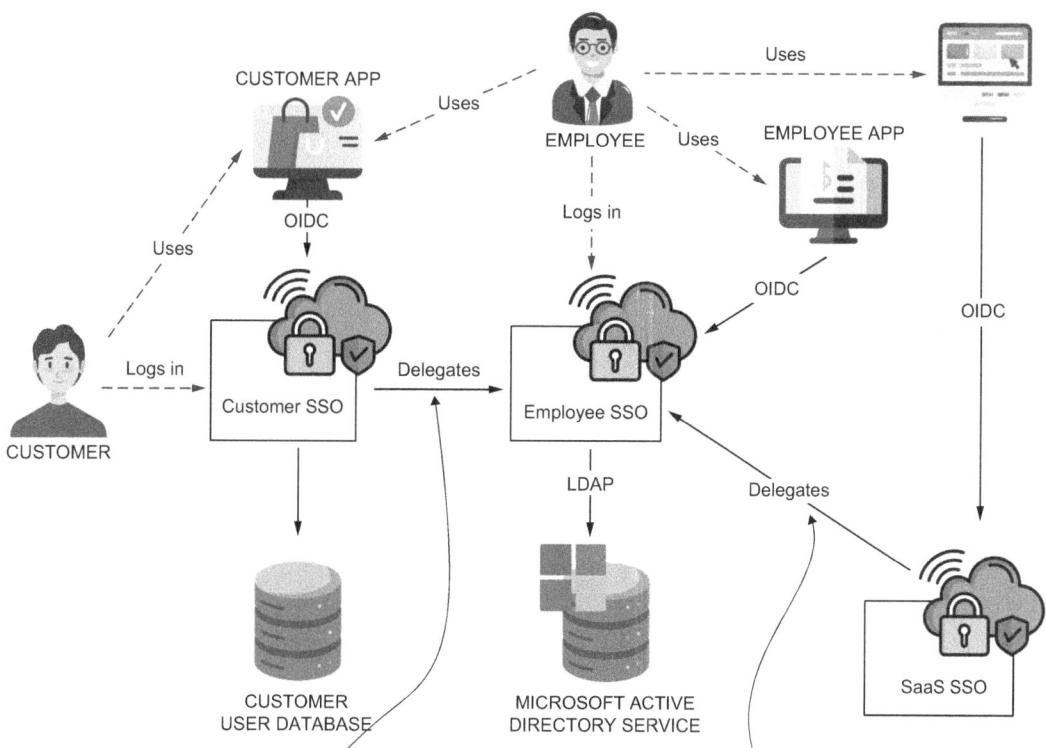

The customer SSO detects that the user is an employee and forwards the login to the internal SSO, granting access to employee-only features.

When accessing a SaaS app, the provider's SSO redirects login to the employee SSO, letting the user log in with corporate credentials.

Figure 2.4 A corporate SSO service allows employees to access customer-facing apps, internal employee-only apps, and external SaaS apps using a single set of credentials.

Companies with more than a handful of employees must implement access controls for corporate systems. When employees are hired, they must be granted access; when employees quit, their access must be revoked. An employee SSO service is critical to the functioning of a modern company. If you're building an employee-facing application, you have to integrate it with the corporate SSO service. What protocol should this integration use?

Modern corporate SSO services support OIDC, which you can use to secure employee-facing apps. If the corporate SSO service doesn't support OIDC, you can deploy a bridge from OIDC to the protocol that the SSO service supports. An OIDC-to-SAML bridge, for example, allows your application to use OIDC and the SSO service to use SAML.

The Lightweight Directory Access Protocol (LDAP) and SAML protocols have been around for decades and are widely deployed in enterprises. We don't cover SAML or LDAP here because they're well covered in other books. We focus on OIDC because it can be used for both customer-facing and employee-facing apps and is easier to work with than LDAP and SAML.

2.1.3 *Partner authentication*

ACME has several partners that have to access its internal systems to assist ACME employees. A vendor's technical support team might need access to ACME's internal systems to help employees during an upgrade, or the company might rely on an external vendor that provides customer support. ACME has two ways to grant partners access to its internal systems:

- *Give partners employee accounts.* Partner employees are given user accounts in ACME's employee directory. This approach is common because it's straightforward to implement. If a partner employee is fired or quits, ACME's IT staff must be notified to revoke that employee's access. The notification mechanism can be slow, introducing the risk that a partner's former employee may still have access to ACME's systems when they shouldn't.
- *Delegate partner-employee authentication to the partner's employee SSO service.* In this approach, ACME configures its employee SSO service to recognize when a partner's employee is trying to log in and delegates the actual login to the partner's SSO service. That way, as soon as a partner's employee loses access to the partner's SSO service, they also lose access to ACME's systems.

2.1.4 *Phishing-resistant authentication*

Hackers can break into systems by attacking machines or the people who use them. When attacking machines, hackers look for technical vulnerabilities in applications and infrastructure that they can exploit. Alternatively, hackers can trick human users who have legitimate access to targeted systems into granting access or performing an unauthorized action. Attacks targeting human users are called phishing attacks, and they're growing rapidly because they're highly effective.

Consider the steps hackers can use to break into ACME's cloud infrastructure. Using a LinkedIn search, hackers identify Joe Smith as the lead cloud DevOps engineer on ACME's online retail team and learn that he can be reached at jsmith@acme.com. Through some online sleuthing, the hackers determine that ACME uses Google Cloud Platform (GCP) to run its online services. Because Joe is ACME's lead DevOps engineer, hackers infer that he likely has administrator access to the GCP console.

The hackers craft an email that looks like one sent by Google Cloud. The email tells Joe that there's a problem in ACME's system and he should click a link to get more details.

Joe has been working for eight hours without a break. He is tired, so he doesn't notice that the convincing email is fake. He clicks the link, which takes him to a replica of the Google login screen. He also misses the fact that the URL in the browser address bar isn't a Google URL. He enters his username, his password, and the one-time password from the authenticator app into the fake login form.

The fake login form captures Joe's credentials and uses them to log in to Google Cloud. It sends Joe to a screen that tells him the email he received was sent in error. Joe is happy because he has no extra work to do. He quickly closes his browser and heads home, unaware that he has just given hackers access to ACME's GCP infrastructure. Over the next few hours, they use Joe's administrator credentials to steal critical data from ACME's systems.

Phishing attacks are highly effective because they target the humans using a computer system. Even the most security-savvy and careful system administrator can be phished by a determined attacker. You can make your application more resistant to phishing attacks like the one outlined above by allowing users to log in with physical security keys such as a YubiKey (figure 2.5).

Phishing-resistant security keys are gaining popularity and should be used to protect high-value user

Figure 2.5 A user has to insert the YubiKey into their laptop and then click the button on the login screen for an application that supports a physical security key. The YubiKey checks whether the URL of the site the user is trying to log in to matches the URL stored on the YubiKey. If the URLs don't match, the login fails. A YubiKey can protect against phishing attacks such as the one described in this section.

accounts. Adding support for phishing-resistant authentication is easy with WebAuthn-compatible keys such as YubiKey. We cover WebAuthn in chapter 15.

2.1.5 *Authentication technology from a developer's perspective*

User authentication is one of the first security features developers add to applications. Externalizing user authentication from a monolithic application into an SSO service is the recommended approach (figure 2.6). Applications interact with SSO services using industry-standard protocols. For developers, the most important protocols to know are OAuth2, OIDC, and WebAuthn.

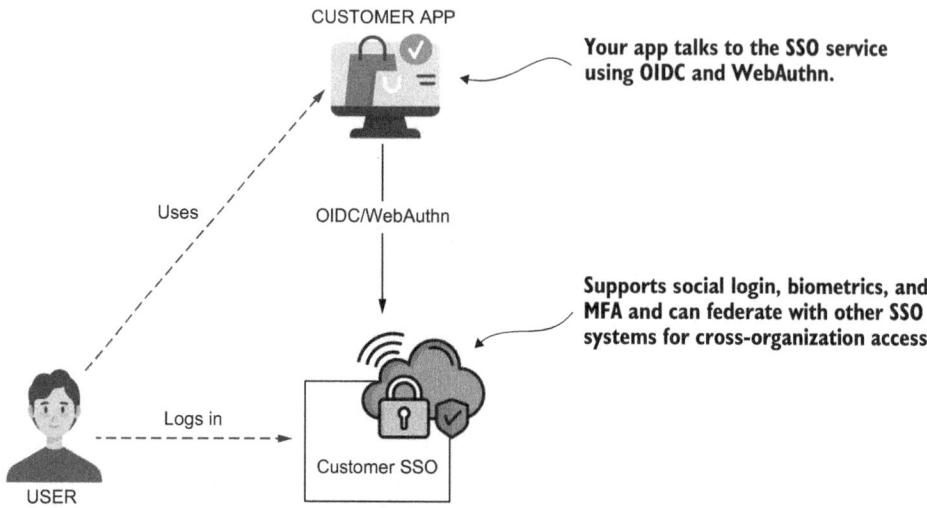

CUSTOMER APP

Your app talks to the SSO service using OIDC and WebAuthn.

Uses

OIDC/WebAuthn

Supports social login, biometrics, and MFA and can federate with other SSO systems for cross-organization access

Logs in

Customer SSO

USER

Figure 2.6   Externalize application authentication into an SSO service that applications can access using OIDC and WebAuthn. If you know OIDC and WebAuthn, you can use all modern SSO services.

OAuth2 and OIDC enable applications to delegate user login to an external service, eliminating the need for an application to manage and store usernames and passwords. All major social networks support OAuth2 and OIDC, allowing users to reduce the number of passwords they need to remember. We'll discuss this subject in more detail in chapters 12 and 13.

The web authentication protocol WebAuthn can be used as an alternative to passwords. Applications can leverage WebAuthn to allow login with biometric scanners such as facial recognition or fingerprint scanners, as well as phishing-resistant physical security keys such as a Yubikey.

OIDC and WebAuthn are supported by high-quality libraries and frameworks across programming languages. Part 5 of the book provides a Spring Security-based set of sample applications that you can use to learn these protocols.

Mastering OIDC and WebAuthn enables you to write applications that work with all modern SSO servers. But you need to be familiar with the material in part 2 of this book, especially TLS, JOSE, X.509 certificates, and public-key infrastructure. Please take the time to review the foundational topics covered in part 2.

> **TIP**   Using an SSO service makes your application more secure and is easier than building your own authentication system. Choose a SaaS, commercial, or well-maintained open source SSO service; keep your SSO service patched and up to date.

Roles and responsibilities

Understanding the roles and responsibilities of different team members is key to successfully implementing SSO services in your organization. This sidebar breaks down the core duties of information security engineers and developers, making the process more transparent and manageable.

- Information-security engineers
  - *Decision Making*—Information security engineers decide which SSO service can be used within the company.
  - *Setup and Configuration*—They are responsible for setting up the SSO service and determining which configurations of OpenID Connect and WebAuthn to enable.
- Developers
  - *Implementation*—Developers must integrate OpenID Connect and WebAuthn libraries into their applications to enable interaction with the chosen SSO service.
  - *Protocol Knowledge*—Understanding OpenID Connect and WebAuthn protocols is essential. Once the protocols are mastered, using a programming language-specific library becomes straightforward. Focus on learning the protocols first to simplify implementation.

Learning the protocols might seem daunting at first, but when you understand the principles, implementing them in your applications is straightforward.

2.1.6 *Exercises*

1 Why are passwords terrible for security and user experience?
2 What protocol makes it possible to log in without a password?
3 What is OIDC used for?
4 What is a phishing attack?
5 Which authentication technology can protect against phishing attacks?
6 What capabilities does an SSO service provide?
7 Should every application use an SSO service?

2.2 *Securing application credentials*

Monolithic applications and microservices must access database servers, message brokers, email servers, and internal and external APIs to provide application functionality. ACME's online shopping application, for example, depends on the services in figure 2.7.

When a customer buys a pair of shoes on ACME's website, the backend makes an API call to a payment processor to charge the customer's credit card. The credit-card processing API requires an API key to authenticate that the call comes from ACME's systems. If hackers get access to the payment API key, they can cause financial damage to ACME.

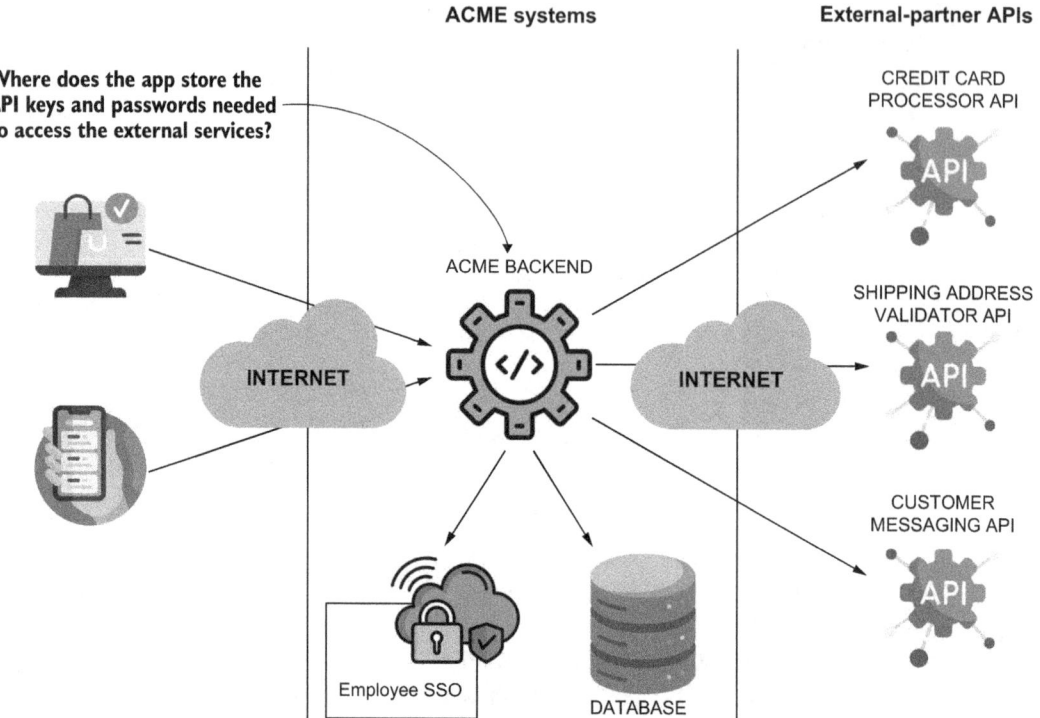

Figure 2.7 **Applications depend on internal and external services that require passwords and API keys. The credentials that enable service access are extremely sensitive and must be protected. How can an application store and access the sensitive credentials it needs to operate?**

Where can the application store the payment API key so that it's accessible only to the application? Our hypothetical payment processor API keys are valid for one month from the date when they're issued. How can ACME implement a reliable process for regularly updating API keys on production servers?

Beyond API keys, applications require a general way to store the secrets they need to operate. Storing secrets in configuration files is a common practice, but it suffers from the following serious drawbacks:

- *Configuration drift*—A highly available application running on 10 servers requires a copy of the configuration file on each server. An update process can fail easily, resulting in 2 of the 10 servers having the wrong configuration settings.
- *Hard to secure*—Operating systems don't provide the fine-grained security controls required to properly lock down configuration files containing sensitive secrets.
- *Difficult to audit*—Filesystems don't provide a sufficiently fine-grained audit trail to allow investigation of security incidents involving stolen credentials.
- *Difficulty of rotating credentials regularly*—Changing credentials on a regular basis is a security best practice. Applications must be able to determine credential expi-

ration dates or be notified when credentials are updated. Implementing credential rotation with configuration files is a difficult, error-prone process.

Putting all application secrets in a centralized credential service is a great alternative to using configuration files (figure 2.8). The primary benefits of using a credential service are

- *One source of truth*—Centralized credential services serve as the single source of truth for all application instances, eliminating configuration drift caused by file-based configuration.
- *Easy updates*—When credentials are updated in the credential service, applications can be notified of the change, enabling them to use the new values without restarting.
- *Simplified credential rotation*—Credential services store metadata about credentials, such as expiration times, so that applications can choose the currently valid credential versions.
- *Comprehensive audit logs*—Credential services offer fine-grained audit logs that are essential for proactively monitoring suspicious activity and investigating security incidents.

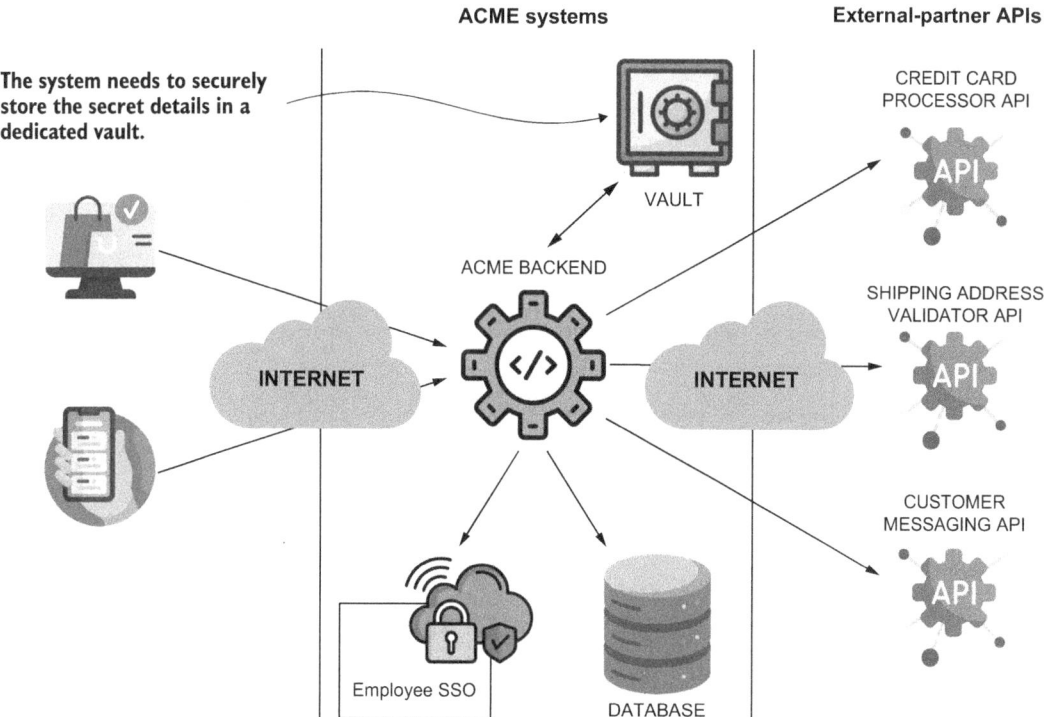

Figure 2.8 A credential vault is a centralized store of sensitive configuration values, such as passwords, API keys, digital certificates, and other secrets the application needs at run time.

- *Hardware security module support*—Credential services typically use specialized hardware security modules to ensure that their secrets are well protected against even the most determined attackers.

Don't write your own credential service. Building and maintaining one requires deep security expertise, and mistakes can cause catastrophic security failures. There are three common approaches to accessing a credential store:

- *Cloud provider credentials service*—Public cloud providers also offer centralized credential management services for applications running in the public cloud. An application running on Microsoft Azure, for example, can use the Azure Key Vault service to manage sensitive credentials. We cover HashiCorp Vault in part 4.
- *Container platform credentials service*—If an application runs on a container platform, it can use the platform's built-in credentials service. Applications running on Cloud Foundry can use CredHub, a credential store built into the Cloud Foundry platform. Kubernetes provides a fundamental credential storage mechanism called Secrets, which we cover in part 3 of the book.
- *Self-deployed credential service*—You can deploy and run many commercial and open source credential management services in your infrastructure. HashiCorp Vault is a widely deployed open source credential management service with a commercial enterprise version.

Unfortunately, no industry-standard protocol or API for accessing a credential service exists. Every credential service product has its own proprietary API and client libraries that you must add to your application.

Applications access credential services over the network, so the credential service must have a way to authenticate the application and receive its request. Thus, we have a bootstrapping problem:

- How does the application obtain the secret to access the credential service?
- Where does the application store the secret to access the credential service?
- How can you change the secret used to access the credential service while the application is still accessing it?

Bootstrapping trust is a complex problem that can be solved only if it's baked into the application platform (figure 2.9).

The techniques for handling secrets securely are the same whether you're writing a million-line monolithic application or a thousand-line microservice. Becoming comfortable with these patterns enables you to do the following:

- Meet corporate security standards and pass security audits
- Protect credentials for accessing your data sources and APIs
- Simplify automated testing and deployment pipelines

The book teaches patterns for handling secrets securely and shows you how to implement them using Spring, Kubernetes, HashiCorp Vault, and public cloud key management services.

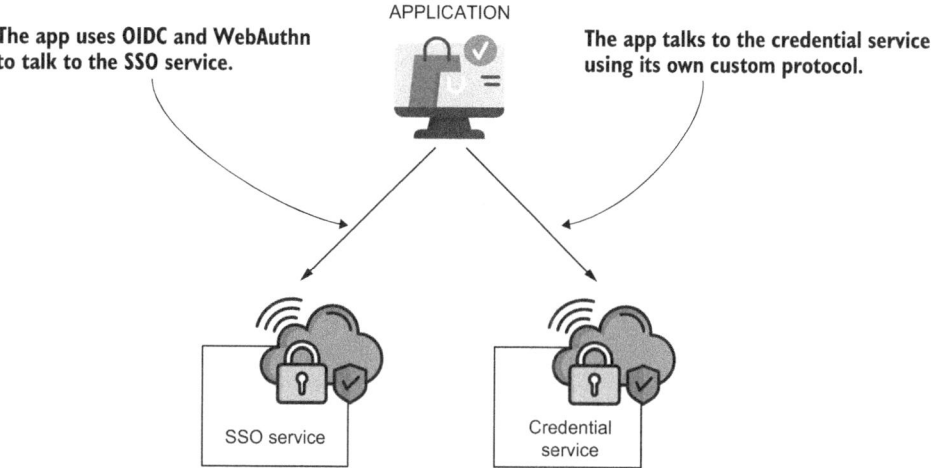

APPLICATION

The app uses OIDC and WebAuthn to talk to the SSO service.

The app talks to the credential service using its own custom protocol.

SSO service

Credential service

Figure 2.9   A credential management service and an SSO service are two foundational components of cloud-native application security. As a developer, you can use the OIDC and WebAuthn protocols to interact with all modern SSO services. But for credential services, there is no industry-standard API, so you have to use a proprietary API provided by the credential service's implementation.

BEST PRACTICE   Always store application credentials in a centralized credential store, such as a SaaS, commercial, or well-maintained open source credential management service.

2.2.1   Exercises

8   Where should application secrets be stored?

9   What problems do you run into when you store application secrets in configuration files?

10   What are the benefits of using a credential-storage service?

11   Should all applications use a credential storage service?

12   Is there an industry standard protocol or API that can be used to access a credential service?

2.3   Exercise answers

1   Why are passwords terrible for security and user experience?

   Passwords are difficult to manage because long, complex passwords are hard to remember. Most users interact with many online services that require passwords, and without a password manager, they often choose weak passwords or reuse a password across multiple accounts. Also, storing passwords securely is both challenging and costly. To improve security and user experience, applications should avoid storing passwords and rely on SSO services instead.

2   What protocol makes it possible to log in without a password?

The WebAuthn protocol enables passwordless login using biometrics, such as a phone's facial recognition or a fingerprint scanner, or using phishing-resistant physical security keys.

3 What is OIDC used for?

OIDC is an industry-standard protocol widely used by SSO services. It provides a universal API for interacting with these services, simplifying authentication and authorization.

4 What is a phishing attack?

A phishing attack tricks users into entering their credentials (such as passwords) on a fake website designed to mimic a legitimate one, allowing hackers to steal sensitive information.

5 Which authentication technology can protect against phishing attacks?

Physical security keys offer protection against phishing attacks by validating the website a user is logging in to. The WebAuthn protocol makes it possible to use these keys in applications for a more secure login process.

6 What capabilities does an SSO service provide?

SSO services handle user authentication on behalf of apps, eliminating the need for each app to store passwords. They enable passwordless login using WebAuthn and provide social login options such as Log in with Facebook. SSO services can also federate with other SSO systems, allowing apps to trust users authenticated by different organizations.

7 Should every application use an SSO service?

Yes. Using an SSO service improves security and reduces effort for both developers and users. Even older applications can benefit from refactoring to integrate with an SSO service.

8 Where should application secrets be stored?

Application secrets should always be stored in a dedicated credential storage service designed for secure management of sensitive data.

9 What problems do you run into when you store application secrets in configuration files?

Storing secrets in configuration files can lead to several issues:

- They're hard to secure and audit.
- Credential rotation becomes cumbersome.
- It's challenging to synchronize secrets across multiple machines, increasing the risk of errors and security breaches.

10 What are the benefits of using a credential storage service?

Credential storage services provide several advantages. A single source of truth does the following:

- Eliminates configuration drift
- Simplifies credential rotation

- Offers comprehensive audit logs for better security oversight
- Supports hardware security modules for additional protection
- Simplifies the implementation of DevSecOps processes

11 Should all applications use a credential storage service?

Yes. Every application should use a credential storage service because it significantly enhances security and simplifies DevSecOps implementation.

12 Is there an industry-standard protocol or API that can be used to access a credential service?

Currently, no universal, industry-standard protocol or API for interacting with credential storage services exists. Developers must rely on provider-specific APIs and libraries.

Summary

- Passwords are weak, often reused across services, and costly to store securely, making them a poor choice for both security and user experience.
- Externalizing authentication to SSO services improves security, reduces development effort, and provides a better user experience across multiple applications.
- Modern applications should support OAuth2/OIDC for social login, WebAuthn for biometric authentication, and password-based multifactor authentication as a fallback.
- Corporate SSO services enable employees to access internal applications, external SaaS services, and customer-facing apps using unified AD credentials.
- Organizations can either give partner employees internal accounts or delegate authentication to the partner's SSO service for improved security.
- Physical security keys using the WebAuthn protocol protect against phishing attacks by validating website URLs before authentication.
- OAuth2, OIDC, and WebAuthn are the essential authentication protocols developers need to master for modern applications.
- Applications should store sensitive credentials like API keys and passwords in centralized credential services rather than configuration files.
- Credential services provide a single source of truth, easy updates, simplified rotation, comprehensive audit logs, and support for hardware security modules.
- No industry standard exists for credential service APIs, so you must use provider-specific APIs and libraries.
- Information-security engineers choose and configure SSO services; developers implement OIDC and WebAuthn integration in applications.

Service-to-service communication

This chapter covers

- Analyzing problems in securing service-to-service calls to uncover vulnerabilities
- Analyzing technologies available to secure the service-to-service call graph
- Compiling a list of security technologies every developer should know

All applications must solve the following four security problems:

- Securing communication channels
- Authentication and authorization
- Handling sensitive credentials, such as API keys required to access external services
- Running the application securely in a cloud environment or on-premises

In a microservice-based application, a single user request can travel through multiple microservices, like a chain of friends trying to pass along a secret. But the whole system falls apart if one friend is a loudmouth or a spy. That's why it's so important to secure the service-to-service call chain.

By the end of this chapter, you'll have a solid list of technologies and patterns every developer should know—your personal cheat sheet on security in development. With this knowledge, you'll be ready to lock down your app tighter than a teenager's diary. In the world of microservices, security isn't just a feature; it's your app's reputation on the line.

3.1   Securing the service-to-service call chain

In a service-oriented architecture, an application is decomposed into features organized around business capabilities. Each capability is delivered as an independently deployable service (or microservice, in a microservice-based architecture). Every service has a user interface or API, along with business logic. If a service requires a database, the database should be private to the service so that services can be deployed independently.

Let's focus on a microservices example because it usually adds more complexity. Consider the amazon.com product page in figure 3.1, which highlights the potential of microservices.

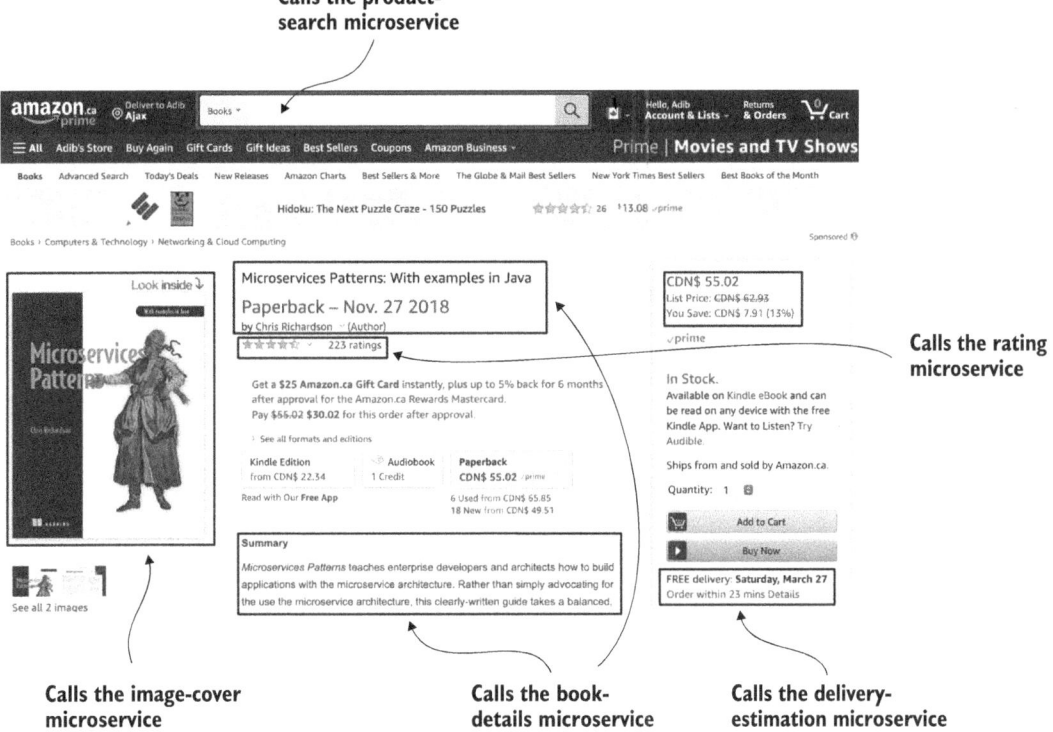

Figure 3.1   Potential microservices that can be spotted on a product page: product-search microservice, look-inside microservice, book-details microservice (title, author, publication date, and summary), product-rating microservice, pricing microservice that can calculate discounts dynamically, and delivery-estimation microservice that estimates when an order will arrive at a customer's address and the shipping costs

You can think of the product-details page in the figure as a microservice. It has a UI: the HTML and JavaScript required to display the page. It has business logic that makes API calls over HTTP to supporting microservices to get all the data required to render the page. Figure 3.2 shows that the product page microservice is composed of other microservices.

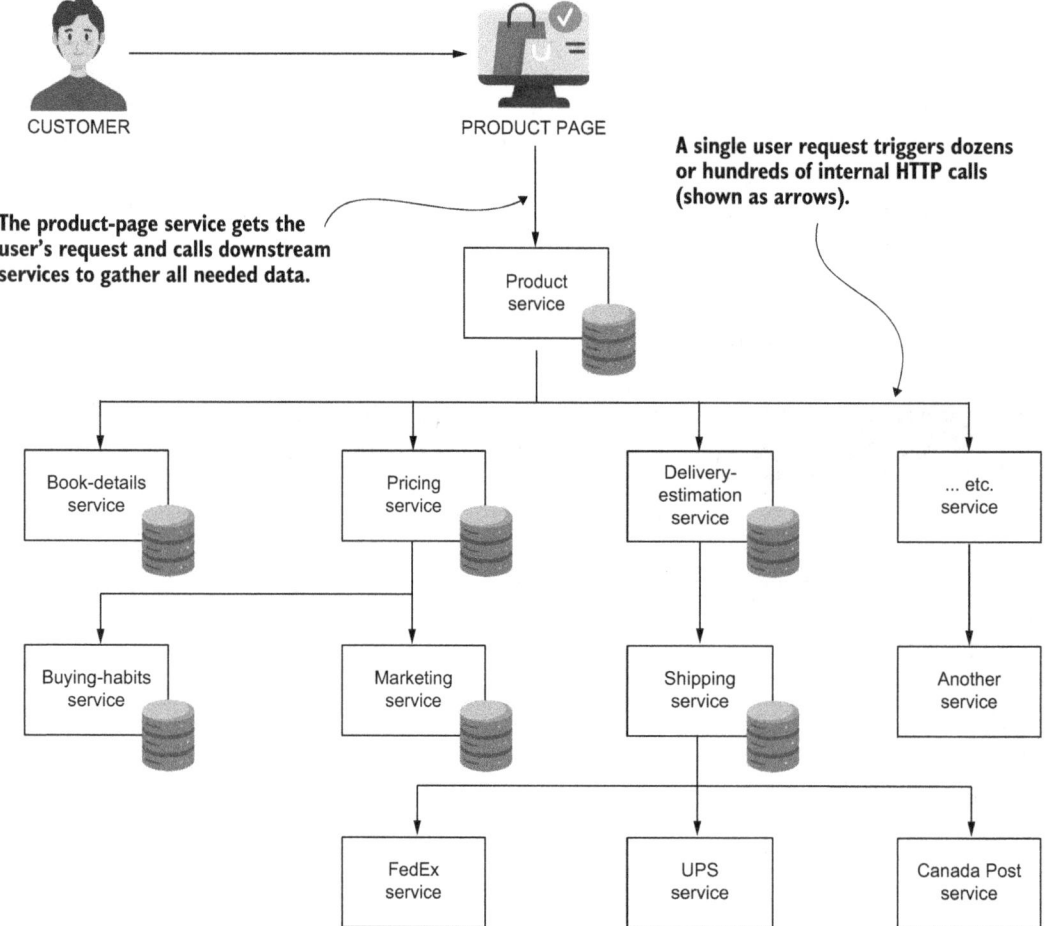

Figure 3.2   An HTTP request to the product-page microservice fans out through multiple layers of supporting microservices; this is what we mean by the service-to-service call graph. Organizations can have hundreds of microservices that interact with one another.

The book-details microservice stores facts about a book that don't change, such as the title, author, and summary. The service offers a REST API for retrieving book details using the product ID. There isn't much business logic in the book-details service—

mostly data access and caching to make the service as fast as possible. Because book details don't change after a book is published, the service uses a document database such as MongoDB to store the details as JSON documents.

The pricing microservice offers a REST API as its user interface for consuming other services. The business logic dynamically computes the discount offered by factoring in inventory levels, buying habits, market intelligence, and other variables to determine the optimal profit-maximizing price for the item being sold to the person viewing the product. The pricing microservices uses an in-memory data grid such as Apache Geode to cache all the data required to make a pricing decision quickly.

The delivery-estimation microservice offers an API to determine how quickly the product can be delivered and the shipping costs, such as "FREE delivery: Saturday March 27 Order within 23 min" as shown in the Amazon product page in figure 3.1 earlier in this chapter. To create the delivery estimate, the service does the following:

- Calls the inventory service to determine which warehouses have the product in stock.
- Computes the shipping cost and delivery time from each warehouse where the product is in stock.
- Selects the optimal warehouse from which to ship the product.
- Returns the delivery estimate with details on shipping cost, delivery date, and order cutoff time so that the product page service can display a message such as "FREE delivery: Saturday, March 27. Order within 23 min."

The look-inside service lets customers flip through a book before purchasing. It uses a JavaScript library to render the book pages and support navigation. The business logic ensures that the user can read only a few pages, not the entire book. The book content can be pulled from an object store or a document database.

Microservices are both a technical and organizational architecture. Technically, a microservices architecture decomposes functionality into smaller services that call one another, as discussed earlier. Organizationally, each microservice is owned by a cross-functional team responsible for every aspect of the microservice, including requirements, design, development, testing, deployment, maintenance, and operations. Organizing teams around microservices enables rapid evolution of features and functionality.

> **TIP** Microservices increase complexity and should be used only where appropriate. Much has been published about microservices over the past few years, covering what they are and how to design and build them, as well as the pros and cons of the approach. If you want to review microservice architecture, check out *Microservices Patterns*, by Chris Richardson (Manning, 2018), and *Cloud Native Patterns: Designing Change-Tolerant Software*, by Cornelia Davis (Manning, 2019). The rest of this book assumes basic familiarity with the concept of microservices. You don't need to be a microservices guru to learn the security aspects.

When one microservice receives a request, it may need to send several requests to other microservices. This creates two problems: how the user's identity can be passed from one microservice to another and how a microservice can know which service sent the request. Figure 3.3 illustrates these two problems.

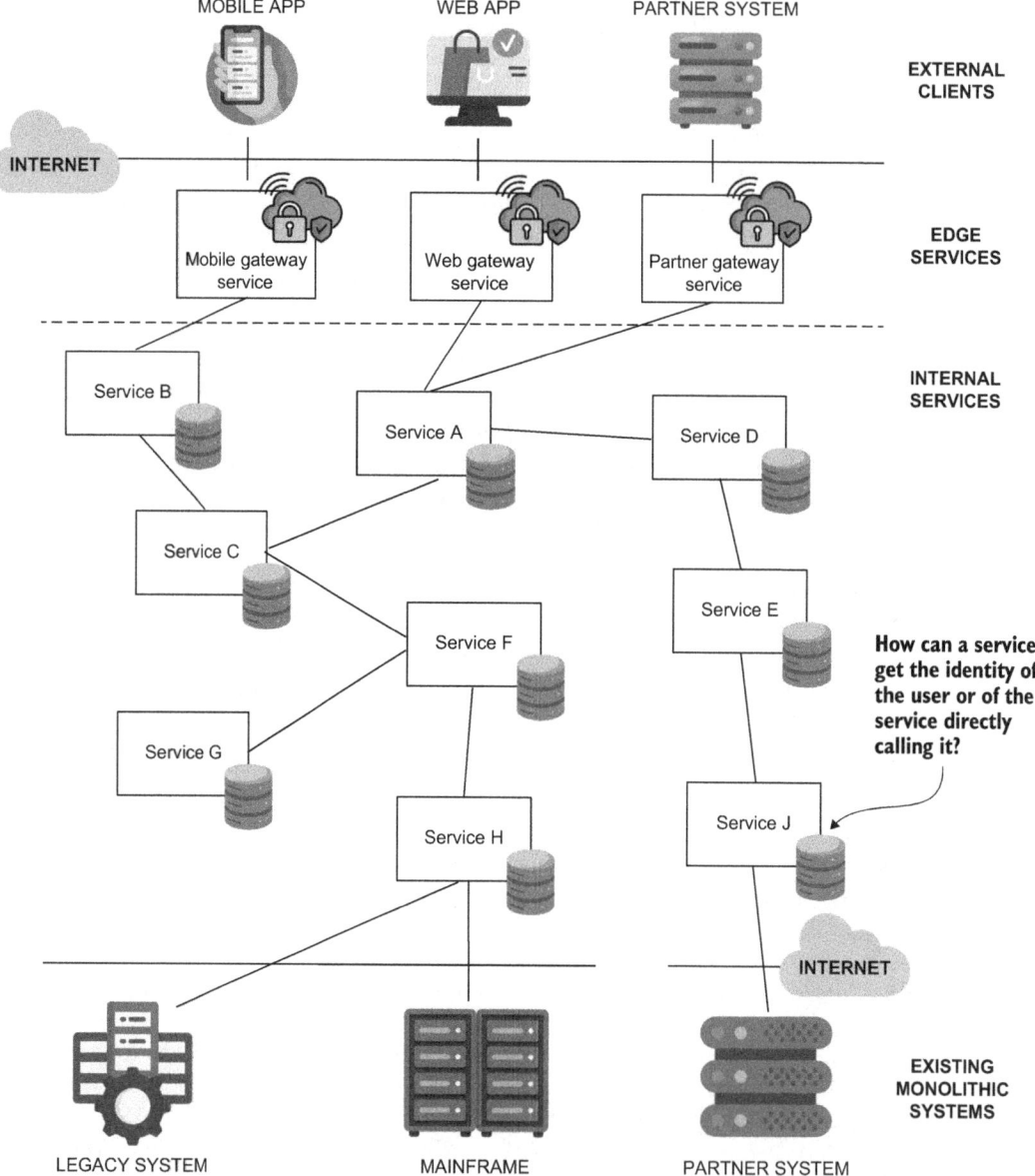

Figure 3.3   A generic call graph showing edge microservices that receive user requests and call internal microservices to handle them. How can a microservice determine the identity of the user who initiated the request? How can it determine the identity of the service that called it?

3.1.1 Propagating user identity through the service call chain

An edge microservice can use OpenID Connect (OIDC) or Web Authentication (WebAuthn) protocols to determine the user's identity because it interacts with the user's device. When the edge microservice calls an internal service, it can do so using one of several interaction patterns and protocols:

- *Synchronous call using HTTP REST*—A straightforward way to request data or perform an operation in which the caller waits for a response
- *Synchronous call using a Remote Procedure Call (RPC) such as gRPC or Thrift*—A method that uses an RPC for faster communication and stricter type checking
- *Asynchronous request-reply using a message broker such as RabbitMQ*—A way to send a request without waiting for an immediate response, allowing the service to send the reply later through a message queue
- *Asynchronous event notification using message brokers such as Kafka*—A way to broadcast events to multiple services without waiting for a direct response

The edge service making the call might be written in Java, and the service that receives the call might be written in JavaScript. As shown in figure 3.4, we need a way to propagate

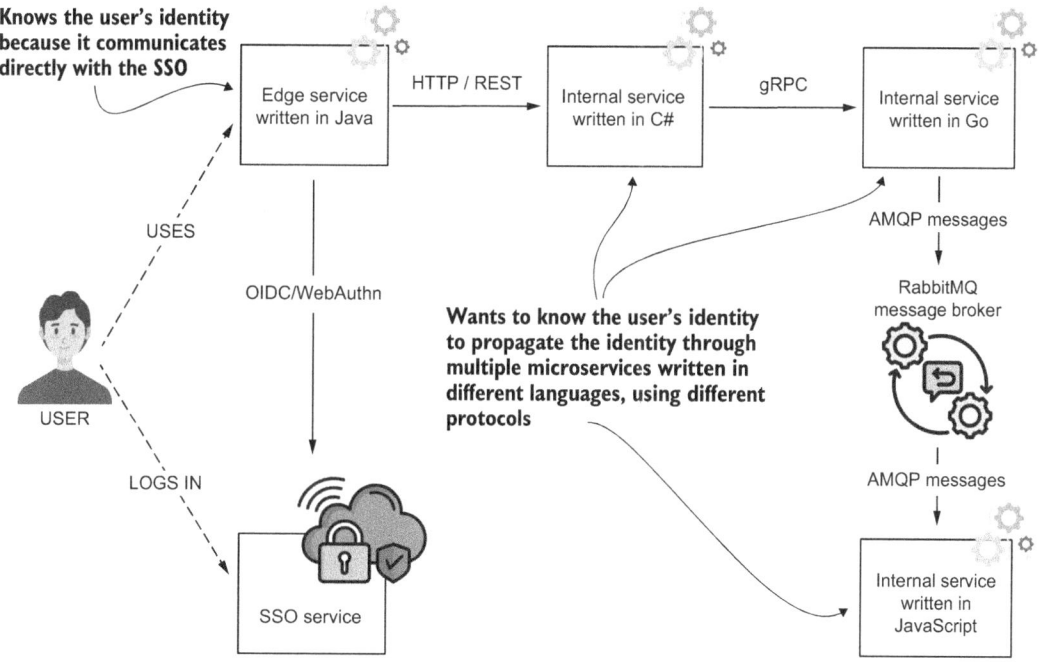

Figure 3.4 The edge service uses OpenID Connect (OIDC) or WebAuthn protocols to determine the identity of the user making the request. It must then propagate the user identity over HTTP to the service written in C#, which must propagate the user identity over gRPC to the service written in Go, which must propagate the user identity over the Advanced Message Queuing Protocol (AMQP) to the service written in JavaScript.

user identity across a service-to-service call chain that uses different network protocols and programming languages.

There is no standard way to solve the user identity-propagation problem. You must assemble a solution from a set of conventions, patterns, and technologies. We present the patterns in the final part of this book so you can build up the prerequisite knowledge of cryptographic primitives, mutual Transport Layer Security (TLS), the JSON Object Signing and Encryption (JOSE) suite of standards, X.509 certificates, Open Authorization (OAuth) 2, OIDC, service mesh, and API gateways. Be patient; there is a lot of complex technology to digest before you can solve this problem.

3.1.2   Determining service identity

Some microservices don't care about the identity of the user who initiated the request. The inventory service shown in figure 3.5, for example, needs the product

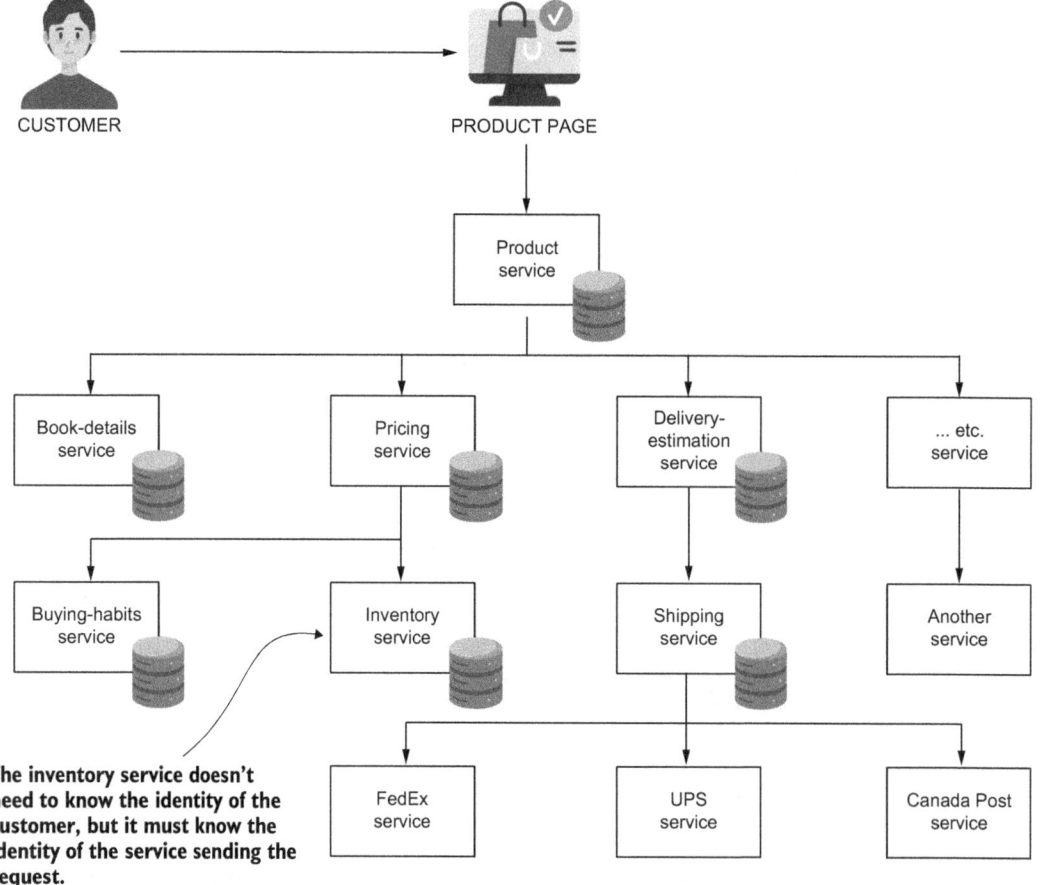

The inventory service doesn't need to know the identity of the customer, but it must know the identity of the service sending the request.

Figure 3.5   Some services, such as inventory, don't need to know the identity of the customer viewing a product page to return the current inventory level.

ID to determine product availability. It doesn't need to know the customer's user ID when browsing the product catalog.

The inventory service needs to know the identity of the requesting service so that it can authorize the operation. Consider the following operations and associated authorization rules:

- *Check product inventory levels*. Any internal service can request product availability.
- *Increase inventory*. Only the warehouse management service can increase the product inventory count
- *Decrease inventory*. Only the checkout service and the warehouse management service can decrease the inventory count of a product

Microservices make authorization decisions based on user identity, service identity, or both. There are two common approaches to establishing service identity:

- *API key*—A unique key shared between services to verify their identity
- *Mutual TLS* (mTLS) *authentication*—A secure protocol in which both services authenticate each other using digital certificates

In the API key approach (which we'll discuss in chapter 16), the microservice expects the caller to include an HTTP header or message header containing an API key that uniquely identifies the caller. How does the caller get an API key? How is an API key revoked? What is the data format of an API key? Are keys created automatically or manually? API gateways can simplify the implementation of the API key pattern.

In the mTLS approach, the caller and the microservice exchange X.509 digital certificates and use them to set up a secure TLS connection. (We'll talk about these certificates in detail in chapter 9.) The microservice can determine the identity of the caller by checking the fields in the X.509 certificate used to establish the connection.

In chapter 1, we discussed the importance of using TLS to secure all communication channels. mTLS is a stronger configuration of TLS that's more complex to configure and use. Service meshes and Secure Production Identity Framework for Everyone (SPIFFE) simplify the deployment and management of mTLS.

We'll explore API gateways and service meshes in part 5 of this book so you can build on your skills in cryptographic primitives, mTLS, the JOSE suite of standards, X.509 certificates, SPIFFE, and OAuth 2.0.

3.1.3 Exercises

1 What is the difference between an edge microservice and an internal microservice?
2 What is the difference between user identity and service identity?
3 Explain the user identity propagation problem.
4 Is there an industry-standard solution to the user-identity-propagation problem?

5 What are two approaches to solving the service identity problem?

6 What technology can help simplify implementing the API key service identity pattern?

7 What technology can simplify the implementation of mTLS between services?

3.2 Securely running services on Kubernetes

Historically, development teams focused exclusively on coding applications. When development was complete, the application was thrown over the wall to an operations team for deployment and maintenance. Developers didn't have to know how to run applications in production, and operators didn't have to learn to write software. The strict division of responsibility between development and operations was a constant source of problems for IT organizations. The DevOps movement rose to break down the wall between developers and operations.

Modern software development teams are expected to deploy and run applications in production on self-service public and private cloud platforms. Operations teams have evolved into platform engineering teams, giving developers a self-service platform for deploying and running applications.

Kubernetes has emerged as enterprises' tool of choice for building self-service platforms. Running applications securely on Kubernetes requires the following:

- Secure container image
- A secure Kubernetes cluster into which to deploy the container image
- Kubernetes deployment manifests configure the application to run in accordance with Kubernetes security best practices

The development team that built a custom application is responsible for containerizing it. Creating an application container is fairly easy; plenty of examples are online. But many of these examples produce insecure container images. Part 4 shows best practices for creating secure images through approaches such as Dockerfiles and cloud-native buildpacks.

Installing and securing a Kubernetes cluster is typically the job of a platform engineering team. Explaining how to deploy, manage, and run a secure Kubernetes cluster is beyond the scope of this book.

Running applications on Kubernetes requires developers to write Yet Another Markup Language (YAML) deployment manifests, which can configure every aspect of how an application runs on Kubernetes. Part 4 of the book shows how to write secure deployment manifests that follow best practices. We assume that you know the basics of using Kubernetes. *Kubernetes in Action*, by Marko Lukša (Manning, 2017) provides an excellent introduction to Kubernetes.

> **TIP** Learn and follow best practices for creating secure container images and writing secure Kubernetes deployment manifests.

> **Roles and Responsibilities**
>
> DevOps platform engineers are essential to designing, implementing, and maintaining secure Kubernetes clusters. Their responsibilities include ensuring that these clusters adhere to rigorous corporate security standards, typically defined and enforced by corporate information-security engineers. These standards encompass policies for access control, network security, resource allocation, and monitoring to help keep the Kubernetes environment robust against potential threats.
>
> As an application developer, your role focuses on securely packaging your application as containers and crafting Kubernetes deployment manifests that follow established security guidelines. This role includes addressing vulnerabilities in your application's dependencies, applying best practices for container configuration, and ensuring that your application's interactions with Kubernetes resources comply with security policies.
>
> This book helps you learn how to package your applications securely and run them on Kubernetes. It covers everything from protecting your container images to writing Kubernetes configuration files that follow security best practices, giving you the knowledge and tools to keep your applications secure.

3.2.1 Exercises

8 What two skills should you possess to run services securely on Kubernetes?

3.3 Security technologies every developer should know

The following list covers the foundational security technologies and standards that every application developer should be familiar with:

- *TLS*—The most widely deployed standard for encrypting data communications between applications. Because you can never trust the network, most other application security standards depend on TLS.
- *OAuth2 and OIDC*—Allow you to extract user authentication from your application and delegate it to a specialized single sign-on (SSO) service that you can configure quickly and easily. OIDC is supported by most security products and programming language frameworks.
- *WebAuthn*—Can eliminate passwords. You can use it to enable users to log in with biometric scans or phishing-resistant physical security keys.
- *Credentials storage service*—Modern applications require credentials (passwords, API keys, digital certificates, and so on) to make calls to external systems. Losing application credentials can lead to catastrophic security failures. Unfortunately, no industry-standard protocol works with all products. You have to learn the generic patterns for working with application credentials securely and the specific details of the credential storage service you're using, such as HashiCorp Vault.

- *API gateway*—Simplifies implementing API keys and can be used to secure edge microservices.
- *Service mesh*—Because a service mesh simplifies the deployment of mTLS between microservices.
- *SPIFFE*—Offers a good way to solve the problem of bootstrapping trust, enabling the implementation of advanced security patterns.
- *Cloud-native buildpacks*—Automate the creation of secure container images that are easy to patch when security vulnerabilities are discovered in the base layers.
- *Kubernetes*—The preferred way to run microservices in production. You'll need to know how to write secure Kubernetes deployment manifests to enable security features.

The standards and technologies in the preceding list depend on those in the following list:

- *Advanced Encryption Standard (AES)*—The most widely deployed data encryption algorithm. TLS and numerous other standards encrypt data using AES. Also, if you need to encrypt data before storing it on disk or in a database, you need to know AES.
- *JOSE*—A collection of standards used by many other standards, such as OICD, and by numerous products. When you code an OAuth 2.0-based resource-server API, you'll have to know JOSE.
- *X.509 Digital Certificates*—Required by TLS and used for numerous other protocols. If you don't know X.509 certificates, you'll get stuck when reading documentation or debugging problems.

All previous standards and technologies rely on a solid understanding of the following cryptographic primitives:

- Cryptographic hash functions
- Message authentication codes
- Symmetric key cryptography
- RSA and elliptic curve public key cryptography
- Diffie-Hellman key exchange

In part 2 of the book, we cover cryptography from a developer-friendly perspective. The goal of this book is to teach developers complex security technologies in an approachable way. But a single book can't cover everything a developer needs to know about security, so we'll focus on the areas in figure 3.6.

> **TIP** Security is a huge topic, with a lot of complex technology to learn. You'll have to be patient and diligent to master it all. If you read the book in chapter order and run the sample applications, we're confident that you'll have fun learning the key application security technologies developers should be familiar with.

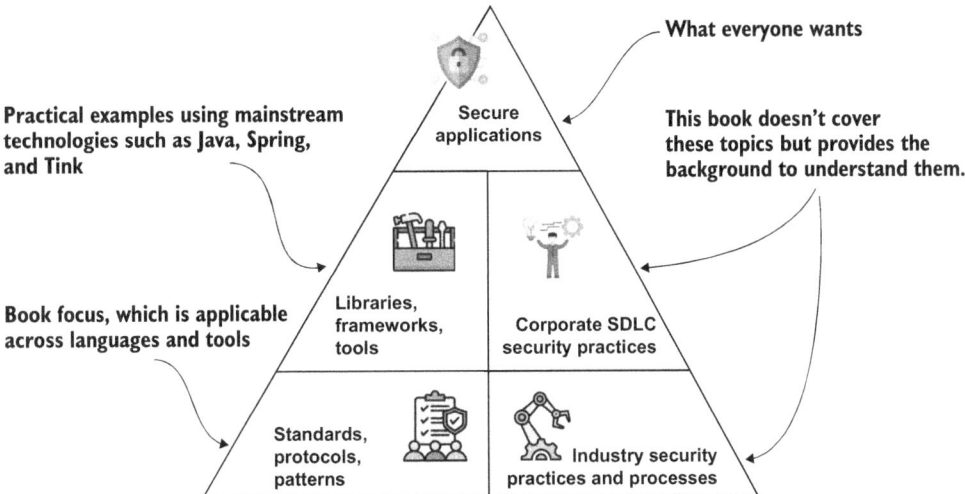

Figure 3.6 The book teaches you the standards, protocols, and patterns for building secure applications through practical sample applications. The goal is to set you up for success on your security learning journey by teaching you foundational technologies that every developer should know.

3.3.1 Exercises

9 Using pen and paper, list all the application technologies a developer should be familiar with, as defined in chapters 1 and 2 of this book.

10 On a scale of 1 to 10, where 1 means you're a novice and 10 means you're an expert, rate yourself on all the technologies listed in the preceding exercise.

3.4 Exercise answers

1 What is the difference between an edge microservice and an internal microservice?

An edge microservice interacts with users or external systems over the internet. It's the entry point for new requests. Internal microservices receive requests from other microservices.

2 What is the difference between user identity and service identity?

User identity is the identity of the entity that initiates a request chain. This is typically a human user, such as a customer, employee, or partner. It can also be a system acting on its own behalf, such as an API consumer making a request. Service identity is the identity of the service making a request on behalf of a user, such as an edge microservice calling an internal service as part of processing a user request. In this case, two identities are active: the user who made the request and the identities of the services in the call chain that fulfill the request.

3 Explain the user-identity-propagation problem.

Passing user identity between services written in different programming languages and using different communication protocols, such as HTTP, gRPC, and AMQP.

4 Is there an industry-standard solution for solving the user-identity-propagation problem?

Unfortunately, there is no industry-standard way to propagate user identity across service-to-service calls. You have to rely on patterns and conventions within your systems.

5 What are two approaches to solving the service-identity problem?

API keys and mTLS are two common approaches to solving the problem.

6 What technology can help simplify the implementation of the API key service identity pattern?

An API gateway, such as Spring Cloud Gateway, can simplify the implementation of the API key pattern.

7 What technology can simplify the implementation of mTLS between services?

A service mesh, such as Istio, can make mTLS connectivity between microservices simple.

8 What two skills should you possess to run services securely on Kubernetes?

Two skills are creating secure container images and writing Kubernetes manifests that follow security best practices.

Summary

- Microservice architectures decompose applications into independently deployable services that communicate through service-to-service calls, creating complex call chains.
- Edge microservices interact directly with users and external systems; internal microservices receive requests from other microservices.
- User identity propagation through service call chains requires passing user credentials across programming languages and network protocols such as HTTP, gRPC, and AMQP.
- No industry standard exists for propagating user identity between services, so custom solutions using patterns and conventions are required.
- Service identity can be established through API keys or mTLS authentication to authorize which services can perform specific operations.
- API gateways simplify implementation of API key patterns for service authentication and authorization.
- Service mesh technologies like Istio simplify the deployment and management of mTLS between microservices.
- Developers must learn to create secure container images and write Kubernetes deployment manifests that follow security best practices.
- Platform engineering teams provide secure Kubernetes clusters. Developers handle secure application packaging and deployment configuration.

- Essential security technologies for developers include TLS, OAuth 2/OIDC, WebAuthn, credential-storage services, API gateways, service meshes, SPIFFE, cloud-native buildpacks, and Kubernetes.
- These technologies depend on foundational knowledge of AES encryption, JOSE standards, X.509 digital certificates, and cryptographic primitives such as hash functions and public-key cryptography.
- DevOps has evolved from separate development and operations teams to integrated teams responsible for both building and running applications in production.

Part 2

Cryptography foundations

Part 1 gave you the big picture of application security: who does what, where to focus your learning, and how all the pieces fit together. Now it's time to zoom in on the foundation: the cryptographic algorithms themselves. These algorithms are the building blocks that make everything else in security possible.

Most developers encounter cryptography when a library throws a confusing error or when they're told to "just add encryption." The math can look intimidating, and the standards read like they're written for rocket scientists. The goal of part 2 is to cut through that complexity. You'll learn just enough to understand the foundations of cryptography in practice.

We'll start with the basics: ensuring integrity and authenticity with hashes and hash-based message authentication codes (HMACs, covered in chapter 4). Then we'll move into encryption with the Advanced Encryption Standard (AES, covered in chapter 5), learning how to protect confidentiality without falling into common traps. From there, you'll explore public-key cryptography with Rivest–Shamir–Adleman (RSA; chapter 6) and elliptic curves (chapter 7), seeing how they solve the key-distribution problem and enable digital signatures.

Along the way, the ACME, Inc. case study will keep you grounded in real-world scenarios, with Java examples you can run and adapt. By the end of part 2, you'll understand the essential algorithms behind modern security protocols and have the confidence to configure and use them correctly in your own systems.

Message integrity
and authentication

This chapter covers
- Guaranteeing data integrity using the Secure Hash Algorithm
- Ensuring sender authenticity with a hash-based message authentication code (HMAC)
- Ensuring data integrity using an HMAC
- Using the Java Cryptography Architecture and Java Cryptography Extensions

This chapter is the first step in a friendly introduction to cryptographic algorithms for application developers. We won't cover the mathematics behind these algorithms. Instead, we'll demonstrate cryptography concepts with working Java examples so you can build the intuition and background you need to understand application security.

Cryptographic algorithms are the foundational security building blocks, no matter what programming language you write code in or which cloud provider you deploy your application on. These documentation and mysterious error messages from security libraries make perfect sense if you understand the basics of cryptography. You'll no longer get stuck or blindly copy and paste from Stack Overflow and blog posts.

> **DEFINITION**   A *cryptographic algorithm* is a set of mathematical rules used to secure information. Depending on its purpose, it can hide data (encryption), detect changes (hashing), prove who created the data (digital signatures), or securely establish shared secrets (key exchange).

Suppose that you want to add a social login button to your application, such as Login with Google. You'll have to use protocols such as OpenID Connect (OIDC) and Open Authorization (OAuth) 2.0. OIDC is built on top of the JSON Web Token (JWT) standard, which means you'll need to understand JSON Web Signature (JWS) and JSON Web Encryption (JWE). To understand JWS, you must understand HMAC. To understand HMAC, you must understand the concept of cryptographic hash functions and message authentication code (MAC). All these names may look foreign right now, but this sort of material is exactly what you'll study in this book. We've prepared a step-by-step approach in which you start with the basics and build your knowledge from the ground up.

You'll work through two example applications in this chapter. The first shows how to use a cryptographic hash function to detect data corruption. The second shows how to use a cryptographic function called an HMAC to determine who created a file and whether it has been tampered with.

> **DEFINITION** A *cryptographic function* is a mathematical operation that secures information by transforming it in a way that's hard (or infeasible) to reverse without a secret, such as a key. Examples include hashing functions, encryption functions, and digital signature functions.

4.1   *The goals of cryptography*

Consider ACME, Inc., a shoe manufacturer. Customers shop for shoes on ACME's e-commerce website and pay for orders using credit cards. For every order placed, ACME's e-commerce system calls the credit card API provided by a payment processing company (figure 4.1).

Cryptography is used to secure HTTP requests from the user's web browser to the e-commerce website and from the e-commerce system to the payments API. As HTTP request/response messages flow back and forth between customers, ACME, and Payment, cryptography solves four fundamental security problems:

- *Integrity*—Ensures that the data sent in messages hasn't been altered during transmission
- *Authentication*—Confirms that the communicating parties are who they claim to be
- *Confidentiality*—Protects data from being read by unauthorized parties, ensuring privacy

- *Nonrepudiation*—Guarantees that the sender can't deny sending the message or transaction

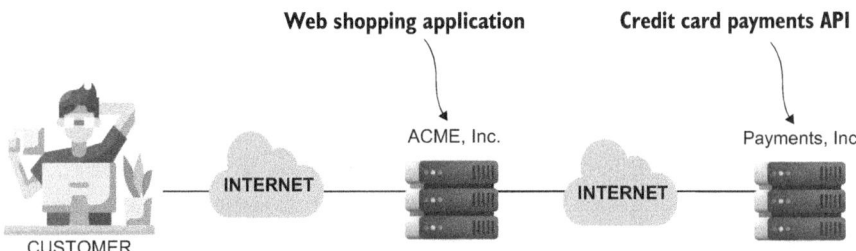

Figure 4.1   A typical high-level e-commerce architecture. Customers place orders using ACME's web applications, which call the Payments, Inc. credit card API to collect payment while processing an order.

Integrity ensures that data isn't tampered with during transmission or storage. An HTTP request from a customer's browser to the e-commerce system can be altered by network hardware problems or by hacker interception and modification. Similarly, a customer address saved to a database can be altered accidentally by disk drive corruption or intentionally by a hacker modifying the database. One fundamental problem that cryptography solves is ensuring message integrity during transmission and storage.

Authentication in the context of cryptography means that the message recipient can determine who sent the message. How can a payment API be sure that a request to charge a credit card came from ACME and not from a hacker pretending to be ACME? How can a customer be sure they are sending their credit card information to ACME's website rather than to a hacker pretending to be ACME?

> **NOTE**   Authentication can refer to user authentication or message authentication. User authentication typically means asking users to prove their identity via a challenge, such as providing a correct username-and-password combination. In this part of the book, when you see the term authentication, we mean message authentication as described in this section, not logging users in to an application.

Confidentiality ensures that data is understandable only by the intended recipients. How can ACME and Payments make sure hackers can't steal credit card details if they intercept network traffic? If an employee of ACME loses a laptop containing customer data, how can a customer be sure that their personal details aren't accessible to anyone who finds the computer?

Nonrepudiation is a legal and technical concept ensuring that a party can't later deny having performed a specific action. In simple terms, it provides proof that an action occurred and shows who performed it.

Suppose that ACME wants to prove in court that its payment API received and approved a request to charge $100 to a customer's credit card. It's not enough for the system to have processed the request; the company must be able to prove that it happened.

Authentication allows two parties to verify each other's identity while communicating. But authentication alone doesn't provide proof to someone outside that interaction. A third party, such as a judge or auditor, can't rely on authentication logs alone to determine what occurred.

Nonrepudiation fills this gap. It allows a party to prove to an independent third party that a specific message was sent or received by a specific party. This is typically achieved with cryptographic mechanisms such as digital signatures.

Nonrepudiation is essential whenever computer systems must establish legally valid, auditable, provable interactions, especially in financial, contractual, or regulatory contexts.

Considering security along the dimensions of integrity, authentication, confidentiality, and nonrepudiation provides a framework for understanding how and when to use different cryptographic algorithms. Table 4.1 shows the types of algorithms required to achieve the goals of cryptography.

Table 4.1 Cryptography goals and algorithm types

Goal	Foundational algorithm required	Standards covered in the book
Integrity	Cryptographic hash function	SHA-2, SHA-3 (this chapter)
Authentication	Cryptographic hash function	HMAC using SHA-2 or SHA-3 (this chapter)
Confidentiality	Symmetric or public-key encryption	AES, RSA, ECC, JWE, Diffie-Hellman, TLS
Nonrepudiation	Public-key encryption	RSA, ECC, X.509, JWS, PKI

Learning the algorithms in table 4.1 will take several chapters. This effort is worthwhile because it will give you programming superpowers. Grab a coffee and your laptop. From here on, we'll teach you how to ensure data integrity and authentication.

4.2   *Cryptographic hash functions*

ACME, an online shoe retailer, allows customers to return shoes they don't like for a full refund. Customers mail the returns to ACME's warehouse, where staff members check that the returned shoes are in good condition before authorizing a refund. Once a day, the warehouse management application generates a `refunds.json` file containing a list of orders and the amount to refund. The payment service issues refunds to customer credit cards based on the data from `refunds.json`. Figure 4.2 illustrates this workflow.

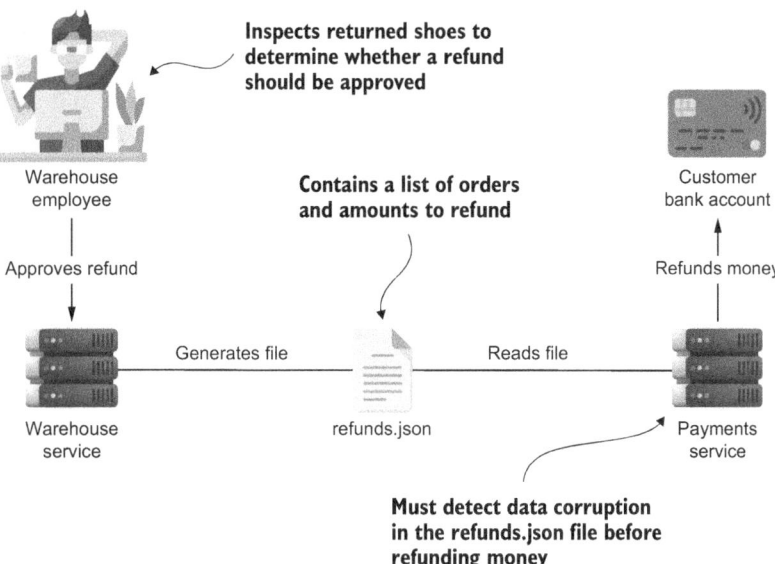

Figure 4.2   ACME staff members approve refunds using the warehouse management application. Once a day, the application generates a refunds.json file. The payment service refunds customer credit cards for the amount specified in that file.

The following code snippet shows an example of the content of the refunds.json file:

```
[ {
  "orderId" : "12345",
  "amount" : 500
}, {
  "orderId" : "56789",
  "amount" : 250
} ]
```

The business wants to ensure customers' happiness, so the payment service must return the correct amount of money to the correct customer's credit card. To accomplish this goal, the payment service must be able to detect data corruption in the refunds.json file before it starts processing refunds. This section explores how to use cryptographic hash functions to detect data corruption.

> **NOTE**   The rest of the book uses the ACME scenario, providing a set of sample applications that implement variations of the scenario using a variety of cryptographic algorithms. All the code for the sample applications is available at https://github.com/Software-Security-For-Developers/software-security-for-developers. Using the same scenario in multiple chapters will make the concepts in the book easier to understand. Figure 4.2 is repeated where necessary later in the book, so you won't have to flip back to this section.

4.2.1 Secure Hash Algorithm

A *hash function* takes an input of any size and maps it to a fixed-size bit string. Executing the SHA-256 hash function on the string "abc" or a 4 GB movie file produces a 256-bit output string. Table 4.2 shows example inputs and outputs from the SHA-256 hash function.

Table 4.2   Hash values using SHA-256 for inputs of varying sizes

Input	SHA-256 hash value represented as hexadecimal number
1-byte lowercase "a"	ca978112ca1bbdcafac231b39a23dc4da786eff8147c4e72b9807785afee48bb
1-byte uppercase "A"	559aead08264d5795d3909718cdd05abd49572e84fe55590eef31a88a08fdffd
2.6GB ubuntu.iso file	b45165ed3cd437b9ffad02a2aad22a4ddc69162470e2622982889ce5826f6e3d

Hash functions are deterministic, meaning that every time you run a hash function on the same input, it produces the same output value. Cryptographic hash functions are special types of hash function with mathematical properties that make them suitable for computer security. Two primary properties of a cryptographic hash function are

- *One-way property*—Given the hash function's output, it isn't feasible to determine the original input on which the function was run (figure 4.3).
- *Collision resistance*—Different input values should produce different output values. It shouldn't be feasible to find two different inputs that produce the same hash value.

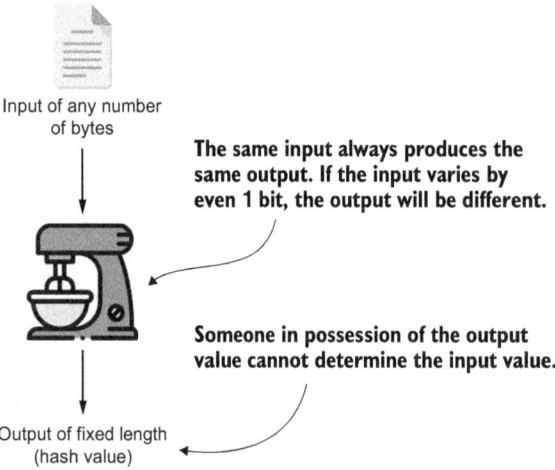

Input of any number of bytes

The same input always produces the same output. If the input varies by even 1 bit, the output will be different.

Someone in possession of the output value cannot determine the input value.

Output of fixed length (hash value)

Figure 4.3   Think of the hash function as a blender: it takes inputs of different sizes and produces outputs of the same size. Different input values produce different output values. Attackers who access the hash value can't determine anything about the input.

A great deal of math is used to design and assess the security of cryptographic hash functions. It takes years of effort, careful scrutiny, and peer review by cryptographers to reach a consensus that a particular hash function is safe for cryptographic use. You should always use standardized, peer-reviewed hash functions.

WARNING Designing and implementing a secure hash function is a huge undertaking and one that's full of pitfalls. Don't design your own cryptographic hash function; use only industry-standard functions that have been peer-reviewed and approved by your corporate information-security team. All programming languages provide excellent implementations of cryptographic hash functions as part of their standard libraries, so you don't need to implement your own.

The Secure Hash Algorithm (SHA) is a family of widely used cryptographic hash functions standardized by the National Institute of Standards and Technology (NIST). NIST defines cryptography standards for applications used by the U.S. government, which is a major technology buyer. Companies that sell software to the U.S. government must adhere to standards produced by NIST, so NIST standards are widely implemented across programming languages. There are four generations of SHA algorithms:

- SHA-0 was published in 1993 and later withdrawn due to security issues.
- SHA-1 was published in 1995 and deprecated in 2011 due to security weaknesses.
- SHA-2 was published in 2001, was widely used at the time of writing, and is still considered secure.
- SHA-3 was published in 2015 and is being adopted in new applications and standards.

As the preceding list shows, algorithms can become insecure over time. Cryptographers continually look for weaknesses in widely used hash functions because breaking one can compromise all the protocols built on top of it. Google security researchers, for example, found a way to generate collisions for the SHA-1 hash function (https://security.googleblog.com/2017/02/announcing-first-sha1-collision.html). As a result, SHA-1 is no longer considered secure.

A collision occurs when two different inputs produce the same hash value. A secure hash function should make this practically impossible. If an attacker can deliberately create two different inputs that result in the same hash, they can trick a system into accepting altered data as genuine. With digital signatures, this could allow an attacker to replace a signed document with a different one that has the same hash without invalidating the signature. That is why the ability to create collisions fundamentally breaks the security guarantees that a hash function provides.

WARNING Today's secure algorithms might be considered insecure tomorrow. Always use an up-to-date, industry-standard hash function that is considered secure by the cryptography community and your corporate information-security team. Be ready to change your code in response to new attacks.

Because it takes a long time to standardize a hash function, NIST thought it was prudent to have a backup hash function in case a successful attack against SHA-2 was discovered. The SHA-3 hash function uses a different mathematical structure from SHA-2, so a mathematical breakthrough affecting SHA-2 shouldn't affect SHA-3.

The SHA-2 and SHA-3 algorithms can be configured to produce 224, 256, 384, or 512 bits of output. The longer the output, the more security you get. Choosing an output size depends on memory, speed, and security tradeoffs. Currently, 256-bit output is the minimum setting considered secure. Research the recommended output size before you write code that uses a cryptographic hash function. The website www .keylength.com aggregates recommendations from various government organizations on the minimum key sizes that should be used for various cryptographic algorithms.

> **TIP** If you've implemented a `hashCode()` method on a Java object, you may wonder how the Java `hashCode()` method relates to cryptographic hash functions. The `hashCode()` defined on a Java object returns a 32-bit integer, which is insufficient for cryptographic use. Never use the Java `hashCode()` method for cryptography.

4.2.2   *Verifying integrity using a cryptographic hash function*

Because cryptographic hash functions produce repeatable output for a given input, they are ideal for detecting data corruption. In the ACME scenario discussed earlier, the warehouse-management application produces two files:

- `refunds.json` contains the order IDs and refund amounts.
- `refunds.json.sha256` contains the SHA-256 hash computed over the contents of the `refunds.json` file.

> **NOTE** SHA-256 isn't a standalone algorithm; it's one member of the SHA-2 family. SHA-256 produces a 256-bit hash. Other SHA-2 variants include SHA-224, SHA-384, and SHA-512. When documentation and standards refer to SHA-2, they mean the entire family, not a single hash function.

The payment service detects data corruption using the following steps:

1. Compute the SHA-256 hash value on the contents of the `refunds.json` file.
2. Compare the computed SHA-256 value to the expected value in the `refunds.json.sha256` file. If the values match, no data corruption occurred. If the values don't match, the `refunds.json` or `refunds.json.sha256` file is corrupt; raise an error, and don't refund any credit cards.

Table 4.3 contains pseudocode for the two apps in our example.

Table 4.3   Pseudocode for using a cryptographic hash function to validate file integrity

Warehouse Management Application	Payments Service

`saveRefunds(Path location, byte[] content)`
`hashValue = CryptoUtils.sha256(content)`
`writeFile(location, content)`
`writeFile(location + ".sha256", hashValue)`
	`isRefundsFileValid(Path location)`
	`content = readFile(location)`
	`expected = CryptoUtils.sha256(content)`
	`actual = readFile(location + ".sha256")`
	`if (expected == actual) return true`
	`else return false`

Figure 4.4 shows the generic validation process.

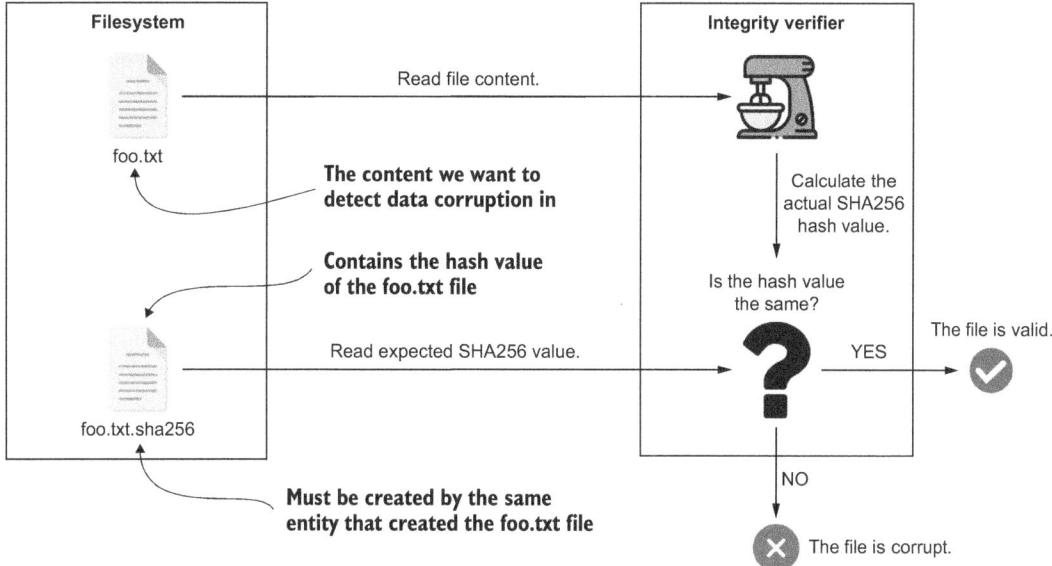

Figure 4.4 Detecting a data integrity violation using a cryptographic hash function. The foo.txt producer computes the hash value of the file contents and writes it to foo.txt.sha256. A consumer computes the SHA-256 value of the contents of foo.txt and compares the computed value with the expected value in foo.txt.sha256. If the expected and actual values match, the file is valid; if not, the file is corrupt.

You may wonder what happens if the `foo.txt` file is valid but `foo.txt.sha256` is corrupt. In such a case, the verification algorithm rejects a valid `foo.txt` file, thinking that it's corrupt. This behavior is OK because our goal is to process the `foo.txt` file if—and only if—we're sure that it's valid. It's better to reject some valid files than process an invalid one.

An attacker can edit the `foo.txt` file, compute a new SHA-256 value, and write it to `foo.txt.sha256`. Will the verification algorithm catch active tampering? The answer is no. The verification algorithm has no way to protect against an attacker who tampers with both `foo.txt` and `foo.txt.sha256`. The algorithm is designed to protect against accidental data corruption caused by network errors, disk failure, and accidental file edits. We'll discuss how to protect against active tampering later. Let's examine how Maven Central and Git use cryptographic hash functions.

MAVEN CENTRAL AND CRYPTOGRAPHIC HASH FUNCTIONS

Maven Central is the Java community's repository for distributing open-source libraries. It contains millions of files that are downloaded millions of times per day. Data corruption can occur due to network errors or disk failure. Maven Central uses cryptographic hash functions so tools can detect data corruption. Figure 4.5 shows the Spring Framework's Web MVC module files stored in Maven Central.

← → C ⌒₀ repo1.maven.org/maven2/org/springframework/spring-webmvc/6.2.10/

org/springframework/spring-webmvc/6.2.10

```
../
spring-webmvc-6.2.10-javadoc.jar              2025-08-14 07:37    2598426
spring-webmvc-6.2.10-javadoc.jar.asc          2025-08-14 07:37        833
spring-webmvc-6.2.10-javadoc.jar.md5          2025-08-14 07:37         32
spring-webmvc-6.2.10-javadoc.jar.sha1         2025-08-14 07:37         40
spring-webmvc-6.2.10-sources.jar              2025-08-14 07:37     854133
spring-webmvc-6.2.10-sources.jar.asc          2025-08-14 07:37        833
spring-webmvc-6.2.10-sources.jar.md5          2025-08-14 07:37         32
spring-webmvc-6.2.10-sources.jar.sha1         2025-08-14 07:37         40
spring-webmvc-6.2.10.jar                       2025-08-14 07:37    1091514
spring-webmvc-6.2.10.jar.asc                   2025-08-14 07:37        833
spring-webmvc-6.2.10.jar.md5                   2025-08-14 07:37         32
spring-webmvc-6.2.10.jar.sha1                  2025-08-14 07:37         40
spring-webmvc-6.2.10.module                    2025-08-14 07:37       4206
spring-webmvc-6.2.10.module.asc                2025-08-14 07:37        833
spring-webmvc-6.2.10.module.md5                2025-08-14 07:37         32
spring-webmvc-6.2.10.module.sha1               2025-08-14 07:37         40
spring-webmvc-6.2.10.pom                       2025-08-14 07:37       2963
spring-webmvc-6.2.10.pom.asc                   2025-08-14 07:37        833
spring-webmvc-6.2.10.pom.md5                   2025-08-14 07:37         32
spring-webmvc-6.2.10.pom.sha1                  2025-08-14 07:37         40
```

File and its associated SHA-1 hash value

Figure 4.5   Files in Maven Central. Notice the .sha1 and .md5 files that contain hash values of the corresponding artifacts. MD5 and SHA-1 are insecure, but Maven Central still uses them for backward compatibility.

When the Maven Central service was released, the SHA-1 and MD5 cryptographic hash functions were considered secure and industry-standard. In figure 4.5, you see files with .md5 and .sha1 extensions for each file stored in Maven Central. Today, both SHA-1 and MD5 are considered insecure. Maven Central still has to support SHA-1 and MD5 for backward compatibility.

GIT AND CRYPTOGRAPHIC HASH FUNCTIONS

The Git source control system uses a cryptographic hash function to identify every file and every commit in the repository. The `git log` command displays a list of all commits in a repository, including the SHA-1 hash of each commit's contents. The following code snippet shows a Git commit identified by the SHA-1 hash of its contents:

```
commit 0303595cb21647b203ae9069a5191cbd4ad0f865        The SHA-1 hash
Author: Adib Saikali <adib@example.com>                value representing
Date:   Sun Aug 23 22:05:34 2020 -0400                 the git commit

    Project Skeleton
```

Git identifies every file in the repository by the SHA-1 hash of its contents. When you add a file to the repository, Git performs the following steps:

1   Computes the SHA-1 of the file being added.
2   Checks to see whether the SHA-1 value already exists in the repository.
    – If the SHA-1 exists in the repo, Git adds an entry in its database where the key is the file path and the value is the SHA-1 of the file. Because the content is already in the repo, Git doesn't have to add it.
    – If the SHA-1 doesn't exist in the repo. Git adds the file content to its database with a key set to the SHA-1 hash. Then it adds an entry linking the path name of the file to the SHA-1 key.

The SHA-1 hash function allows Git to store a single instance of a file in the repository even if the file exists in multiple directories. Without cryptographic hash functions, source control systems like Git are difficult to implement.

Git was designed in 2005, and its code and data structures were hardcoded to use SHA-1. SHA-1 was deprecated in 2011. In 2018, the Git team selected SHA-256 to replace SHA-1. The change from SHA-1 to SHA-256 is a massive undertaking, and the Git team has been working on the upgrade for several years (https://lwn.net/Articles/811068/).

4.2.3   *Design for hash function change*

The Maven Central and Git examples discussed in the preceding section demonstrate the need for applications to upgrade their hash functions. If you're designing a system that uses a cryptographic hash function, assume that it's only a matter of time before you need to change it.

Design your code, data structures, file formats, and database schemas so that you can change the hash function as needed. You can include a version number in your data format, for example, so that consumers can determine which hash algorithm was used.

> **WARNING**   Attackers will set version fields to known old values to weaken the security of a data exchange. Applications that read the version field should be able to upgrade old data from an insecure algorithm version to a more secure one. Applications should take special care to ensure that it's impossible to downgrade from a secure version to an insecure version of an algorithm. Any versioning scheme must go through a proper security analysis.

Cryptographic hash functions are useful for many applications. They show up in security protocols and standards you'll encounter as a developer, including AES, Transport Layer Security (TLS), JSON Web Token (JWT), JSON Web Encryption (JWE), and JSON Web Signature (JWS). Getting comfortable with cryptographic hash functions adds a superpower to your programming toolbox. These functions can help you achieve the cryptographic objectives outlined in table 4.4.

Table 4.4   Cryptography goals and algorithms matrix

Goal	SHA-2	SHA-3
Integrity	Yes	Yes
Authentication	No	No
Confidentiality	No	No
Non-repudiation	No	No

All programming languages have excellent implementations of cryptographic hash functions in their standard libraries. The samples in this book are written in Java. Section 4.3 provides an overview of the Java Cryptography Architecture and Java Cryptography Extensions, which we use in many samples throughout the book.

4.2.4   *Exercises*

1 What are the four main goals of cryptography?
2 How is a cryptographic hash function different from the hashCode() method in Java?
3 What problem does using SHA-256 on a file solve, and what problem does it not solve?

4.3   *Java Cryptography Architecture and Java Cryptology Extensions*

The *Java Cryptography Architecture* (JCA) and the *Java Cryptography Extensions* (JCE) support cryptography in Java. Java's cryptography support is split between the JCA and JCE libraries due to U.S. government cryptography export-control laws that were in effect when Java was released. The JCA contains interfaces and algorithms that can be exported without restrictions; the JCE implementations are subject to export controls.

JCA and JCE are designed using a modular, provider-based architecture. The API interfaces and classes, defined in the java.security and javax.crypto packages, are included in the standard Java distribution. Implementations of the JCA and JCE APIs are packaged as providers and added to the Java Runtime Environment (JRE).

Developers write application code to interact with the standard API layer, which routes calls to the algorithm implementations in the installed providers (figure 4.6).

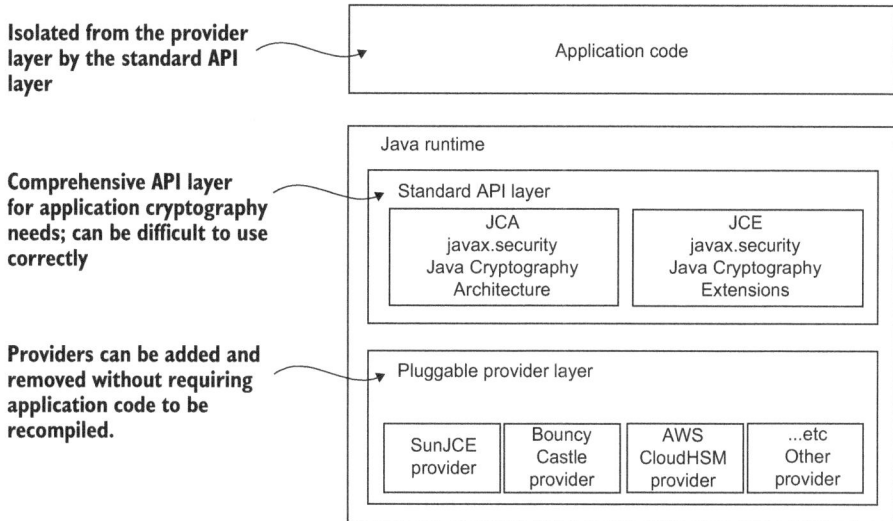

Isolated from the provider layer by the standard API layer

Comprehensive API layer for application cryptography needs; can be difficult to use correctly

Providers can be added and removed without requiring application code to be recompiled.

Figure 4.6 Application code calls the standard JCA and JCE APIs, making the code independent of the crypto algorithm implementation. The JCA and JCE layer routes calls to a provider's implementation. Java 11-based OpenJDK ships with 13 providers out of the box.

How USA export control laws affected the design of the Java crypto libraries

The SunJCE provider (https://www.oracle.com/java/technologies/javase-jce8-downloads.html) is the default provider shipped with most Java distributions derived from OpenJDK. In Java 8 and earlier, the default SunJCE provider was configured with weak algorithms to comply with export controls. An unlimited-strength JCE extension .jar was available as a download add-on to the JRE. It enabled strong cryptography for Java users in countries considered friendly to the U.S. government.

The Bouncy Castle (https://www.bouncycastle.org/) JCE provider was created by Australian developers who aren't subject to U.S. export-control laws and can offer strong cryptography support to all Java users. Bouncy Castle was also optimized for embedded low-power devices with limited CPU resources. Bouncy Castle implements more algorithms than ship with the default SunJCE provider.

After cryptography export-control laws in United States were relaxed, Java 9 (released in 2017) and later versions shipped with unlimited-strength encryption.

A *hardware security module* (HSM) implements cryptographic algorithms in hardware to increase security. HSMs are used in highly sensitive secure environments such as financial and government applications. Many HSM vendors ship JCE implementations to make their HSM modules usable from Java code without requiring developers to learn the vendor's proprietary API. Amazon offers a cloud-based HSM and ships the CloudHSM JCE provider (https://mng.bz/oZyN) for users to add to Java applications deployed to Amazon Web Services (AWS).

Multiple providers can be installed in the same JRE, meaning that developers can choose among multiple implementations of the same algorithm. The Java 21 OpenJDK bundles 13 security providers by default. Developers access algorithms using names that are standardized and documented in the JCA (https://docs.oracle.com/en/java/javase/11/docs/specs/security/standard-names.html). SHA-256, for example, is the JCA standard name for the SHA-2 hashing algorithm with a 256-bit output.

Cryptographic hash functions are sometimes called message digests because they take an arbitrary-size input and turn it into a fixed-size output. The JCA uses the `java.security.MessageDigest` abstract class to define the API for working with cryptographic hash functions.

You can obtain an instance of `MessageDigest` using the static method `Message-Digest.getInstance()`. `MessageDigest.getInstance("SHA-256")`, for example, requests an implementation of the SHA-256 hash function from the default provider installed in the JRE.

The following listing shows a simple use of SHA in a plain Java implementation. As you can see, the code is straightforward because Java provides the tools required to apply basic cryptographic functions. You can find this example in the ssfd_ch4_ex1 project provided with this book.

> **Listing 4.1   Using SHA-3 to get a hash for a given file**

```
static String sha3HexOfResource(String resourceName)
    throws IOException, NoSuchAlgorithmException {        Getting an input stream
    try (InputStream is =                                 to read a given file
      Main.class.getClassLoader().getResourceAsStream(resourceName)) {

        if (is == null) {                              Defining MessageDigest object
            throw new IllegalArgumentException(         that implements the needed
                "Error: Resource '" + resourceName +    cryptographic algorithm and
                "' not found on classpath.");           applying the transformation
        }
                                                Reading all content of
        byte[] data = is.readAllBytes();        the file as a byte array
        byte[] digest = MessageDigest.getInstance("SHA3-256")
                                    .digest(data);

        return HexFormat.of().formatHex(digest);    Returning the value as
    }                                               hexadecimal formatted string
  }
}
```

When you run the project, you'll see the output shown in the following code snippet. The string starting with 542b49… is the SHA-3 hash of the `refunds.json` file, which you can find in the project's resources folder. Try applying the same code to different files and comparing the results; then run it multiple times on the same file. You'll see that the result is always the same for a given file.

```
SHA3-256(refunds.json) =
542b49a04073502046b0de5751d5f7a9afe7c1ff2d63524c0863233a53de0c14
```

The `java.security.MessageDigest` class provides access to a variety of industry-standard hashing algorithms. Java supports the insecure MD2, MD5, and SHA-1 hashing algorithms for backward compatibility; use them only when working with historical data. SHA-2 and SHA-3 algorithms are considered secure; use them for new-application development.

The "Java Security Standard Algorithm Names" document contains a list of algorithm names that can be passed to the `MessageDigest.getInstance()` method. SHA-224, SHA-256, SHA-384, and SHA-512 refer to the SHA-2 algorithm with different output sizes. You can look up the SHA-3 algorithm, in various output sizes, using the names SHA3-224, SHA3-256, SHA3-384, and SHA3-512.

> **TIP** The JCA and JCE are powerful low-level generic APIs that aren't developer-friendly. It's easy to misconfigure or accidentally misuse them. The rest of this chapter and subsequent chapters use JCA and JCE because they're the standard libraries in Java and are available to every Java program. You should be able to read code written with JCA and JCE. For production code, though, you should use a developer-friendly crypto library such as Google Tink (https://github.com/google/tink).

Tink is designed to reduce common programming errors when working with cryptography libraries. Tink provides Java, C++, Objective-C, Go, Python, and JavaScript implementations, so you can learn the library once and use it across multiple programming languages. The Java version of Tink is built as a developer-friendly layer on top of JCA and JCE, with some extra features that aren't available in the core Java libraries.

The following listing shows how to do the same encoding using the Tink library. You can find this example in the ssfa_ch4_ex2 project.

Listing 4.2 Hashing the refunds.json file using Tink

```
public static String hashRefundsJsonWithSha3(String resourceName)
  throws IOException, GeneralSecurityException {

  try (InputStream in =                                    Get an input stream to
        Main.class.getClassLoader()                        read the file contents.
             .getResourceAsStream(resourceName)) {    Define a MessageDigest
                                                       object which implements
    MessageDigest md =                                 the hashing algorithm.
        EngineFactory.MESSAGE_DIGEST.getInstance("SHA3-256");
                                                          Read the file content
    byte [] fileContent = in.readAllBytes();              as a byte array.
    byte [] digested =  md.digest(fileContent);       Apply the hashing function
    return HexFormat.of().formatHex(digested);        to the file content.
  }
}                                                     Return the digested content as
                                                      hexa formatted string.
```

When you run the project, you see that it produces the same result as the application you worked on earlier in this chapterl, ssfd_ch4_ex1:

```
SHA3-256(refunds.json) =
542b49a04073502046b0de5751d5f7a9afe7c1ff2d63524c0863233a53de0c14
```

Cryptographic algorithms are CPU-intensive. As you scale your applications to handle more users, you require more CPU cores, which increases operational costs. OpenJDK provides fast, portable implementations of cryptographic algorithms in Java. Low-level optimization techniques are possible in C and assembly language but not in Java. These optimizations can speed cryptographic operations at the expense of a more complex deployment.

Amazon and Google offer two highly optimized JCA providers: Amazon Corretto Crypto Provider (ACCP) and Google Conscrypt. ACCP (https://aws.amazon.com/blogs/opensource/introducing-amazon-corretto-crypto-provider-accp/) is a JCA implementation built on the highly optimized OpenSSL libcrypto native C library. Google Conscrypt (https://conscrypt.org/) is a JCA provider implemented on top of BoringSSL (https://boringssl.googlesource.com/boringssl/), which is Google's fork of the OpenSSL native library. One of the main advantages of Conscrypt is that it supports Android devices and OpenJDK.

It's easy to add the ACCP or Conscrypt provider to your deployment without rewriting your code. Starting with the default JCA provider implementations that ship with OpenJDK usually is best. You can switch providers when the cost savings from a nondefault provider outweigh the complexity of adding it to your deployment pipeline.

4.4   *Implementing message integrity in Java*

Over the past few pages, you've learned about cryptographic hash functions and the JCA. Now you're ready to implement the ACME scenario discussed earlier in this chapter. The scenario is reproduced here so you don't have to flip back.

ACME customers mail newly purchased shoes they don't like to the ACME warehouse for a refund. Members of the warehouse staff use the warehouse management application to authorize refunds after verifying that the returned shoes are in good condition. Once a day, the generated refund file is sent to the payment service for processing, as shown in figure 4.7.

The sample application discussed in this section implements the ACME data-corruption-detection scenario. You can find the code at https://github.com/Software-Security-For-Developers/software-security-for-developers. The GitHub repository contains detailed instructions on how to run the application on a developer's laptop. We recommend that you run the sample application to deepen your understanding of the topic. The sample repository includes two projects: `ssfd_ch4_ex3-warehouse` and `ssfd_ch4_ex3-payments`:

- *Warehouse* is a Java application that writes the `refunds.json` file and the `refunds.json.sha256` file containing the hash value of the `refunds.json` contents.

- *Payments* contains a Spring Boot application that reads the `refunds.json` file, computes the SHA-256 hash of its contents, and compares the computed value with the expected value stored in `refunds.json.sha256`. If the values match, the refunds file is processed (its values are displayed in the endpoint response); otherwise, an exception is thrown.

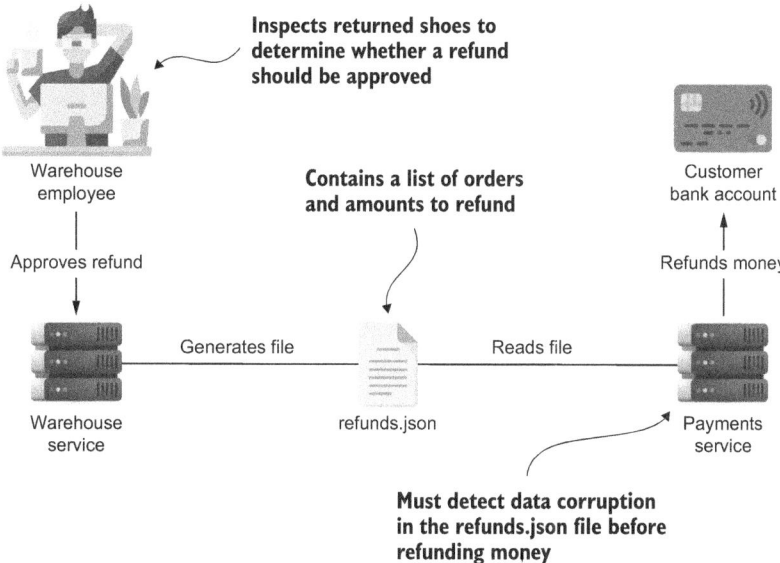

Figure 4.7   ACME staff members approve refunds using the warehouse management application. Once a day, the warehouse management application generates a refunds.json file. The payment service issues refunds to customers' credit cards for the amount specified in the refunds.json file.

Start by running Warehouse, which is a plain Java application. The project already provides a demo refunds.json file in the resources folder. Running the app generates another file containing the SHA-3 hash of the refunds.json file. It hashes the file the way we discussed previously.

The payments service uses the `Refund` record in the following snippet as the Java representation of refundable orders:

```
public record Refund(String orderId, BigDecimal amount) {
}
```

We kept the `Refund` record to the bare minimum so we could demonstrate cryptographic hash function concepts without making the sample application complex. The Payments app exposes an endpoint that receives both the refunds.json file and its hash. You'll find the endpoint's implementation in the next listing.

Listing 4.3 The refunds endpoint

```
@RestController
@RequestMapping("/api/refunds")
@AllArgsConstructor
public class RefundController {

  private final RefundService refundService;

  @PostMapping(consumes = MediaType.APPLICATION_JSON_VALUE,
          produces = MediaType.APPLICATION_JSON_VALUE)
  public List<Refund> uploadRefunds(
    @RequestHeader("X-Content-SHA3") String sha3,
    @RequestBody byte[] body) {
      return refundService.verifyAndReturnRefunds(body, sha3);
  }
}
```

The endpoint gets both the file (as a request body) and a hash string (as a HTTP header).

The controller further delegates to a service that implements the business case.

The next listing shows a simple implementation of the refunds service. The service method takes an input file along with its hash. It recalculates the hash of the received data and compares the result with the provided hash value. If the two match, the data is considered valid, and the application returns the orders in the response. If the hash is missing or the computed and provided hash values don't match, the application throws an exception.

Listing 4.4 The service that validates the received file by computing its hash

```
@Service
@AllArgsConstructor
public class RefundService {

  private final ObjectMapper objectMapper;
  private final HashManager hashManager;

  public List<Refund> verifyAndReturnRefunds(
    byte[] bodyBytes, String providedHashHex) {

    if (providedHashHex == null || providedHashHex.isBlank()) {
      throw new InvalidHashException(
              "Missing X-Content-SHA3 header");
    }

    String computed = hashManager.computeSha3Hex(bodyBytes);
    if (!computed.equalsIgnoreCase(providedHashHex.trim())) {
      throw new InvalidHashException(
              "Invalid SHA3 hash for provided refunds file");
    }

    try {
        return objectMapper.readValue(
            bodyBytes, new TypeReference<List<Refund>>(){});
    } catch (IOException e) {
```

The service compares its own calculated hash with the one it received. If they are not the same, it throws an exception.

```
      throw new IllegalArgumentException(
        "Invalid refunds JSON format", e);
    }
  }
}
```

Now it's time to try the example yourself. Run the Payments project, and call the endpoint. You can find detailed instructions in the project's README file. First, send the file along with the hash value generated by the Warehouse application. This call should succeed without exceptions. Next, modify the contents of the refunds.json file, but don't recalculate the hash. When you send the request again, the endpoint will throw an exception.

By computing the SHA-256 hash of the `refunds.json` file and comparing it with the expected hash stored in the `refunds.json.sha256` file, the payment service can detect accidental data corruption. But it can't detect whether a hacker changed `refunds.json` and generated a corresponding `refunds.json.sha256`. Detecting active tampering is the focus of section 4.5.

4.5   *Message authentication code*

In the preceding section, we detected accidental data corruption. But a hacker can fool the payment service into refunding the wrong amount by modifying `refunds.json` and the associated `refunds.json.sha256` file. To stop this type of attack, the payment service must validate two things before processing refunds:

- *Authenticity*—The `refunds.json` file was created by the warehouse service, not a hacker.
- *Integrity*—The `refunds.json` file was not modified after it was created.

We can extend the integrity-detection algorithm to construct a *message authentication code* (MAC) that provides integrity and authenticity. The MAC can be computed only by the sender and receiver of a message. An attacker can view and modify the message body but can't compute the MAC. A MAC enables the following data exchange:

- The sender generates the message body, computes the MAC on the message body, and sends the message and MAC to the recipient.
- The recipient receives the message body, computes the MAC on the received message body, and compares the computed MAC with the expected MAC. If the computed and expected MACs match, the message came from the sender and is unmodified. Figure 4.8 depicts the MAC.

The sender, the receiver, and a hacker can compute the cryptographic hash of a message's content because all anyone needs to compute the hash value is the message body. But computing the MAC requires both the message body and a secret key. The secret key is known to the sender and receiver but not the hacker, so the hacker can't compute a MAC. A MAC can be built from a cryptographic hash function, as shown in figure 4.9.

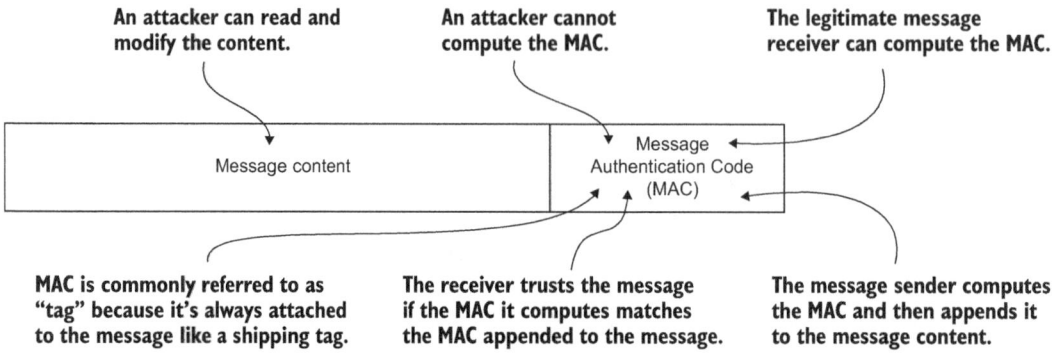

Figure 4.8   The MAC is data added to the end of a message that the receiver can use to verify who sent the message and whether it was tampered with.

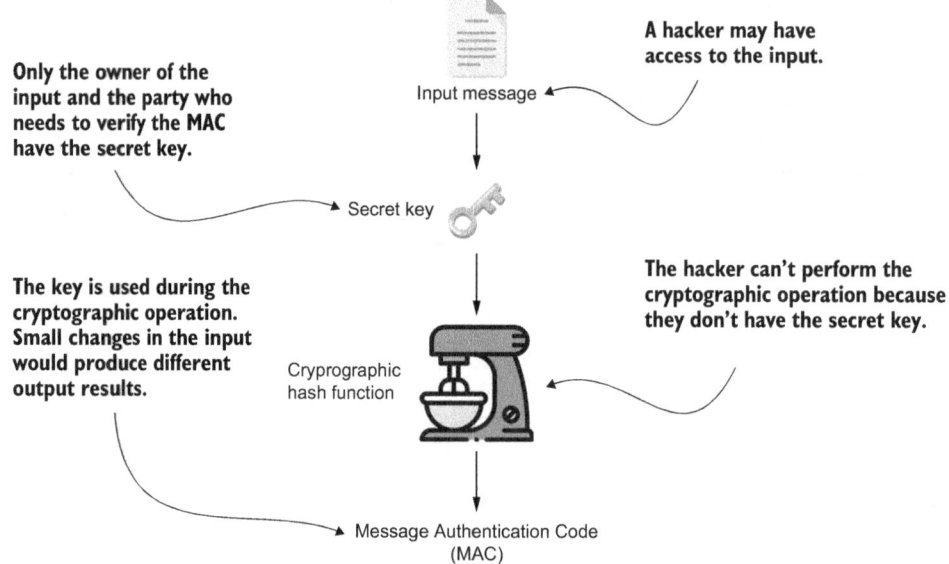

Figure 4.9   Computing the MAC requires both the secret key and the input message. If a hacker modifies the input, they can't compute a valid MAC because they don't know the secret key used in the computation. Without a valid MAC, they can't fool the receiver with a fake message body.

You can use many algorithms to implement a MAC. One popular approach is to build the MAC using a cryptographic hash function, as illustrated in figure 4.9. But be careful how the secret key is mixed with the input.

A simple approach to mixing the secret key into the input is concatenating the message body with the secret key and then computing the hash of the resulting string. If the input is "abc", the secret key is "123", and the hash function is SHA3-512, the MAC value is the result returned by SHA3-512("abc123").

WARNING   The concatenation approach for mixing the secret with the input is secure with some hash functions and insecure with others. SHA-2, for example, is unsafe with the concatenation approach, whereas SHA-3 is secure. Section 4.5 discusses a secure way to build a MAC from a hash function.

4.5.1   Hashed message authentication code

Hashed Message Authentication Code (HMAC) is a widely used approach to implementing a message authentication code using a cryptographic hash function and a secret key. HMAC works with SHA-2, SHA-3, and other hash functions. The output of the HMAC function is the same size as the output of the hash function it's configured to use. An HMAC based on SHA-256, for example, produces 256 bits of output.

The details of how the HMAC algorithm mixes the secret key with the input are beyond the scope of this book. Fortunately, programming language libraries have excellent out-of-the-box HMAC implementations, so you don't have to know how the HMAC algorithm works. All you have to know is when and how to use it.

TIP   In cryptographic literature, || indicates concatenation. "abc" || "123" results in the string "abc123", for example. The concatenation notation is used frequently in this book. A common mistake is assuming that an HMAC is computed by first concatenating the input bytes with the secret key and then hashing the result. If the input is "abc" and the secret key is "123", for example, SHA256("abc123") is not equal to HMAC("abc", "123", SHA256). HMAC uses a more elaborate algorithm.

4.5.2   Java support for HMAC

Java 21 supports computing HMACs using the MD5, SHA-1, SHA-2, and SHA-3 hash functions. Because MD5 and SHA-1 are insecure, they should be used only for processing historical data that relies on these older functions.

The following code shows a simple utility function that takes a byte array and a key, computes the HMAC of the input bytes using SHA-256, and returns the result as a hexadecimal string. You'll find this function in the ssfd_ch4_ex4 project provided with the book.

Listing 4.5   Computing an HMAC using SHA-256 in Java

```
public static byte[] hmacSha256(byte[] key, byte[] data) throws Exception {
  Mac mac = Mac.getInstance("HmacSHA256");
  mac.init(new SecretKeySpec(key, "HmacSHA256"));
  return mac.doFinal(data);
}
```

The javax.crypto.Mac class provides access to a variety of industry-standard HMAC algorithms. "HmacSHA256" is the standard name for an HMAC based on SHA-256. The "Java Security Standard Algorithm Names" document (https://docs.oracle.com/en/java/javase/11/docs/specs/security/standard-names.html) contains a list of all the algorithm names that can be passed to the `Mac.getInstance()` method. The `SecretKeySpec` class is a versatile way to store a key's bytes along with the algorithm for which it was designed. Its generic design allows it to be used with a variety of algorithms.

The key on the HMAC function should contain enough randomness to make it hard to guess. A 256-bit key for SHA-256 is a reasonable default. Because the HMAC key is effectively a password, you should treat it with care to make sure that it isn't stolen. Your corporate information-security team may have standards and recommendations on the minimum size of an HMAC key and which hash function to use with it. Consult the team before using an HMAC in your application.

HMAC is a key building block in many common industry-standard protocols, such as TLS and JWT. Developing an intuitive understanding of HMAC and how it's used will make security documentation much easier to understand.

4.5.3   *Exercises*

4 What extra guarantee does HMAC provide over a plain hash function?

5 Why is concatenating a secret key with a message and hashing it (for example, `SHA256("message" + "secret")`) not the same as HMAC?

6 Which cryptographic goals do SHA-2, SHA-3, and HMAC fulfill?

7 What risk exists if you hardcode HMAC secret keys in configuration files?

8 In the ACME refunds scenario, what happens if the refunds.json file is changed but the HMAC doesn't match?

4.6   *Guaranteeing authenticity using HMAC*

In this section, we'll review the implementation of the ACME scenario using an HMAC in Java. Recall that the Warehouse application sends a `refunds.json` file to the payments service so that the payments service can issue refunds to customers' credit cards. The payments service wants to ensure that the warehouse application created the `refunds.json` and that the file wasn't tampered with after it was created (figure 4.10).

When the payments service retrieves the `refunds.json` file, it computes `HMAC-SHA256(refunds.json, secret key)` and compares it with the expected value in `refunds.json.hs256`. If the values match, the data wasn't corrupted, and the creator of `refunds.json` and `refunds.json.hs256` must have known the secret key required to compute the HMAC. Because the secret key is known only to the warehouse application and the payments service, the payments service can assume that the `refunds.json` file was created by the warehouse application.

You can find this example implemented in the ssfd_ch4_ex5-warehouse and ssfd_ch4_ex5-payments projects provided with this book. The warehouse project is a plain Java application that calculates the HMAC for a refunds.json file stored in its resources folder. This application simulates the request payload generated by the warehouse service in the system. The payments project is a Spring Boot application that exposes an endpoint. It receives the refunds file in the HTTP request body, validates the HMAC, and processes the refunds (which in our simplified model means returning them in the HTTP response body). Figure 4.11 depicts the validation flow.

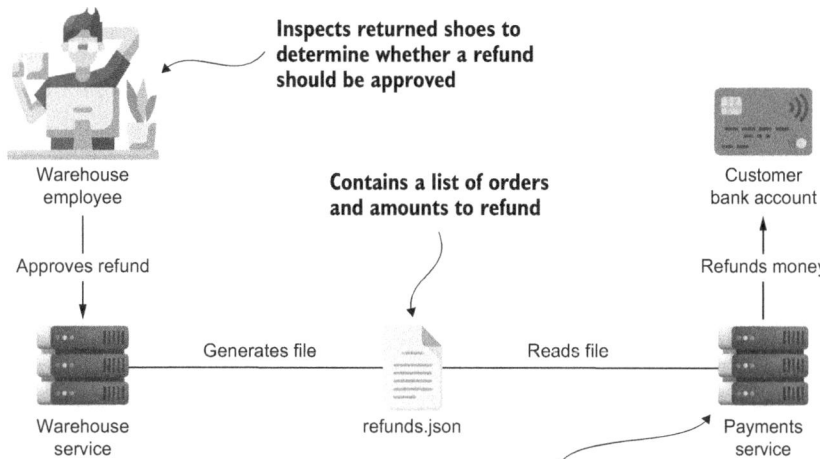

Figure 4.10 ACME staff members approve refunds in the warehouse management application. Once a day, the application generates a refunds.json file. Then the payment service issues refunds to customers' credit cards for the amounts specified in that file.

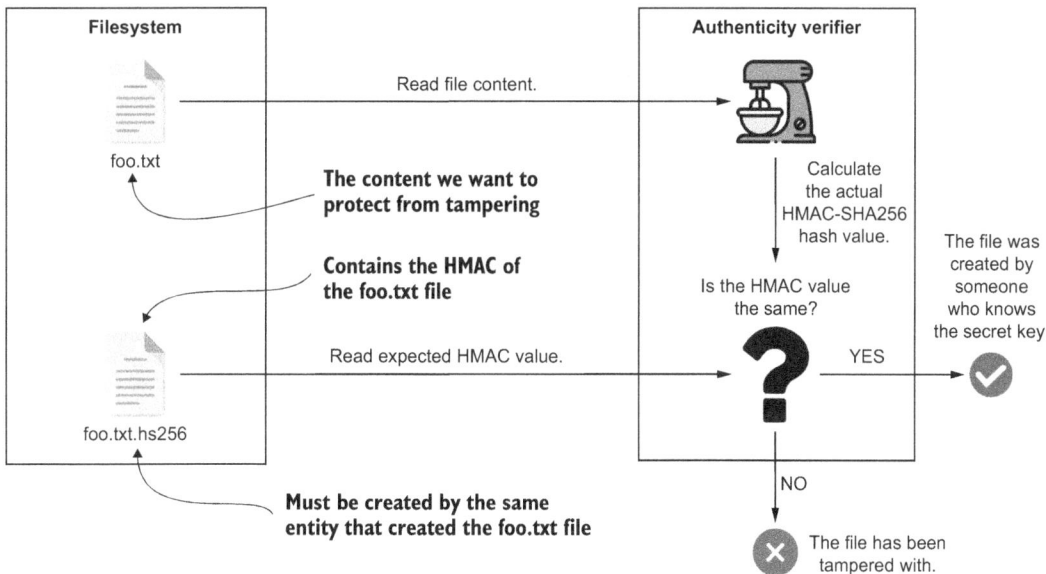

Figure 4.11 Determine who created a file and whether the file was tampered with by using an HMAC. The producer of the foo.txt file computes the HMAC-SHA-256 value of the content and writes it to foo.txt.hs256. A consumer computes the SHA-256 value of the contents of foo.txt and compares the computed value with the expected value in foo.txt.hs256. If the computed and expected HMAC values differ, the file has been tampered with, and an error should be raised.

An HMAC requires a *secret key* to be shared between the Warehouse application and the payments service. How do the Warehouse application and the payments service agree on the value of this secret key? For now, we simplify by assuming that the owners of the payments and warehouse services met in person and agreed on a secret key during the meeting. Meeting in person to agree on a shared key is problematic; we'll show how to solve the key-agreement problem in a later chapter.

> **WARNING**   Storing a key in a configuration file in plain text (especially if it's hardcoded) is a security antipattern. This book is dedicated to storing secrets securely in credential storage services. To keep the examples simple and focus on the concepts, we'll store secrets alongside the examples.

As you did in section 4.4, first run the Warehouse application to generate the `refunds.json.hs256` file. Then start the Payments project and call the `/api/refunds` endpoint. See the project README file for details.

By computing the HMAC-SHA256 hash of the refunds file and comparing it with the expected hash stored in the `refunds.json.hs256` file, the payment service can detect data corruption and ensure that the file was generated by someone who had the secret key used to create the MAC. The following listing shows the service method implementation in our example project.

Listing 4.6   Validating the HMAC before processing refunds

```
public List<Refund> verifyAndReturnRefunds(
  byte[] bodyBytes, String providedHmacHex) {

  if (providedHmacHex == null || providedHmacHex.isBlank()) {
    throw new InvalidHashException("Missing X-Content-HMAC header");
  }

  String computed = hmacManager
                  .computeHmacHex(bodyBytes);
  if (!computed.equalsIgnoreCase(providedHmacHex
                  .trim())) {
    throw new InvalidHashException(
      "Invalid HMAC for provided refunds file");
  }
  try {
    return objectMapper.readValue(
      bodyBytes, new TypeReference<List<Refund>>(){});
  } catch (IOException e) {
    throw new IllegalArgumentException("Invalid refunds JSON format", e);
  }
}
```

The payments service computes the HMAC on the received data.

The received HMAC is compared with the computed one. If they are not equal the service throws an exception and the request is rejected.

HMAC is widely used in many security protocols, including TLS. The knowledge you've gained in this chapter will help you better understand security protocols and libraries. Table 4.5 highlights the cryptographic goals that HMAC fulfills.

Table 4.5   Cryptography goals and algorithms matrix

Goal	SHA-2	SHA-3	HMAC
Integrity	Yes	Yes	Yes
Authentication	No	No	Yes
Confidentiality	No	No	No
Non-repudiation	No	No	No

Pat yourself on the back. You've learned a lot about cryptographic hash functions and MACs.

TIP   Even though HMAC doesn't provide content confidentiality, it's still a critical component of the security toolbox. You'll see some applications of HMAC in upcoming chapters.

4.7   *Exercise answers*

1 What are the four main goals of cryptography?

   Integrity (data isn't changed), authentication (you know who sent it), confidentiality (only the right people can read it), and nonrepudiation (senders can't deny sending it).

2 How is a cryptographic hash function different from the `hashCode()` method in Java?

   A cryptographic hash function produces a long, fixed-size output (such as 256 bits) designed for security, with properties such as being one-way and collision-resistant. The Java hashCode() method simply returns a 32-bit integer for use in hash tables and isn't secure for cryptography.

3 What problem does using SHA-256 on a file solve, and what problem does it not solve?

   It detects accidental corruption (such as network errors or disk corruption) because any change to the file changes the hash. It doesn't prevent active tampering; an attacker could change both the file and the hash.

4 What extra guarantee does HMAC provide over a plain hash function?

   HMAC ensures authenticity in addition to integrity. Only parties with the secret key can generate or validate the HMAC, so attackers can't forge a valid one.

5 Why is concatenating a secret key with a message and hashing it (e.g., `SHA256("message" + "secret")`) not the same as HMAC?

   HMAC uses a carefully designed algorithm to combine the key and message. Simple concatenation is insecure with some hash functions (such as SHA-2), but HMAC remains secure with algorithms such as SHA-2 and SHA-3.

6 Which cryptographic goals do SHA-2, SHA-3, and HMAC fulfill?

   – SHA-2 and SHA-3—Integrity only

– HMAC—Integrity and authentication

– None—Confidentiality and nonrepudiation

7 What risk exists if you hardcode HMAC secret keys in configuration files?

Attackers who gain access to the code or config can steal the secret key. A best practice is to store keys in a secure credential store, not in plain text.

8 In the ACME refunds scenario, what happens if the `refunds.json` file is changed but the HMAC doesn't match?

The payments service rejects the file, throws an exception, and processes no refunds.

Summary

- Cryptography solves four fundamental security problems: integrity (whether data is unchanged), authentication (sender identity), confidentiality (data privacy), and nonrepudiation (legal proof of a transaction).
- Cryptographic hash functions like SHA-2 and SHA-3 produce fixed-size outputs for any input and have one-way and collision-resistant properties, making them ideal for detecting data corruption.
- Hash functions are deterministic: the same input always produces the same output, but different inputs produce different outputs.
- SHA-1 and MD5 are deprecated due to security vulnerabilities, whereas SHA-2 and SHA-3 are generally considered secure for new applications.
- Cryptographic hash functions can detect accidental data corruption but can't prevent active tampering by attackers who modify both data and hash files.
- A MAC uses a secret key shared between sender and receiver to ensure message integrity and authenticity.
- HMAC is a secure way to build a MAC using cryptographic hash functions and secret keys and is widely used in protocols such as TLS and JWT.
- JCA and JCE provide cryptographic support through a provider-based architecture with standardized APIs.
- Simply concatenating secret keys with messages before hashing is insecure with some algorithms, but HMAC provides a secure mixing method across all supported hash functions.
- Applications should design for hash function upgrades because algorithms become insecure over time, requiring version fields and migration strategies.
- HMAC enables detection of both accidental corruption and active tampering because attackers can't forge a valid HMAC value without knowing the secret key.
- To prevent theft, store secret keys for HMAC securely in credential management systems rather than hardcoded in configuration files.

Advanced Encryption Standard

This chapter covers

- Using Advanced Encryption Standard (AES) to protect data confidentiality
- Selecting a safe AES operating mode for typical application development needs
- Using AES in Galois/Counter Mode to provide confidentiality, integrity, and authenticity

Users expect applications to protect their data and keep it confidential according to the laws where they live. Citizens of the European Union (EU), for example, expect applications to comply with the General Data Protection Regulation (GDPR). Encryption is required in most applications because most countries have laws governing data confidentiality. As a developer, you must be able to use encryption to protect user data.

The Advanced Encryption Standard (AES) is the most widely used technology for ensuring data confidentiality. All public cloud providers, including Amazon, Google, and Microsoft, use AES extensively to secure their APIs and services.

Windows, Linux, and macOS use AES for disk encryption. Foundational networking protocols such as Internet Protocol Security (IPsec), Transport Layer Security (TLS), and Secure Shell (SSH) also use AES to deliver security.

Working with AES is a critical security skill for an application developer. This chapter provides a developer-friendly introduction to AES. We won't cover the mathematical details that underpin AES. Instead, we'll show you how to use AES through a series of Java sample applications, building the intuition you need to use AES successfully.

5.1   AES overview

To keep data safe during transmission or storage, you must encrypt it. *Encryption* scrambles data using a key, making it look like a random sequence of bits. This ensures that no one can understand the data without the correct key.

Decryption is the process of reversing the scrambling to turn encrypted data back into its original form. The original data is called plaintext, and the scrambled, encrypted version is called ciphertext. Figure 5.1 depicts the relationship between encryption and decryption.

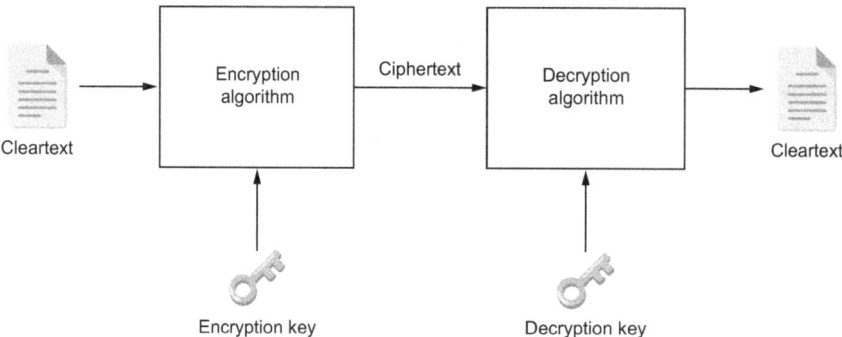

Figure 5.1   A cipher consists of an algorithm and a key for encrypting and decrypting data. The details of the encryption and decryption algorithm are public knowledge; the key is secret. If the same key is used to encrypt and decrypt, the cipher is called a symmetric cipher; otherwise, it's called an asymmetric cipher.

DEFINITION   *Encryption* is the process of transforming readable data (plaintext) into an unreadable form (ciphertext) using a key, so that only someone with the right key can turn it back into its original form.

DEFINITION   *Decryption* is the process of transforming encrypted data (ciphertext) back into its original, readable form (plaintext) with the correct key.

Encryption algorithms can be classified in two families: symmetric and asymmetric. Symmetric ciphers use the same key to encrypt and decrypt data; they're covered in this chapter. Asymmetric ciphers use a pair of keys, one for encrypting data and another for decrypting data; they're covered in chapter 6.

Designing a secure encryption algorithm for use in industry and government on a wide range of devices, from low-power IoT devices to phones and supercomputers, is a huge engineering effort. AES is the de facto standard for symmetric key encryption algorithms used in all applications, including cloud-native applications. All major CPU architectures—Intel, ARM, and others—provide hardware support and acceleration for AES, so you don't need to worry about performance when using AES.

History of AES

In 1997, the National Institute of Standards and Technology (NIST) ran an open competition to select "an unclassified, publicly disclosed encryption algorithm capable of protecting sensitive government information well into the next century." The competition attracted 15 submissions, which were put through rigorous analysis before a winner was selected. Rijndael, an algorithm designed in 1998 by Belgian academics Vincent Rijmen and Joan Daemen, was selected as the AES standard in 2001. Before AES, the *Data Encryption Standard* (DES) was the official encryption algorithm of the U.S. government. DES was designed by IBM and the U.S. cyber spies at the National Security Agency (NSA). Many researchers and organizations outside the United States were suspicious that the NSA had engineered a weakness in DES. The open process used to select the winning AES algorithm contributed to confidence in AES's security, even among those who were suspicious of the NSA's intentions.

The AES algorithm requires its input to be 128 bits (16 bytes) long. If the input is shorter than 128 bits, you must add extra bits to make the input exactly 128 bits. Adding extra bits is called *padding*. If the input is longer than 128 bits, you must break it into a series of 128-bit blocks.

> **DEFINITION** Encryption algorithms like AES, which work on a fixed-size input, are called *block ciphers*. A *block-cipher algorithm* is a method of encrypting data by dividing it into fixed-size blocks (such as 128 bits) and transforming each block into ciphertext using a secret key.

Because AES uses the same secret key for encryption and decryption, that key is classified as a symmetric block cipher (figure 5.2). AES supports key sizes of 128, 192, and 256 bits, which determine the encryption's security level. Larger key sizes provide greater resistance to brute-force attacks but don't make the algorithm more correct or fundamentally different. In practice, AES-128 is considered secure for most real-world applications; AES-256 is typically chosen when long-term confidentiality or regulatory requirements demand a higher security margin. Larger keys have a performance cost, but that cost is usually modest on modern hardware, especially when hardware acceleration is available. As a result, selecting a key size is primarily a tradeoff among required security assurance, compliance requirements, and acceptable performance overhead.

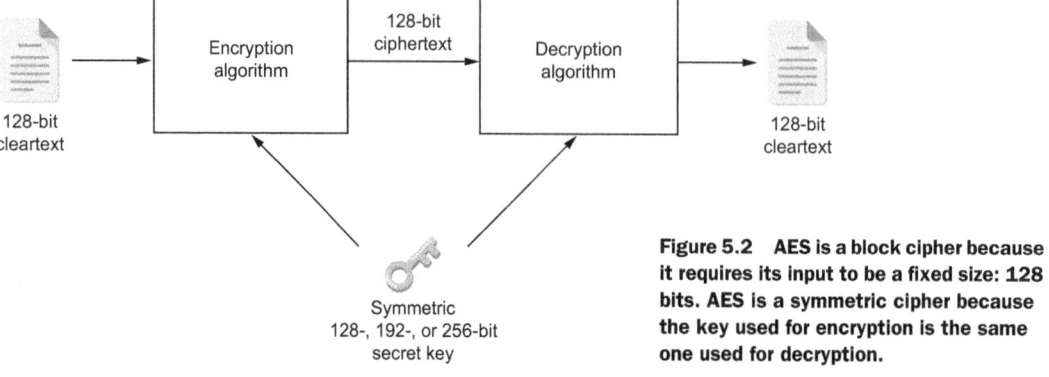

Figure 5.2 **AES is a block cipher because it requires its input to be a fixed size: 128 bits. AES is a symmetric cipher because the key used for encryption is the same one used for decryption.**

WARNING AES offers multiple configuration options. Unfortunately, some AES configurations are insecure and shouldn't be used. Using a secure AES configuration is critical. How do you determine whether a particular AES configuration is secure? The rest of this chapter provides an overview of the key AES configuration settings, along with recommendations that are considered safe today. Corporate security teams publish recommendations on AES configurations that developers should use. Consult your information-security team for its recommended AES configurations.

5.2 Modes of operation

The mode of operation is the most complex and essential topic for an application developer to understand for AES. We've broken this section into small subsections to make the learning journey easier. You may want to come back to review this section when you've finished the chapter.

Suppose that you want to encrypt a 1,605-byte message with AES. Because AES works only on 16-byte blocks, you must break the message into 1,001 blocks—1,000 16-byte blocks plus a final block with 5 bytes of message content and 11 bytes of padding. Then you need a way to apply AES to each of the 1,001 blocks. The algorithm for breaking input into blocks of 16 bytes and applying AES to each block is called the *mode of operation*.

DEFINITION A *mode of operation* is a method that describes how to apply a block-cipher algorithm to encrypt or decrypt data larger than a single block.

In Electronic Codebook (ECB) mode, for example, each 16-byte block is encrypted independently with the secret key. Then the ciphertext blocks are concatenated to produce the encrypted output (figure 5.3).

If the input blocks repeat, the ciphertext will repeat because the AES encryption function is deterministic. Given the same input block and the same secret, it always produces the same output. An attacker can count how many times a ciphertext repeats, gaining information about repeating patterns in the cleartext.

Input of arbitrary length is broken into blocks of 16 bytes (128-bits) so that each block can be encrypted. Additional padding is needed if the initial contenent cannot be split exactly and the last block is smaller.

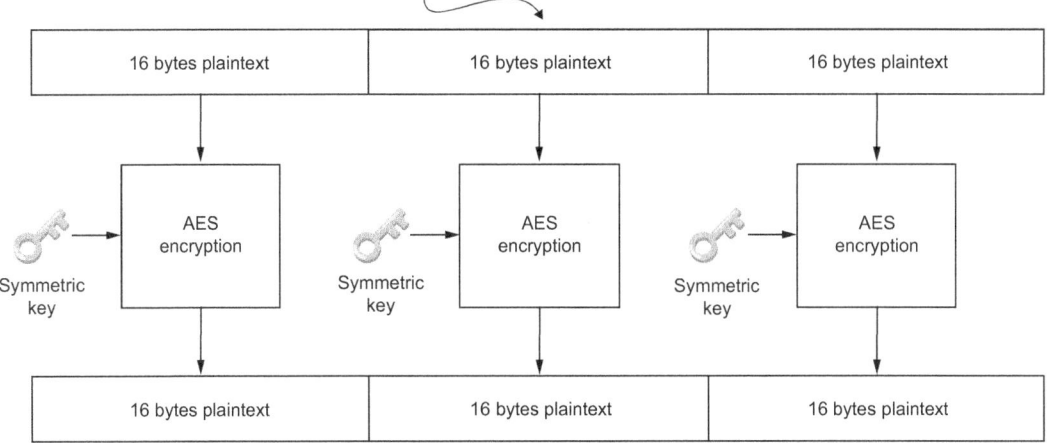

Figure 5.3   ECB mode encrypts each input block independently using the secret key and concatenates the resulting ciphertext. ECB mode is simple but insecure; never use it.

Suppose that the ECB mode of operation is used to encrypt HTTP requests and responses. The attacker knows that every successful HTTP response starts with the line HTTP/1.1 200 OK, which is 15 characters. Adding the newline character yields a 16-byte block. AES is deterministic, so encrypting HTTP/1.1 200 OK 100 times with the same key produces the same ciphertext every time. The attacker looks for repeating patterns in the ciphertext to deduce that a particular sequence of ciphertext corresponds to HTTP/1.1 200 OK. The attacker can manipulate HTTP responses by substituting the ciphertext that corresponds to HTTP/1.1 200 OK in places where the response code should not have been 200 OK. The attacker can change the meaning of the response without having to crack the encryption key. The ECB mode of operation is part of the AES standard, but it isn't secure and shouldn't be used.

> **WARNING**   Never use ECB mode in your applications. When searching online for code samples that implement AES in your favorite programming language, you'll run into samples that use AES/ECB mode. Don't just copy and paste code and accidentally use ECB mode. Don't use ECB mode unless you're reading historical data encrypted in ECB mode and have to decrypt it so you can re-encrypt it with a better AES mode.

A block-cipher mode of operation is a generic concept that works with any encryption algorithm that operates on fixed-sized input blocks. You can choose among many modes of operation. AES supports the following:

- *ECB*—Encrypts each block of data independently, but it's insecure because identical plaintext blocks produce identical ciphertext blocks

- *Cipher-block chaining (CBC)*—Encrypts each block based on the previous block, making it more secure than ECB but requiring an initialization vector (IV)
- *Cipher feedback (CFB)*—Converts a block cipher to a stream cipher, allowing encryption of data smaller than the block size
- *Output feedback (OFB)*—Similar to CFB but generates the keystream independently of the plaintext, making it resistant to error propagation
- *Counter (CTR)*—Transforms a block cipher into a stream cipher by encrypting a counter value for each block, providing high efficiency and parallelism
- *Galois/Counter mode (GCM)*—Combines CTR mode for encryption with Galois field multiplication for authentication, ensuring both confidentiality and integrity
- *Synthetic initialization vector (SIV)*—Resistant to IV misuse, ensuring security even if the IV is repeated
- *AES-GCM-SIV*—A variant of GCM that offers better protection against nonce reuse while maintaining high performance

Applications always use AES in a specific mode of operation. Data encrypted with one mode can't be decrypted with another mode. Each mode of operation makes different security, usability, and performance tradeoffs.

> **NOTE**   If you get a statement such as "This application encrypts data using an AES-256 key," you must ask, "Which AES operating mode is the application using?" Unless you know which mode is in use, you can't evaluate the security of the encrypted data.

AES supports many operating modes because it's designed for use in a variety of situations that demand different tradeoffs among security, power consumption, and simplicity. A low-power temperature sensor installed in an office building, for example, has different security requirements from a public-facing credit card processing API, but both can use an AES operating mode that makes the right tradeoffs.

Unfortunately, some modes of operation, such as ECB, are insecure, and you should never use them. Other modes are covered by patents, so they're not widely deployed. Explaining all the AES operating modes is beyond the scope of this book. We'll focus on two commonly used modes, CBC and GCM, because you are likely to encounter them in enterprise applications.

> **TIP**   If you're unsure what AES mode to use and your company doesn't have a published recommendation, go with GCM or one of its variations, such as AES-GCM-SIV.

5.2.1   CBC mode

CBC is a mode of operation for AES encryption, designed to make each ciphertext block appear random even when the same plaintext is encrypted multiple times. This helps prevent attackers from spotting patterns in the ciphertext that could reveal clues about the original data. If a message contains repeated sections, for example, CBC ensures that those repetitions are invisible in the encrypted output.

CBC achieves this by chaining data blocks together during encryption. Each plaintext block is combined with the previous block's ciphertext before it is encrypted, ensuring that the encryption of each block depends on the one before it and making patterns difficult to detect.

To use AES in CBC mode, you need two essential components:

- *Secret key*—Used to encrypt and decrypt data. It must be shared securely between the sender and receiver.
- *IV*—A random value used to start the encryption process for the first block, ensuring that the encryption is different each time even if the same plaintext and key are used.

The secret key is known only to the parties that should have access to the data. The IV is a random 128-bit value used in CBC mode to ensure that the generated ciphertext has no repeating patterns even if the plaintext being encrypted does. The word vector might remind you of college mathematics. Rest assured that in the context of AES initialization, a vector is a random value that should be used only once.

In cryptographic terminology, a number that's used only once is called a *nonce*. Figure 5.4 provides a visual explanation of the CBC mode of operation.

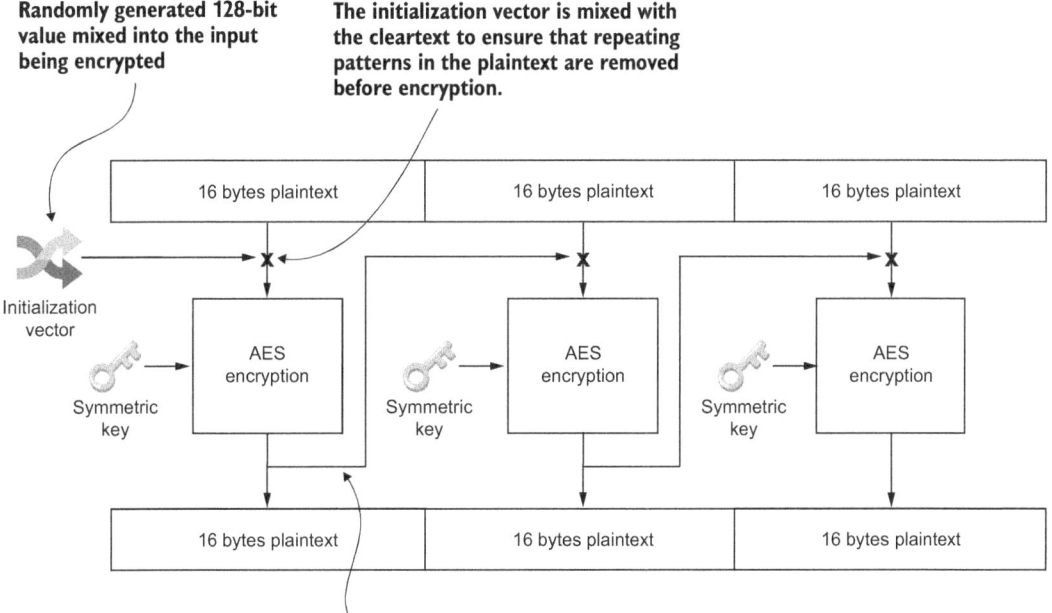

Figure 5.4 CBC takes the output of one block and feeds it into the next. The net result is that even if you encrypt the same data multiple times, the ciphertext looks random. An attacker can't determine patterns in the underlying data by looking for patterns in the ciphertext.

The IV is combined with the first 128-bit plaintext block to generate the first cipher block. Then the first cipher block is combined with the second plaintext block, and the result is encrypted using AES. This chaining process repeats for all blocks.

To decrypt data encrypted with AES CBC mode, you need both the key and the IV. Only the key is treated as a secret value; the IV is stored as cleartext so that the ciphertext can be decrypted later. You should use the IV only once with a specific key.

> **NOTE** If you want to encrypt two different files with the same AES key, you must use a different IV for each one.

A good mental model for understanding AES in CBC mode is a black box that takes an input message of any length, a secret key, and a random IV. The purpose is to produce an output consisting of the IV followed by the ciphertext. Figure 5.5 depicts AES in CBC mode.

> **WARNING** If a key and IV combination is reused, you can end up with catastrophic encryption failure. An attacker might be able to compute the original encryption key or recover the ciphertext, for example. The exact consequences of reusing an initialization vector depend on the mathematics underlying the mode of operation. The detailed implications are beyond the scope of this book. The key takeaway is that you should never reuse an IV across encryption operations.

> **TIP** Every time you call the AES encryption function, you should generate a new random IV using a cryptographically secure random-number generator such as `java.security.SecureRandom`.

Another interesting aspect of AES-CBC to consider is that if a file is encrypted with AES-CBC, an attacker can tamper with it by randomly modifying some bits. Upon decryption, AES-CBC will return corrupt plaintext, causing problems for the user.

In a blog post (https://cybergibbons.com/reverse-engineering-2/why-is-unauthenticated-encryption-insecure/), Andrew Tierney demonstrates how an attacker with access to the AES-CBC-encrypted ciphertext for the message "A dog's breakfast" can modify it to say "A cat's breakfast" without knowing the encryption key or breaking AES. AES-CBC mode guarantees the confidentiality of the encrypted data (table 5.1); it doesn't protect the integrity or authenticity of the data. Table 5.1 shows which security goals AES-CBC mode provides.

Table 5.1 Cryptography goals and algorithms matrix

Goal	SHA-2	SHA-3	HMAC	AES-CBC
Integrity	Yes	Yes	Yes	No
Authentication	No	No	Yes	No
Confidentiality	No	No	No	Yes
Nonrepudiation	No	No	No	No

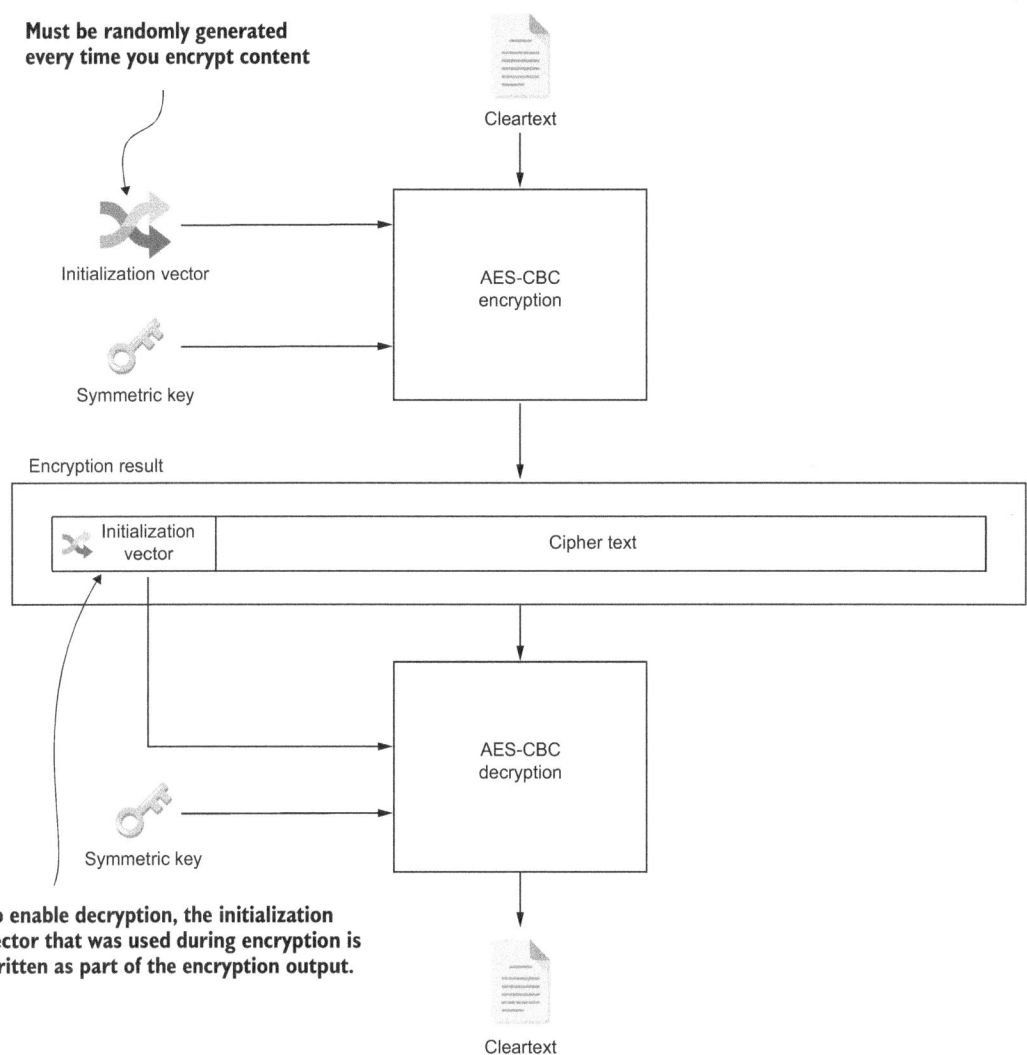

Figure 5.5 AES in CBC mode can be visualized as a black box that takes three inputs: plaintext, key, and IV. The IV is written to the output in plaintext, followed by the ciphertext computed by AES in CBC mode. The decryption process requires three inputs: IV, ciphertext, and key. The IV and ciphertext can be read from the output bytes; the key must be provided by the party performing the decryption.

WARNING   AES-CBC mode provides confidentiality only. In practice, security also requires integrity and authentication. So don't use AES-CBC mode; instead, use AES-GCM mode, which we explain in section 5.2.3.

5.2.2   Authenticated encryption

As you saw earlier, data confidentiality alone is insufficient. An attacker can tamper with encrypted data in highly detrimental ways to compromise applications. Authenticated encryption refers to any encryption scheme that provides data integrity, authenticity, and confidentiality.

Authenticated encryption can be implemented by combining message authentication codes (MACs) with an encryption algorithm. Data is encrypted using AES-CBC, for example, and then a hash-based message authentication code (HMAC) is computed over the ciphertext. Before decryption, the HMAC of the ciphertext is used to ensure that it hasn't been tampered with. There are three ways to combine encryption and MACs:

- *Encrypt-and-MAC*—Encrypt the plaintext and calculate the MAC of the plaintext. The Secure Shell (SSH) protocol takes this approach. Only cryptography experts should use Encrypt-and-MAC because it can lead to subtle security bugs.
- *MAC-then-Encrypt*—Compute the MAC over the plaintext and then encrypt both the plaintext and the MAC. The TLS 1.2 protocol takes this approach. Only cryptography experts should use MAC-then-Encrypt because it can lead to subtle security bugs.
- *Encrypt-then-MAC*—Encrypt the plaintext and then compute the MAC of the encrypted text. The IPsec protocol takes this approach, which is the most secure option for combining encryption and MACs.

Combining encryption and MACs correctly is tricky. Cryptographers designed several modes of operation for AES that provide authenticated encryption.

> **WARNING** The designers of major protocols such as SSH and TLS made mistakes when combining encryption with MACs, which caused vulnerabilities in early versions of these protocols. Use an authenticated-encryption mode such as GCM instead of rolling your own authenticated-encryption scheme.

5.2.3   *GCM*

AES-GCM is an operating mode that ensures integrity, authenticity, and confidentiality. AES-GCM provides security equivalent to encrypting with AES-CBC mode and then computing MAC over the ciphertext. Explaining the mathematical details of how GCM mode works is beyond the scope of this book, so we'll focus instead on the essential details developers should know.

Think of AES-GCM mode as a black box that takes three inputs: plaintext, a secret key, and a random initialization vector to produce an output consisting of the IV followed by the ciphertext and MAC. Figure 5.6 shows AES in GCM mode.

GCM is popular because it's fast and provides both encryption and data integrity. But it also has some drawbacks that developers must be aware of.

The most serious problem is nonce reuse. GCM requires a unique, never-repeated nonce for every encryption performed with the same key. If the same nonce is accidentally reused even once, the security of the encrypted data can be severely compromised. An attacker may learn information about the plaintext or even create forged messages that appear to be valid.

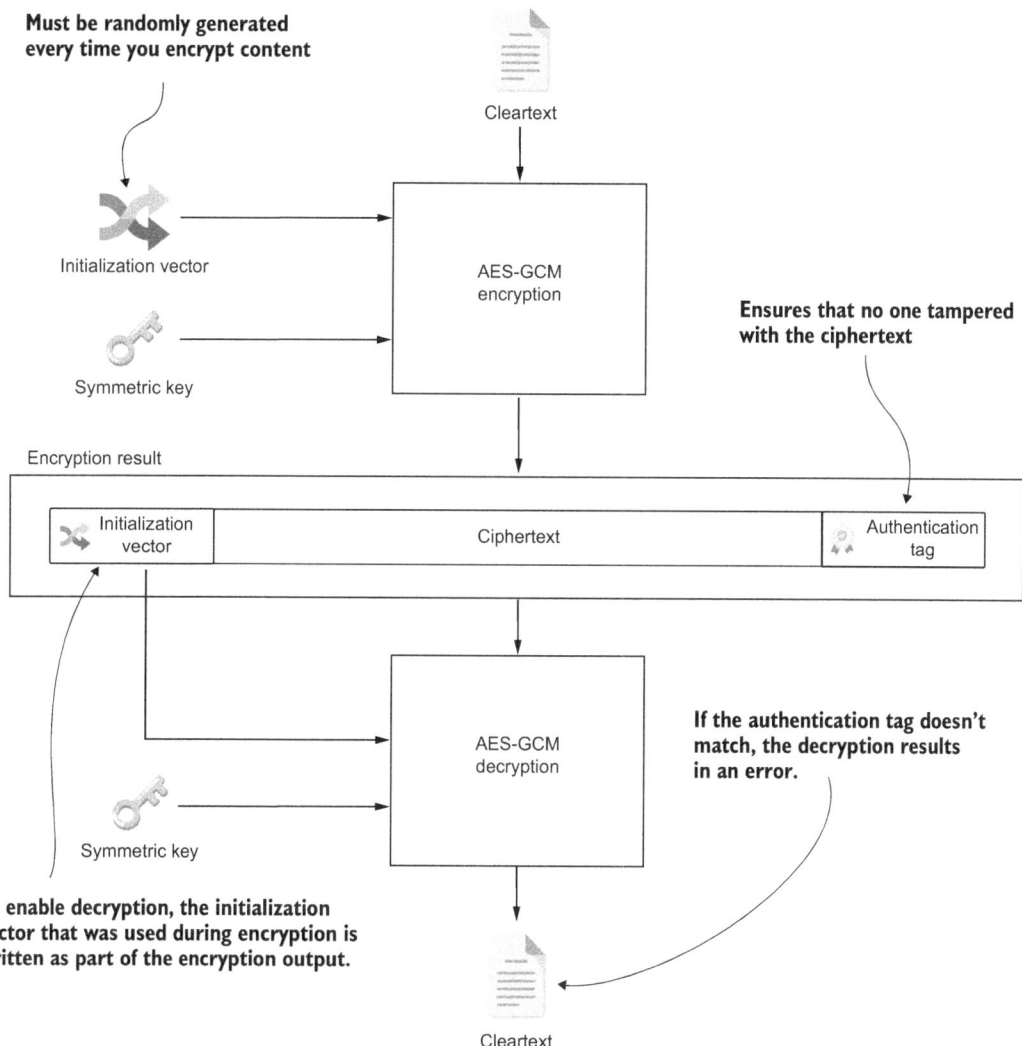

Must be randomly generated every time you encrypt content

Cleartext

Initialization vector

AES-GCM encryption

Ensures that no one tampered with the ciphertext

Symmetric key

Encryption result

| Initialization vector | Ciphertext | Authentication tag |

AES-GCM decryption

If the authentication tag doesn't match, the decryption results in an error.

Symmetric key

To enable decryption, the initialization vector that was used during encryption is written as part of the encryption output.

Cleartext

Figure 5.6 **AES in GCM mode, shown as a black box that processes three inputs: plaintext, key, and IV. The algorithm outputs the IV (used in plaintext) followed by the ciphertext it computes and the authentication code generated by GCM mode. To decrypt, you provide four inputs: IV, ciphertext, key, and authentication code. The algorithm uses these inputs to verify the data's integrity and recover the original plaintext.**

Another downside is that GCM is fragile when misused and doesn't fail gracefully when implemented incorrectly. Small mistakes—such as using predictable nonces, truncating authentication tags, or reusing keys for too long—can undermine its security guarantees. Unlike some other modes, GCM offers little protection against developer errors.

Finally, although GCM is very efficient on modern hardware, its correct use requires careful handling of details such as nonce generation, key management, and error checking. For this reason, GCM works best when you use it through well-tested cryptographic libraries and high-level APIs rather than implement it manually.

In GCM mode, the decryption algorithm first verifies that the authentication code is valid. If the code is invalid, it raises an error and doesn't attempt decryption. You should always use an authenticated encryption mode. AES-GCM is widely implemented, so GCM should be your default mode whenever you use AES. AES in GCM mode delivers three of the four goals of cryptography (table 5.2).

Table 5.2   **Cryptography goals and algorithms**

Goal	SHA-2	SHA-3	HMAC	AES-CBC	AES-GCM
Integrity	Yes	Yes	Yes	No	Yes
Authentication	No	No	Yes	No	Yes
Confidentiality	No	No	No	Yes	Yes
Nonrepudiation	No	No	No	No	No

WARNING   Reusing an initialization vector (IV) with GCM is catastrophic. Never reuse IVs with AES-GCM. Also, IVs must be unique and unpredictable. Although AES is very secure, it's easy to make mistakes when writing code that uses it, such as reusing an IV, not using enough randomness, or making other implementation errors. Secure coding practices and code reviews help ensure that you don't accidentally introduce a vulnerability.

5.2.4   *Exercises*

1 What extra guarantees does AES-GCM provide compared with AES-CBC?
2 Why is reusing an IV in AES-GCM dangerous?
3 Which cryptographic goals do AES-CBC and AES-GCM fulfill?
4 In the ACME-refunds scenario, what happens if the encrypted refunds.json file is tampered with?

5.3   *Java support for AES*

Java 21 ships with first-class support for AES in several operating modes, including CBC and GCM. Working with AES requires generating IVs, which are random sequences of bytes. The utility method in the following listing generates the requested number of random bytes using a cryptographically secure random number generator. You can find this method in the `ssfd_ch5_ex1` project provided with the book.

Listing 5.1   Generating secure random numbers

```
import java.security.SecureRandom;

public class CryptoUtils {

  private static final SecureRandom secureRandom
  ➥= new SecureRandom();
```

Always use a secure source of randomness when generating initialization vectors for AES.

```
private static byte[] randomBytes(int length) {          ◄─┐  Securely generate the
  byte[] bytes = new byte[amount];                          │  specified number of
  secureRandom.nextBytes(bytes);                            │  random bytes.
  return bytes;
}
```

WARNING In Java, java.util.Random isn't cryptographically secure and should never be used to generate random bytes for cryptographic use. Always use java.security.SecureRandom instead. When coding in an IDE, be careful not to import Random instead of SecureRandom by accident.

The following utility function takes an array of bytes and encrypts it using AES in GCM mode with a 256-bit key. You can find this method in the ssfd_ch5_ex2 project provided with the book.

Listing 5.2 Encrypting with AES-GCM

```
public static byte[] encryptAes256GCM(
  byte[] clearText,
  byte[] key) {

  try {                                                   Get a random
    byte[] iv = generateRandomBytes(12);         ◄───────  initialization vector.

    Cipher cipher = Cipher
    ⇒.getInstance("AES/GCM/NoPadding");          ◄─┐  Get an implementation of
                                                    │  the AES algorithm in GCM
    GCMParameterSpec gcmSpec =                       │  mode with no padding.
      new GCMParameterSpec(128, iv);
                                                        Configure the cipher to
    SecretKeySpec keySpec = new SecretKeySpec(key, "AES");  encrypt and generate
                                                           │ 128-bit authentication
    cipher.init(Cipher.ENCRYPT_MODE,                       │ tags and to use a 12-byte
    ⇒keySpec, gcmSpec);                          ◄─────────┘ initialization vector.

    byte[] cipherText = cipher.doFinal(clearText);   ◄──┤ Encrypt the plain text.

    byte[] result = new byte[iv.length               ┌─  Add the initialization vector
    ⇒+ cipherText.length];                       ◄───┘  just before the cipher text.

        System.arraycopy(iv, 0, result, 0, iv.length);
    System.arraycopy(cipherText, 0, result, iv.length, cipherText.length);

    return result;

  } catch (Exception e) {
    throw new RuntimeException("AES-256-GCM encryption failed", e);
  }
}
```

The code starts by obtaining an instance of javax.crypto.Cipher using the Cipher.getInstance() method. Cipher is the Java Cryptography Extensions (JCE) API for encrypting and decrypting data; it's a stateful object and not thread-safe.

The algorithm name follows the pattern algorithm/mode/padding—as in "AES/ GCM/NoPadding". The Java Security Standard Algorithm Names document (https:// docs.oracle.com/en/java/javase/11/docs/specs/security/standard-names.html) lists all the algorithm names that can be passed to the `Cipher.getInstance()` method. Before the cipher can be used, it must be initialized with three parameters:

- The mode to configure the cipher in encrypt or decrypt mode.
- The AES key to use.
- The GCM configuration, which in this case uses a 128-bit message authentication tag and a 12-byte IV. A 12-byte IV is the NIST-recommended size, but always check with your infosec team on important algorithm choices such as IV size.

You can encrypt all the data at the same time by calling `doFinal()`. Alternatively, you can call `update()` and pass the data in chunks, which can be useful for encrypting a large file that you don't want to read into a byte array. The `Cipher` class defines methods for processing associated data. Please consult the Javadoc on `Cipher` for details.

The IV must be available to the code that decrypts the cipher text. The preceding sample concatenates the 12-byte IV with the cipher text. The decryption code has to break the input byte array into two parts—the 12-byte IV and the ciphertext—as shown in the following listing.

Listing 5.3   Decryption of AES-GCM encrypted data

```
public static byte[] decryptAes256GCM(byte[] ivAndCiphertext, byte[] key) {
  try {
    byte[] iv = new byte[12];
    byte[] cipherText
      = new byte[ivAndCiphertext.length - 12];

    System.arraycopy(ivAndCiphertext, 0, iv, 0, 12);
    System.arraycopy(ivAndCiphertext, 12,
        cipherText, 0, cipherText.length);

    Cipher cipher
      = Cipher.getInstance("AES/GCM/NoPadding");
    GCMParameterSpec gcmSpec
      = new GCMParameterSpec(128, iv);
    SecretKeySpec keySpec
      = new SecretKeySpec(key, "AES");
    cipher.init(Cipher.DECRYPT_MODE,
      keySpec, gcmSpec);

    return cipher.doFinal(cipherText);
  } catch (Exception e) {
    throw new RuntimeException("AES-256-GCM decryption failed", e);
  }
}
```

Separate the input into the initialization vector and the cipher text.

Configure the cipher.

Decrypt the input.

TIP   As discussed in chapter 4, you can use alternative libraries that sometimes make the code cleaner and simpler. One such library is Google Tink, available at https://github.com/google/tink.

The next listing shows how to use Tink to encrypt and decrypt with AES-GCM. We're simply using the methods defined by the library; we don't have to implement the cryptographic operations ourselves. This example is in the ssfd_ch5_ex3 project provided with the book.

Listing 5.4 Encryption and decryption with AES in GCM mode using Tink

```
public static void main(String[] args) throws Exception {
  AeadConfig.register();

  KeysetHandle keysetHandle = KeysetHandle.generateNew(
    AesGcmKeyManager.aes256GcmTemplate());

  Aead aead = keysetHandle.getPrimitive(Aead.class);

  byte[] plaintext = "Hello, Tink AES-GCM!"
    .getBytes(StandardCharsets.UTF_8);

  byte[] ciphertext                              ⟵─┐ Encrypting the
    = aead.encrypt(plaintext, null);                │ plain text

  byte[] decrypted                               ⟵─┐ Decrypting
    = aead.decrypt(ciphertext, null);               │ the cipher

  // Print results
}
```

5.3.1 *The ACME scenario*

Recall the ACME refund-processing scenario from chapter 4. Customers mail shoes they don't like to ACME's warehouse. Warehouse employees verify that the returned shoes are in good condition before authorizing a credit card refund using the warehouse management app. Once a day, the application produces a refunds.json file and sends it to the payments service to refund customers' credit cards (figure 5.7).

The following code snippet shows the content of this file. Chapter 4 used the same content scheme and discussed hashing functions, MACs, and HMACs.

```
[ {
  "orderId" : "12345",
  "amount" : 500
}, {
  "orderId" : "56789",
  "amount" : 250
} ]
```

In chapter 4, we used HMAC to detect data corruption or tampering with the refunds.json file. In this chapter, we want to protect the integrity, authenticity, and confidentiality of the refunds.json file.

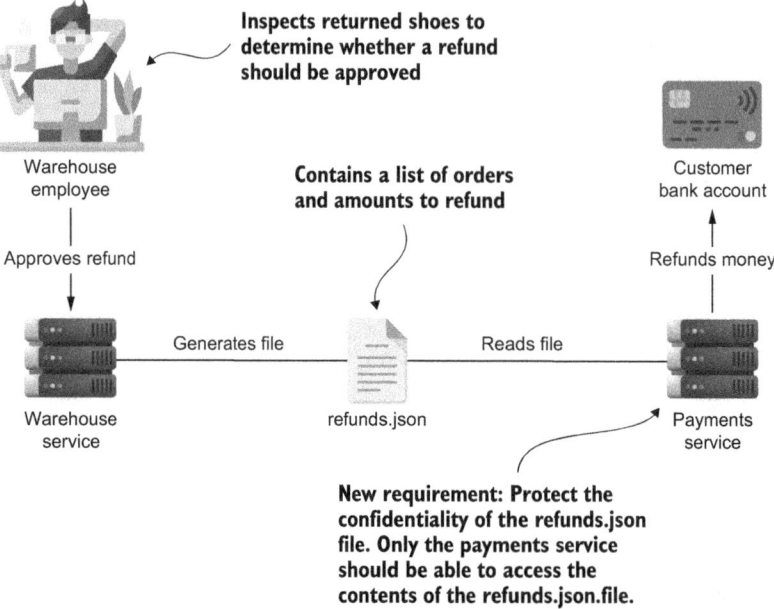

Figure 5.7   ACME staff members approve refunds using the warehouse management application. Once a day, the application generates a refunds.json file. The payment service refunds customers' credit cards for the amount specified in the file.

5.3.2   *Implementing the ACME scenario*

In the ACME scenario, the warehouse service sends a refunds.json file to the payments service so that it can issue refunds to customers' credit cards. To guarantee the integrity, authenticity and confidentiality of the refunds.json file, the warehouse service (project ssfd_ch5_ex4-warehouse provided with the book) encrypts it using AES-GCM mode with a 256-bit key.

The payments service (project ssfd_ch5_ex4-payments) decrypts refunds.json using AES-GCM, which throws an error if the ciphertext has been tampered with or the key is wrong. Because only the warehouse and payment services know the secret key, the payments service can assume that the warehouse service created refunds.json.

The next listing shows a simple implementation of the service class in the payments service. The service decrypts the data with AES-GCM using the secret configured in the application.properties file. The plaintext result is returned as the response body.

> **WARNING** We may repeat ourselves throughout the book, but this point is important: never configure secrets directly in property files or hardcode them in a real-world project. Never! In a real-world scenario, all secret details must be stored securely in a security vault such as HashiCorp Vault (https://www.hashicorp.com/).

Listing 5.5 The RefundService class decrypts the data

```
@Service
@RequiredArgsConstructor
public class RefundService {

  private final ObjectMapper objectMapper;
  private final AesGcmManager aesGcmManager;

  public List<Refund> decryptAndReturnRefunds(byte[] encryptedBodyBytes) {
    byte[] plainBytes =
      aesGcmManager
      ➥.decrypt(encryptedBodyBytes);              ⟵┐  Decrypting the
    try {                                            │  request body
     return objectMapper.readValue(plainBytes,
        new TypeReference<List<Refund>>(){});
    } catch (IOException e) {
     throw new IllegalArgumentException("Invalid
     ➥refunds JSON format", e);
    }
  }
}
```

The steps for testing this example are

1 Run the Warehouse application to generate the refunds.json.aesgcm file, which contains the AES-GCM encryption of the refunds.json file's contents.

2 Run the payment service, a Spring Boot application that exposes an endpoint that decrypts the content and returns the plaintext in the response.

3 Call the endpoint exposed by the payment service to confirm that the decryption works. Write a few different tests to make sure you understand the example:

– Change the key in the application.properties file and observe that the decryption no longer works.

– Alter the contents of refunds.json.aesgcm and observe that the endpoint fails to decrypt the data.

You can find detailed instructions for running the example in the payments project's README.md file.

With AES in GCM mode, any file corruption triggers an error during decryption, ensuring that the problem is detected. In CBC mode, the decryption process still completes, but the resulting file is corrupted, and the error might go unnoticed.

5.4 Authenticated Encryption with Associated Data

Consider a scenario in which a message must be sent securely between two systems. The message has a header containing metadata that intermediary systems use to route it to its final destination. The message body contains content that must be kept confidential, so it's encrypted (figure 5.8). Because the intermediary systems don't have access to the message encryption key, the header must be in plaintext so they can read it and route the message.

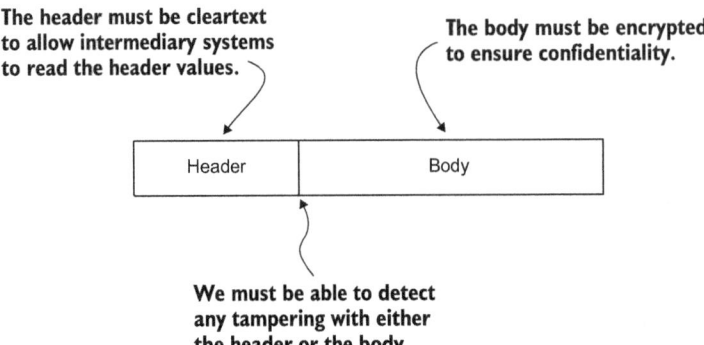

The header must be cleartext to allow intermediary systems to read the header values.

The body must be encrypted to ensure confidentiality.

Header | Body

We must be able to detect any tampering with either the header or the body.

Figure 5.8   A message with a plaintext header and an encrypted body is common.

In some situations, attackers can manipulate messages in ways that could disrupt an application:

- *Tampering with the header*—An attacker could intercept the message, modify its header, and potentially route it to the wrong recipient.
- *Swapping message bodies*—An attacker might intercept two messages, swap their encrypted bodies, and send them to their original recipients, causing confusion or errors in the receiving applications.

To prevent these types of attacks, the receiving application must be able to detect whether the header has been altered or the encrypted body has been swapped. In security terminology, the header is called additional authenticated data (AAD). This term means that the header is plaintext data that is associated with, and bound to, the encrypted portion (ciphertext) of the message. Ensuring this association is crucial to security.

A common approach is to use a MAC to ensure the integrity of both the header and the body. This approach involves the following steps:

1 Encrypt the body using AES.
2 Create a MAC over the combined header and encrypted body, often using HMAC.

Although this method is effective, it requires two separate algorithms (HMAC for the MAC and AES for encryption), which can add complexity.

As mentioned earlier, an authenticated encryption mode combines encryption and MAC creation into a single process. This type of mode is known as Authenticated Encryption with Associated Data (AEAD). AEAD allows you to do the following:

- Leave some data (like the header) as plaintext.
- Encrypt the rest of the data, such as the body.
- Compute a MAC over both the plaintext (header) and the ciphertext (body) to ensure that they are tightly bound and haven't been tampered with.

Essentially, AEAD achieves the same result as performing HMAC(header ‖ AES(body)) but with one algorithm.

AES in GCM is one of the most popular encryption modes because it supports AEAD. It simplifies the process by combining encryption and authentication in a single operation (figure 5.9), making it easier and more efficient to secure messages while protecting against tampering and message-swapping attacks.

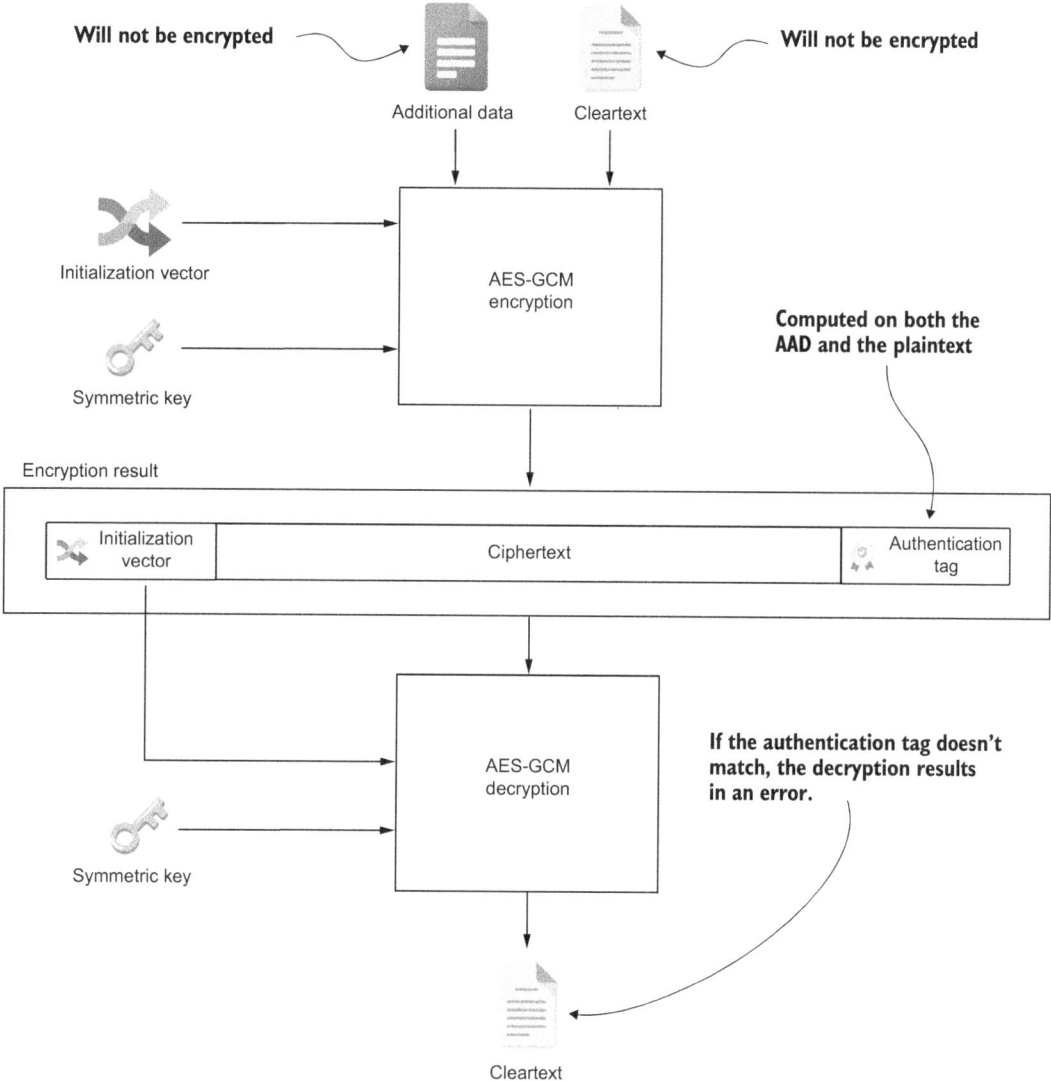

Figure 5.9   AES in GCM mode is a black box that takes four inputs: plaintext, a secret key, an IV, and optional AAD. The authentication tag is computed using the AAD and the ciphertext. The IV, ciphertext, and authentication tag are saved to the output. To decrypt, you must provide both the encryption key and the AAD; otherwise, an error is raised.

AEAD is useful outside the context of messages in transit. Consider a payment API that stores information about transactions in a SQL database. The transactions table has columns for the transaction ID, credit card number, amount, and date.

To comply with security standards, we use AES to encrypt the credit card number before storing it in the database. A malicious DBA, a hacker, or a buggy piece of code can take the encrypted credit card number from one row and swap it with the encrypted credit card number in another row. The hacker doesn't have to decrypt the credit card number; they can cause havoc by corrupting the database. By running AES in GCM mode, we can encrypt the credit card number and compute an authentication code that factors in the transaction ID, amount, and date; this way, we can detect whether the data in a row has been tampered with. Some databases, such as Google BigQuery, have native support for AEAD (https://cloud.google.com/bigquery/docs/reference/standard-sql/aead-encryption-concepts).

The following listing shows a simple example of encryption with AES in GCM mode using AEAD. You can find this example in the ssfd_ch5_ex5 project provided with the book.

Listing 5.6 AEAD encryption with AES-GCM in Java

```java
public static byte[] encryptAes256GCM(byte[] clearText,
byte[] key,
byte[] aad) {                                    AAD can be provided along with
  try {                                          the clear text to be encrypted.
    byte[] iv = generateRandomBytes(12);

    Cipher cipher = Cipher.getInstance("AES/GCM/NoPadding");
    GCMParameterSpec gcmSpec = new GCMParameterSpec(128, iv);

    SecretKeySpec keySpec = new SecretKeySpec(key, "AES");
    cipher.init(Cipher.ENCRYPT_MODE, keySpec, gcmSpec);

    if (aad != null && aad.length > 0) {         If AAD is provided,
      cipher.updateAAD(aad);                     set it on the cipher.
    }

    byte[] cipherText = cipher.doFinal(clearText);

    byte[] result = new byte[iv.length + cipherText.length];
    System.arraycopy(iv, 0, result, 0, iv.length);
    System.arraycopy(cipherText, 0, result, iv.length, cipherText.length);
            return result;
  } catch (Exception e) {
    throw new RuntimeException("AES-256-GCM encryption failed", e);
  }
}
```

The next listing shows the decryption for ciphers with AAD.

Listing 5.7   AEAD decryption with AES-GCM in Java

```
public static byte[] decryptAes256GCM(byte[] ivAndCiphertext,
                                       byte[] key,
                                       byte[] aad) {
  try {
    byte[] iv = new byte[12];
    byte[] cipherText = new byte[ivAndCiphertext.length - 12];
    System.arraycopy(ivAndCiphertext, 0, iv, 0, 12);
    System.arraycopy(ivAndCiphertext, 12,
        cipherText, 0, cipherText.length);

    Cipher cipher = Cipher.getInstance("AES/GCM/NoPadding");
    GCMParameterSpec gcmSpec = new GCMParameterSpec(128, iv);
    SecretKeySpec keySpec = new SecretKeySpec(key, "AES");
    cipher.init(Cipher.DECRYPT_MODE, keySpec, gcmSpec);

    if (aad != null && aad.length > 0) {      ⟵  If exists, the AAD is configured on
      cipher.updateAAD(aad);                       the cipther before decryption
    }

    return cipher.doFinal(cipherText);
  } catch (Exception e) {
    throw new RuntimeException("AES-256-GCM decryption failed", e);
  }
}
```

Compressing the data

Compressing data before sending it over the network or storing it can reduce costs and improve performance. Often, we want to combine encryption and compression to meet security, performance, and cost requirements. As a developer, you have to make a choice: compress data first and then encrypt it or encrypt it first and then compress it?

Compression algorithms replace frequently repeating data patterns with shorter ones. Encryption algorithms provide security by making the output look like a random data stream without repeating patterns. As a result, compression algorithms perform poorly on encrypted ciphertext. It's better to compress data first and then encrypt it to get the maximum compression ratio.

5.4.1   Exercises

5 Why should compression be applied before encryption, not after?

6 What happens to compression ratios if you try to compress encrypted data?

7 In a system in which messages are both compressed and encrypted, what risk exists if encryption is applied before compression?

5.5   AES best practices

We've covered a lot of details about AES. As you may have noticed from the various warning boxes in this chapter, it's easy to use AES incorrectly and build an insecure system. Without professional advice from a security specialist, you should opt for AES-GCM with a 256-bit key. In the following sections, we discuss this recommendation in detail.

5.5.1 Selecting the AES key size

The AES secret key can be 128, 192, or 256 bits long. Which key size is best? An attacker can write a program that tries every possible key in the hope of finding the correct encryption key. Trying every possible key is called a brute-force attack.

Using a computer to brute-force a 128-bit AES key requires quadrillions of years of computing time. A quadrillion is 1 million billion. The sun will explode in 5 billion years, so there's no practical way to brute-force a 128-bit AES key using the computers available at the time of writing. But what if you have a quantum computer?

Quantum computers can perform computations that aren't feasible on a classical electronic computer. In theory, a quantum computer running Grover's algorithm can speed a brute-force attack against AES. With a quantum computer, a 128-bit AES key has the same strength as a 64-bit key, and a 256-bit key has the strength of a 128-bit key.

The theory of quantum computing is well understood, but building a practical quantum computer remains an unsolved engineering challenge at the time of writing. Cryptographers are building encryption algorithms that can resist quantum computers, but none has been standardized so far.

The AES algorithm is considered mathematically secure. But in real life, you need an AES implementation, which may contain bugs that weaken security. The AES encryption key must be stored somewhere, so hackers often look for ways to steal the key rather than try to break AES mathematically.

There have been many cases of developers publishing secret keys to GitHub repos accidentally or through ignorance (https://qz.com/674520/companies-are-sharing-their-secret-access-codes-on-github-and-they-may-not-even-know-it/). A 256-bit AES key won't keep data secure if the attacker steals the key. Managing keys securely is both a human and technical problem. This book shows you how to use Vault and public cloud key management services to store encryption keys; human processes for handling secret keys are beyond the scope of this book.

> **TIP** Use 256-bit AES keys.

5.5.2 Checklist for using AES-GCM correctly in Java

Here are best practices developers should follow to use AES correctly in GCM mode:
- Use a 256-bit key for optimal security.
- Generate the key with a cryptographically secure random number generator such as `java.security.SecureRandom`.
- Keep the key secret, store it in a secure key storage system, and follow a secure process for handling key material.
- Use a 96-bit IV for AES-GCM. If you use a longer IV, AES-GCM derives a 96-bit value from it.

- Generate the IV using a cryptographically secure random number generator such as `java.security.SecureRandom`.
- Never reuse an IV. Reusing a key-IV combination with AES-GCM can result in a catastrophic security failure. Always generate a new random IVr before calling the`Cipher.init()` method in Java.
- Use a 128-bit tag size, configured via the `javax.crypto.spec.GCMParameterSpec` class in Java. This is the largest authentication tag size possible with AES-GCM.
- The maximum amount of data that can be encrypted by a key-IV combination is approximately 68 GB, or ($2^{39} - 16$) bytes. If you have to encrypt more than 68 GB with a single AES key-IV combination, use a different AES mode or split the data into 68 GB chunks.

TIP The preceding list is challenging to follow in your application code. Use a library that implements these best practices and offers a developer-friendly API that's hard to misuse accidentally. Tink is a good choice because it has implementations in Java, C++, Objective-C, Go, Python, and JavaScript and is maintained by the security team. Chapter 7 covers Tink.

5.5.3 Exercises

8 What is the recommended AES key size for strong security?

9 How does a quantum computer change the effective strength of AES keys?

10 Why is it dangerous to store AES keys directly in source code or configuration files?

11 What IV size and policy should you use with AES-GCM?

12 Why is it better to use a library such as Tink instead of writing your own AES-GCM code in production?

5.6 Exercise answers

1 What extra guarantees does AES-GCM provide compared with AES-CBC?

AES-GCM provides integrity, authenticity, and confidentiality, whereas AES-CBC provides only confidentiality.

2 Why is reusing an IV in AES-GCM dangerous?

Reusing an IV with AES-GCM is catastrophic because it can allow attackers to recover the key or forge messages.

3 Which cryptographic goals do AES-CBC and AES-GCM fulfill?

AES-CBC provides only confidentiality. AES-GCM provides confidentiality, integrity, and authentication. Neither provides nonrepudiation.

4 In the ACME-refunds scenario, what happens if the encrypted refunds.json file is tampered with?

The paymens service will detect tampering during decryption (an authentication tag mismatch) and throw an error. No refunds will be processed.

5 Why should compression be applied before encryption, not after?

Because encryption produces random-looking data with no patterns, it's nearly impossible for compression algorithms to reduce size effectively.

6 What happens to compression ratios if you try to compress encrypted data?

Compression ratios drop dramatically (often, there's no size reduction) because ciphertext appears random and has no repeating sequences.

7 In a system in which messages are both compressed and encrypted, what risk exists if encryption is applied before compression?

Compression after encryption wastes CPU cycles and may lead to inefficient or misleading system design because the data won't shrink.

8 What AES key size is recommended for strong security?

For long-term security, 256-bit keys are recommended.

9 How does a quantum computer change the effective strength of AES keys?

Quantum computers running Grover's algorithm halve the effective strength of AES keys. AES-128 becomes effectively 64-bit; AES-256 becomes effectively 128-bit.

10 Why is it dangerous to store AES keys directly in source code or config files?

If attackers gain access to your code repository or configuration files, they can steal the key and decrypt all your data.

11 What IV size and policy should be used with AES-GCM?

A 96-bit (12-byte) IV should be generated fresh with a cryptographically secure random-number generator (RNG) for every encryption operation. Reuse of an IV is catastrophic.

12 Why is it better to use a library like Tink rather than write AES-GCM code by hand in production?

Because libraries like Tink implement best practices automatically, they reduce the risk of developer mistakes that introduce security flaws.

Summary

- AES is the most widely used symmetric encryption algorithm, supported by all major cloud providers and operating systems to protect data confidentiality.
- AES is a block cipher that encrypts fixed 128-bit blocks and requires a mode of operation to handle data larger than one block.
- ECB mode is insecure because identical plaintext blocks produce identical ciphertext blocks, revealing patterns to attackers.
- CBC mode chains blocks together using an IV to prevent pattern detection, but it provides only confidentiality, not integrity or authenticity.
- IVs must be random, unique for each encryption operation, and never reused with the same key to prevent catastrophic security failures.
- Authenticated encryption combines encryption with message authentication to provide confidentiality, integrity, and authenticity in a single operation.

- GCM is the recommended AES mode because it provides authenticated encryption, ensuring confidentiality, integrity, and authenticity.
- AES-GCM requires a secret key and a random IV and produces ciphertext with an authentication tag that detects tampering.
- AEAD authenticates plaintext headers along with encrypted message bodies without encrypting the headers.
- Java provides AES support via the Cipher class, but developers should use cryptographically secure RNGs and follow specific configuration requirements.
- Best practices include using 256-bit keys, 96-bit IVs, and 128-bit authentication tags and never reusing IVs.
- Compression should be applied before encryption because encrypted data appears random and therefore can't be effectively compressed.
- Quantum computers could halve AES key strength using Grover's algorithm, making 256-bit keys roughly equivalent to 128-bit security today.
- Prefer developer-friendly libraries like Tink over hand-coding AES to avoid common security mistakes.

Public key encryption and digital signatures: Unleashing RSA

This chapter covers

- Using RSA to encrypt data
- Using RSA for digital signatures

When you buy products online, look up directions to a restaurant, interact with friends and strangers on a social network, or collaborate with co-workers on a video conference call, you depend on public key cryptography. Without it, the Internet as we know it wouldn't exist.

Secure communication on the internet relies on the Transport Layer Security (TLS) protocol, which is built on public key cryptography. With a solid understanding of public key cryptography, configuring and troubleshooting TLS connections becomes straightforward. Without this knowledge, you may blindly copy commands from blog posts, hoping that your changes will fix the problem. Public key cryptography isn't only a tool but also an essential foundation for any developer working with secure applications.

This chapter offers application developers a friendly introduction to public key cryptography. Its goal is to teach you how to use it to solve real-world security problems. The mathematics behind public key cryptography is extremely interesting but beyond the scope of this book. You won't find any equations in this chapter; instead, you'll see sample code that uses popular Java libraries to help you develop an intuitive understanding of public key cryptography and apply it in your applications.

> **NOTE**   This chapter assumes that you're familiar with the material in chapters 3, 4, and 5—in particular, hash-based message authentication code (HMAC), the Java Cryptography Architecture (JCA), the Advanced Encryption Standard (AES), and authenticated encryption using Galois/Counter mode (GCM). If you need a refresher, please review chapters 3, 4, and 5.

6.1   The secret-key distribution problem

To understand public key cryptography, start by exploring the key distribution problem using a variation of the ACME, Inc. scenario from previous chapters. ACME, an online shoe retailer, allows customers to return shoes they don't like for a full refund. Customers mail the returns to ACME's warehouse, where staff members check that the returned items are in good condition and authorize a credit card refund using the warehouse management app (figure 6.1).

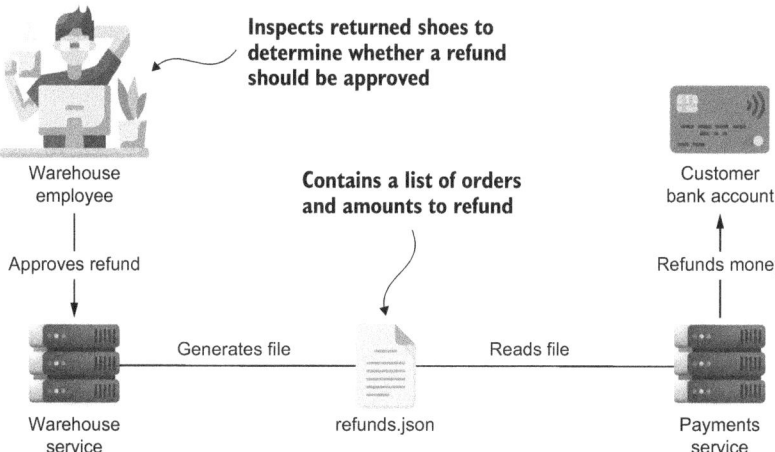

Figure 6.1   ACME staff members inspect returned merchandise and approve refunds using the warehouse management service. The payment service issues a refund to customers' credit card accounts.

The warehouse management service creates a file listing all newly approved refunds. Once a day, the payment service retrieves this file from the warehouse to issue refunds to customers' credit cards. The following code snippet shows an example of the refunds.json file's content:

```
[ {
  "orderId" : "12345",
```

```
   "amount" : 500
}, {
   "orderId" : "6789",
   "amount" : 250
} ]
```

In previous chapters we used a symmetric secret key which we stored in the Spring Boot `application.properties` configuration files of the warehouse and payment services.

Because the AES secret key is a configuration file, an administrator must set the same key value in both the payment service's `application.properties` file and the warehouse service's `application.properties` file. This isn't hard to do for only two applications, but multiple applications will have to talk to one another when the system grows. The accounting application, for example, needs the data from the warehouse to keep the corporate books up to date.

The inventory management system needs access to refund data to track inventory accurately. The marketing application needs the same data to look for patterns in products that customers don't like (figure 6.2).

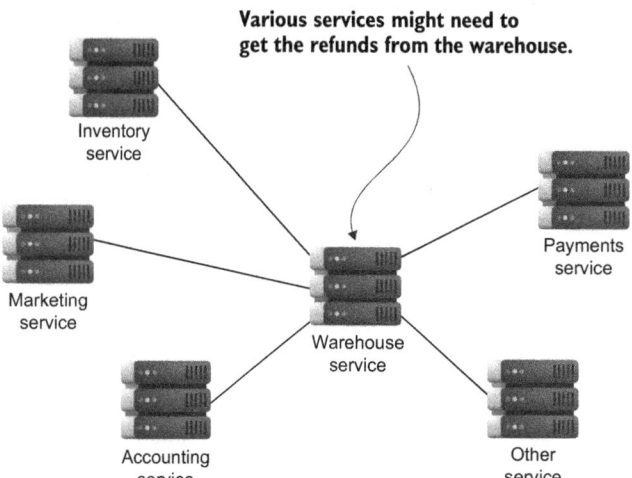

Figure 6.2 In a service-oriented system, more than one application needs to communicate with others. This complicates key distribution.

Administrators must set the secret key in all applications that must interact with the warehouse service. In an enterprise with hundreds of services, managing encryption keys in configuration files is hard. We need a better approach to key management.

Storing a secret key in plain text in `application.properties` is dangerous. A hacker can steal the configuration file and the encryption key, gaining access to encrypted data. Also, after we know that a key has been stolen, we must assume that all keys have been stolen and must change every encryption key we use in every configuration file across every system we run without disrupting business operations. This effort is huge but important.

> **WARNING** Storing a secret key in plain text in a properties file or hardcoding it is dangerous. Never store secrets in configuration files. Instead, use a vault and infrastructure that protect secret values.

The problem of sharing a secret key among applications is called *the key-distribution problem.* Trying to solve it by storing keys in configuration files creates high management costs and security risks. We need a way to share encryption keys without using configuration files. Public key cryptography provides the tools to solve the problem.

6.1.1 Exercises

  1 What problem does public key cryptography solve compared with symmetric key cryptography?

  2 Why is it safe to share a public key but not a private key?

  3 If a hacker steals a private key, what should you do?

  4 Why do systems use digital certificates when sharing public keys?

6.2 Public key cryptosystems

For centuries, governments, militaries, and diplomats have relied on encryption to protect their secrets. Early examples of encryption include the Spartans' use of the scytale, a simple device that wrapped a strip of parchment around a rod to encode messages. The Romans employed the Caesar cipher, shifting letters by a fixed number to disguise their communications. These early methods, though primitive, laid the foundation for securing sensitive information.

As empires expanded and conflicts grew more complex, the challenge of key distribution emerged. Without secure ways to share encryption keys, the secrecy of messages could easily be compromised. In medieval Europe, royal courts and military commanders sent couriers carrying handwritten keys or codebooks to their counterparts. These couriers faced great peril because if they were captured by the enemy, the entire cryptographic system could be exposed.

By the Renaissance, ciphers became more sophisticated. The Vigenère cipher, described as unbreakable for centuries, required both parties to possess the same keyword to encode and decode messages. Despite its ingenuity, the cipher still relied on secure key exchange, often requiring trusted envoys or meetings to deliver these critical keys in person.

During World Wars I and II, encryption reached new heights of complexity. The Germans employed machines like Enigma, which relied on intricate key systems that were updated daily. Even so, the distribution of keys presented a monumental challenge. Codebooks were delivered under armed guard, often at great risk, and their loss or theft could jeopardize entire operations.

This long history of ingenuity and danger highlights the critical importance of secure key distribution. It wasn't until 1976, with the groundbreaking work of

Whitfield Diffie and Martin Hellman, that the world saw a revolutionary shift. Diffie's and Hellman's paper, "New Directions in Cryptography," introduced the concept of *public-key cryptography*, rendering the age-old reliance on secret courier systems obsolete. This innovation marked a turning point and paved the way for secure communications in the digital era.

The key insight in public key cryptography is the introduction of public and private keys. Public keys are freely shared with the world; it's OK for anyone to possess a copy of the public key. Private keys are kept secret and never shared with anyone.

The private and public key form a pair, mathematically bound to each other in such a way that the private key works only with its public key and the public key works only with the private key. Plaintext encrypted with the public key can be decrypted only with the private key. Security rests on keeping the private key secret. If the private key is compromised, a new key pair must be generated. Figure 6.3 illustrates the concept of public–private key pairs.

Key pair

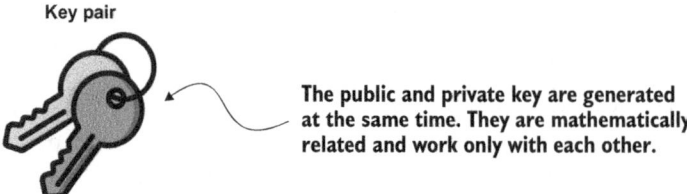

The public and private key are generated at the same time. They are mathematically related and work only with each other.

Figure 6.3   A key pair, consisting of a private and a public key. The keys are numbers that are related by means of a mathematical equation. The private key works only with the public key in the same key pair, and the public key works only with the private key from the same key pair. The private key must be kept secret, but the public key can be shared with anyone, including friends, enemies, and hackers. Security in a public key cryptosystem depends on keeping private keys private.

In a system with many services, each service must have its own public–private key pair. The service's private key is stored securely in a key vault to protect it from theft. Two services that want to communicate securely exchange public keys over an insecure network. After the public keys are exchanged, they can be used to encrypt communications between the services (figure 6.4).

We assume that a hacker can read and modify network traffic. A hacker can intercept an HTTP request containing a public key, modify the public key's value, and forward the HTTP request to the recipient, for example. We encode the public key inside a digital certificate to protect it from modification during transit. Chapter 8 covers digital certificates, which are essential for establishing trust that the public key being used is the correct one.

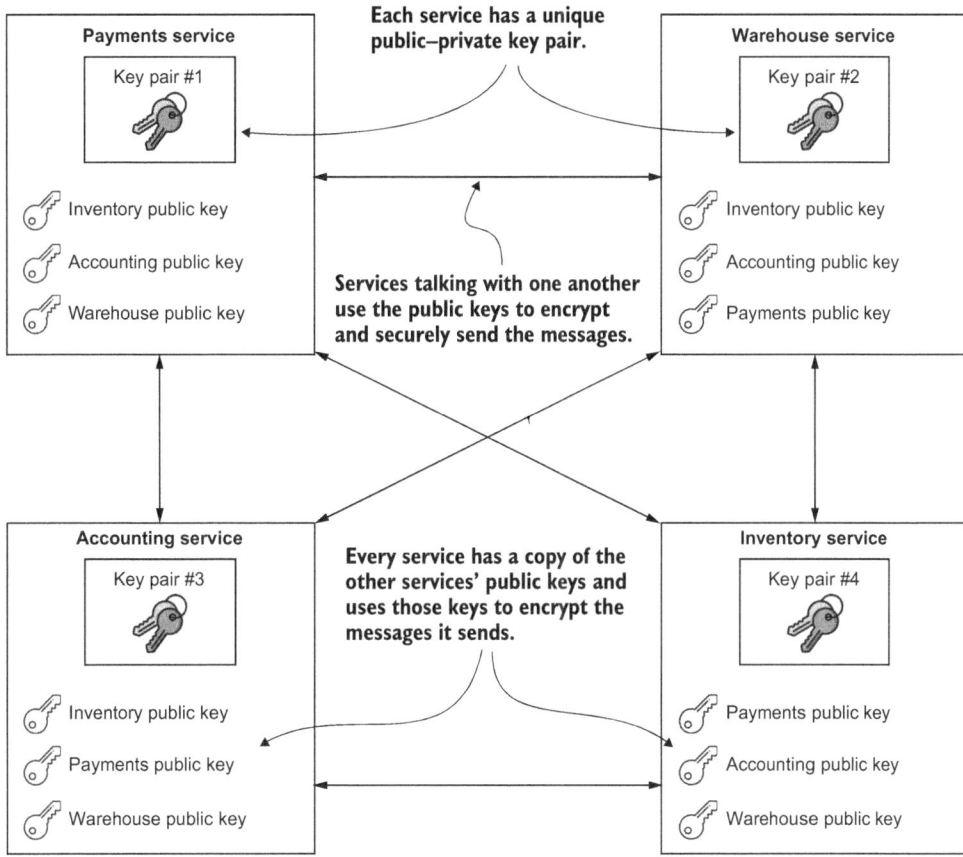

Figure 6.4 **Each service has a unique public–private key pair; it freely shares its public key over the network with any other service that might ask for it. When two services want to communicate, they exchange public keys and use those keys to secure the communication link. If a hacker steals a private key, only the communication link using that private key is compromised. A hacker that has access only to the public keys can't compromise the system's security.**

WARNING Digital certificates are critical to the security of a public key cryptosystem. You must understand and be comfortable with them before using public key cryptography in a production application. To make this chapter easier to follow, we don't use digital certificates in the sample applications. Read chapter 7 before using public key cryptography in your application.

Public key cryptosystems are built on top of a trapdoor mathematical function. A trapdoor function is one for which you can quickly compute a result from the input parameters but it's not easy to compute the parameters from the result. Given two large prime numbers, for example, you can easily and quickly multiply them; given the result of the multiplication, though, it's infeasible to work out which original prime numbers were used.

Two public key cryptography systems are widely used:

- *RSA*—Based on the difficulty of factoring the product of two large prime numbers
- *Elliptic curves*—Based on the challenge of solving the elliptic-curve discrete logarithm problem

The rest of this chapter provides sample applications using RSA to encrypt and sign content in plain Java. We cover elliptic curves in chapter 7. The samples focus on important use patterns in public key cryptography.

6.2.1 Exercises

  5 What math problem is RSA security based on?

  6 Why would quantum computers break RSA?

  7 Which RSA key sizes are considered safe today?

  8 What is the difference between RSAES-PKCS1-v1_5 and RSA-OAEP?

6.3 RSA public key cryptosystem

The RSA public key encryption algorithm (named after the initials of its inventors, Ron Rivest, Adi Shamir, and Leonard Adleman) was invented in 1977. RSA also refers to a company called RSA Security LLC, founded in 1982 by the inventors of the RSA algorithm to commercialize their invention. Being first to market with security products based on the RSA algorithm led to widespread adoption and implementation of the RSA cryptosystem across programming languages and in numerous security protocols.

The mathematical details of RSA are beyond the scope of this book. But it's important to know the following facts about the RSA algorithm:

- The RSA algorithm is based on the mathematical problem of factoring a large integer into a product of prime numbers.
- Integer-factoring algorithms are slow when the number being factored is large. The slowness of integer factoring is the basis of security for the RSA algorithm.
- If mathematicians discover a fast integer-factoring algorithm, RSA will no longer be secure.
- Computers are getting faster, and implementations of factoring algorithms are improving. At the time of writing, the largest number ever factored is a 250-decimal-digit (829-bit) number from the RSA factoring challenge called RSA-250.
- Quantum computers will break RSA because they can factor integers much more quickly than classical computers. At the time of writing, however, quantum computers aren't powerful or widespread enough to be practical threats.

6.3.1 Configuring RSA

Now that we've covered the theory, we'll dive into configuring RSA. Using RSA requires choosing two critical settings:

- *Key size*—Determines the length of the key, typically measured in bits (e.g., 2,048 or 4,096). Larger keys offer stronger security but require more computational resources.

- *Padding scheme*—Protects against certain cryptographic attacks by adding random data to the plaintext before encryption. Common schemes include PKCS#1 v1.5 and Optimal Asymmetric Encryption Padding (OAEP).

The larger the key size, the more security you get. Today, RSA 2048-bit keys are considered secure, but you should use longer keys, such as 3,072- or 4,096-bit keys. Your corporate security standards should provide guidance on the minimum RSA key length.

There are two RSA-based encryption schemes:

- *RSAES-PKCS1-v1_5*—An older RSA encryption scheme that uses PKCS #1 v1.5 padding. It's simple but considered less secure against chosen-ciphertext attacks, so OAEP has mostly replaced it in modern systems.
- *OAEP*—A padding scheme for RSA that mixes the message with random data using hash functions. It provides stronger security guarantees and is recommended instead of PKCS #1 v1.5.

Using RSAES-PKCS1-v1_5

RSAES-PKCS1-v1_5 is an RSA encryption scheme, defined in the Public Key Cryptography Standards (PKCS) version 1.5 and later in RFC 2313. Although it was widely adopted at the time, researchers eventually discovered serious vulnerabilities that made it insecure. As a result, you should never use it for encryption today.

Unfortunately, many older systems and products still support RSA PKCS#1 v1.5 for the sake of backward compatibility. This creates a risk of downgrade attacks, in which an attacker tricks a system into using this older, less secure protocol instead of a more secure one. By exploiting these weaknesses, attackers can compromise the confidentiality of encrypted messages.

To protect your systems and data, configure your applications to reject PKCS#1 v1.5. This configuration ensures that you're not exposed to downgrade attacks and that you rely only on secure encryption schemes.

Using OAEP

OAEP was designed to fix the security weaknesses in PKCS#1 v1.5. One of its key improvements is the addition of randomized padding to the plaintext before encryption. Padding involves adding extra data to the original message to make it a fixed length. In OAEP, this padding is randomized.

This randomness ensures that even if the same plaintext is encrypted multiple times, the resulting ciphertext will be different each time. This is important because predictable patterns in plaintext, such as repeated structures or identical encrypted messages, can give attackers clues to reverse-engineer the encryption. (Remember AES-CBC mode from chapter 5.) This approach is how the British, through Alan Turing's research, broke Germany's Enigma messages during World War II.

OAEP eliminates these patterns by randomizing the padding, making it far more difficult for an attacker to analyze and exploit the ciphertext.

These improvements significantly strengthen RSA encryption by preventing vulnerabilities like chosen-ciphertext attacks, in which an attacker manipulates ciphertexts to extract information about the plaintext. With its robust design, OAEP has become the standard padding scheme for RSA encryption, ensuring stronger protection for sensitive data.

If you're developing or maintaining applications, always use RSA-OAEP as the padding scheme for RSA encryption. RSA-OAEP is widely regarded as the modern, secure standard for ensuring the confidentiality of data and protecting against potential exploits.

> **TIP** Always use RSA-OAEP, turn off RSA-PKCSv1.5 in everything you're using, and use 4,096-bit RSA keys for maximum security. Many professional cryptographers prefer elliptic-curve cryptography (ECC) to RSA, so read chapter 7 to learn about ECC as well.

6.3.2 *Hybrid encryption*

The implementation of the RSA encryption algorithm is significantly slower than that of AES (discussed in chapter 5), especially because processors provide special instructions for hardware-accelerated AES and the mathematics for RSA encryption is CPU-intensive. Therefore, AES is commonly combined with RSA in a hybrid symmetric–asymmetric scheme.

The key idea is to use AES to encrypt the content and then use RSA to encrypt the AES encryption key. Key wrapping indicates that an encryption key is itself encrypted. Hybrid encryption and decryption consists of the following steps (illustrated in figure 6.5):

- *Sender encryption process—*
  - Generate a random AES key called the content encryption key (CEK).
  - Execute AES encryption on content using the CEK from step 1 as the key.
  - Wrap the CEK by encrypting it with the RSA public key.
  - Send the encrypted CEK and the encrypted content to the recipient.

- *Recipient decryption processes—*
  - Unwrap the CEK by decrypting it with the RSA private key.
  - Execute AES decryption on the content, using the CEK to recover the original content.

Widely deployed security protocols such as TLS, Internet Protocol Security (IPsec), JSON Web Encryption (JWE), and Secure Shell (SSH) use hybrid encryption. Chapter 10 covers TLS, and chapter 11 covers JWE with RSA, which implements the hybrid encryption scheme we just described. When using hybrid encryption, you have to configure two algorithms:

- Use AES for bulk data encryption. Review chapter 5 for best practices on configuring AES. AES-GCM with a 256-bit key is one example configuration.
- Use RSA for wrapping the AES CEK. Always use RSA-OAEP mode. Key sizes should be 2,048-bit or larger.

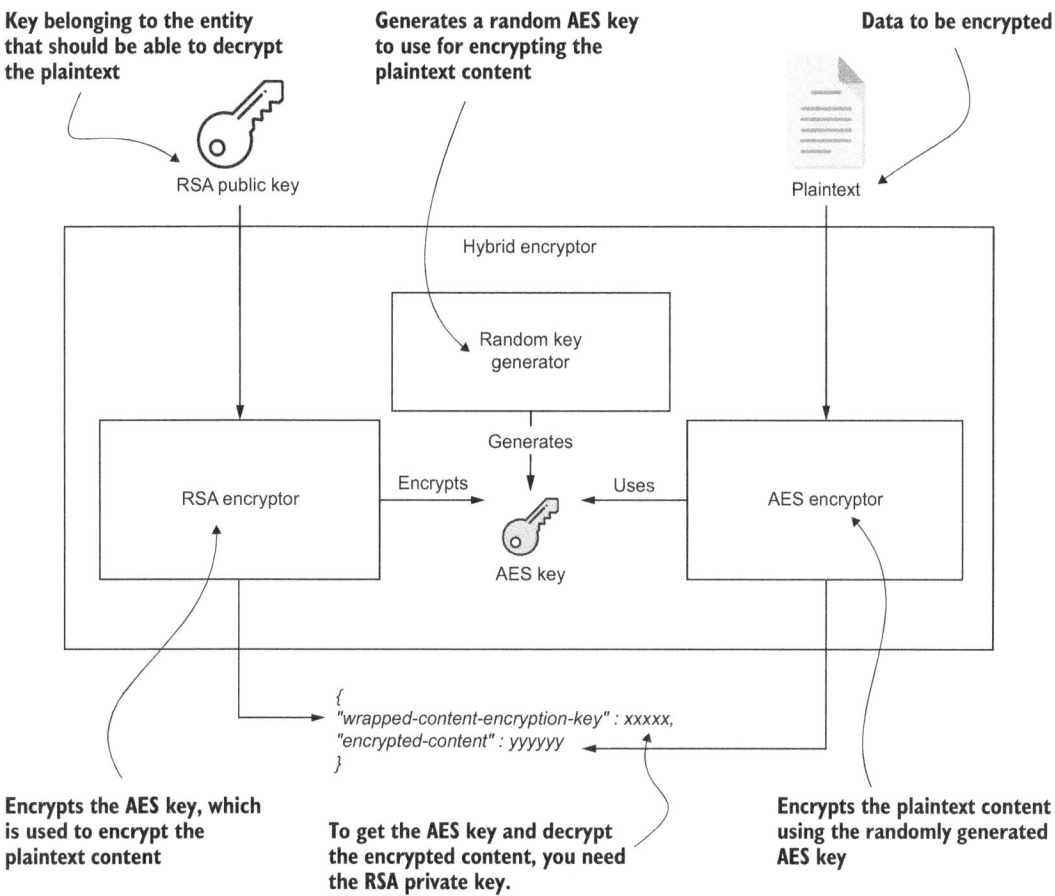

Key belonging to the entity that should be able to decrypt the plaintext

RSA public key

Generates a random AES key to use for encrypting the plaintext content

Data to be encrypted

Plaintext

Hybrid encryptor

Random key generator

RSA encryptor

Encrypts · Generates · Uses

AES key

AES encryptor

{
"wrapped-content-encryption-key" : xxxxx,
"encrypted-content" : yyyyyy
}

Encrypts the AES key, which is used to encrypt the plaintext content

To get the AES key and decrypt the encrypted content, you need the RSA private key.

Encrypts the plaintext content using the randomly generated AES key

Figure 6.5 Hybrid encryption uses a high-performance symmetric algorithm such as AES to encrypt content. Then the AES CEK is encrypted with the recipient's RSA public key, allowing the recipient to use their private key to first the CEK and then decrypt the content.

6.3.3 Signing data with RSA

Chapter 4 discusses message authentication codes (MACs) and HMACs, which are great tools for checking integrity and authentication. Both work with a shared secret key (symmetric key).

Digital signatures also provide integrity and authentication, but they're built on asymmetric key pairs (a private key and a public key). Like encryption, this approach has the advantage of making key distribution easier and applying the principle of least privilege more effectively.

A digital signature is a cryptographic mechanism that identifies the creator of a piece of data and proves that the data hasn't been changed since creation. It allows anyone to verify that a message or document truly came from the claimed sender and that its contents remain intact (figure 6.6).

NOTE   The private key is always used for the sensitive action. In the case of encryption and decryption, it's used for decryption. Anyone can encrypt data with the public key, but only the holder of the private key can decrypt it. For digital signatures, the private key is used for signing, and the matching public key is used for verification. This way, anyone can check the signature using the public key, but only the owner of the private key can create the signature.

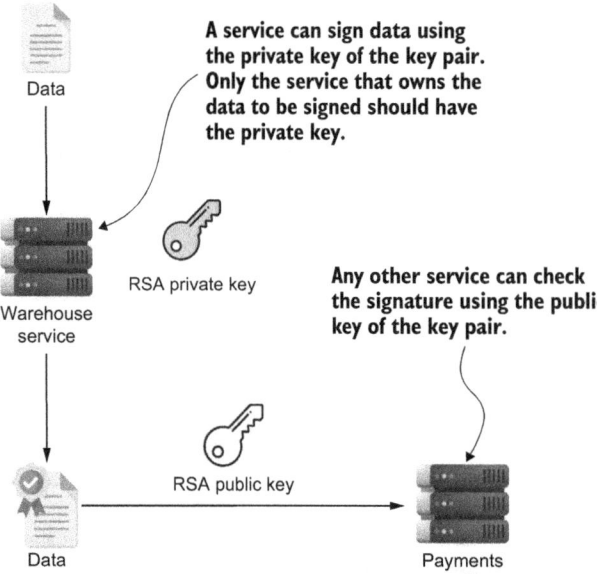

A service can sign data using the private key of the key pair. Only the service that owns the data to be signed should have the private key.

Any other service can check the signature using the public key of the key pair.

Figure 6.6   Using RSA for digital signatures. The warehouse service signs data with its private key, and the payment service (or any other service) can verify the signature using the corresponding public key. This approach ensures integrity and authenticity because only the service that holds the private key can create the signature.

One important difference is nonrepudiation. Nonrepudiation means that after someone signs a message, they can't deny that they signed it. Digital signatures give you this property because only the owner of the private key could have produced the signature, but anyone can verify it using the public key. With HMACs, this verification isn't possible because both sides have the same secret key; either side could have created the code, so you can't prove which one did.

Another important difference is performance. HMACs are fast because they're based on hashing, which is lightweight and efficient even for large amounts of data. Digital signatures are slower because they use the heavy math of public key cryptography. HMACs are a good choice when speed matters, such as when many API requests must be signed; digital signatures are better suited to cases in which performance is less critical but strong guarantees (such as nonrepudiation) are required.

6.3.4   *Exercises*

9   Why is RSA often combined with AES in a hybrid scheme?

10   What is the term for encrypting an encryption key?

11 List the steps a sender follows in hybrid encryption.

12 Which widely used protocols rely on hybrid encryption?

13 Which key of a key pair (private or public) is used to sign data?

14 List the main important differences between HMAC and RSA digital signatures.

6.4 Java support for RSA

Now let's get back to our ACME scenario. Using AES to encrypt the refunds.json file, as we did in chapter 5, works (figure 6.7). But now ACME engineers face two problems:

- Handling key rotations
- Keeping the same secret key on both sides of the communication channel

The engineers think this approach gives the payment service too much control and goes against the zero-trust principle, so they decide to redesign the code to use RSA instead. With RSA, key rotation is easier because they can simply create an endpoint that exposes the public keys instead of updating each service manually. This approach also eliminates the need to share secret keys everywhere.

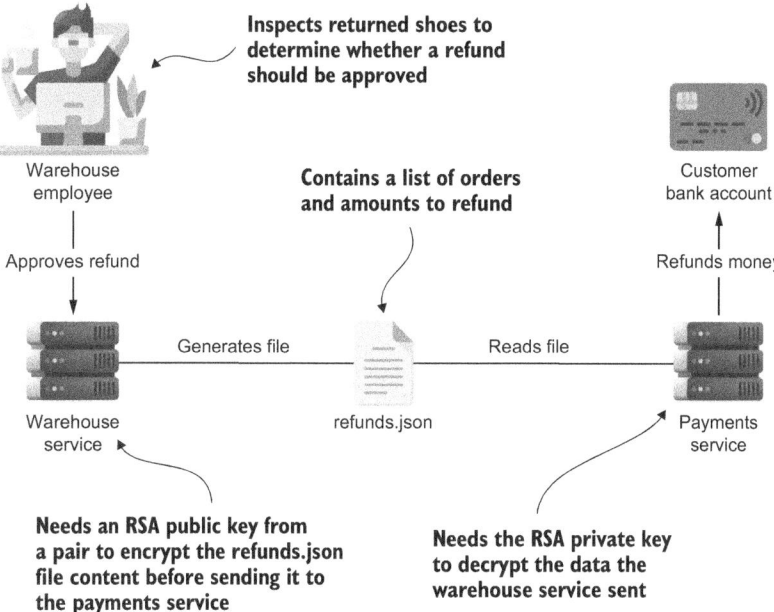

Figure 6.7 The Warehouse service uses the public key from a key pair to encrypt the content of the refunds.json file. The Payments service uses the private key from the pair to decrypt the data it receives.

In a real-world setup, the payment service would hold the key pair (both the private and public keys) and expose the public key through an endpoint. This way, it wouldn't be necessary to rotate keys in two places (as discussed in chapters 11 and 12).

To keep this example simple (for now), we decided to generate a key pair separately and then configure the public key in the warehouse service and the private key in the payment service. This example teaches you to do the following:

- Generate an RSA key pair with plain Java.
- Encrypt data with RSA using a public key in plain Java.
- Decrypt data with RSA using a private key in plain Java.

You'll follow these steps:

1   Generate an RSA key pair using a small Java application called the key generator.
2   Encrypt the refund details in the warehouse application using the public key from step 1.
3   Decrypt the refund details in the payment application using the private key from step 1.

The following listing shows how to generate a key pair with Java. You can find the full implementation in the project ssfd_ch6_ex1-keygenerator. Running this simple app saves the public and private keys in the project's root folder. Then you configure the public key in the warehouse service (ssfd_ch6_ex1-warehouse) and the private key in the payment service (ssfd_ch6_ex1-payments).

Listing 6.1   Generating an RSA key pair

```java
public class RsaKeyPairGenerator {

  private final int keySize;
  private final SecureRandom secureRandom;

  public RsaKeyPairGenerator(int keySize, SecureRandom secureRandom) {
    this.keySize = keySize;
    this.secureRandom = secureRandom;
  }

  public KeyPair generate() throws Exception {
    KeyPairGenerator kpg =
      KeyPairGenerator.getInstance("RSA");
    kpg.initialize(keySize, secureRandom);
    return kpg.generateKeyPair();
  }
}
```

Getting a key generator manager object

Specifying the key size and a random seed to generate the key pair

Generating the key pair

The key generator application saves the keys in two separate files. Place the public key file in the warehouse application's `resources` folder.

The warehouse application also includes an example `refunds.json` file, similar to the ones you used in earlier chapters. When you run the warehouse application (a simple Java app), it creates a new file in the project's root folder. This file, called `refunds.json.rsa`, stores the RSA-encrypted content.

The next code snippet shows an example refund in plaintext:

```
[
  {
    "orderId": "10001",
    "amount": 120
  }
]
```

The next listing shows the Java code for RSA encryption. You can find the full app implementation in the ssfd_ch6_ex1-warehouse project provided with the book.

Listing 6.2   Encryption using the RSA public key

```
public static byte[] rsaEncryptChunked(
  byte[] data,
  PublicKey key) throws Exception {

  Cipher cipher = Cipher.getInstance("RSA/ECB/
  ⟲OAEPWithSHA-256AndMGF1Padding");
  cipher.init(Cipher.ENCRYPT_MODE, key);

  int modulusBytes = ((RSAPublicKey) key).getModulus().bitLength();
  modulusBytes = (modulusBytes + 7) / 8;
  int maxBlock = modulusBytes - 11;

  ByteArrayOutputStream out = new ByteArrayOutputStream();
  for (int off = 0; off < data.length; off += maxBlock) {
    int len = Math.min(maxBlock, data.length - off);
    out.write(cipher.doFinal(data, off, len));
  }

  return out.toByteArray();
}
```

Getting a Cipher object that knows how to encrypt and decrypt with RSA. We need to specify both the mode and the padding.

Setting the cipher into the encryption mode

Encrypting the chunks

Returning the encrypted content

Splitting the file into smaller chunks which will be one by one encrypted

Now copy the encrypted content file and to the payment service's resources folder. Place the private key file you generated earlier in the same folder. When you run the payment application, it uses the private key to decrypt the encrypted contain and produce the plaintext file, as shown in the next listing.

Listing 6.3   Decryption using the RSA private key

```
public static byte[] rsaDecryptChunked(
  byte[] ciphertext,
  PrivateKey privateKey) throws Exception {

  Cipher cipher = Cipher.getInstance("RSA/ECB/
  ⟲OAEPWithSHA-256AndMGF1Padding");
  cipher.init(Cipher.DECRYPT_MODE, privateKey);

  int keySizeBytes =
    (((RSAPrivateKey) privateKey).getModulus().bitLength() + 7) /8;
```

Getting a cipher object capable of decrypting with RSA

Setting the cipher object in decrypting mode

Identifying the block sizes of the blocks of data to decrypt

```
try (ByteArrayOutputStream baos = new ByteArrayOutputStream()) {
  for (int offset = 0; offset < ciphertext.length;) {
    int len = Math.min(keySizeBytes, ciphertext.length - offset);
    baos.write(cipher.doFinal(ciphertext, offset, len));
    offset += len;
  }
  return baos.toByteArray();
}
}
```

Decrypting the blocks of data

Returning the decrypted data

This example shows a straightforward way to use RSA encryption with plain Java. Most programming languages also provide standard cryptographic algorithms, so you can apply the same ideas to implement RSA encryption and decryption in other technologies.

Let's extend our scenario. For this demo, we want the warehouse app to sign the encrypted content using RSA. The payments app will verify the signature before trying to decrypt the data.

We separated this example into the projects ssfd_ch6_ex2-warehouse and ssfd_ch6_ex2-payments provided with this book. Follow these steps:

1 Generate a new key pair using the key pair generator app (project ssfd_ch6_ex1-keygenerator).

2 Copy the private key to the warehouse application and name it signing_private_key.pem.

3 Copy the public key to the payments application and name it signing_public_key.pem.

NOTE Encryption uses the public key, and signing uses the private key. This means the warehouse app will use a public key to encrypt data but a private key to sign it.

Pay close attention because the apps use two separate key pairs, one for encryption/decryption and another for signing/verification. It wouldn't make sense to use the same key pair for both tasks. If you did, both apps would need access to both the private and public keys, which would reduce security and make the setup almost the same as using a single shared secret. In fact, it would be worse than a symmetric approach because asymmetric algorithms like RSA are slower and less efficient. The following listing shows how the warehouse app signs the refunds data using a plain Java implementation.

Listing 6.4   Signing the data with RSA using a private key

```
public static byte[] signSha256Rsa(
    byte[] data,
    PrivateKey privateKey) throws Exception {

    Signature sig = Signature.getInstance("SHA256withRSA");
```

Getting a Signature object capable of generating signatures with RSA

```
sig.initSign(privateKey);
sig.update(data);

    return sig.sign();
}
```

Setting the private
key for signing

Setting the data
to be signed

Generating and
returning the signature

The next listing shows how to use plain Java to verify an RSA signature using the public key from the pair, which the payments service does before decrypting the data. If
the signature can't be verified, the service rejects the data.

Listing 6.5   Verifying the RSA signature using the public key

```
public static boolean verify(
    byte[] data,
    byte[] signature,
    PublicKey publicKey) throws Exception {

    Signature sig = Signature.getInstance("SHA256withRSA");
    sig.initVerify(publicKey);
    sig.update(data);

    return sig.verify(signature);
}
```

Getting a Signature
object capable of
verifying an RSA
signature

Setting the public
key needed to verify
the signature

Setting the signed data whose
signature is to be checked

Verifying the signature for the
data and returning true if it
matches or false otherwise

That's all for asymmetric key encryption and signing with RSA for now. You've seen
how to use RSA for encrypting data and creating digital signatures, and you've
learned its strengths and limitations. In chapter 7, you'll learn about ECC, which uses
a different mathematical foundation but aims to provide the same guarantees with
smaller keys and better performance.

6.5   *Exercise answers*

1   What problem does public key cryptography solve compared to symmetric key
    cryptography?

    It solves the key-distribution problem. You no longer have to secretly share
    the same key with every service.

2   Why is it safe to share a public key but not a private key?

    The public key only encrypts or verifies; it can't unlock the data by itself. The
    private key must stay secret to protect the system.

3   If a hacker steals a private key, what should you do?

    Generate a new key pair and replace the compromised one.

4   Why do systems use digital certificates when sharing public keys?

    Certificates protect against tampering and impersonation by proving that the
    public key belongs to the claimed service.

5   What math problem is RSA security based on?

    It's based on the difficulty of factoring large numbers into their prime factors.

6 Why would quantum computers break RSA?

Quantum computers can run algorithms that factor numbers much faster than classical computers.

7 Which RSA key sizes are considered safe?

Today, 2,048-bit keys are safe, but security experts recommend 3,072- or 4,096-bit keys for long-term use.

8 What is the difference between RSAES-PKCS1-v1_5 and RSA-OAEP?

PKCS1 v1.5 is older, weaker, and vulnerable to chosen-ciphertext attacks. OAEP uses random padding, making it the modern, secure option.

9 Why is RSA often combined with AES in a hybrid scheme?

RSA is slow for large data, whereas AES is fast and efficient.

10 What is the term for encrypting an encryption key?

This process is called key wrapping.

11 List the steps a sender follows in hybrid encryption.

– Generate an AES key.

– Encrypt the data with AES.

– Encrypt the AES key with RSA.

– Send both the encrypted data and the encrypted key.

12 Which widely used protocols rely on hybrid encryption?

Protocols like TLS, IPsec, JWE, and SSH use hybrid encryption.

13 Which key of the key pair (private or public) is used for signing data?

The private key is used to sign the data. Only the owner of the data has the private key, which ensures nonrepudiation.

14 List the main differences between HMAC and RSA digital signatures.

Keys—

– HMAC—A shared secret key (symmetric)

– RSA—A public/private key pair (asymmetric)

Who can verify—

– HMAC—Only parties that share the secret key

– RSA—Anyone who has the public key

Nonrepudiation—

– HMAC—Not possible because both sides share the same key

– RSA—Possible because only the private key holder could sign

Performance—

– HMAC—Fast and based on hashing

– RSA—Slow and uses heavy math

Use cases—

– HMAC—Efficient checks between trusted parties (e.g., API calls)

– RSA—Signatures that must be verified by many parties or require proof of authorship (e.g., certificates or software signing)

Summary

- Public key cryptography solves the key-distribution problem by using mathematically related public–private key pairs in which public keys can be freely shared and private keys remain secret.

- RSA public key encryption is based on the mathematical difficulty of factoring large numbers into prime factors. Security depends on this computational challenge.

- RSA keys should be at least 2,048 bits, with 3,072 or 4,096 bits recommended for long-term security against advancing computational power.

- Avoid RSAES-PKCS1-v1_5, which is an old, insecure RSA padding scheme. RSA-OAEP provides secure randomized padding and is the recommended standard.

- Hybrid encryption combines fast AES for content encryption and RSA for encrypting the AES key, providing performance and security benefits.

- Key wrapping refers to encrypting an encryption key and is commonly used in hybrid schemes in which RSA encrypts AES content encryption keys.

- RSA digital signatures use the private key to sign data and the public key to verify signatures, providing integrity, authenticity, and nonrepudiation.

- Digital signatures differ from HMACs by enabling nonrepudiation because only the private key holder can create valid signatures and anyone can verify them with the public key.

- RSA signatures are slower than HMACs due to the heavy mathematical operations involved, but they provide stronger guarantees, including proof of authorship for legal purposes.

- Use separate RSA key pairs for encryption/decryption versus signing/verification to maintain security and avoid compromising either function.

- Private keys are used for sensitive operations such as decryption and signing. Public keys are used for encryption and signature verification.

- RSA encryption requires splitting large data into chunks because RSA can encrypt only data smaller than the key size minus padding overhead.

- Quantum computers could break RSA by efficiently factoring large numbers, making current key sizes inadequate against future quantum threats.

- Digital certificates are essential for validating public key authenticity and preventing man-in-the-middle attacks during key exchange.

- Sharing symmetric encryption and signing keys between applications incurs high management costs and security risks.

- Public key cryptography algorithms use key pairs to perform encryption and signing operations.

- Key pairs have two mathematically related keys: private and public keys. Public keys are freely shared with the world, so it's OK for anyone to possess a copy of a public key. Private keys are kept secret and never shared.

- RSA and ECC are the two most widely used public key cryptosystems.

- Quantum computers will break RSA and ECC because they solve the mathematical problems RSA and ECC use much more quickly than classical computers can. But quantum computers aren't yet powerful or widespread enough to be practical threats.

- Key warping describes a widely used technique in which a content encryption key is used to encrypt content. Then the content encryption key is encrypted to protect it during transit or storage.

- A hybrid encryption scheme combines symmetric and public key cryptography. A symmetric cipher such as AES is used to encrypt content; then the AES content-encryption key is wrapped using RSA encryption.

- RSA signatures use the private key to sign and the public key to verify, ensuring that only the private key holder can create a valid signature, but anyone can check it with the public key.

- Digital signatures provide integrity, authenticity, and nonrepudiation. With HMAC, you get integrity and authentication but not nonrepudiation because both sides share the same secret.

- RSA signing and RSA encryption use different key pairs. Use one pair for encryption/decryption and another for signing/verification to avoid weakening security.

- RSA signatures are slower than HMACs. They rely on heavier math operations, so they're often reserved for cases in which nonrepudiation or public verification is required.

- Always consult your information-security team to ensure that you're using corporate-recommended configurations of common cryptographic algorithms.

Public key encryption and digital signatures: Using ECC

7

This chapter covers

- Using elliptic curve encryption
- Using elliptic curve digital signatures
- Selecting a public key cryptosystem

In chapter 6, we explored the mechanics of RSA, a foundational cryptographic system that has safeguarded digital communications for decades. But although RSA is the wise elder of public key cryptography, it has challenges, particularly in performance. In this chapter, we shift gears to focus on elliptic curve cryptography (ECC), a sleek, modern alternative that offers the same level of security with far smaller keys and better performance.

Before diving in, let's take a moment to appreciate how far we've come. Back in the 1970s, Whitfield Diffie and Martin Hellman introduced the world to public key cryptography, sparking a revolution. Little did they know that decades later, we'd be exploring mathematical curves to protect everything from online shopping to encrypted cat memes. As cryptographers like to joke, using ECC is like trading in your vintage station wagon (RSA) for a high-performance sports car, which is sleek, efficient, and built for the demands of the modern world.

So grab your gear. First, we'll unravel the mysteries of ECC; explore how it builds on concepts from RSA; and discuss why it has become the cryptographic tool of choice in the age of smartphones, cloud computing, and high-stakes digital security.

7.1 *Elliptic-curve public key cryptosystems*

ECC, invented in 1985 by Victor Miller and Neal Koblitz, started gaining widespread adoption in 2004 as an alternative to RSA because it provides better performance. The mathematics of elliptic-curve cryptography is beyond the scope of this book, but it's important to know the following facts about the mathematics behind ECC algorithms:

- ECC is based on the mathematical problem of computing the discrete logarithm of a point on an elliptic curve (figure 7.1). If you aren't a mathematician, don't bother with the equations and fancy mathematical notions. We leave this here because it gives the problem the difficulty that makes ECC secure. An attacker would need immense computational power to figure out the solution.
- Computing the discrete logarithm of a point on an elliptic curve is slow. This difficulty is the basis for the security of ECC.
- If mathematicians discover a fast way to solve the discrete-logarithm problem, ECC will no longer be secure.
- Quantum computers will break elliptic-curve cryptography eventually, but they're not yet powerful or widespread enough to pose a threat.

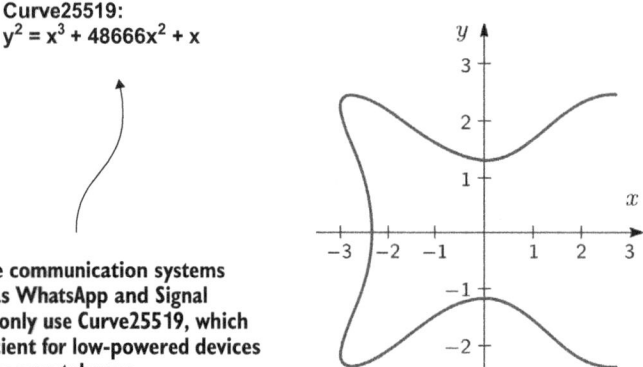

Curve25519:
$y^2 = x^3 + 48666x^2 + x$

Secure communication systems such as **WhatsApp and Signal** commonly use **Curve25519**, which is efficient for low-powered devices such as smartphones.

Figure 7.1   An example elliptic curve. This curve, named Curve25519, is one of the curves most used with the ECC algorithm.

7.1.1 *Configuring ECC*

Imagine an elliptic curve to be a fancy type of graph drawn by solving a mathematical equation. Elliptic curves are special because they have unique mathematical properties that allow operations such as "adding" two points or "multiplying" a point by a number while staying on the curve. These operations form the backbone of ECC.

There are countless ways to define an elliptic curve by tweaking the variables of the equations. Each tweak produces a new curve. But not all curves are safe for cryptography for the following reasons:

- Some curves are easy to break, potentially enabling attackers to figure out your secret keys.
- To ensure security, cryptographers carefully test and approve specific curves for use in encryption.

NOTE Not all mathematically possible elliptical curves can be used in cryptography. Cryptographers carefully test and approve specific curves for use in encryption.

To make developers' life easier, these approved curves are given names (sometimes long and strange ones) instead of long equations. Here are a few examples:

- Curve25519—Known for speed and security; commonly used in secure messaging apps
- Curve448-Goldilocks—Offers very high security
- P-256—A widely used curve standardized by the U.S. government
- secp256k1—Famous for being used in Bitcoin and other cryptocurrencies

For ECC to work, the sender and receiver must use the same elliptic curve. If they don't, their encrypted messages won't make sense to each other. The result would be like trying to play a piano duet when one person is using the wrong sheet music.

When setting up encryption, you configure which elliptic curve to use. This decision boils down to choosing one of the preapproved named curves based on your needs. Cryptographers and security experts consider several tradeoffs when selecting a curve:

- *Security level*—Different curves have different security levels. Curve25519, for example, provides the equivalent of 128 bits of security, whereas Curve448-Goldilocks provides 224 bits of security.
- *Computational efficiency*—Some curves have special mathematical properties that make them computationally efficient. Therefore, the choice of curve affects performance. Curve25519, for example, is faster and more efficient than the P-256 curve.
- *Implementation safety*—Some curves are harder than others to code, increasing the risk of implementation bugs that affect security.
- *Trust in the curve designer*—The number of elliptic curves is infinite, but only a few curves are standardized. When you use a specific curve, you're trusting the designer of the curve to pick a secure one. It's best to use a curve that is widely peer-reviewed and considered safe by many independent cryptographers.

The choice of curve has real-world implications for security. Curve25519, for example, designed by independent cryptographer Daniel J. Bernstein, is now widely used and considered to have good security and performance. Consult your corporate security standards to see which curves are recommended for use in your application.

7.1.2   Diffie-Helman key agreement

Elliptic-curve encryption combines two techniques to keep your data secure. As discussed in chapter 6, this is called a hybrid encryption scheme because it uses two different methods:

- Advanced Encryption Standard (AES)—A fast, secure way to encrypt the actual content, such as your message or file
- Elliptic Curve Diffie-Hellman (ECDH)—A clever way to generate the AES encryption key securely so that only the intended parties can use it even if someone is watching the communication

Using ECDH is like creating a super-secret key that only you and the person you're talking to know, and AES is the lock that uses that key to keep your data safe.

You're already comfortable with AES from chapter 5, but before you dive into how elliptic-curve encryption works, you need to understand the Diffie-Hellman (DH) algorithm, which is the foundation of ECDH. It's the magic behind creating a shared secret key securely even when you're communicating over an insecure network.

Let's examine some network traffic to understand how a DH key exchange works. We'll use the ACME scenario from the previous chapters (figure 7.2).

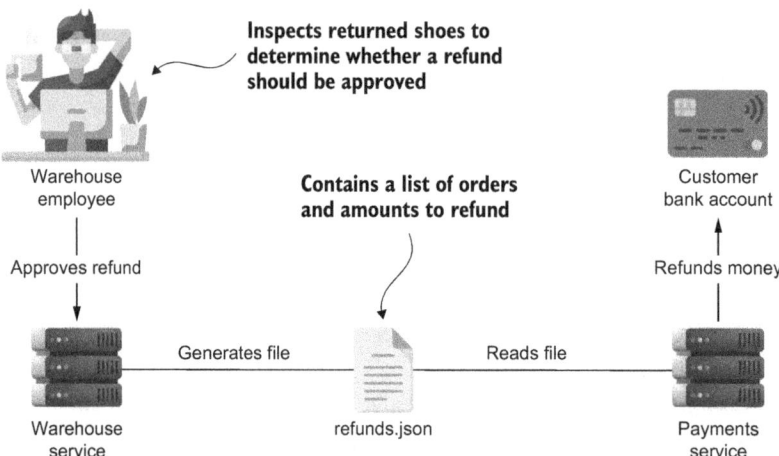

Figure 7.2   ACME staff members inspect returned merchandise and approve refunds using the warehouse management service. Once a day, the payment service asks the warehouse management service to return a JSON array containing the credit cards and refund amounts. The payment service issues refunds to customers' credit card accounts.

DH key agreement is a foundational algorithm used in Transport Layer Security (TLS) and Secure Shell (SSH) to turn an insecure communication channel into a secure one by adding encryption. DH starts with two systems exchanging their public keys and configuration parameters over an insecure network channel. Then each system can use the DH algorithm to compute the same shared secret, which is never transmitted over the network. This shared secret can be used as an AES encryption key.

Suppose that you and a friend want to agree on a secret number, but you can talk only through a public chat room where everyone can see your messages. If you send the secret directly, anyone can steal it. Instead, DH gives you a clever way to create the same secret on both sides without sending the secret itself.

Each of you has a public–private key pair. You exchange the public keys (figure 7.3). The private keys remain under each person's control and are never shared.

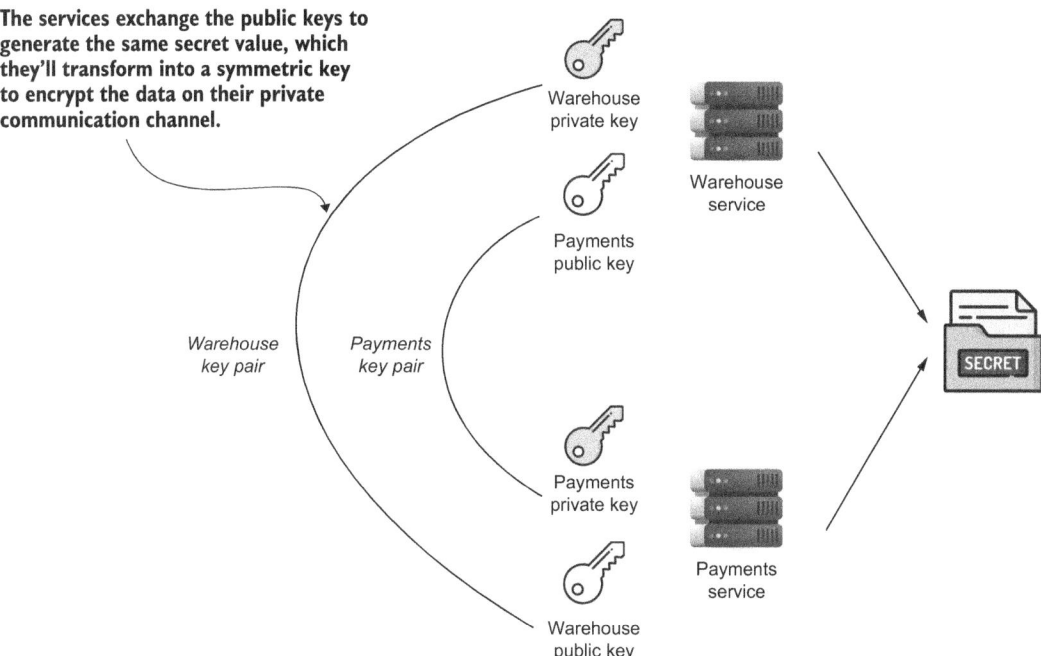

Figure 7.3 The DH algorithm computes the same result from the (payment private key, warehouse public key) and (warehouse private key, payment public key) key combinations.

You mix your friend's public key with your own private key using the DH formula. Your friend mixes your public key with their private key using the DH formula. Because of the way the math for this algorithm is designed, both sides end up with the same result:

```
sharedSecret = f(privateA, publicB) = f(privateB, publicA)
```

No one else can calculate this unless they know one of the private keys. The shared-Secret is just a big number. You won't use it directly; usually, you'll run it through a key-derivation function (a formula that turns it into a proper encryption key). The result is an AES key (or multiple AES keys) used to encrypt all future communications.

> **NOTE**   Often, you'll see code and documentation that refers to a DH key exchange, which is another name for a DH key agreement.

Secure communication protocols such as TLS and SSH use key exchange/agreement algorithms to generate symmetric encryption keys to protect data in transit. You'll use DH indirectly when you make HTTPS requests to a remote API; you don't have to write code that calls the DH algorithm.

You must decide which DH variant to choose only when you configure a TLS connection. Part 3 of the book covers TLS from a developer's perspective. For now, it's important to know that the DH algorithm has two variants:

- DH—The original 1976 algorithm based on the discrete-logarithm problem over the integers. It requires keys that are thousands of bits long, leading to slow computation.
- ECDH—A version of DH based on the discrete-logarithm problem for a point on an elliptic curve. It provides better performance than the original DH because it requires shorter keys. Modern protocols such as TLS 1.3 use this DH variant.

7.1.3   Exercises

1   What hard mathematical problem is ECC security based on?
2   Why aren't all elliptic curves safe to use in cryptography?
3   What is the difference between the original DH and ECDH algorithms?
4   Why do developers rarely implement the DH algorithm directly in their code?

7.2   Java support for elliptic curves

Java provides built-in support for working with elliptic curves, making it possible to apply this powerful cryptography in real-world applications with a few lines of code. In this section, we'll explore two common uses of elliptic curves:

- *Encryption with ECC*—Applying elliptic-curve cryptography to protect data
- *Signatures with the Elliptic Curve Digital Signature Algorithm (ECDSA)*—Using elliptic curves to generate and verify digital signatures

Together, these examples will give you a practical understanding of how ECC fits into the Java security APIs and how you can apply it in your own projects.

7.2.1   Java support for encryption with elliptic curves

Following our usual ACME example, let's assume that the development team decided to change the RSA encryption—decryption (chapter 6) with ECC. This example is illustrated in figure 7.2 earlier in this chapter. Java provides good tooling for implementing

ECC encryption and decryption as well. We'll use three projects provided with the book:

- ssfd_ch7_ex1-keygenerator—Generates the public–private key pair
- ssfd_ch7_ex1-warehouse—Encrypts the refunds data with the public key from the pair generated by the app ssfd_ch7_ex1-keygenerator
- ssfd_ch7_ex1-payments—Decrypts the encrypted file produced by the warehouse app using the private key from the pair

We'll follow these steps to encrypt and decrypt with ECC:

1 Generate a new key pair with the key-pair generator app.
2 Set the public key from the pair and the refunds file in the resources folder of the warehouse app.
3 Run the warehouse app to generate the encrypted file.
4 Store the encrypted file and the private key in the resources folder of the Payments appp.
5 Run the payments app to demonstrate that the decryption works.

You can also experiment by decrypting with a different key or modifying the encrypted content slightly, but both attempts will fail, proving the integrity of the process. The next code snippet shows how refunds are stored in the `refunds.json` file:

```
[
  {
    "orderId": "10001",
    "amount": 120
  },
  {
    "orderId": "10002",
    "amount": 450
  }
]
```

The following code produces the key pair. You must specify the curve to use along with a random seed value.

Listing 7.1 Generating the key pair for encryption

```
public class EcKeyPairGenerator {

  private final String curveName;
  private final SecureRandom secureRandom;

  public EcKeyPairGenerator(
    String curveName,
    SecureRandom secureRandom) {

    this.curveName = curveName;
    this.secureRandom = secureRandom;
  }
```

```
public KeyPair generate() throws Exception {
  KeyPairGenerator kpg = KeyPairGenerator.getInstance("EC");
  ECGenParameterSpec ecSpec =
    new ECGenParameterSpec(curveName);
  kpg.initialize(ecSpec, secureRandom);
  return kpg.generateKeyPair();
}
}
```

Getting a key pair generator object able to generate ECC key pairs

Setting the curve and a random seed

Generating the key pair

Configuring the curve we want to use to generate the key pair

The next listing shows the code the warehouse project uses to encrypt the refunds.json file. Although you can implement ECC directly in plain Java, the process requires quite a few more lines of code. We chose to use the Bouncy Castle provider to simplify the example. (Chapter 5 covers providers and the Java security API architecture; feel free to revisit that chapter for a refresher.)

Listing 7.2   Encryption using the ECC public key from the pair

```
public final class EccEncryptor {

  public static byte[] eccEncrypt(
    byte[] data,
    PublicKey recipientPublic) throws Exception {

    if (Security.getProvider("BC") == null) {
      Security.addProvider(new BouncyCastleProvider());
    }

    Cipher ecies = Cipher.getInstance("ECIES", "BC");
    ecies.init(Cipher.ENCRYPT_MODE, recipientPublic);
    return ecies.doFinal(data);
  }
}
```

Getting a cipher object capable of encypting data with ECC

Setting the cipher object mode to encyption

Encrypting the data and returning the encryption result

Place the public key and the file you want to encrypt in the warehouse app's resources folder; then run the application. The encrypted version of the file, refunds.json.ecc, is generated in the root of the project.

The next listing shows the decryption logic in the payments app. As before, we used the Bouncy Castle provider to keep the implementation straightforward. To try it, copy the private key from your key pair and the encrypted file you generated with the warehouse project to the resources folder of the payments app. When you run the application, the decrypted file, refunds.json, is created in the project's root folder.

Listing 7.3   Decryption using the ECC private key from the pair

```
public class EccDecryptor {

  public static byte[] eciesDecrypt(
    byte[] ciphertext,
    PrivateKey privateKey) throws Exception {
```

```
    if (Security.getProvider("BC") == null) {
        Security.addProvider(new BouncyCastleProvider());
    }

    Cipher cipher = Cipher.getInstance("ECIES", "BC");
    cipher.init(Cipher.DECRYPT_MODE, privateKey);
    return cipher.doFinal(ciphertext);
  }
}
```

Getting a cipher object capable of decrypting data with ECC

Setting the cipher object mode to decryption

Decrypting the encrypted data and returning the clear text result

Experiment with a few scenarios to better understand how the process works:

- Try using a private key from a different pair. Notice that decryption fails.
- Modify the encrypted file. Observe how the payments app reacts.

That wraps up the demonstration of encrypting and decrypting files with ECC in Java. Now you know how to use public and private keys with the Bouncy Castle provider to secure data. Section 7.2.2 takes matters further, discussing how to create and verify digital signatures using electronic counter-countermeasures (ECCM).

7.2.2 Java support for signing with elliptic curves

You can also use elliptic curves to generate digital signatures. Chapter 6 introduced digital signatures and demonstrated them with RSA. This section builds a similar example, but this time, the application generates signatures using ECDSA, an algorithm that relies on elliptic curves to create digital signatures. You can think of ECDSA as the elliptic-curve-based alternative to RSA for digital signatures.

The next listing shows a Java implementation of ECDSA. In this example, the warehouse project signs the encrypted data, allowing the payments project to verify its authenticity before attempting decryption.

Listing 7.4   Signing the data with a private key

```
public final class EccSigner {

  public static byte[] sign(
    byte[] data,
    PrivateKey privateKey) throws Exception {

    Signature sig = Signature.getInstance("SHA256withECDSA");
    sig.initSign(privateKey);
    sig.update(data);

    return sig.sign();
  }
}
```

Getting a Signature object capable of signing data with SHA256 and ECDSA

Configuring the private key for signing

Setting the data to be signed

Generating and returning the signature

The identifier of the algorithm we'll use is SHA256withECDSA. This name means that first the data is hashed using SHA256 to produce a fixed output; only then is the signature produced with ECDSA. You can find this implementation in project ssfd_ch7_ex2-warehouse provided with the book.

We generated a separate key pair for the signing process, just as we did in chapter 6 with the RSA example. The warehouse app uses the private key of this pair for signing. The payments app will need the public key to verify the signature.

We use a separate key pair for signing because the purpose of signing is different from that of encryption. An encryption key pair protects confidentiality, whereas a signing key pair ensures authenticity and integrity. Keeping these pairs separate reduces risk because even if an encryption key is compromised, the attacker can't create valid signatures, and vice versa. The following listing shows the implementation in the payments app for validating the signature with the public key.

> **Listing 7.5   Verifying a signature with the public key**

```
public class EccSignatureVerifier {

    public static boolean verifyResourceSignature(          Getting a Signature object
        byte[] data,                                        capable of verifying the
        byte[] sigBytes,                                    ECDSA signature
        PublicKey publicKey) throws Exception {
          Signature verifier = Signature.getInstance("SHA256withECDSA");  ◄──┘
          verifier.initVerify(publicKey);              ◄─         Configuring the public
          verifier.update(data);        ◄─  Setting the data       key to be used to
                                            that was signed        verify the signature

          return verifier.verify(sigBytes);   ◄─  Verify and return the
      }                                           result of verification
}
```

That's it for our ECDSA demo in Java. We generated a dedicated signing key pair, signed the data with the warehouse app, and verified the signature in the payments app before attempting decryption. The flow is simple: Hash → Sign with the private key → Send data + signature → Verify with the public key. Keep the signing keys separate from encryption keys, and always verify first to avoid wasting work on tampered content.

Next, we'll explore the key differences between RSA and ECC. As we move forward, we'll revisit asymmetric encryption and digital signatures in several chapters, each time from a new perspective and in more advanced scenarios.

7.3   *RSA vs. ECC*

Today, RSA and ECC are considered secure. Both are used in widely deployed security protocols such as SSH and TLS. You can find high-quality implementations of RSA and ECC in all popular programming languages' libraries. But take care to use ECC and RSA correctly by picking the right configuration and key size and by following best practices. Your corporate security standards should have up-to-date guidance on recommended RSA and ECC configurations.

RSA and ECC are based on mathematical problems that can be solved quickly on a quantum computer. But quantum computers are in their infancy. At the time of writing, scientists and engineers think we're years away from practical, powerful quantum computers that can break RSA and ECC. Cryptographers are developing quantum-resistant public key cryptosystems that they hope will be available before quantum computers are powerful enough to crack RSA and ECC.

A mathematical breakthrough that provides a fast algorithm for factoring large integers will break RSA. A breakthrough algorithm for computing the discrete logarithm of a point on an elliptic curve will break ECC. Mathematicians don't know whether such fast algorithms exist, will ever be discovered, or can be proved impossible to create. Having two mature public key cryptosystems gives us insurance: if one cryptography system falls to a mathematical breakthrough, we have a backup.

Secure RSA keys are large numbers, sometimes 4,096 bits long. Performing arithmetic operations on large numbers is slow and consumes battery power on mobile devices such as phones and tablets. ECC keys are much smaller than RSA keys. A 256-bit ECC key, for example, is thought to provide the same security as an RSA-3072 key. https://www.keylength.com provides up-to-date key-size recommendations using various methodologies. Overall, ECC's performance is better than RSA's. Therefore, ECC started gaining widespread adoption in 2004 with the rise of smartphones, on which battery life is a priority. On the server side, the performance advantage of ECC is welcome because it lowers operating costs.

Today, most cryptographers recommend ECC instead of RSA for new applications. Defaulting to ECC using Curve25119 is a safe choice in 2026, but you should consult your corporate security standards when deciding between ECC and RSA.

7.3.1   Exercises

5 What size ECC key provides security roughly equal to a 3,072-bit RSA key?

6 What would break RSA, and what would break ECC?

7 Why did ECC adoption grow strongly starting around 2004?

8 Which cryptosystem do most cryptographers recommend for new applications today?

7.4   Exercise answers

1 What hard mathematical problem is ECC security based on?

> ECC is based on the elliptic-curve discrete-logarithm problem, which is extremely hard to solve.

2 Why aren't all elliptic curves safe to use in cryptography?

> Some curves have weaknesses or can be broken. Cryptographers approve only specific curves (such as Curve25519) that have been tested for safety.

3 What is the difference between the original DH and the ECDH algorithm?

> DH works with large integers and requires long keys. ECDH works with elliptic curves and provides the same security with much shorter keys and faster performance.

4 Why do developers rarely implement the DH algorithm directly in their code?

Secure protocols like TLS and SSH already use DH/ECDH under the hood. Developers need only configure which variant to use, not reimplement the math.

5   What size ECC key provides security roughly equal to a 3,072-bit RSA key?

A 256-bit ECC key is considered equivalent in strength to a 3,072-bit RSA key.

6   What would break RSA, and what would break ECC?

A fast integer-factoring algorithm would break RSA. A fast algorithm for solving the elliptic-curve discrete-logarithm problem would break ECC.

7   Why did ECC adoption grow strongly starting around 2004?

Smartphones and mobile devices need strong security with small keys that use less CPU and battery power.

8   Which cryptosystem do most cryptographers recommend for new applications today?

ECC, often with Curve25519, is efficient and secure for most modern use cases.

Summary

- ECC is a modern alternative to RSA that provides the same level of security with smaller keys and better performance.
- ECC is based on the elliptic-curve discrete-logarithm problem, which is hard to solve with today's computers.
- Like RSA, ECC will eventually be broken by powerful quantum computers, but those computers don't yet pose a practical threat.
- Different elliptic curves offer different levels of security, efficiency, and trust. Widely used safe curves include Curve25519, P-256, and secp256k1.
- ECDH is used to securely generate shared symmetric keys over insecure networks and is the variant used in modern TLS.
- Java supports ECC directly, and libraries like Bouncy Castle make it easier to use ECC to encrypt and decrypt content.
- ECC is also used for digital signatures through ECDSA. Signing and encryption must use separate key pairs to avoid weakening security.
- Digital signatures with ECC provide authenticity, integrity, and nonrepudiation while remaining more efficient than RSA for mobile devices and high-scale systems.
- Today, most cryptographers recommend ECC over RSA for new applications because of its performance and security tradeoffs.

Part 3

Securing
communication channels

By now you've seen the cryptographic building blocks—hashes, HMACs, AES, RSA, and elliptic curves—and you know how they work in isolation. But security isn't just about the math; it's also about trust. Who are you really talking to? Can you be sure that the keys you're using belong to the right person or system? How do you keep conversations private when the network itself can't be trusted?

Part 3 connects the building blocks into systems that establish trust and protect communication over hostile networks. You'll start by learning how digital certificates and public key infrastructure solve the "who are you talking to?" problem (chapter 8). You'll follow the life cycle of a certificate from creation to validation, renewal, and even revocation. You'll see how to handle self-signed certificates and set up your own certificate authority for local development (chapter 9). Finally, you'll see it all come together with Transport Layer Security (TLS; chapter 10), the protocol that secures the modern internet, protects against eavesdropping and impersonation, and keeps data safe in motion.

Throughout Part 3, the ACME, Inc. case study keeps you grounded in real-world software systems. You'll experiment with tools like OpenSSL, configure Spring Boot apps with certificates, and understand how tools such as Kubernetes ingress controllers and service meshes handle TLS at scale.

Public key infrastructure and X.509 digital certificates: Know who you're talking to

This chapter covers

- Inspecting X.509 digital certificates for key fields that developers need to know
- Verifying X.509 certificates to decide whether a certificate is trustworthy
- Understanding common reasons why certificate validation fails

In chapter 7, we explored how public key cryptography addresses the challenge of securely sharing a secret by using a key pair: a public key and a private key. The private key must remain confidential and securely stored, but the public key can be freely distributed without special protection.

Now let's imagine that we need to establish a secure connection between a client and a server at ACME, Inc. At first glance, this might sound straightforward, but we have important details to consider. When the client and server set up their connection, for example, they exchange public keys. This exchange happens before encryption is in place, so it takes place over an unsecured channel.

You might think "Isn't that fine? After all, they're called public keys; anyone can have them!" That's true. Public keys are designed to be openly shared. The critical question, though, isn't whether you can receive a public key but whose public key you're getting.

During this initial exchange, an attacker could intercept the communication and substitute their own public key in place of the one you expected. If that happens, the attacker could trick you into encrypting or verifying messages with their key instead of the server's legitimate key (see figure 8.1). This type of attack is known as a man-in-the-middle attack, and it highlights a key challenge: although cryptography solves the mathematics of securing data, it doesn't by itself solve the problem of trust.

That's where certificates and public key infrastructure (PKI) come in. In the next section, we'll see how digital certificates and trusted authorities help ensure that the public key you're using really belongs to the server you intend to talk to.

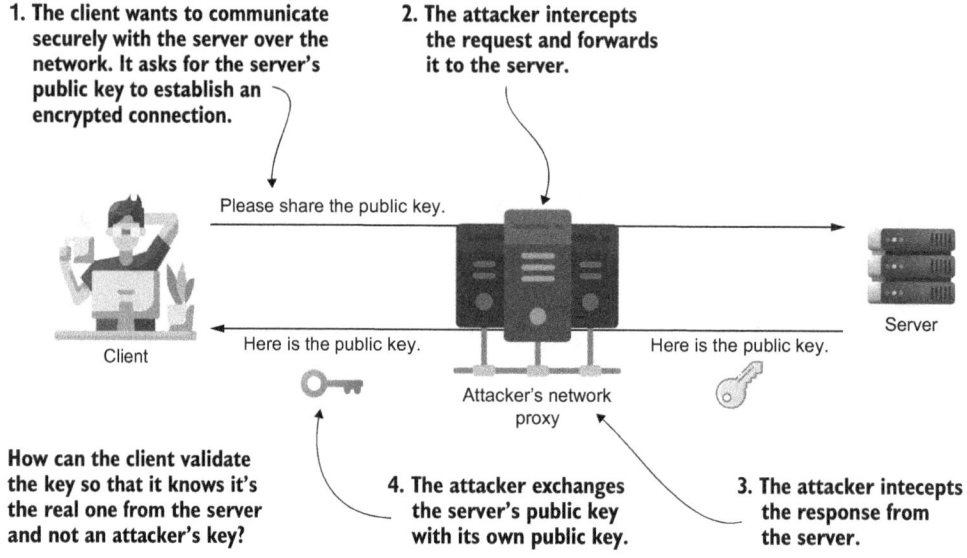

1. The client wants to communicate securely with the server over the network. It asks for the server's public key to establish an encrypted connection.

2. The attacker intercepts the request and forwards it to the server.

Please share the public key.

Here is the public key.

Client

Server

Attacker's network proxy

Here is the public key.

How can the client validate the key so that it knows it's the real one from the server and not an attacker's key?

4. The attacker exchanges the server's public key with its own public key.

3. The attacker intecepts the response from the server.

Figure 8.1   Public keys are exchanged over an insecure connection and can be modified by a man-in-the-middle attacker. The client needs a way to validate that the public key it received from the server hasn't been tampered with. By using an X.509 digital certificate, the client can determine who the public key belongs to.

If the client is fooled into using the attacker's public key to set up the connection, the attacker can observe and modify data exchanged over the encrypted connection. Before using a public key to set up an encrypted communication channel, a client needs a way to determine that the key hasn't been modified by an attacker and to verify the identity of the server it belongs to.

To make it easy to determine who a public key belongs to, the key is stored inside a tamperproof X.509 digital certificate. X.509 is a widely used standard for attaching metadata to a public key. A user of the public key inspects the X.509 certificate to determine who owns the public key and whether the public key can be trusted.

The rest of the chapter teaches everything a developer needs to know about X.509 digital certificates. We'll start by learning how to inspect X.509 certificates and then see an example of verifying certificate validity.

WARNING Never trust a public key until you've verified who the key belongs to.

8.1 Inspecting X.509 digital certificates

An X.509 certificate is a data structure with standardized field names and semantics defined in RFC 5280. All programming languages and application servers provide libraries for working with X.509 certificates. Command-line utilities that interact with remote services over the network, such as curl, kubectl, and git, use flags to configure which X.509 certificates to use and how to handle validation. Cloud services, load balancers, and APIs use X.509 certificates. A solid working knowledge of X.509 certificates is essential for a software developer.

The best way to understand X.509 is to explore a real-world public X.509 certificate. This section is a guided tour of the github.com X.509 certificate using the OpenSSL command-line utility. We'll take a step-by-step approach, introducing key concepts of X.509 along the way, so make sure to read this section sequentially from start to finish.

8.1.1 Inspecting X.509 certificates with OpenSSL

OpenSSL (https://www.openssl.org/) is a popular open source cryptography toolkit with a powerful command-line interface (CLI) called openssl. We'll use that CLI to explore X.509 certificates in this chapter.

Most operating systems ship with the openssl CLI, but the version can be different, which means that the output or command-line options may be different. You can check the version of OpenSSL on your machine using the command openssl version. The samples used in the book were produced with OpenSSL version 3.0.13 running on Ubuntu 24.04 in a Docker container. The following listing shows the Dockerfile used to create the container image.

Listing 8.1 Dockerfile with OpenSSL

```
FROM ubuntu:24.04
RUN apt-get update \
   && apt-get install -y \
      ca-certificates \
      openssl wget curl vim \
   && rm -rf /var/cache/apt/archives /var/lib/apt/lists/*
COPY examples /examples
```

If you want to follow along with the commands shown in this chapter, you can build the container image on your machine using the instructions at https://mng.bz/26YN.

Alternatively, you can run the prebuilt container published in GitHub packages using the following command:

```
docker run -ti ghcr.io/securing-cloud-applications/openssl:main
```

8.1.2 Downloading a website's X.509 digital certificate using the OpenSSL CLI

In this chapter, we'll take a public website and download and analyze the certificate it uses. Transport Layer Security (TLS), which we'll explore in chapter 10, secures communication over the Internet.

The TLS protocol uses X.509 certificates to set up an encrypted connection, which makes it possible to use the openssl s_client command to download the X.509 certificate of any public website. The command openssl s_client -servername github.com -connect github.com:443, for example, opens a TLS connection to github.com and prints lots of details (100+ lines of text), including the X.509 certificate and the TLS connection configuration.

The openssl s_client command is interactive; it waits for user input. If you type GET /, the command sends an HTTP GET request to the server over the TLS connection. You can avoid waiting for keyboard input by echoing an empty string and sending it through a pipe.

The command echo | openssl s_client -servername github.com -connect github .com:443 2>/dev/null prints out the TLS connection information without waiting for user input. But the output contains more information than just the X.509 certificate, so we filter the output of the openssl s_client command by piping it to the openssl x509 subcommand to extract only the X.509 certificate:

```
echo | openssl s_client -servername github.com -connect
github.com:443 2>/dev/null | openssl x509
> github-cert.pem
```

We combine two invocations of the OpenSSL client to extract the website's certificate. The openssl s_client command opens a secure connection and prints out the certificate to the screen. The second invocation, openssl x509 > github-cert.pem, filters out the X.509 certificate and puts it in a file called github-cert.pem, whose content is shown in the following listing.

Listing 8.2 PEM-encoded X.509 github.com certificate at time of writing

```
-----BEGIN CERTIFICATE-----
MIIFajCCBPCgAwIBAgIQBRiaVOvox+kD4KsNklVF3jAKBggqhkjOPQQDAzBWMQsw
CQYDVQQGEwJVUzEVMBMGA1UEChMMRGlnaUNlcnQgSW5jMTAwLgYDVQQDEydEaWdp
Q2VydCBUFMgSHlicmlkIEVDQyBTSEEzODQgMjAyMCBDQTEwHhcNMjIwMzE1MDAw
MDAwWhcNMjMwMzE1MjM1OTU5WjBmMQswCQYDVQQGEwJVUzETMBEGA1UECBMKQ2Fs
aWZvcm5pYTEWMBQGA1UEBxMNU2FuIEZyYW5jaXNjbzEVMBMGA1UEChMMR2l0SHVi
LCBJbmMuMRMwEQYDVQQDEwpnaXRodWIuY29tMFkwEwYHKoZIzj0CAQYIKoZIzj0D
AQcDQgAESrCTcYUh7GI/y3TARsjnANwnSjJLitVRgwgRI1JlxZ1kdZQQn5ltP3v7
KTtYuDdUeEu3PRx3fpDdu2cjMlyAOaOCA44wggOKMB8GA1UdIwQYMBaAFAq8CCkX
```

```
jKU5bXoOzjPHLrPt+8N6MB0GA1UdDgQWBBR4qnLGcWloFLVZsZ6LbitAh0I7HjAl
BgNVHREEHjAcggpnaXRodWIuY29tgg53d3cuZ2l0aHViLmNvbTAOBgNVHQ8BAf8E
BAMCB4AwHQYDVR0lBBYwFAYIKwYBBQUHAwEGCCsGAQUFBwMCMIGbBgNVHR8EgZMw
gZAwRqBEoEKGQGh0dHA6Ly9jcmwzLmRpZ2ljZXJ0LmNvbS9zEaWdpQ2VydFRMU0h5
YnJpZEVDQ1NIQTM4NDIwMjBDQTEtMS5jcmwwRqBEoEKGQGh0dHA6Ly9jcmw0LmRp
Z2ljZXJ0LmNvbS9zEaWdpQ2VydFRMU0h5YnJpZEVDQ1NIQTM4NDIwMjBDQTEtMS5j
cmwwPgYDVR0gBDcwNTAzBgZngQwBAgIwKTAnBggrBgEFBQcCARYbaHR0cDovL3d3
dy5kaWdpY2VydC5jb20vQ1BTMIGFBggrBgEFBQcBAQR5MHcwJAYIKwYBBQUHMAGG
GGh0dHA6Ly9vY3NwLmRpZ2ljZXJ0LmNvbTBPBggrBgEFBQcwAoZDaHR0cDovL2Nh
Y2VydHMuZGlnaWNlcnQuY29tL0RpZ2lDZXJ0VExTSHlicmlkRUNDU0hBMzg0MjAy
MENBMS0xLmNydDAJBgNVHRMEAjAAMIIBfwYKKwYBBAHWeQIEAgSCAW8EggFrAWkA
dgCt9776fP8QyIudPZwePhhqtGcpXc+xDCTKhYY069yCigAAAX+Oi8SRAAAEAwBH
MEUCIAR9cNnvYkZeKs9JElpeXwztYB2yLhtc8bB0rY2ke98nAiEAjiML8HZ7aeVE
P/DkUltwIS4c73VVrG9JguoRrII7gWMAdwA1zxkbv7FsV78PrUxtQsu7ticgJlHq
P+Eq76gDwzvWTAAAAX+Oi8R7AAAEAwBIMEYCIQDNckqvBhup7GpANMf0WPueytL8
u/PBaIAObzNZeNMpOgIhAMjfEtE6AJ2fTjYCFh/BNVKk1mkTwBTavJlGmWomQyaB
AHYAs3N3B+GEUPhjhtYFqdwRCUp5LbFnDAuH3PADDnk2pZoAAAF/jovErAAABAMA
RzBFAiEA9Uj5Ed/XjQpj/MxQRQjzG0UFQLmgwWlc73nnt3CJ7vskCICqHfBKlDz7R
EHdV5Vk8bLMBW1Q6S7Ga2SbFuoVXs6zFMAoGCCqGSM49BAMDA2gAMGUCMCiVhqft
7L/stBmv1XqSRNfE/jG/AqKIbmjGTocNbuQ7kt1Cs7kRg+b3b3C9Ipu5FQIxAM7c
tGKrYDGt0pH8iF6rzbp9Q4HQXMZXkNxg+brjWxnaOVGTDNwNH7O48+s/hT9bUQ==
-----END CERTIFICATE-----
```

The github.com X.509 certificate shown in listing 8.2 uses the Privacy Enhance Mail (PEM) format to represent the certificate as a string of ASCII characters. PEM certificates start with a marker line containing the string `-----BEGIN CERTIFICATE-----` followed by the Base64-encoded certificate followed by a marker line `-----END CERTIFICATE-----`. PEM-formatted certificates are widely used because they're easy to store in text configuration files. Non-PEM formats exist as well, and we'll cover them later in this chapter.

8.1.3 Viewing the fields of an X.509 digital certificate

To gain a better understanding of X.509 certificates, it's best to examine the fields of an actual X.509 certificate. This hands-on approach reveals the certificate's structure and the associated validation rules. The `openssl x509` command is a powerful tool for this purpose because it can read PEM-encoded certificates and display all their fields in a human-readable format. The command in the next snippet generates well-organized textual output, showing the fields of the X.509 certificate in the PEM-encoded GitHub certificate from listing 8.2:

```
openssl x509 -in github-cert.pem -noout -text
```

> **NOTE** Certificates have expiry dates. If you're following along with the sample repo, you'll get different output unless you use the certificate files from the repo.

As shown in listing 8.3, the number of fields in an X.509 can feel overwhelming. Fortunately, as an application developer, you have to be familiar with only three types of fields:

- Subject—Identifies the public key and its owner
- Issuer —Indicates who created the certificate
- Validity—Indicates the time range in which the certificate is valid

The remaining fields in X.509 certificates are crucial for developers who are building libraries to process certificates, but we'll cover them only briefly. Take a moment to review the details presented in the following listing to get familiar with the structure and content of a certificate.

Listing 8.3   Contents of github.com X.509 certificate on March 5, 2023

```
Certificate:
  Data:
    Version: 3 (0x2)
    Serial Number:
      0c:d0:a8:be:c6:32:cf:e6:45:ec:a0:a9:b0:84:fb:1c
    Signature Algorithm: ecdsa-with-SHA384
    Issuer: C = US, O = DigiCert Inc, CN
      = DigiCert TLS Hybrid ECC SHA384 2020 CA1
    Validity
      Not Before: Feb 14 00:00:00 2023 GMT
      Not After : Mar 14 23:59:59 2024 GMT
    Subject: C = US, ST = California, L = San Francisco,
      O = "GitHub, Inc.", CN = github.com
    Subject Public Key Info:
      Public Key Algorithm: id-ecPublicKey
        Public-Key: (256 bit)
        pub:
          04:a3:a4:03:46:03:df:46:51:56:cb:c9:39:ab:22:
          cd:e7:6c:59:96:7a:93:a0:fb:b9:40:1c:90:32:88:
          36:c6:09:76:9c:50:f5:55:f7:76:5e:68:20:9c:ee:
          22:ed:83:0c:15:30:10:41:44:5e:32:ac:90:a1:d5:
          aa:f2:e5:43:b3
        ASN1 OID: prime256v1
        NIST CURVE: P-256
    X509v3 extensions:
      X509v3 Authority Key Identifier:
        0A:BC:08:29:17:8C:A5:39:6D:7A:0E:CE:33:C7:2E:B3:ED:FB:C3:7A
      X509v3 Subject Key Identifier:
        C7:07:27:78:85:F2:9D:33:C9:4C:5E:56:7D:5C:D6:8E:72:67:EB:DE
      X509v3 Subject Alternative Name:
        DNS:github.com, DNS:www.github.com
      X509v3 Key Usage: critical
        Digital Signature
      X509v3 Extended Key Usage:
        TLS Web Server Authentication, TLS Web Client Authentication
      X509v3 CRL Distribution Points:
        Full Name:
          URI:http://crl3.digicert.com
            /DigiCertTLSHybridECCSHA3842020CA1-1.crl
        Full Name:
          URI:http://crl4.digicert.com
            /DigiCertTLSHybridECCSHA3842020CA1-1.crl
```

```
        X509v3 Certificate Policies:
          Policy: 2.23.140.1.2.2
            CPS: http://www.digicert.com/CPS
        Authority Information Access:
          OCSP - URI:http://ocsp.digicert.com
          CA Issuers - URI:http://cacerts.digicert.com
          ➥/DigiCertTLSHybridECCSHA3842020CA1-1.crt
        X509v3 Basic Constraints:
          CA:FALSE
        CT Precertificate SCTs:
          Signed Certificate Timestamp:
            Version   : v1 (0x0)
            Log ID    : EE:CD:D0:64:D5:DB:1A:CE:C5:5C:B7:9D:B4:CD:13:A2:
                  32:87:46:7C:BC:EC:DE:C3:51:48:59:46:71:1F:B5:9B
            Timestamp : Feb 14 16:58:33.338 2023 GMT
            Extensions: none
            Signature : ecdsa-with-SHA256
                  30:46:02:21:00:E4:16:AE:D3:E2:2C:BA:82:9F:A9:79:
                  F2:4B:C6:94:52:ED:4D:E0:87:CC:50:CA:69:B1:B4:8F:
                  05:77:3A:94:EB:02:21:00:B5:9F:C3:F9:CB:0F:AD:D0:
                  60:F2:30:1B:71:05:72:12:0D:BD:65:1F:07:A9:9C:53:
                  4B:76:95:12:04:A6:BF:2E
          Signed Certificate Timestamp:
            Version   : v1 (0x0)
            Log ID    : 48:B0:E3:6B:DA:A6:47:34:0F:E5:6A:02:FA:9D:30:EB:
                  1C:52:01:CB:56:DD:2C:81:D9:BB:BF:AB:39:D8:84:73
            Timestamp : Feb 14 16:58:33.387 2023 GMT
            Extensions: none
            Signature : ecdsa-with-SHA256
                  30:45:02:20:1E:3C:60:32:7E:20:51:F5:D6:E1:AF:7D:
                  4D:F5:97:C4:48:2E:46:57:6B:86:05:37:32:4F:25:04:
                  36:B1:F7:B7:02:21:00:FC:09:7E:C0:7C:03:83:26:36:
                  BD:A7:5B:EB:1D:13:59:F6:62:20:8E:6D:6F:B7:0D:31:
                  EB:DB:F5:11:EE:5B:D4
          Signed Certificate Timestamp:
            Version   : v1 (0x0)
            Log ID    : 3B:53:77:75:3E:2D:B9:80:4E:8B:30:5B:06:FE:40:3B:
                  67:D8:4F:C3:F4:C7:BD:00:0D:2D:72:6F:E1:FA:D4:17
            Timestamp : Feb 14 16:58:33.402 2023 GMT
            Extensions: none
            Signature : ecdsa-with-SHA256
                  30:46:02:21:00:CC:E0:6B:F4:E6:74:FB:A3:92:67:21:
                  53:8B:2C:0D:EB:83:F2:B0:DD:05:2D:E2:D1:C8:BE:63:
                  98:4B:18:AC:36:02:21:00:EE:D2:3B:60:5A:23:08:29:
                  4E:82:33:47:4A:72:A5:16:2E:46:85:13:6D:DC:DA:25:
                  80:85:80:07:AA:B1:51:47
Signature Algorithm: ecdsa-with-SHA384
Signature Value:
  30:64:02:30:04:dc:0d:d4:de:34:99:0a:9c:1f:a8:e1:c1:76:
  5c:62:f4:04:a0:29:35:3e:c2:0d:2a:c3:71:6a:b5:f4:37:d4:
  ec:0b:60:57:71:87:43:25:36:4f:c7:c2:48:d1:49:68:02:30:
  56:d0:bc:c9:17:10:fb:cd:be:fe:2d:df:42:ba:c6:da:46:db:
  aa:a6:67:ee:8e:88:84:81:20:85:cc:96:35:a7:b2:26:11:d6:
  0c:99:9d:3c:c8:83:70:10:4b:0e:15:9b
```

8.1.4   Subject field: Identifying the public key and its owner

Every X.509 certificate contains a public key. The owner of the public key is called the subject. The Subject fields contain the public key's value and metadata about who owns the public key. If we compare a certificate to a passport, the Subject fields contain the person's name, birthdate, photo, height, and so on. The key Subject fields from the github.com certificate in listing 8.3 are extracted in the next listing.

Listing 8.4   Subject fields for the github.com certificate as of March 5, 2022

```
Subject: C=US,ST=California,L=San Francisco,O="GitHub, Inc.",CN=github.com
Subject Public Key Info:
Public Key Algorithm: id-ecPublicKey
  Public-Key: (256 bit)
  pub:
    04:a3:a4:03:46:03:df:46:51:56:cb:c9:39:ab:22:
    cd:e7:6c:59:96:7a:93:a0:fb:b9:40:1c:90:32:88:
    36:c6:09:76:9c:50:f5:55:f7:76:5e:68:20:9c:ee:
    22:ed:83:0c:15:30:10:41:44:5e:32:ac:90:a1:d5:
    aa:f2:e5:43:b3
  ASN1 OID: prime256v1
  NIST CURVE: P-256
X509v3 extensions:
X509v3 Subject Alternative Name:
    DNS:github.com, DNS:www.github.com
```

The Subject Public Key Info section specifies the public key's value and the type of key being used. In the github.com certificate shown in listing 8.4, the public key is a 256-bit elliptic curve key derived from the P-256 NIST curve. Libraries and frameworks are designed to handle the various types of public keys supported by X.509 certificates. If you need a refresher on the two most commonly used public key types, RSA and elliptic curves, refer to chapters 6 and 7.

Two fields define the public key's owner:

- Subject—Identifies the main entity (person, organization, or server) the certificate was issued to.
- Subject Alternative Name (SAN)—Extends the Subject field by allowing multiple identifiers such as additional domain names, IP addresses, and emails.

To intuitively understand the subject fields, you must understand the historical context in which X.509 was developed.

The International Telecommunications Union (ITU) originally designed X.509 certificates with a specific use case in mind: issuing digital certificates for individuals and storing them in a phone directory. This work was carried out in the late 1980s, before the invention of the World Wide Web and HTTP. As a result, the Subject field in X.509 certificates includes subfields that resemble a mailing address rather than a Domain Name System (DNS) name. Take a look at the next snippet for an example of the Subject field from the github.com certificate:

```
Subject: C=US,ST=California,L=San Francisco,O="GitHub, Inc.",CN=github.com
```

The subfields are attributes of the entity that owns the public key:

- `C`—Country
- `ST`—State
- `L`—Locality (city, town, or village)
- `O`—Organization
- `CN`—Common name

If the certificate represents a human, you might see a person's name, such as `Adib Saikali`. But when the certificate belongs to a website, it's typical to use the DNS name of the website in the `Subject` field's `CN` section. More subfields can be used in the subject name, but we'll ignore them because they're uncommon.

SAN is a required extension field that contains a network address of the owner of the public key. The allowed network address types are DNS names, email addresses, IP addresses, and URIs. The github.com certificate in listing 8.2 contains the names `DNS:github.com, DNS:www.github.com`. Here are typical use cases for the allowed network address types:

- DNS name—Widely used to identify server identity, it's used by clients to ensure that they're talking to the right server. Web browsers, for example, use the SAN DNS field to check that the certificate used for a TLS connection has a DNS name that matches the URL the user typed in the browser address bar. Wildcard DNS names such as *.example.com are allowed.
- IP address—An IP address can be used to identify servers. But the supply of IPv4 addresses is limited, so companies and cloud providers reuse IP addresses. If you see an IP address in an X.509 certificate, you can't tell who owns that IP address. Using an IP address in a certificate is a bad idea.
- Email—Email can be used to create certificates that represent humans, but it's not common to create email-based certificates. You'll likely see an X.509 certificate with an email SAN in the context of code signing using the popular sigstore.dev project.
- Uniform Resource Identifier (URI)—A URL can be used for application identity in a service-to-service call chain. In part 5 of this book, when we cover Secure Production Identity Framework for Everyone (SPIFFE), you'll encounter URI-based SANs.

EXTRACTING THE PUBLIC KEY USING THE OPENSSL CLI

As we've been discussing, each certificate has a public key. You can use the `openssl x509` command to extract a certificate's public key. For the github.com certificate in listing 8.2, stored in the file `github-cert.pem`, you can use the command in the next snippet to print the public key to the console:

```
openssl x509 -in github-cert.pem -pubkey -noout
```

The next snippet shows the command's result:

```
-----BEGIN PUBLIC KEY-----
MFkwEwYHKoZIzj0CAQYIKoZIzj0DAQcDQgAEo6QDRgPfRlFWy8k5qyLN52xZlnqT
```

oPu5QByQMog2xgl2nFD1Vfd2Xmggn04i7YMMFTAQQUReMqyQodWq8uVDsw==
-----END PUBLIC KEY-----

Notice that the key is output in PEM format as a Base64-encoded string with a marker line indicating what is in the encoded string. We can decode the public key string with `openssl pkey` by processing the output from the preceding command. The following listing shows you how to decode the public key using `openssl` commands.

Listing 8.5   Decoding the public key

```
openssl x509 -in github-cert.pem -pubkey -noout | openssl pkey -pubin -text

-----BEGIN PUBLIC KEY-----
MFkwEwYHKoZIzj0CAQYIKoZIzj0DAQcDQgAEo6QDRgPfRlFWy8k5qyLN52xZlnqT
oPu5QByQMog2xgl2nFD1Vfd2Xmggn04i7YMMFTAQQUReMqyQodWq8uVDsw==
-----END PUBLIC KEY-----
Public-Key: (256 bit)
pub:
    04:a3:a4:03:46:03:df:46:51:56:cb:c9:39:ab:22:
    cd:e7:6c:59:96:7a:93:a0:fb:b9:40:1c:90:32:88:
    36:c6:09:76:9c:50:f5:55:f7:76:5e:68:20:9c:ee:
    22:ed:83:0c:15:30:10:41:44:5e:32:ac:90:a1:d5:
    aa:f2:e5:43:b3
ASN1 OID: prime256v1
NIST CURVE: P-256
```

The github.com certificate we decoded contains an elliptic curve public key based on the NIST P-256 curve. Recall from chapters 6 and 7 that RSA and elliptic curve are two commonly used types of public keys. An X.509 certificate can contain an RSA or an elliptic curve key but not both.

8.1.5   *Issuer field: Identifies who created the certificate*

A certificate authority (CA) is like an official organization that gives out digital certificates (X.509 certificates). The `Issuer` field in a certificate tells you which CA created it. Knowing who issued the certificate is important because it helps you decide whether the certificate should be trusted.

Think of a passport: the certificate itself is the passport, and the CA is the country that issued it. If you don't trust the country, you won't trust the passport either.

Deciding whether to trust a CA isn't always simple; it involves several factors that we'll discuss in the next section. For now, let's focus on the X.509 fields that point to the CA: `Issuer` and `Authority Information Access` (AIA). The following snippet shows an example of the `Issuer` field taken directly from a certificate:

`Issuer: C=US, O=DigiCert Inc, CN=DigiCert TLS Hybrid ECC SHA384 2020 CA1`

The Issuer field is a string with a well-defined structure, using the same format as the `Subject` field, such as `C=US, O=DigiCert Inc, CN=DigiCert TLS Hybrid ECC SHA384 2020 CA1`. The Issuer string typically contains the following fields:

- C—Country where the CA is located
- O—Name of the organization that owns the CA
- CN—Common name of the CA

In the case of the github.com certificate, we see that an organization called DigiCert Inc., based in the United States, issued the certificate using a CA called DigiCert TLS Hybrid ECC SHA384 2020 CA1. The Issuer field contains the first breadcrumb required to validate the certificate. We'll see how to follow the breadcrumbs later in this chapter. We can extract the issuer from an X.509 certificate using the command in the next snippet:

```
openssl x509 -in github-cert.pem -noout -issuer -ext authorityInfoAccess
```

In the following snippet, you see the result of running the preceding command:

```
Issuer=C = US, O = DigiCert Inc,
➥CN = DigiCert TLS Hybrid ECC SHA384 2020 CA1
```

8.1.6 Validity fields

Like passports, X.509 certificates are valid for a specific time range. The certificate should be considered valid if the current time is within the time range set in the Not Before and Not After fields. The Validity field specifies the date range, as shown in the next snippet:

```
Validity
      Not Before: Feb 14 00:00:00 2023 GMT
      Not After : Mar 14 23:59:59 2024 GMT
```

Certificate lifespans vary from a few minutes to a few years. In the case of the github.com certificate, we see that it's valid for one year, from February 14, 2023, to March 14, 2024. Long-lived certificates are a security risk because protecting a private key that long is difficult.

> **NOTE** The longer a certificate is valid, the more opportunity there is for the private key to be stolen, leaked, or lost.

A best practice is to create certificates with the shortest time span reasonable for the certificate's use case. Code-signing certificates issued by the https://sigstore.dev project, for example, are valid for only 10 minutes, which is long enough to sign an executable or container image in a build pipeline. Certificates issued by the Let's Encrypt CA are valid for 90 days and are typically used to secure websites. We'll cover some practices for certificate expiry later in this chapter.

You can extract the validity date range using the openssl command, as shown in the following snippet:

```
openssl x509 -in github-cert.pem -noout -dates
```

The command produces output similar to that shown in the next snippet:

```
notBefore=Feb 14 00:00:00 2023 GMT
notAfter=Mar 14 23:59:59 2024 GMT
```

The `notBefore` and `notAfter` fields in the output represent the validity period of the X.509 certificate:

- `notBefore`—The start date and time (when the certificate becomes valid). Before this date, the certificate is not considered trustworthy or usable. In this case, the certificate is valid starting February 14, 2023 at 00:00:00 GMT.
- `notAfter`—The expiration date and time (when the certificate ceases to be valid). After this date, the certificate is considered expired and should no longer be used. In this case, the certificate expires March 14, 2024 at 23:59:59 GMT.

Together, these fields define the certificate's validity period, ensuring that it can be used only within this specific timeframe.

8.1.7 X.509 digital certificate encoding formats

Common sources of frustration for developers working with X.509 certificates are the various encoding formats and the tools used to work with them. In section 8.1.2, we looked at PEM-encoded X.509 certificates. Although PEM is the most commonly used certificate format today, you may run across other formats. No matter what data format is used to store an X.509 certificate, the fields and the meaning of the fields inside the file are the same. Following are some X.509 file formats you might encounter:

- DER—Raw binary, typically formatted using Distinguished Encoding Rules (DER) defined by the ASN.1 standard. If you see a certificate file with a .der extension, it probably contains the raw bytes of a certificate. When you decode a Base64 string in a PEM certificate, you end up with a DER file.
- PKCS#12—A binary cryptography file format that can store certificates and private keys. A single PKCS#12 file can store multiple certificates and their associated private keys. If you see a file with a .p12 or .pfx extension, it's typically a PKCS#12-formatted file. PKCS#12 is an industry standard, so lots of tools understand how to process it.
- JKS—A binary format for storing a collection of certificates and private keys used by the Java programming language. Java supports PKCS#12 files, and many Java-based frameworks can use PEM files, so it's better to use PKCS#12-formatted files when working with Java. Many blog posts and Stack Overflow answers show examples using JKS files. In chapter 9, we show you how to use PEM and PKCS#12 files with Java.

Tools like OpenSSL can convert one certificate format to another. Stay focused on the meanings of the fields in the certificate; those fields will have the same meanings now and in the future. Over time, you're likely to need to deal only with PEM files.

8.1.8 Exercises

1 What are the three main X.509 certificate fields that application developers need to be familiar with?
2 What information is contained in the `Subject` field and in the SAN extension?

3 Why is using an IP address in the SAN field generally considered bad practice?

4 What do the `Validity` fields `notBefore` and `notAfter` represent?

5 Name two common certificate-encoding formats other than PEM.

8.2 Verifying X.509 digital certificates

The big question we're answering in this chapter is: "Who owns a public key?" We solved part of the problem by placing the public key inside an X.509 certificate. This certificate has a set of standard fields, each with a clear meaning. By looking at these fields, we can see who the owner of the public key is. But here's the next challenge: can we trust what the certificate says?

In everyday life, people sometimes use fake IDs, such as fake driver's licenses, fake passports, or other forged documents. The same risk exists online: attackers can create fake digital certificates. That's why in this section, we'll focus on how to check whether a certificate is authentic and can be trusted. When a digital certificate is verified, you know who issued it and that it wasn't tampered with, but you still can't trust it. To trust a certificate, you must trust the CA that issued it— a complex situation that we'll explore in this section.

If you trust the CA and the certificate is valid, is the certificate safe to use? Unfortunately, the answer depends on the certificate owner's security practices. Recall from chapters 6 and 7 that a public key has a corresponding private key. If the private key is stolen, the thief can pretend to be the certificate owner.

There's no algorithmic way to determine whether a private key has been stolen until the real owner reports the theft to the CA, which adds the certificate to a certificate revocation list (CRL). Ideally, the owner of an X.509 certificate follows all the recommended best practices for protecting private keys. Those best practices are beyond the scope of this book, but we'll cover some important patterns in upcoming chapters.

> **TIP** You can trust an X.509 digital certificate only if the certificate hasn't been tampered with, the CA that issued the certificate can be trusted, and the owner of the certificate can be trusted to keep the private key private. Trusting a certificate has two components: risk assessment and algorithmic verification. The rest of this section teaches you the algorithmic component of certificate verification.

8.2.1 Verifying the github.com X.509 certificate

How can we be sure that an X.509 certificate is still valid and hasn't been damaged or changed? Sometimes, certificates get corrupted accidentally, perhaps because of hardware failures, network transmission errors, or problems in saving to disk. At other times, an attacker who wants to trick the system tampers with them on purpose.

In chapter 4, we learned that both corruption and tampering can be detected with the help of digital signatures, which are created with hash functions. A digital signature works like a security seal: if the data changes, the seal no longer matches.

But here's the key question: which signature algorithm should you use to verify the certificate? Every X.509 certificate includes this information inside the `Signature`

`Algorithm` field. This field tells you which algorithm was used to sign the certificate and what value you should expect when verifying its authenticity. The following listing shows the part of the certificate (from listing 8.2) where you can find the details about the signature.

Listing 8.6   Signature section of github.com X.509 certificate on March 5, 2023

```
Certificate:
  Data:
    [Remvoved for brevity]                          The cryptographic algorithm
    Signature Algorithm: ecdsa-with-SHA384    ◄─┘  used to sign the data
    Signature Value:                                ◄─┐  The signature
      30:64:02:30:04:dc:0d:d4:de:34:99:0a:9c:1f:a8:e1:c1:76:  │  value in hex
      5c:62:f4:04:a0:29:35:3e:c2:0d:2a:c3:71:6a:b5:f4:37:d4:
      ec:0b:60:57:71:87:43:25:36:4f:c7:c2:48:d1:49:68:02:30:
      56:d0:bc:c9:17:10:fb:cd:be:fe:2d:df:42:ba:c6:da:46:db:
      aa:a6:67:ee:8e:88:84:81:20:85:cc:96:35:a7:b2:26:11:d6:
      0c:99:9d:3c:c8:83:70:10:4b:0e:15:9b
```

The github.com certificate is signed with an Elliptic Curve Digital Signature Algorithm (ECDSA) using the SHA-384 cryptographic hash function. We discussed ECDSA in chapter 7, where we also implemented a small Java app that signed data sent between two apps. This information is sufficient for libraries to validate that the certificate hasn't been tampered with. The `openssl verify` command, for example, can be used to verify a certificate, as shown in the next snippet:

```
$ openssl verify  github-cert.pem
```

The output of running the `openssl verify` command is

```
C = US, ST = California, L = San Francisco,
➥O = "GitHub, Inc.", CN = github.com
error 20 at 0 depth lookup: unable to get local issuer certificate
error github-cert.pem: verification failed
```

Notice that errors output with the message `unable to get local issuer certificate error`. This type of error is common, but the wording of the error message depends on the verification tool or framework used.

Understanding the root cause of this verification failure is critical for developers. To get to that root cause, you have to understand a set of related concepts:

- *Root certificates*—Self-signed certificates issued by trusted CAs that serve as the foundation of the certificate trust hierarchy
- *Intermediate certificates*—Certificates issued by root or higher-level intermediate CAs to create a bridge between the root certificate and end-user certificates, adding an extra layer of security
- *Chain of trust*—The hierarchical relationship that links an end-user certificate to a trusted root certificate through intermediate certificates, enabling the verification of the certificate's authenticity

Grab a strong cup of coffee. These concepts are challenging but critical to understand. We'll explore the concepts using OpenSSL and the github.com certificate; then we'll take a step back and generalize what we've learned.

Verifying an X.509 certificate requires validating its digital signature, which in turn requires the public key of the CA that issued it. That public key is stored inside an X.509 certificate, which raises a couple of issues:

- Where to get the CA's certificate
- How to validate the CA's certificate

This problem feels self-referential, similar to the famous question "Which came first, the chicken or the egg?" In our case, the answer is that CAs' certificates are preinstalled as part of the operating system, browser, or language runtime. Here, we're using an Ubuntu-based Docker image.

Ubuntu ships with a trusted CA in a package called `ca-certificates`. We can inspect the contents of the package using the `dpkg -L ca-certificates` command as follows to determine the directory location of the trusted CAs.

Listing 8.7   CAs preinstalled in Ubuntu 24.04

```
$ dpkg -L ca-certificates
/.
/etc
/etc/ca-certificates
/etc/ca-certificates/update.d
/etc/ssl
/etc/ssl/certs
/usr
/usr/sbin
/usr/sbin/update-ca-certificates
/usr/share
/usr/share/ca-certificates
/usr/share/ca-certificates/mozilla          <--| Directory contains all certificates
/usr/share/ca-certificates/mozilla/ACCVRAIZ1.crt    of the certificate authorities
/usr/share/ca-certificates/mozilla/AC_RAIZ_FNMT-RCM.crt   trusted by Ubuntu 24.04
/usr/share/ca-certificates/mozilla/AC_RAIZ_FNMT-RCM_SERVIDORES_SEGUROS.crt
/usr/share/ca-certificates/mozilla/ANF_Secure_Server_Root_CA.crt
/usr/share/ca-certificates/mozilla/Actalis_Authentication_Root_CA.crt
/usr/share/ca-certificates/mozilla/AffirmTrust_Commercial.crt
/usr/share/ca-certificates/mozilla/AffirmTrust_Networking.crt
/usr/share/ca-certificates/mozilla/AffirmTrust_Premium.crt
/usr/share/ca-certificates/mozilla/AffirmTrust_Premium_ECC.crt
/usr/share/ca-certificates/mozilla/Amazon_Root_CA_1.crt
/usr/share/ca-certificates/mozilla/Amazon_Root_CA_2.crt
/usr/share/ca-certificates/mozilla/Amazon_Root_CA_3.crt
/usr/share/ca-certificates/mozilla/Amazon_Root_CA_4.crt
/usr/share/ca-certificates/mozilla/Atos_TrustedRoot_2011.crt
… etc extra output trimmed
```

Notice that the `/usr/share/ca-certificates/mozilla` directory contains many files, each corresponding to a trusted CA. The filenames seem to contain the names of the

CAs. Because the github.com certificate we're using was signed by DigiCert, we can search /usr/share/ca-certificates/mozilla for filenames containing the string Digi, as shown in the following snippet:

```
root@c6044a0470f5:/usr/share/ca-certificates/mozilla# ls -1 DigiCert*
DigiCert_Assured_ID_Root_CA.crt
DigiCert_Assured_ID_Root_G2.crt
DigiCert_Assured_ID_Root_G3.crt
DigiCert_Global_Root_CA.crt
DigiCert_Global_Root_G2.crt
DigiCert_Global_Root_G3.crt
DigiCert_High_Assurance_EV_Root_CA.crt
DigiCert_TLS_ECC_P384_Root_G5.crt
DigiCert_TLS_RSA4096_Root_G5.crt
DigiCert_Trusted_Root_G4.crt
```

Recall that the CA used to sign the GitHub certificate is called DigiCert TLS Hybrid ECC SHA384 2020 CA1, which is not in the preceding list. That's why we get the error message lookup: unable to get local issuer certificate. A web search for DigiCert TLS Hybrid ECC SHA384 2020 CA1 leads to the DigiCert Trusted Root Authority Certificates page of the DigiCert website (figure 8.2; https://mng.bz/15OZ).

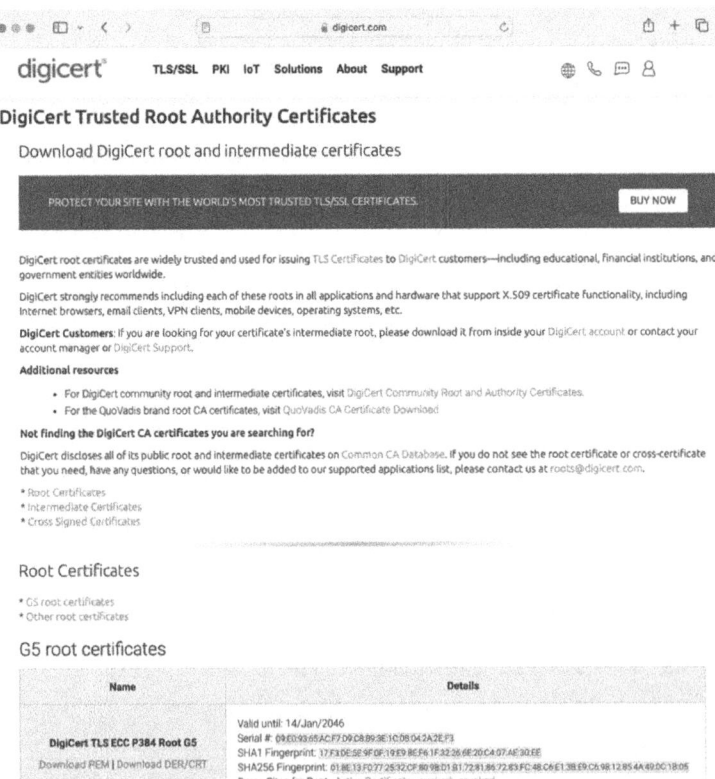

Figure 8.2 DigiCert CA with a full list of certificates

On the DigiCert Trusted Root Authority Certificates page, search for the string `DigiCert TLS Hybrid ECC SHA384 2020 CA1` to find details about the CA's certificate (figure 8.3).

DigiCert TLS Hybrid ECC SHA384 2020 CA1

Download PEM | Download DER/CRT

Issuer: DigiCert Global Root CA
Valid until: 13/Apr/2031
Serial #: 07:F2:F3:5C:87:A8:77:AF:7A:EF:E9:47:99:35:25:BD
SHA1 Fingerprint: AE:C1:3C:DD:5E:A6:A3:99:8A:EC:14:AC:33:1A:D9:6B:ED:BB:77:0F
SHA256 Fingerprint: F7:A9:A1:82:F0:96:4A:3F:26:70:BD:66:8D:56:1F:B7:C5:5D:3A:A9:AB:83:91:E7:E1:69:70:2D:B8:A3

Figure 8.3   Details and links for the certificate of the DigiCert TLS Hybrid ECC SHA384 2020 CA1 CA

Using the data on the page and the `wget` CLI tool, we download the X.509 certificate of the CA that issued the certificate for githhub.com by using the following command:

```
wget https://cacerts.digicert.com/
⇒DigiCertTLSHybridECCSHA3842020CA1-1.crt.pem
```

The following listing shows the result of inspecting the downloaded certificate with `openssl` commands.

Listing 8.8   DigiCert TLS Hybrid ECC SHA384 2020 CA1 X.509 certificate

```
$ openssl x509 -text -noout -in
⇒DigiCertTLSHybridECCSHA3842020CA1-1.crt.pem
Certificate:
    Data:
        Version: 3 (0x2)
        Serial Number:
            07:f2:f3:5c:87:a8:77:af:7a:ef:e9:47:99:35:25:bd
        Signature Algorithm: sha384WithRSAEncryption
        Issuer: C = US, O = DigiCert Inc,                        ⎤ The certificate's
        ⇒OU = www.digicert.com, CN = DigiCert Global Root CA  ⟵──┘ issuer
        Validity                                         ⟵── Validity time range
            Not Before: Apr 14 00:00:00 2021 GMT              of the certificate
            Not After : Apr 13 23:59:59 2031 GMT
        Subject: C = US, O = DigiCert Inc,
        ⇒CN = DigiCert TLS Hybrid ECC SHA384 2020 CA1    ⟵── The subject which
        Subject Public Key Info:                              identifies the public
            Public Key Algorithm: id-ecPublicKey              key and its owner
                Public-Key: (384 bit)
                pub:
                    04:c1:1b:c6:9a:5b:98:d9:a4:29:a0:e9:d4:04:b5:
                    db:eb:a6:b2:6c:55:c0:ff:ed:98:c6:49:2f:06:27:
                    51:cb:bf:70:c1:05:7a:c3:b1:9d:87:89:ba:ad:b4:
                    13:17:c9:a8:b4:83:c8:b8:90:d1:cc:74:35:36:3c:
                    83:72:b0:b5:d0:f7:22:69:c8:f1:80:c4:7b:40:8f:
                    cf:68:87:26:5c:39:89:f1:4d:91:4d:da:89:8b:e4:
                    03:c3:43:e5:bf:2f:73
```

```
                    ASN1 OID: secp384r1
                    NIST CURVE: P-384
            X509v3 extensions:
                X509v3 Basic Constraints: critical
                    CA:TRUE, pathlen:0
                X509v3 Subject Key Identifier:
                    0A:BC:08:29:17:8C:A5:39:6D:7A:0E:CE:33:C7:2E:B3:ED:FB:C3:7A
                X509v3 Authority Key Identifier:
                    03:DE:50:35:56:D1:4C:BB:66:F0:A3:E2:1B:1B:C3:97:B2:3D:D1:55
                X509v3 Key Usage: critical
                    Digital Signature, Certificate Sign, CRL Sign
                X509v3 Extended Key Usage:
                    TLS Web Server Authentication, TLS Web Client Authentication
                Authority Information Access:
                    OCSP - URI:http://ocsp.digicert.com
                    CA Issuers -
                    URI:http://cacerts.digicert.com/
                    DigiCertGlobalRootCA.crt
                X509v3 CRL Distribution Points:
                    Full Name:
                      URI:http://crl3.digicert.com/DigiCertGlobalRootCA.crl
                X509v3 Certificate Policies:
                    Policy: 2.16.840.1.114412.2.1
                    Policy: 2.23.140.1.1
                    Policy: 2.23.140.1.2.1
                    Policy: 2.23.140.1.2.2
                    Policy: 2.23.140.1.2.3
        Signature Algorithm: sha384WithRSAEncryption
        Signature Value:
            47:59:81:7f:d4:1b:1f:b0:71:f6:98:5d:18:ba:98:47:98:b0:
            7e:76:2b:ea:ff:1a:8b:ac:26:b3:42:8d:31:e6:4a:e8:19:d0:
            ef:da:14:e7:d7:14:92:a1:92:f2:a7:2e:2d:af:fb:1d:f6:fb:
            53:b0:8a:3f:fc:d8:16:0a:e9:b0:2e:b6:a5:0b:18:90:35:26:
            a2:da:f6:a8:b7:32:fc:95:23:4b:c6:45:b9:c4:cf:e4:7c:ee:
            e6:c9:f8:90:bd:72:e3:99:c3:1d:0b:05:7c:6a:97:6d:b2:ab:
            02:36:d8:c2:bc:2c:01:92:3f:04:a3:8b:75:11:c7:b9:29:bc:
            11:d0:86:ba:92:bc:26:f9:65:c8:37:cd:26:f6:86:13:0c:04:
            aa:89:e5:78:b1:c1:4e:79:bc:76:a3:0b:51:e4:c5:d0:9e:6a:
            fe:1a:2c:56:ae:06:36:27:a3:73:1c:08:7d:93:32:d0:c2:44:
            19:da:8d:f4:0e:7b:1d:28:03:2b:09:8a:76:ca:77:dc:87:7a:
            ac:7b:52:26:55:a7:72:0f:9d:d2:88:4f:fe:b1:21:c5:1a:a1:
            aa:39:f5:56:db:c2:84:c4:35:1f:70:da:bb:46:f0:86:bf:64:
            00:c4:3e:f7:9f:46:1b:9d:23:05:b9:7d:b3:4f:0f:a9:45:3a:
            e3:74:30:98
```

We downloaded a certificate from the internet, where hackers like to do malicious things. How do we know that this certificate wasn't tampered with in some way? We have to use openssl to verify it, as shown in the following snippet:

```
openssl verify DigiCertTLSHybridECCSHA3842020CA1-1.crt.pem
```

The following snippet shows the response to the given command. The certificate is valid.

```
DigiCertTLSHybridECCSHA3842020CA1-1.crt.pem: OK
```

Success! We can trust that `DigiCertTLSHybridECCSHA3842020CA1-1.crt.pem` hasn't been tampered with.

But how did `openssl` do the verification? OpenSSL checked the digital signature of `DigiCertTLSHybridECCSHA3842020CA1-1.crt.pem` using the public key of the CA that issued the `DigiCertTLSHybridECCSHA3842020CA1-1.crt.pem` certificate.

What CA issued a certificate for another CA? We can discover the answer by inspecting `DigiCertTLSHybridECCSHA3842020CA1-1.crt.pem` using `openssl`:

```
openssl x509 -noout -issuer -in DigiCertTLSHybridECCSHA3842020CA1-1.crt.pem
```

Running the `openssl x509` command produces these certificate details:

```
issuer=C = US, O = DigiCert Inc, OU = www.digicert.com,
  CN = DigiCert Global Root CA
```

When we examine the `CN` field, it looks as though "DigiCert Global Root CA" issued the `DigiCertTLSHybridECCSHA3842020CA1-1.crt.pem` certificate. Recall that the Ubuntu operating system ships with CA files installed in the /usr/share/ca-certificates/Mozilla directory containing `DigiCert_Global_Root_CA.crt`. We can observe that by inspecting `DigiCert_Global_Root_CA.crt` using `openssl` as shown in the next snippet:

```
openssl x509 -noout -subject -in /usr/share/
  ca-certificates/mozilla/DigiCert_Global_Root_CA.crt
```

The result of running the command is

```
subject=C = US, O = DigiCert Inc, OU = www.digicert.com,
  CN = DigiCert Global Root CA
```

Notice that the subject of the `DigiCert_Global_Root_CA.crt` certificate matches the issuer of the `DigiCertTLSHybridECCSHA3842020CA1-1.crt.pem` certificate. We can ask `openssl` to print out the steps it's taking to verify the certificate by using the `-show_chain` option. The following snippet shows the command we run to display the certificate chain for github.com, and listing 8.9 shows the output after running the command.

```
openssl verify -show_chain  -CAfile
  DigiCertTLSHybridECCSHA3842020CA1-1.crt.pem github-cert.pem
```

Listing 8.9   The certificate chain

```
github-cert.pem: OK    ⟵—┤ Indicates successful verification        The subject of the certificate
Chain:                                                               that openssl is verifying
depth=0: C = US, ST = California, L = San Francisco, O = "GitHub, Inc.",
  CN = github.com (untrusted)                                        ⟵
depth=1: C = US, O = DigiCert Inc,
  CN = DigiCert TLS Hybrid ECC SHA384 2020 CA1       ⟵        The Intermediate
depth=2: C = US, O = DigiCert Inc, OU = www.digicert.com,           certificate authority
  CN = DigiCert Global Root CA      ⟵—┐ The root certificate        that issued the
                                       │ authority                  GitHub certificate
```

We asked openssl to verify that the github.com certificate hasn't been tampered with. openssl validated the digital signature in the github.com certificate using the DigiCert TLS Hybrid ECC SHA384 2020 CA1 X.509 certificate, which was in turn validated using the "DigiCert Global Root CA." This root CA is trusted because it's preinstalled in Ubuntu 24.04. Three certificates were involved, each certificate playing one of the following roles:

- *End entity*—The github.com certificate used to establish a secure connection to GitHub.
- *Intermediate CA*—The certificate used to issue the github.com certificate.
- *Root CA*—The certificate used to issue the intermediate CA's certificate. This certificate is trusted because it's installed by the operating system.

Figure 8.4 shows the three certificates and relationships among them.

> **TIP**   The certificate chain of trust is critical. Wrapping your head around this concept can be challenging. If you're struggling, try using the commands in this chapter to download the certificate for amazon.com and then try to replicate what you've seen so far. Hands-on engagement with concepts can clarify the ideas.

This section dealt with the details of the github.com certificate. In the next section, we dive deeper into CAs and the chain of trust. We hope that this chapter whetted your appetite and left you with more questions about the subject, such as these:

- Why does the root certificate have a 25-year lifespan, whereas the intermediate certificate has a 10-year lifespan and the end-entity certificate has a 1-year lifespan?
- What's the difference between an intermediate CA and a root CA?
- Why are intermediate CAs required?
- How do CAs issue certificates?

Chapter 9 focuses on answering these questions.

8.2.2   Exercises

6   What role does the Signature Algorithm field play in an X.509 certificate?

7   What is the purpose of a root CA versus an intermediate CA?

8   Why do operating systems and browsers ship with a collection of preinstalled root certificates?

9   What three types of certificates are involved in the certificate chain of trust?

10   Why can't we always know whether a private key has been stolen, and how is revocation handled when this happens?

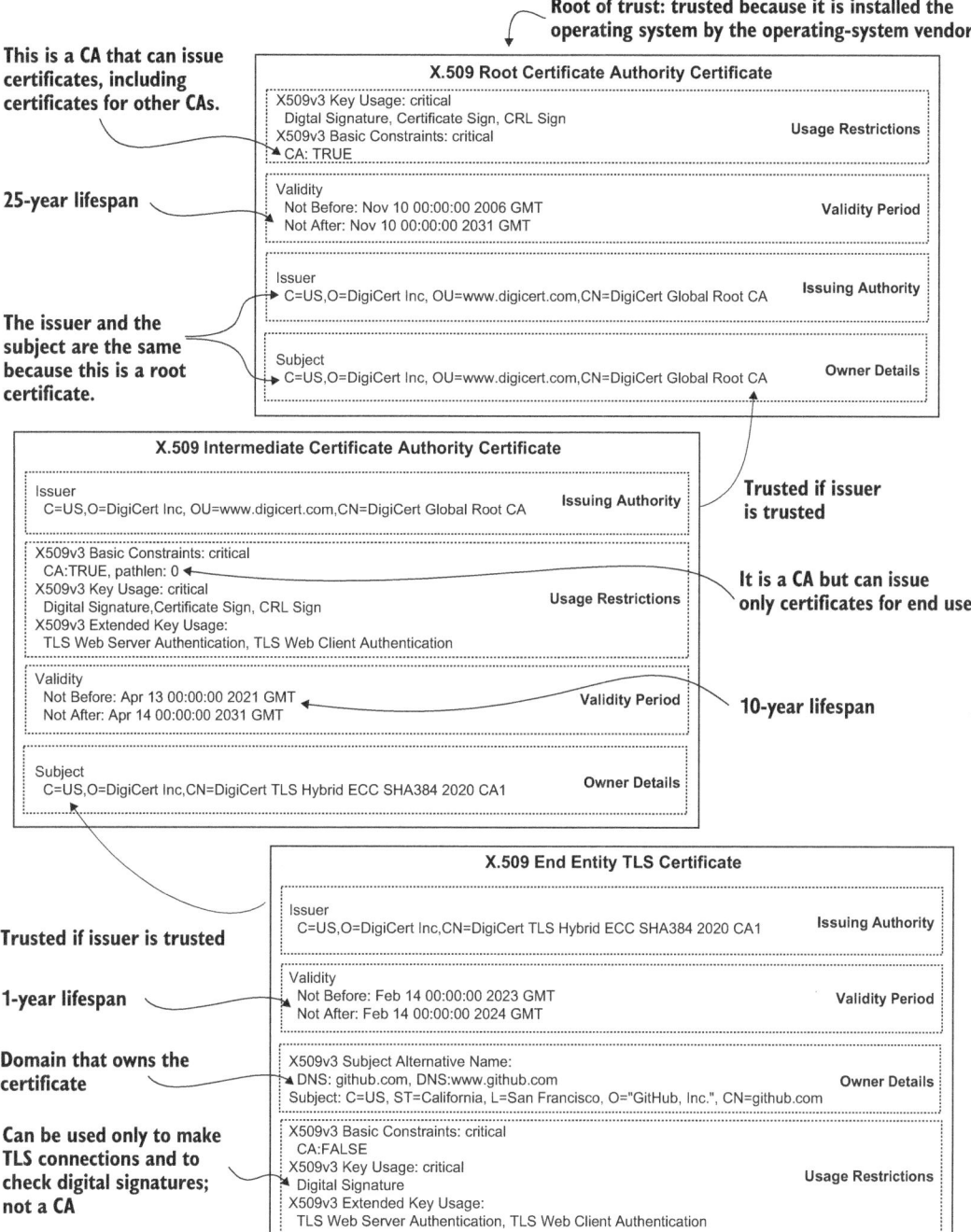

Figure 8.4 Seeing how trust is established by following the certificate chain to a trusted root CA. (Hint: read this figure from bottom to top.)

8.3   Exercise answers

1 What are the three main X.509 certificate fields that application developers need to be familiar with?

The three key fields are Subject, Issuer, and Validity.

2 What information is contained in the `Subject` field and in the `Subject Alternative Name` (SAN) extension?

The Subject field identifies the entity the certificate was issued to (organization, domain, or individual). The SAN field extends this by listing additional identifiers, such as DNS names, IP addresses, URIs, or emails.

3 Why is using an IP address in the SAN field generally considered a bad practice?

Because IP addresses can be reassigned and reused, an IP in a certificate doesn't reliably identify the server owner.

4 What do the `Validity` fields `notBefore` and `notAfter` represent?

The `notBefore` date marks when the certificate becomes valid, and the `notAfter` date marks when it expires.

5 Name two common certificate encoding formats other than PEM.

Two other common formats are DER (binary ASN.1 encoding) and PKCS#12 (often with .p12 or .pfx extensions).

6 What role does the `Signature Algorithm` field play in an X.509 certificate?

It specifies the cryptographic algorithm used to sign the certificate (e.g., ECDSA with SHA-384) and is required to verify authenticity.

7 What is the purpose of a root CA versus an intermediate CA?

A root CA is a self-signed, widely trusted authority. Intermediate CAs issue end-entity certificates and create a safer trust hierarchy so that root certificates aren't used directly.

8 Why do operating systems and browsers ship with a collection of preinstalled root certificates?

Preinstalled root certificates enable applications and users to instantly verify certificates without fetching and manually trusting each CA. This collection is called the trust store.

9 What three types of certificates are involved in the certificate chain of trust?

The three types are end-entity (e.g., github.com), intermediate, and root.

10 Why can't we always know when a private key has been stolen, and how is revocation handled when this happens?

Key theft leaves no technical trace. Revocation is handled through CRLs or the Online Certificate Status Protocol (OCSP) after the owner reports the theft.

Summary

- X.509 certificates contain a public key and metadata about who owns the key and who issued it.

- The three key certificate fields developers need to know are `Subject` (owner identity), `Issuer` (CA), and `Validity` (time range).
- The SAN extension lists network addresses such as DNS names, emails, IP addresses, and URIs.
- CAs digitally sign certificates to prove authenticity and prevent tampering.
- Root CAs are self-signed and preinstalled in operating systems, whereas intermediate CAs create a safer trust hierarchy.
- Certificate verification follows a chain of trust from end-entity certificate to intermediate CA to trusted root CA.
- Common certificate formats include PEM (text-based), DER (binary), and PKCS#12 (can store multiple certificates and keys).
- Certificate validation checks digital signatures and validity dates, and determines whether the CA is trusted.
- CRLs track stolen or compromised certificates that should no longer be trusted.
- OpenSSL command-line tools can inspect, verify, and create certificates for testing and development.

Working with X.509 certificates: Life cycle and self-signing

This chapter covers

- Doing local development using a laptop-scoped certificate authority
- Creating X.509 digital certificates with the Automated Certificate Management Environment (ACME) protocol
- Renewing X.509 digital certificates using ACME

In chapter 8, we looked at what's inside an X.509 certificate. Essentially, it has two things: a public key and a bunch of extra info about that key. We poked around in some of the most important bits, such as who the certificate belongs to (the subject), who gave it out (the issuer), how long it's good for, and a few rules and restrictions.

We also learned how to check whether a certificate is legitimate: follow the trail of who issued it step by step all the way up to a trusted root certificate. The process is like checking whether someone's ID was signed by someone you trust.

So we know who gives out these certificates: the certificate authorities (CAs). But how do they do it? Good question. Let's find out. In this chapter, we'll refine our understanding of CAs by learning about the certificate life cycle, from issuance to expiry or revocation, and the use of self-signed certificates. We'll continue our exploration using the `openssl` CLI to build up our CA. Although developers don't need to create and manage their own CAs, the key to developer certificate superpowers lies in understanding the complex ideas that we'll explore in this chapter. So grab another cup of coffee, and let's dive in.

9.1   Certificate life cycle: Issuance to revocation

Let's start by taking a closer look at how certificates are born, live, and eventually retire or get kicked out. We'll walk through the whole journey, step by step, as illustrated in figure 9.1.

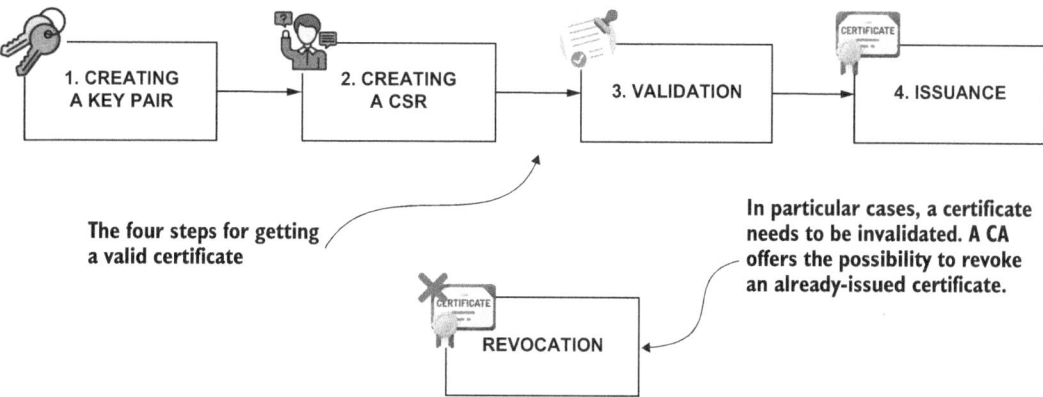

Figure 9.1   The certificate life cycle. This figure walks you through the four main steps of getting a valid digital certificate: generating a key pair, creating a CSR, having it validated by a CA, and receiving the issued certificate.

In section 9.1.1, we'll talk about creating a key pair. Think of this process as making a lock and key: one part (the private key) stays secret with you, but the other part (the public key) is something you can safely share with the world. You need both parts to make the certificate magic happen.

Next, we'll look at how to create a certificate signing request (CSR). It's like filling out a form and sending it to the CA with your digital signature on it.

In section 9.1.3, we dive into validation, which is the CA's way of asking "Wait a sec—are you really who you say you are?" Depending on the type of certificate, this process may be a quick check or a full-on investigation. No trench coats or magnifying glasses are involved (usually), but it's still serious business.

Next, we get to the good part: issuance. If everything checks out, the CA creates your certificate and hands it over. Congrats—you're officially certified. You can show off your public key proudly, and people can trust that it belongs to you.

Finally, section 9.1.5 covers revocation, a sad but important part of the story. Sometimes, things go wrong. Maybe your private key gets leaked, or you're no longer supposed to have the certificate. In that case, the certificate must be revoked—put on a digital "do not trust" list so others know not to use it anymore.

9.1.1 Creating a key pair

An X.509 certificate contains a public key, which means there must be a corresponding private key. The first step in creating a certificate is creating a public/private key pair (figure 9.2).

**The first step is creating a key pair.
The key pair will be used in the creation
request you send to the CA.**

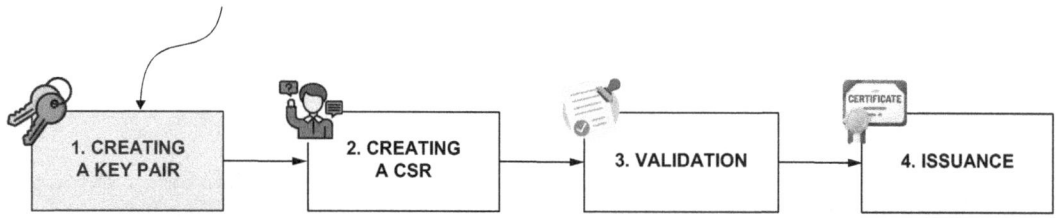

Figure 9.2   Step 1: beginning with a key pair. The life cycle of a certificate kicks off with generating a key pair: one public key and one private key. This pair becomes the foundation of your CSR, which you'll send to the CA to prove that you're legitimate.

We can use the `openssl genpkey` command to perform this task:

```
$ openssl genpkey -algorithm Ed25519 -outform PEM -out private_key.pem
```

We set three parameters. The `-algorithm` parameter sets the type of public key encryption algorithm. In this case, we choose the elliptic curve called Ed25519 and output the key to a file called private_key.pem (in PEM file format). Ed25519 keys are small.

Remember elliptic curves? We talked about them in chapter 7. Don't worry if your recollection is a bit fuzzy; they're a clever bit of math used to create secure keys much smaller than old-school RSA keys. Instead of relying on giant prime numbers, elliptic curve algorithms use points on a special kind of curve (yep, an actual curve from math class) to do the job.

Names like Ed25519 and secp256r1 are different types of elliptic curves. Each curve has its own shape and properties. Ed25519 in particular is known for being fast, secure, and compact, which is why we're using it here. When you set the -algorithm parameter to something like Ed25519, you're saying "Hey, let's use that tiny but mighty curve for our key."

To show the file's content, use the `cat` command:

```
$ cat private_key.pem
```

You get the following output:

```
-----BEGIN PRIVATE KEY-----
MC4CAQAwBQYDK2VwBCIEIAgbK6DGz3JC02saDwhzhdxBr/GjTVDTIw0Po7vEN//d
-----END PRIVATE KEY-----
```

Did you expect the `genpkey` command to generate a public key? The output file contains a private key because every public key requires a corresponding private key. Although it's possible to store these keys in separate files, managing them separately can be cumbersome. For practical reasons, it's often more efficient for the owner of the private key to store the key pair in a single file. You can view the file's contents by using the appropriate command, shown in the following snippet:

```
$ openssl pkey -in private_key.pem -text -noout
```

The following listing shows the public/private key pair generated by running the command discussed earlier. The public key is derived from the private key generated earlier in this section. Notice that the output contains both the private key and the public key.

> **Listing 9.1 The generated public/private key pair**

```
ED25519 Private-Key:
priv:                                          ◁─┤ The private key
    08:1b:2b:a0:c6:cf:72:42:d3:6b:1a:0f:08:73:85:
    dc:41:af:f1:a3:4d:50:d3:23:0d:0f:a3:bb:c4:37:
    ff:dd
pub:                                           ◁─┤ The public key
    0a:76:42:f1:fa:55:57:a0:c2:b9:de:79:d3:0c:4a:
    50:b8:07:bf:78:ee:0f:45:99:a5:ec:cd:98:07:50:
    c1:33
```

9.1.2 Creating a CSR

As you saw in chapter 8, certificates are issued by a CA. This means you have to send the public key and metadata about it to a CA so that it can issue a certificate (figure 9.3).

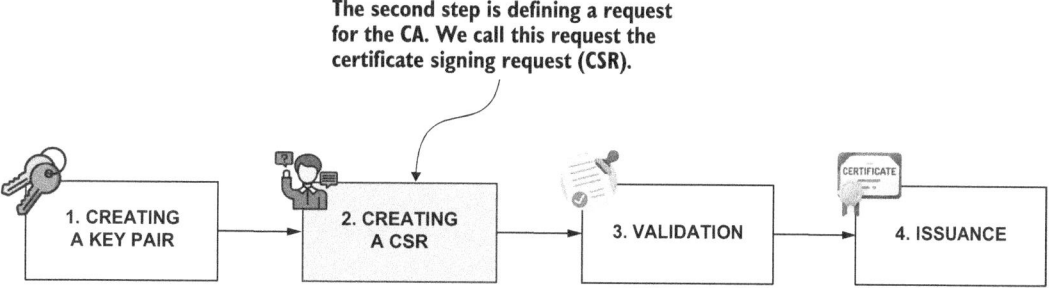

Figure 9.3 Step 2: submitting a CSR. When you've got your key pair, the next move is creating a CSR. This process is like filling out a form saying, "Hey, CA, here's who I am, and here's my public key. Can I have a certificate, please?" The CA will use this info to decide whether you're worthy.

A CSR is a file containing a public key and metadata about the key, sent by the owner of the public key to a certificate authority. We can create a CSR using the openssl req command:

```
$ openssl req -new -key private_key.pem -out request.csr
```

The following interactive input form appears in response to the openssl req command used in the preceding snippet. The user is prompted to provide the details required to create the certificate. These prompts typically include fields such as the country name, state or province, organization name, email address, and other relevant information. Each input contributes to the certificate's distinguished name (DN), which uniquely identifies the entity associated with the certificate.

Listing 9.2   Creating a CSR in the terminal

```
You are about to be asked to enter information that will be incorporated
into your certificate request.
What you are about to enter is what is called a Distinguished Name or a DN.
There are quite a few fields but you can leave some blank
For some fields there will be a default value,          Interactive input from
If you enter '.', the field will be left blank.          the keyboard in
-----                                                     response to questions
Country Name (2 letter code) [AU]:CA
State or Province Name (full name) [Some-State]:ON
Locality Name (eg, city) []:Toronto
Organization Name (eg, company) [Internet Widgits Pty Ltd]:Example Inc.
Organizational Unit Name (eg, section) []:
Common Name (e.g. server FQDN or YOUR name) []:example.com
Email Address []:admin@example.com

Please enter the following 'extra' attributes
to be sent with your certificate request
A challenge password []:
An optional company name []:
```

To generate the request, the openssl req command prompts the user for the details of the subject that should be associated with the public key. It generates a file called request.csr that contains the public key and the metadata about the key collected from the answers. The next snippet presents the content of the certificate request file:

```
-----BEGIN CERTIFICATE REQUEST-----
MIH7MIGuAgEAMHsxCzAJBgNVBAYTAkNBMQswCQYDVQQIDAJPTjEQMA4GA1UEBwwH
VG9yb250bzEVMBMGA1UECgwMRXhhbXBsZSBJbmMuMRQwEgYDVQQDDAtleGFtcGxl
LmNvbTEgMB4GCSqGSIb3DQEJARYRYWRtaW5AZXhhbXBsZS5jb20wKjAFBgMrZXAD
IQAKdkLx+lVXoMK53nnTDEpQuAe/eO4PRZml7M2YB1DBM6AAMAUGAytlcANBAFGD
OpEOiql2WESusN6kPHtQvWQMb/+tbm/zl+o+GfIC8w+3ihzBaduzjzWebehKL8h6
zvLfbz7mgIcnfxpkxAE=
-----END CERTIFICATE REQUEST-----
```

You can print out the details of the CSR using this command:

```
$ openssl req -in request.csr -text -noout
```

The next listing shows the certificate request details in response to the `openssl req` command used in the preceding snippet.

Listing 9.3 The certificate request details

```
Certificate Request:
    Data:
        Version: 1 (0x0)
        Subject: C = CA, ST = ON, L = Toronto,
        ↪O = Example Inc., CN = example.com,
        ↪emailAddress = admin@example.com
        Subject Public Key Info:
            Public Key Algorithm: ED25519
                ED25519 Public-Key:
                pub:
                    0a:76:42:f1:fa:55:57:a0:c2:b9:de:79:d3:0c:4a:
                    50:b8:07:bf:78:ee:0f:45:99:a5:ec:cd:98:07:50:
                    c1:33
        Attributes:
            (none)
            Requested Extensions:
    Signature Algorithm: ED25519
    Signature Value:
        51:83:3a:91:0e:8a:a9:76:58:44:ae:b0:de:a4:3c:7b:50:bd:
        64:0c:6f:ff:ad:6e:6f:f3:97:ea:3e:19:f2:02:f3:0f:b7:8a:
        1c:c1:69:db:b3:8f:35:9e:6d:e8:4a:2f:c8:7a:ce:f2:df:6f:
        3e:e6:80:87:27:7f:1a:64:c4:01
```

The CSR's `Subject` field includes the details you entered during the certificate request creation process. You send the CSR to the CA using a web interface, a proprietary API, email, or an industry-standard protocol such as Automated Certificate Management Environment (ACME). The CA uses these details to validate your request and issue the certificate.

9.1.3   CSR validation

Upon receipt of a CSR, the CA must determine whether the request is legitimate (figure 9.4). A hacker can make a CSR and send it to a CA. The CA must verify the identity

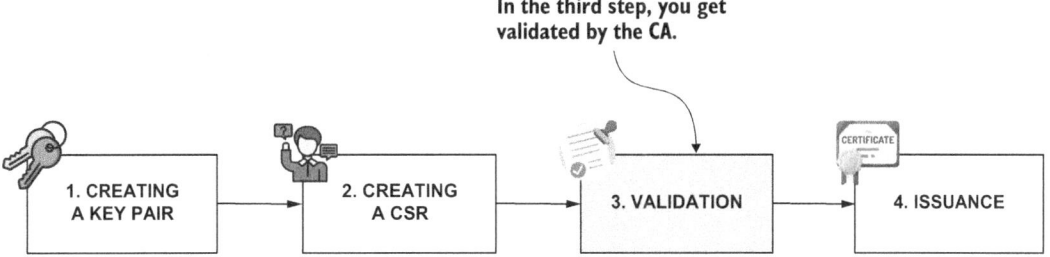

Figure 9.4   Step 3: time for a background check. In the validation step, the CA uses your CSR to make sure that you are who you say you are. This process might involve checking your domain ownership or verifying your organization's identity

of the entity that created the CSR. If the CA can establish the identity of the certificate requester, it can decide whether to issue the certificate.

How does the CA determine the identity of the CSR requester? The CSR we created is for a certificate for the example.com domain. The CA must validate that the sender of the CSR is the owner of the example.com domain. This type of validation is called domain validation because the CA checks whether the requester of the CSR controls the domain that the CSR is about. There are three common ways to perform domain validation:

- *Email*—The CA sends a verification email to a registered domain contact.
- *HTTP-01 challenge*—The CA verifies a specific file hosted on the domain's web server.
- *DNS-01 challenge*—The CA checks a specific Domain Name System (DNS) TXT record added to the domain.

In the email challenge, the CA sends a validation email to the administrator of the domain listed with the domain registrar. If the request is legitimate, the domain administrator clicks the validation link and follows the CA's instructions to complete the verification process.

The key assumption is that if someone has access to the domain's official admin email, they're authorized to request that certificates for the domain to be issued. This validation process is like the email verification process you encounter when creating an account in an online service such as Facebook or X (figure 9.5).

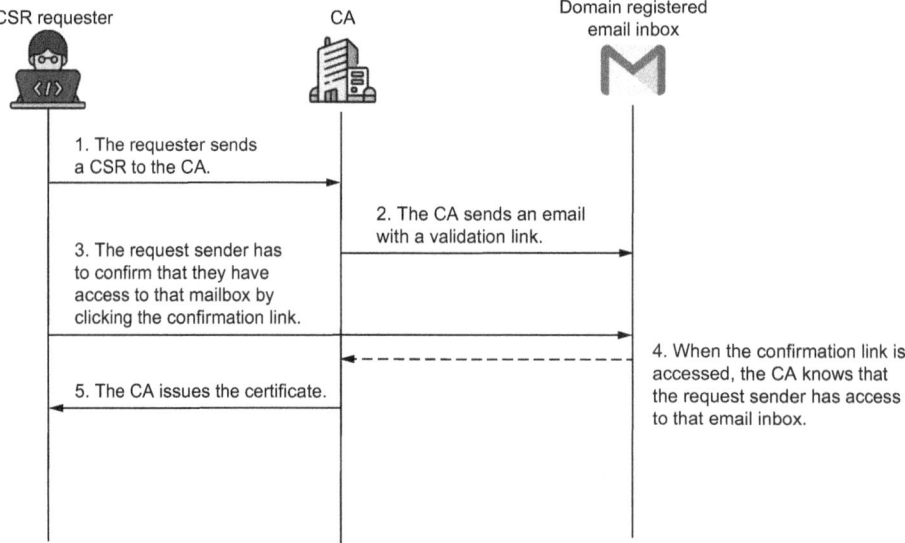

Figure 9.5   Domain validation via email. This figure shows how a CA verifies that the CSR requester controls the domain. After receiving the CSR, the CA sends a validation email. The requester must click a link to prove access to the domain's registered inbox. After verification, the CA issues the certificate.

A primary drawback of email-based domain validation is that it's hard to automate. When verification is complete, the CA issues a certificate and sends it to the requester by email or through a web interface.

HTTP-01 is an industry standard automated way to perform domain validation. HTTP-01 is defined in the ACME protocol in RFC 8555 (https://datatracker.ietf.org/doc/html/rfc8555). This model consists of the following steps (figure 9.6):

1 The requester makes an API call to the CA over HTTPS to deliver the CSR.
2 The CA responds with a small file and a challenge to make the file accessible via HTTP GET on a specific URL on the requester's website.
3 The requester deploys the challenge file to their website at the specified challenge URL.
4 The requester makes an API call to the CA to inform the CA that it has deployed the challenge file at the challenge URL.
5 The CA makes an HTTP GET request to the challenge URL from multiple locations worldwide.
6 If the location contains the challenge file, the CA concludes that the requester controls the domain's website and that it's OK to issue a certificate. If the CA can't use HTTP GET to obtain the challenge file, it concludes that the requester doesn't control the domain and that no certificate should be issued.

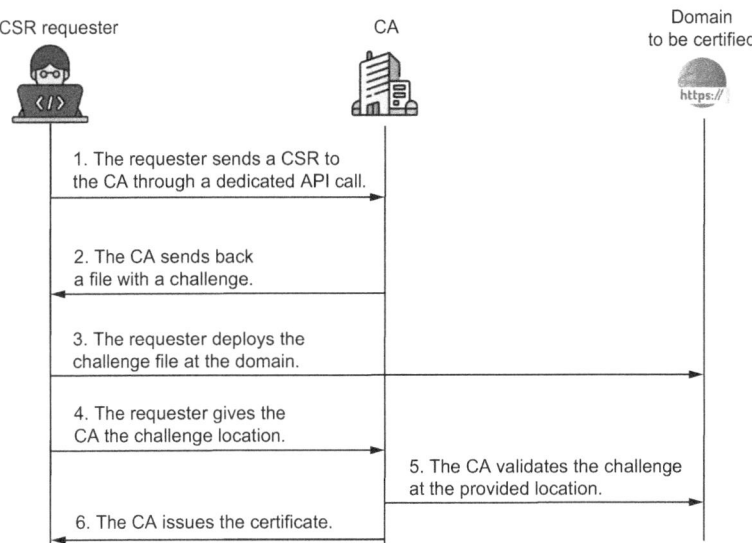

Figure 9.6 Domain validation via HTTP challenge. This flow illustrates how a CA validates domain ownership using an HTTP challenge. The requester sends a CSR, receives a challenge file from the CA, and places it at a specific location on their website. When the CA finds the file at that location, it confirms domain control and issues the certificate.

The primary advantage of the HTTP-01 domain validation challenge is that it's an industry standard with prebuilt automation, making it possible to request short-lived certificates and renew them automatically, which is a security best practice.

Much like the HTTP-01 challenge, the ACME protocol defines the DNS-01 domain validation challenge. This challenge consists of the following steps (figure 9.7):

1   The requester makes an API call to the CA over HTTPS to deliver the CSR.
2   The CA responds with a challenge that requires the requester to add a specific record to the domain's DNS configuration.
3   The requester performs the updates to the domain's DNS configuration.
4   The requester makes an API call to the CA to inform it that the requested DNS configuration change is complete.
5   The CA checks the domain's DNS configuration.
6   If the CA finds the DNS record it's looking for, it concludes that the requester has control of the domain because they were able to modify its DNS configuration and that it's safe to issue a certificate.

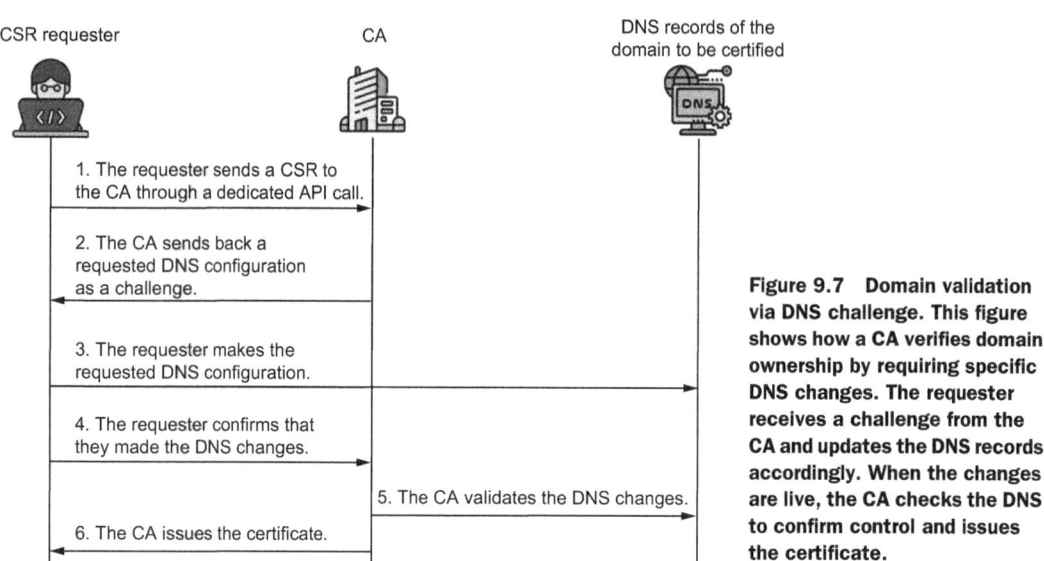

Figure 9.7   Domain validation via DNS challenge. This figure shows how a CA verifies domain ownership by requiring specific DNS changes. The requester receives a challenge from the CA and updates the DNS records accordingly. When the changes are live, the CA checks the DNS to confirm control and issues the certificate.

The primary advantage of the DNS-01 challenge is that it doesn't require the requester to have a website that's accessible from the CA. It can work in situations in which the HTTP-01 challenge fails.

To conclude, the creator of a CSR proves that they can own a certificate for a domain by solving a challenge issued by the CA. The solution to the challenge proves that the requestor has control of the domain in the CSR. There are three common challenge types:

- *Email*—Prove control of a domain by demonstrating the ability to receive emails at the administrative email address listed in the domain registration.
- *HTTP-01*—Prove control over a domain by making a challenge file available over HTTP at a URL chosen by the CA.
- *DNS-01*—Prove control of a domain by making changes to the domain's DNS configuration.

HTTP-01 and DNS-01 are fully automated approaches. In Kubernetes, for example, you can use the `cert-manager` package to implement the HTTP-01 and DNS-01 solvers. We'll cover `cert-manager` in the next section.

> **NOTE**   Most CAs charge a fee to issue a certificate. The cost can range from a few dollars to thousands of dollars, depending on the CA and the type of certificate. Operating a public CA is complex. It requires a dedicated staff and costs millions of dollars annually, so CAs charge fees to cover their operating costs. Let's Encrypt (https://letsencrypt.org/) is a not-for-profit CA that provides certificates at no cost. It was created in 2012 to increase the adoption of Transport Layer Security (TLS) on the internet. Let's Encrypt performs domain validation using the HTTP-01 and DNS-01 challenges.

9.1.4   Certificate issuance

After the certificate authority validates that a CSR was created by a legitimate entity that controls the domain of the requested certificate, the CA creates the certificate and signs it with its private key (figure 9.8). Clients can validate the certificate's authenticity by following the steps described in chapter 8.

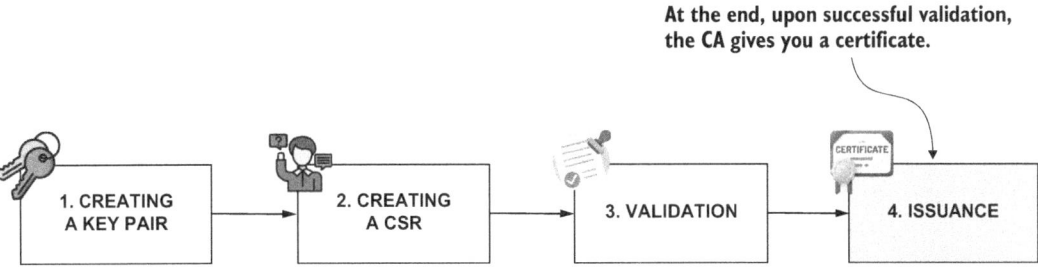

Figure 9.8   Mission accomplished: the certificate is issued. After your identity checks out, the CA gives you the digital certificate. This certificate is proof that you're trustworthy (at least digitally). Now you can use it to secure communications and earn some internet street cred.

But what if you want to create a certificate without going through a public CA? A checkout microservice calls an inventory microservice over HTTPS. Because both microservices are part of the same application, inside the same company, it might make sense to save the cost of obtaining certificates from a public CA by building an internal CA or using a self-signed certificate.

> **DEFINITION**   A *self-signed certificate* is one in which the subject and issuer of the certificate are the same. You can use `openssl` to create a self-signed certificate.

The next snippet shows how to create a self-signed certificate:

```
$ openssl x509 -req -days 365 -in request.csr -signkey private_key.pem
➥-out certificate.pem
```

You get a response similar to the following:

```
Certificate request self-signature ok
subject=C = CA, ST = ON, L = Toronto, O = Example Inc.,
➥CN = example.com, emailAddress = admin@example.com
```

The command creates an X.509 certificate from the request.csr file by signing it with the private key generated in section 9.1.3. Self-signed certificates are easy to create but are not part of the chain of trust. If you use a browser to access a website secured with a self-signed certificate, you see a scary warning page. Command-line tools like curl and kubectl have options to turn off certificate validation, but doing that defeats the point of using certificates.

> **TIP**   Don't use a self-signed certificate; instead, create a private CA and add it to your systems' trust store. Then your private CA will issue certificates that can be used inside your organization. In section 9.2, you'll learn how to create your own CA.

9.1.5   Certificate revocation

Recall that every certificate has a private key that goes with the public key stored in the certificate. What happens if the private key is accidentally published on the internet or stolen before the certificate expires?

In such situations, the certificate owner asks the CA to revoke the certificate. The CA puts the certificate on its certificate revocation list. During the certificate validation process, the browser and other clients check whether the certificate has been revoked before deciding to trust the certificate.

Certificate revocation is a concept you should understand as a developer, but you don't have to know how to perform it. Typically, DevOps specialists or platform engineers take care of certificate revocation.

9.1.6   Exercises

1 What's the first step in creating a certificate?
2 What is a CSR?
3 Why does the CA have to validate the CSR?

4   How does a CA check domain ownership?

5   What is certificate revocation, and why is it important?

9.2   Private CA for local development

Most developers use HTTP during local development and don't try developing with TLS and HTTPS, which can lead to `if` statements in application logic and scripts to account for an application's on-laptop versus on-cluster deployment. When TLS is used, developers often use self-signed certificates. Still, self-signed certificates generate many errors when they're consumed, which leads to more command-line options being passed to tools to ignore certificate validation errors. Worse, it can lead to application code that turns off certificate validation; the code gets into production and can lead to security breaches.

> **TIP**   Use TLS for local development on your laptop by creating a personal CA for your laptop. Install the CA on your laptop and create as many certificates as you need, and you should end up with no certificate validation errors without turning off certificate validation.

9.2.1   Creating a self-signed root certificate

Let's create a self-signed certificate. The first step is using `openssl` to generate a key pair for use as the CA's private key:

```
openssl genpkey -algorithm RSA -outform PEM -out ca/ca_private_key.pem
```

This command outputs the key pair to the file at the path `ca/ca_private_key.pem`. Then we can use the `openssl` command to create an authority certificate that's valid for a given period. Use the following code to create an authority certificate that's valid for 10 years:

```
openssl req -x509 -new -key ca/ca_private_key.pem
➥-days 3650 -out ca/ca_cert.pem -subj "/CN=local-dev CA"
```

We can inspect the generated CA certificate using the command in the next snippet to understand what the certificate contains and verify that it was created correctly. This inspection confirms important details such as the subject (who the certificate is for), the issuer (who signed it; for a self-signed CA, this should be the same as the subject), the validity period (when it starts and when it expires), and the public key associated with it.

We can also check the certificate extensions to ensure that they include the necessary flags for a CA, such as `Basic Constraints: CA:TRUE`, and appropriate key use. This information gives us confidence that the CA certificate is valid and configured as expected before it's used to sign other certificates. Using this command, we can read the certificate details:

```
openssl x509 -in ca/ca_cert.pem -noout -text
```

The preceding command prints the following details on the console.

Listing 9.4   The details of the generated certificate

```
Certificate:
    Data:
        Version: 3 (0x2)
        Serial Number:
            0d:0f:db:21:94:67:c0:cb:cd:10:cf:58:ba:d8:c8:5f:49:58:70:ce
        Signature Algorithm: sha256WithRSAEncryption
        Issuer: CN=local-dev CA
        Validity
            Not Before: Jun 21 15:30:50 2024 GMT
            Not After : Jun 19 15:30:50 2034 GMT
        Subject: CN=local-dev CA
        Subject Public Key Info:
            Public Key Algorithm: rsaEncryption
                Public-Key: (2048 bit)
                Modulus:
                    00:ba:fa:3e:66:1f:a2:12:e2:ca:75:cb:23:55:0e:
                    39:46:b5:61:de:2b:2d:46:56:0c:b9:cc:9c:b7:87:
                    5d:c3:2b:4a:58:f2:e2:1e:07:01:d6:f6:a6:5d:77:
                    bd:84:5b:1d:9c:c9:ea:49:5b:36:0e:2f:75:ea:0c:
                    68:fa:e2:c8:a3:c7:9a:a3:cb:5f:cd:f1:bb:5c:b3:
                    41:8d:34:81:d8:53:38:5b:aa:95:85:44:3b:d0:9d:
                    93:58:06:a8:29:5a:00:91:4a:ab:a0:7c:31:30:fc:
                    cb:1d:76:60:28:71:e0:a0:8f:fd:cf:08:d3:29:1a:
                    f9:1a:af:2c:bb:06:01:50:a8:d7:86:6d:2f:ff:25:
                    2f:29:91:bf:18:ce:63:5e:32:a7:a9:d1:17:1a:0e:
                    b9:3b:54:fe:40:2d:36:75:b2:03:f4:05:51:24:36:
                    51:d1:74:60:77:48:a7:a4:b3:72:f2:2d:32:0e:7c:
                    84:04:a9:a3:9f:0c:d3:55:f4:14:17:30:b2:1c:e6:
                    e2:82:18:29:a4:27:d2:23:0e:70:54:30:60:79:ca:
                    c5:dc:cc:18:46:b3:b6:48:3a:b8:19:71:3c:00:f4:
                    b9:93:bd:15:96:b8:34:25:8d:1a:6d:16:ee:a4:80:
                    d4:40:93:10:6a:45:d4:2e:d0:61:08:f8:c9:c7:c6:
                    33:3b
                Exponent: 65537 (0x10001)
        X509v3 extensions:
            X509v3 Subject Key Identifier:
                B2:93:61:82:15:EC:9C:BA:AD:17:EF:C2:48:87:22:FE:80:14:7A:5B
            X509v3 Authority Key Identifier:
                B2:93:61:82:15:EC:9C:BA:AD:17:EF:C2:48:87:22:FE:80:14:7A:5B
            X509v3 Basic Constraints: critical
                CA:TRUE                                            Notice that the
    Signature Algorithm: sha256WithRSAEncryption                   certificate is
    Signature Value:                                               allowed to sign
        1e:98:1d:ba:02:92:03:28:73:da:db:79:a1:ee:9f:09:e2:50:     other certificates.
        56:14:0b:f6:2d:09:86:12:94:0a:ec:16:cd:fd:a8:10:73:a8:
        b4:d7:7c:e6:6a:18:e7:fd:d9:13:fc:04:f1:02:d4:fb:d9:e0:
        3d:79:8c:dc:c9:64:e1:17:2a:1b:3f:4c:82:cd:e2:1b:10:dd:
        3d:4b:d4:6e:c6:f5:be:0d:e4:79:c0:fc:e2:ac:b2:35:52:c7:
        8d:0d:43:50:f6:e6:dc:76:5e:b0:fc:32:69:c3:a0:a1:2f:0d:
        2a:79:c3:58:15:ec:fa:73:8e:bc:4d:4b:7a:28:d0:d1:c2:30:
```

```
40:b8:90:c2:4e:f7:89:72:ec:c2:95:ba:60:94:e4:29:ad:61:
01:13:e0:d1:1c:f2:94:ae:ee:1b:fe:76:b1:43:b2:be:1a:01:
fb:da:34:07:5e:c9:e8:c2:e1:41:18:d6:71:b5:72:ff:64:e1:
f9:df:66:ba:5a:aa:ff:bc:ee:17:f5:b9:67:e0:28:48:58:3f:
21:e1:8a:7c:10:c2:eb:2d:77:a2:7c:a4:28:97:03:31:20:c1:
79:f6:d9:e7:6c:92:46:76:aa:6b:4a:3e:f8:ad:b8:66:67:74:
7b:9a:4f:94:50:3e:8c:eb:30:49:13:ea:84:12:95:7d:5f:5b:
4e:80:24:12
```

9.2.2 Installing the CA in the operating system's trust store

We've created a CA certificate, but no one trusts it yet. As explained in chapter 8, operating systems come with a preinstalled list of trusted CAs provided by the OS vendor. To make our CA certificate trusted, we must add it to the operating system's list of trusted CAs. Thereafter, any certificate that our CA issues will pass validation.

Keep in mind that the process for installing the CA certificate varies depending on the operating system. You'll have to follow specific instructions for macOS, Windows, or Linux.

For macOS, install the CA using this command:

```
sudo security add-trusted-cert -d -r trustRoot
➥-k "/Library/Keychains/System.keychain" ca/ca_cert.pem
```

On Linux systems, the steps for adding a CA certificate vary among distributions. In Ubuntu, copy the CA certificate file to the directory where Ubuntu stores CA certificates; then run a command to reload the trusted certificates, as in the following example:

```
sudo cp ca/ca_cert.pem /usr/local/share/ca-certificates/myCA.crt
sudo update-ca-certificates
```

On Windows machines, you use the Microsoft Management Console, which is a GUI application. Check the Microsoft documentation at https://mng.bz/Pwg2 for details on installing the certificate.

Installing a local development certificate authority is specific to each operating system, so the instructions provided here may become outdated over time. The key point is that every operating system maintains a list of trusted CAs.

When you add our development CA to this list, the operating system will trust any certificates you issue. A quick web search usually provides up-to-date, step-by-step instructions for installing CA certificates. When you understand the key concepts, the process is straightforward.

9.2.3 Issuing a certificate using the personal CA

Now that we have a CA for our development machine, we can issue a server certificate to use in our application, such as adding it to a Spring Boot application to turn on TLS. We start by creating a key pair for the server certificate, as shown in the next snippet:

```
openssl genpkey -algorithm RSA -outform PEM -out server_key.pem
```

The certificate must have a Subject Alternative Name field defined; otherwise, we'll get an error message from the browser. We must create an OpenSSL configuration file to pass as an input parameter in the command.

Listing 9.5   OpenSSL configuration file ca/server-cert.cnf

```
[ req ]
distinguished_name = req_distinguished_name
req_extensions    = req_ext
x509_extensions   = v3_ca
prompt            = no

[ req_distinguished_name ]
C            = Canada
ST           = Ontario
L            = Toronto
O            = Adib Saikali
OU           = MacBook Pro
CN           = localhost

[ req_ext ]
subjectAltName = @alt_names

[ v3_ca ]
subjectAltName = @alt_names

[ alt_names ]
DNS.1    = localhost
```

Using the configuration file, we can create a CSR based on the inputs in the file:

```
openssl req -new -key server_key.pem -out server_csr.pem
➥-config ca/server-cert.cnf
```

Next, we sign CSR using the CA certificate we created earlier:

```
openssl x509 -req -in server_csr.pem -CA ca/ca_cert.pem
➥-CAkey ca/ca_private_key.pem -CAcreateserial
➥-out server_cert.pem -days 365 -sha256 -extensions req_ext
➥-extfile ca/openssl.cnf
```

We can use OpenSSL to check whether the certificate is valid:

```
openssl verify server_cert.pem
```

This command produces the following output:

```
server_cert.pem: OK
Chain:
depth=0: C=CA, ST=Ontario, L=Toronto, O=Adib Saikali,
➥OU=MacBook Pro, CN=localhost (untrusted)
depth=1: CN=local-dev CA
```

Now you have a server certificate that you can use in your applications. In chapter 10, you'll use the certificate and the CA to explore the TLS. Give yourself a pat on the back; you've learned a lot about certificates in this chapter, and now you have the background to do something real with them.

9.2.4 Exercises

6 Why would you create a local CA?

7 What's a self-signed certificate?

8 Why not use self-signed certificates for everything?

9 How can you make your operating system trust your local CA?

10 What's the benefit of using your CA instead of skipping TLS locally?

9.3 Exercise answers

1 What's the first step in creating a certificate?

You start by creating a key pair: a private key (you keep this secret) and a public key (you can share). This is the foundation of every certificate.

2 What's a CSR?

A CSR is like a digital application form. You send your public key and some personal info to a CA and ask for a certificate.

3 Why does a CA need to validate the CSR?

The CA must verify that you're not a random person trying to get a certificate for something you don't own, such as someone else's website.

4 How does a CA check domain ownership?

It can send you a special email, ask you to put a file on your website (HTTP challenge), or update your DNS settings (DNS challenge). Each challenge is designed to prove that you control the domain.

5 What is certificate revocation, and why is it important?

Revocation means telling everyone "Don't trust this certificate anymore," maybe because the private key was stolen or the cert is no longer needed. It's a way to undo trust.

6 Why would you create a local CA?

A local CA allows you to issue your own certificates for development without paying or waiting on a public CA. It's great for testing but bad for public use.

7 What's a self-signed certificate?

A self-signed certificate is one that you sign yourself instead of having a public CA sign it. It works for testing, but browsers don't trust it by default.

8 Why not use self-signed certificates for everything?

Those certificates aren't part of the global chain of trust. Most systems and browsers throw scary warnings or reject them.

9 How can you make your operating system trust your local CA?

Install the CA certificate into your operating system's list of trusted CAs. The method depends on whether you use macOS, Linux, or Windows.

10 What's the benefit of using your CA instead of skipping TLS locally?

You can test real-world HTTPS setups, avoid writing if TLS hacks in your code, and keep your security behavior consistent from development to production.

Summary

- The certificate life cycle includes critical steps such as generating a key pair, creating a CSR, validating the request, issuing the certificate, and revoking it when necessary.
- OpenSSL enables the creation of a key pair consisting of a private key and its corresponding public key, which form the foundation of an X.509 certificate.
- A CSR includes the public key and metadata about the certificate, which is sent to a CA to request certificate issuance.
- Domain control is verified using one of three methods: email-based validation, hosting a challenge file on the website (HTTP-01), or adding a specific DNS TXT record (DNS-01).
- The CA validates the CSR, ensures that the requester controls the domain, and issues a signed certificate that can be used for secure communication.
- Self-signed certificates allow independent creation of certificates without a public CA, but they're not trusted by browsers or systems without additional configuration.
- A local CA can be established for development environments, allowing developers to issue trusted certificates within their own systems.
- Adding a local CA certificate to the operating system's trusted-certificates list ensures that all certificates issued by the local CA are recognized and validated by the system.
- Developers can use their private CAs to issue certificates for internal applications, eliminating the need to rely on external CAs for testing purposes.

Transport Layer Security: How the internet is secured

The internet is like a noisy city full of people who love to listen in. Every time your phone or computer sends something, logging into your bank, ordering sushi, or sending a file, it's a bit like whispering a secret in a crowded Starbucks. If you're not careful, anyone nearby can hear. Even worse, someone might grab the message, change your tiramisu to cheesecake, or pretend to be your bank.

TLS gives you an encrypted briefcase (so no one can read your message), a signature wax seal (so the recipient knows it's from you), and a way to confirm that the recipient isn't some villain in disguise. TLS is the technology behind that little padlock in your browser. Without it, the web would be a free-for-all of stolen passwords, fake websites, and identity theft (figure 10.1).

Figure 10.1   When surfing the internet from a public network, you never know who's sharing the network with you. For this reason, all communications must be secured.

We'll start in section 10.1 by looking at how TLS builds trust in a hostile network, where anyone could be listening or tampering with your data. In section 10.2, we'll break down what TLS protects you against, including eavesdropping, data tampering, and impersonation. Section 10.3 gets practical, showing how TLS is used in real applications, how it's configured on servers, and what can go wrong if it's set up poorly. By the end of the chapter, you'll clearly understand how TLS works and why it's a critical foundation for securing the modern internet.

10.1   Securing communication with TLS

The internet wasn't built with trust in mind. It was built to send messages from point A to point B, even if that meant crossing through point C, D, and some random router in Iceland. Along the way, your data can pass through dozens of machines you don't control or even know about (figure 10.2).

The problem is that on the internet, you don't get to choose who carries your messages. You have to assume that the network is hostile because it might be. Hackers, spyware, compromised Wi-Fi networks, and misconfigured routers can become uninvited middlemen. So how do you build trust in a place like that?

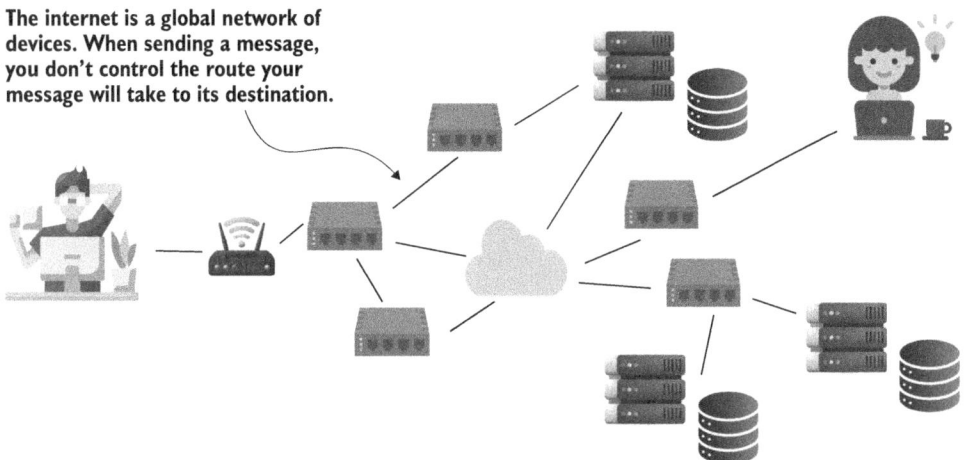

Figure 10.2   The internet is a massive, unpredictable network. When you send a message, it travels through many unknown devices and routers before reaching its destination, which is why encryption such as TLS is essential.

That's where TLS comes in. It doesn't try to make the network safe; it works even though the network is unsafe. It gives your app a way to talk in code, prove who it's talking to, and ensure that the message wasn't changed along the way. In this section, we'll explore why this kind of trust is so hard to get and how TLS pulls it off.

10.1.1 How TLS started

If you're old enough, you may have heard about the Secure Sockets Layer (SSL). Before TLS became the quiet guardian of secure internet connections, there was SSL. Think of SSL as the clunky but brave ancestor of TLS: it had the right idea, but its armor had a few holes. SSL works like this (figure 10.3):

1 Alice (your browser) says "Hi!" and tells Bob (the server) what types of secret codes (encryption methods) she understands.
2 Bob replies with his own list and sends Alice a certificate: a digital ID card that proves who he is and gives her his public key.
3 Alice checks this ID (using a certificate authority she trusts) and uses Bob's public key to send back a shared secret.
4 From that point on, they use the same secret key to encrypt and decrypt their messages.

This sounds good enough, but hackers found problems. They found a way to trick browsers into using weaker encryption (a downgrade attack). They also found that sometimes, they could steal parts of the session key by analyzing patterns or exploiting code bugs.

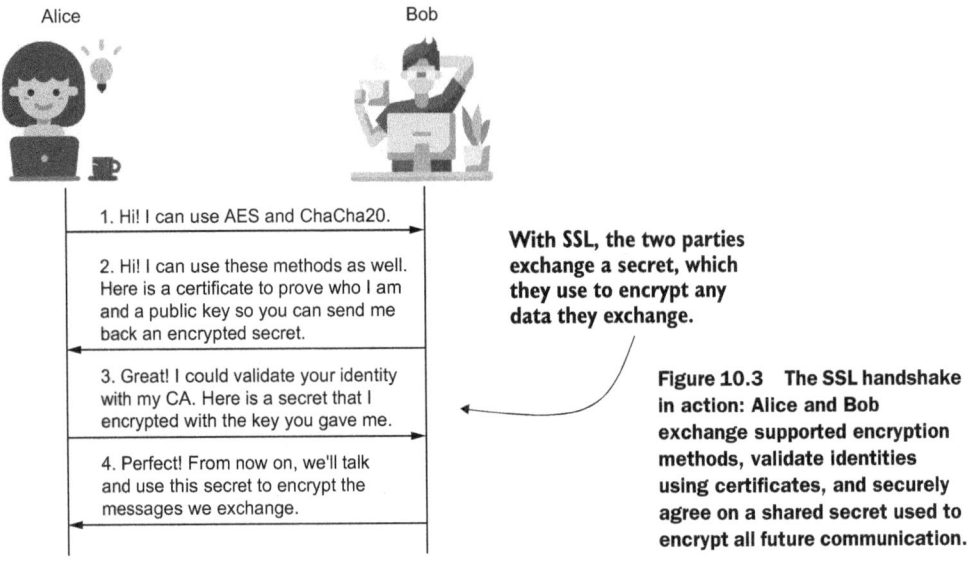

With SSL, the two parties exchange a secret, which they use to encrypt any data they exchange.

Figure 10.3   The SSL handshake in action: Alice and Bob exchange supported encryption methods, validate identities using certificates, and securely agree on a shared secret used to encrypt all future communication.

TLS works a bit differently. Each step has been upgraded to be a lot more robust than SSL (figure 10.4):

1   Alice (your browser) wants to talk securely with Bob (a website).

Hi, Bob! I'd like to talk in private. Here are the encryption methods I support.

2   Bob replies with his digital certificate.

Hi, Alice! Here's my digital certificate to prove I'm Bob. Let's use this encryption method.

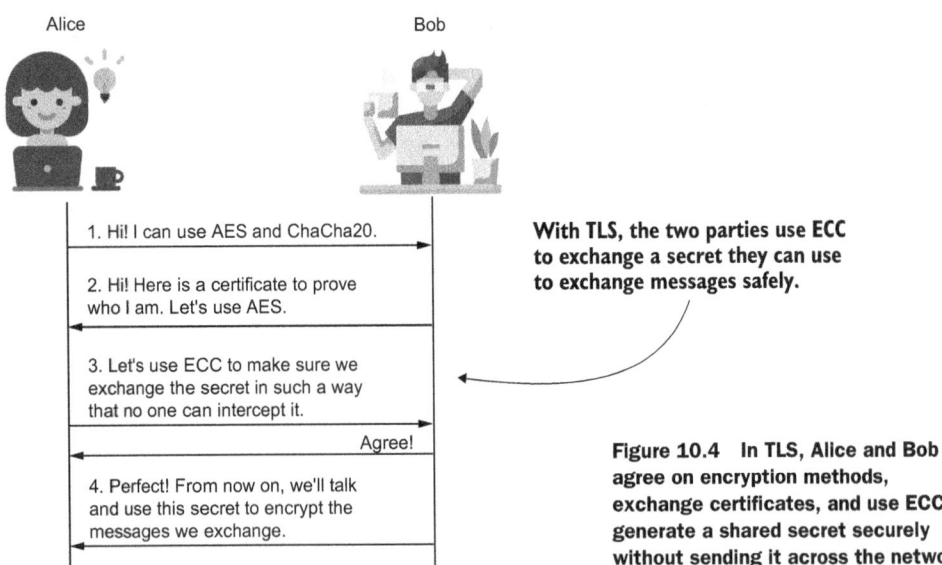

With TLS, the two parties use ECC to exchange a secret they can use to exchange messages safely.

Figure 10.4   In TLS, Alice and Bob agree on encryption methods, exchange certificates, and use ECC to generate a shared secret securely without sending it across the network.

3 They use some clever math (such as elliptic-curve cryptography [ECC]) to agree on a shared secret without sending the secret over the network.

4 When both of them have the secret, they use it to encrypt everything they say.

We know what you're thinking: point 3 sounds like magic. After Alice and Bob agree on an encryption method, how do they use that "clever math"? This math isn't simple to explain, but we'll use an analogy to give you a top-of-the-mountain picture of how it works.

Suppose that Alice and Bob's secret is a color. How can they decide on a color that no one else knows, even if someone is listening? To start, they agree on a common color: yellow. This color is public, and everyone can see it.

Next, Alice picks her own secret color: blue. She mixes her blue with the public yellow and gets green. She sends this green mixture to Bob.

Meanwhile, Bob picks his secret color: red. He mixes it with the same public yellow and ends up with orange. He sends the orange mix to Alice.

Alice takes Bob's orange mix (yellow+red) and adds her secret blue. Bob takes Alice's green mix (yellow+blue) and adds his secret red. Even though they're mixing things independently, they end up with the same final color.

Anyone eavesdropping on this exchange sees only the yellow, green, and orange. They can't re-create the final shared color without knowing Alice's blue or Bob's red. That's how Alice and Bob agree on a secret without revealing it (figure 10.5).

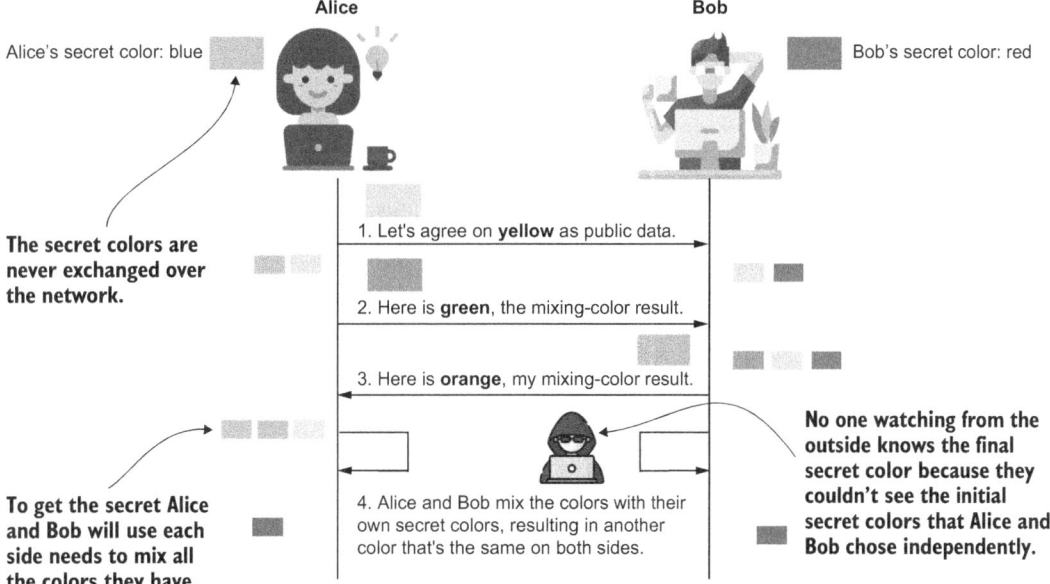

Figure 10.5 Color mixing as an analogy for key exchange in TLS. Alice and Bob each choose a private color, mix it with a public one, and exchange the results. Then they mix again locally to arrive at the same final color without revealing their secret. An outsider, even one who's seeing the entire exchange, can't reconstruct the final shared secret.

TLS uses the same idea, but instead of colors, Alice and Bob use numbers. These numbers are combined using special math functions. They're designed to be easy to compute in one direction (mixing) but nearly impossible to reverse (unmixing). One of the most common methods used for this purpose today is ECC, which is both fast and secure. We talked about ECC in chapters 6 and 7.

At the heart of ECC is a special type of math function called an elliptic curve. It's not a stretched-out oval, as the name suggests, but an actual curve defined by this equation:

$$y^2 = x^3 + ax + b$$

This equation draws a smooth, looping curve with interesting properties on a graph. To help you visualize such a curve, figure 10.6 shows an example called Curve25519, which is often used by systems running on low-powered devices.

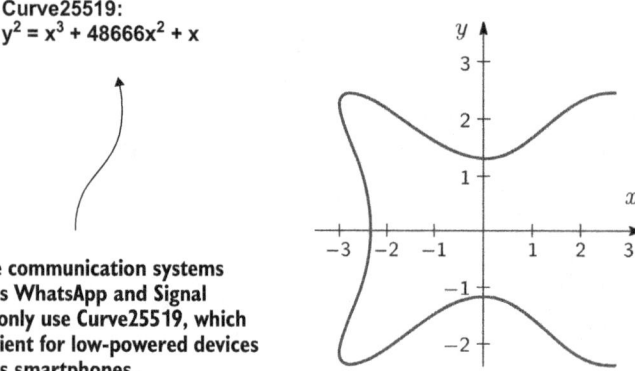

Curve25519:
$y^2 = x^3 + 48666x^2 + x$

Secure communication systems such as WhatsApp and Signal commonly use Curve25519, which is efficient for low-powered devices such as smartphones.

Figure 10.6 Curve25519 is an elliptic curve that's widely used in secure communication systems like WhatsApp and Signal. Its equation provides both high security and efficient performance, making it ideal for modern encryption on low-powered devices such as smartphones.

What makes this curve useful for cryptography is that you can take two points on the curve, "add" them together, and get another point on the curve. This "addition" isn't like normal math; it's geometric. You draw a line through the two points, and where it intersects the curve again, you reflect that point over the x axis. That's the result.

If you keep adding the same point to itself over and over—doubling, tripling, and so on—you predictably move along the curve. But if someone sees only the final result, it's hard to figure out how many times you added the point to get there. This situation, called the Elliptic Curve Discrete Logarithm Problem, makes ECC secure.

ECC turns simple curve math into a one-way trap-door function. It's easy to go forward but nearly impossible to reverse without the key. That's why it's used in TLS, secure messaging, cryptocurrencies, and similar applications.

Even if someone on the network sees all the messages being exchanged, like someone watching the color mixing, they still can't figure out the final shared secret because the private parts (such as Alice's blue and Bob's red) are never sent. Only the mixed results are visible.

The beauty of this approach is that the shared secret never travels across the network. Each side calculates it independently, using the public information and its own private key. This makes the communication secure even if the entire exchange happens over an insecure or hostile network.

TLS isn't just a better version of SSL but also the modern standard. All versions of SSL are now considered unsafe and officially retired. TLS picked up where SSL left off, fixing its flaws and strengthening every part of the handshake. Since 2018, TLS 1.3 has been the preferred version.

10.1.2 TLS and mTLS

TLS is the technology that puts the S in HTTPS. It makes sure that when your browser connects to a website, no one can read or change the information being exchanged. TLS does three main things: encrypts the data so others can't see it, checks whether the data was tampered with, and verifies that the server you're talking to is the real one and not an impostor.

This is how most internet connections work: your browser checks the server's certificate, verifies that it's talking to the right website, and then sends data securely. But notice that only the server proves who it is. Your browser doesn't have to prove anything about itself. This works fine for many public-facing websites where the user doesn't need to be authenticated through the connection itself. (They'll log in with a password later.) But this one-sided trust isn't enough in more secure environments, especially in backend systems in which services talk to other services. That's where mutual TLS (mTLS) comes in.

With mTLS, both the client and the server present certificates and verify each other. mTLS is like a secret handshake: each side must prove their identity before the conversation starts, ensuring that both the server and the client are trusted. It's extremely useful in microservice architectures, APIs exposed to trusted partners, or any system in which you want to block unknown or rogue clients from establishing a connection. Figure 10.7 shows how mTLS works.

1 Alice (a client service) wants to talk securely with Bob (a server service).

> *Hi, Bob! I'd like to talk in private. Here are the encryption methods I support. Also, here's my digital certificate to prove who I am.*

2 Bob replies with his own certificate.

> *Hi, Alice! Thanks for your certificate. Here's mine to prove I'm Bob. Let's use a strong encryption method.*

They check each other's certificates, making sure that they're valid and trusted.

> *Alice checks whether Bob's certificate was signed by someone she trusts. Bob does the same for Alice's certificate.*

3 They use some clever math (like ECC) to agree on a shared secret without sending it across the network.

4 When both of them have the shared secret, they use it to encrypt everything they say.

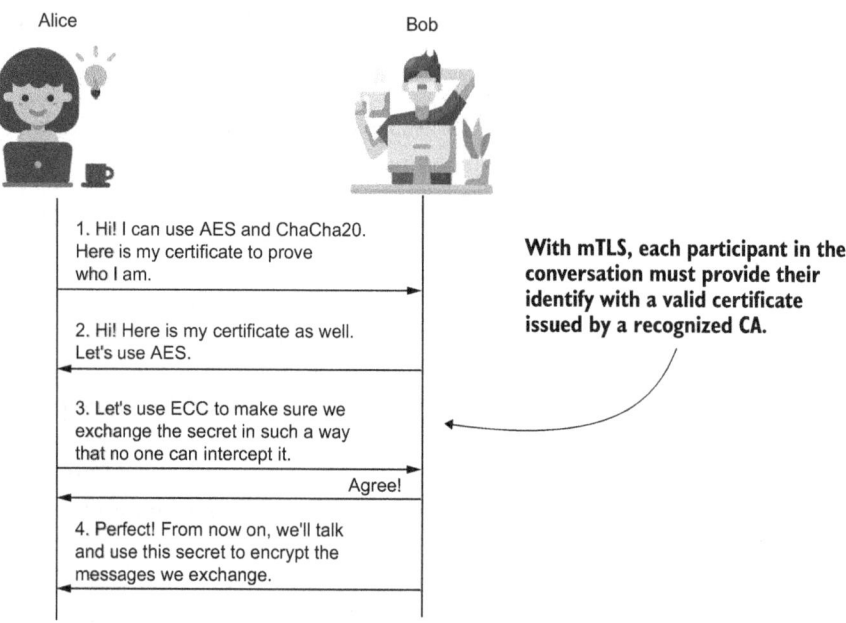

Figure 10.7 In mTLS, Alice and Bob present valid certificates to prove their identities before establishing a secure connection. When their identities are verified, they use ECC to safely agree on a shared secret for encrypting their communication.

Setting up mTLS is more complex than setting up regular TLS because both the client and the server need certificates. In standard TLS, only the server has to prove who it is. You get a certificate for the server—usually from a certificate authority (CA) like Let's Encrypt (https://letsencrypt.org/)—and install it, and you're good to go. But with mTLS, every client also needs its own certificate—a digital ID that proves who it is when connecting. That means you must create, distribute, and store client certificates safely. You also need to track which certificates are trusted and which are expired, and you must what to do when a client's certificate is compromised. In practice, you have to run your own CA.

The extra work gives you a big security boost: you can control which clients can connect to your services. If a device or service doesn't present a valid certificate, the connection is rejected immediately, even before any data is exchanged. This approach is much stronger than relying on usernames, passwords, or API keys, which can be leaked or guessed.

Although mTLS adds complexity, it gives you fine-grained, cryptographic control of who can talk to whom in your system. That's why it's often used in internal microservices and in financial and health-care environments, where trust must be explicit and verified at every connection.

In chapter 16, we'll dive deeper into these service-to-service communication patterns, including best practices for using mTLS. Table 10.1 summarizes our discussion of TLS and mTLS.

Table 10.1   A comparison between TLS and mTLS

	TLS	mTLS
Encrypts data	Yes	Yes
Server proves identity	Yes	Yes
Client proves identity	No	Yes
Common uses	Web browsing	Service-to-service communication and secure APIs
Client certificate required	No	Yes

10.1.3 Exercises

1 Why do we need TLS on the internet?
2 What is the TLS handshake?

10.2   What TLS protects you against

When you browse a website, send an email, or use an app, your device tosses sensitive information into a network you don't control. TLS acts like a shield, protecting that data in three key ways (figure 10.8):

- Eavesdropping (keeping things private)
- Tampering (making sure that nothing changes)
- Impersonation (knowing who you're talking to)

Eavesdropping   **Tampering**   **Impersonation**

 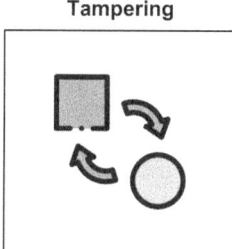 

Figure 10.8   TLS protects against three major threats: eavesdropping (unauthorized listening), tampering (modifying data in transit), and impersonation (using fake credentials to pretend to be someone else).

10.2.1 *Protection from eavesdropping*

Without TLS, anyone sitting between you and the server can read your messages, including Wi-Fi snoopers in a café, compromised routers, and malicious internet service providers. TLS solves this problem by encrypting everything you send or receive. Even if someone intercepts the data, all they see is nonsense.

This isn't just theory. On an unsecured public Wi-Fi network (like one in an airport, hotel, or café), someone using freely available tools can sniff the traffic and see what websites people are visiting, what forms they're filling out, and what files they're downloading. The same thing can happen if an attacker has access to a router or Domain Name System (DNS) server somewhere along the path. Worse, attackers can modify what you receive, injecting fake pages, pop-ups, or malware.

TLS protects against all that by encrypting the connection from start to finish. Using TLS is like sealing your message in a locked, tamperproof envelope that only the real recipient can open. When TLS is in place, even if someone manages to intercept the traffic, they see a stream of random-looking encrypted data. They don't know what you sent, and they can't change it without being detected.

In high school, we ran a tool called Cain & Abel on the school network. It was a network sniffer—a piece of software that let us intercept and read the messages our classmates were sending to one another over Yahoo Messenger and other chat apps during class. Yes, it worked. We could see their full conversations plain as day. Why? Most of those apps didn't use encryption at the time. There was no TLS or SSL—just raw, readable text floating through the networks.

Cain & Abel tricked the network into trusting our computer as though it were the main router by faking the MAC address (a kind of hardware ID) of the real router. As a result, all the internet traffic on the classroom's local network— messages, websites, and everything else—got rerouted through my machine before going out to the internet (figure 10.9). This situation is called a *man-in-the-middle (MITM) attack*. The other students' devices thought they were talking directly to the internet, but in reality, they were talking to us first, and we could read everything before passing it along (including passwords). It was like standing in front of a mailbox, opening each letter, and then resealing it and sending it on its way.

The attacks worked because most services didn't use encryption then. Without TLS or SSL, the messages were plain text. We didn't need to hack anything; we intercepted what was out in the open.

Today, that kind of attack would be much harder to pull off because TLS is everywhere (figure 10.10). It encrypts the connection between your device and the server, so even if someone intercepts the data, all they get is encrypted gibberish. TLS turns open messages into sealed boxes that only the right recipient can unlock. Without it, you're essentially shouting secrets in a crowded room.

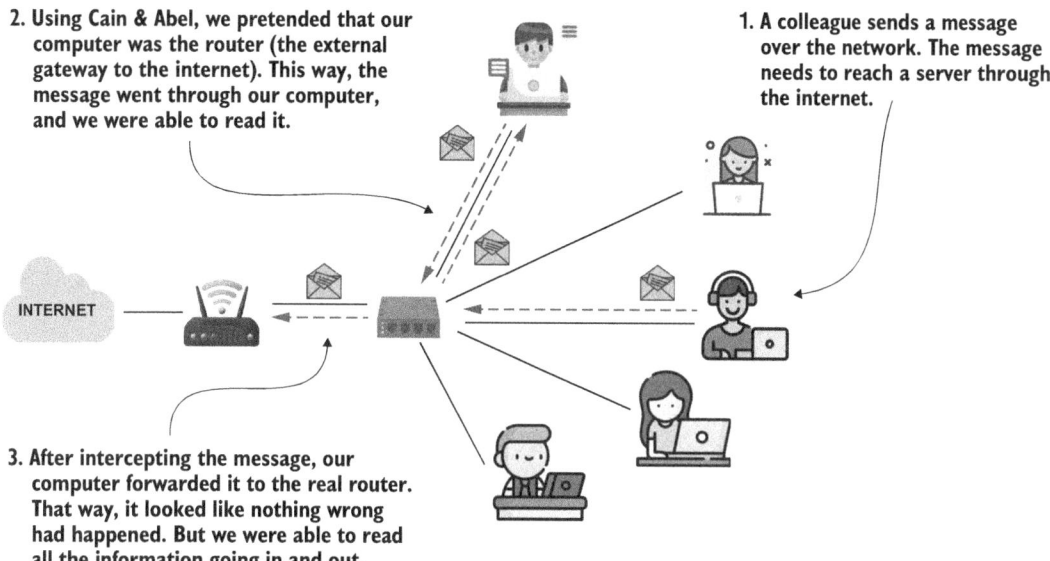

2. Using Cain & Abel, we pretended that our computer was the router (the external gateway to the internet). This way, the message went through our computer, and we were able to read it.

1. A colleague sends a message over the network. The message needs to reach a server through the internet.

3. After intercepting the message, our computer forwarded it to the real router. That way, it looked like nothing wrong had happened. But we were able to read all the information going in and out.

Figure 10.9   A MITM attack using Cain & Abel. By impersonating the router, an attacker silently intercepts messages between users and the internet. The traffic is forwarded normally to prevent suspicion, but the attacker can read all data in and out.

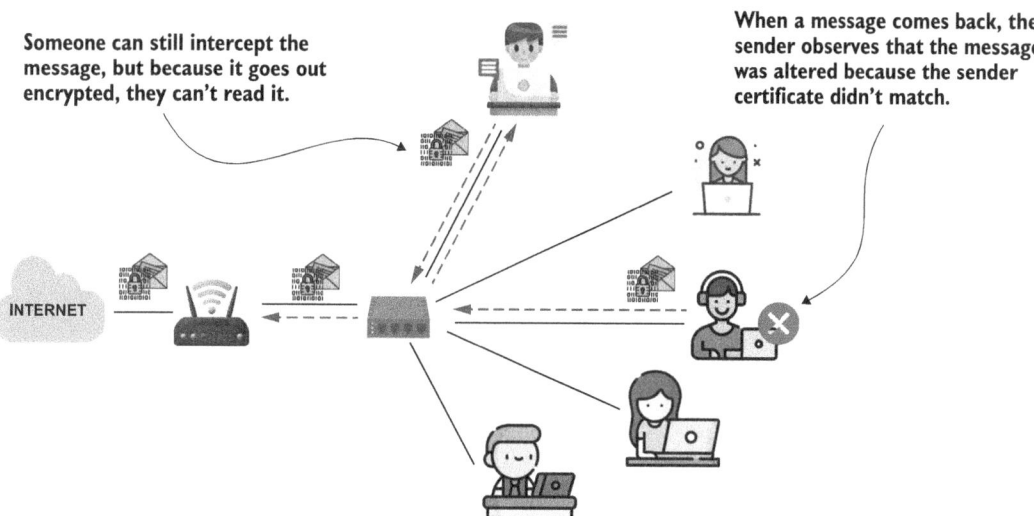

Someone can still intercept the message, but because it goes out encrypted, they can't read it.

When a message comes back, the sender observes that the message was altered because the sender certificate didn't match.

Figure 10.10   With TLS enabled, intercepted messages are encrypted and unreadable by attackers. Even if someone tries to alter the message, the recipient will detect the tampering because the digital signature won't match the sender's certificate. This is how TLS ensures both confidentiality and integrity.

10.2.2 *Making sure that no tampering occurred*

Even if no one reads your data, what if they silently change it? Suppose that you're downloading a file, such as a software update or bank statement, and someone in the middle swaps it with something else, such as a virus or a fake version. Or think about filling out a payment form online. You enter the correct bank-account number, but a hidden attacker quietly replaces it with their own. You click Send, and your money goes to the wrong person.

> **NOTE** Tampering is usually harder to notice than eavesdropping because everything looks normal to the user.

TLS protects against this situation with something called message integrity. Every piece of data you send or receive is digitally signed using something like a cryptographic checksum (also called a MAC or an HMAC). We discussed message integrity in detail in chapter 4. You can think of TLS as a tamper-evident seal on a package. If someone opens the box or changes what's inside, the seal breaks, and TLS knows that something isn't right.

When your browser sees that the message doesn't match the expected integrity check, it discards it immediately. TLS doesn't just keep your data private but also makes sure that what you receive is what the sender intended, no matter how many routers, servers, or unknown devices it passed through.

10.2.3 *Mitigating impersonation*

What if the server you're talking to isn't your bank but a clever fake—same logo, same login page, same everything? You could type your password and credit card number without realizing that you're sending them straight to an attacker. This situation is called spoofing or server impersonation, and it's a real threat, especially on open Wi-Fi networks or in phishing attacks.

TLS solves this problem by using digital certificates. When your browser connects to a secure site (one that starts with https://), the server sends its certificate as part of the TLS handshake. That certificate includes important information: who the website claims to be; when the certificate expires; and most important, a digital signature from a trusted CA.

Your browser already knows and trusts a list of these CAs. So when it sees a certificate from a website, it doesn't take the site's word for it. It checks whether the certificate is

- Valid and not expired
- Properly signed by a trusted CA
- Issued for the right hostname (e.g. bank.com, not bánk.com; observe the small difference in the letter a)

If anything looks off (e.g. expired, forged, or mismatched name), your browser throws up a big red warning or blocks the connection. This protects you from accidentally talking to a fake website that's trying to steal your data (figure 10.11).

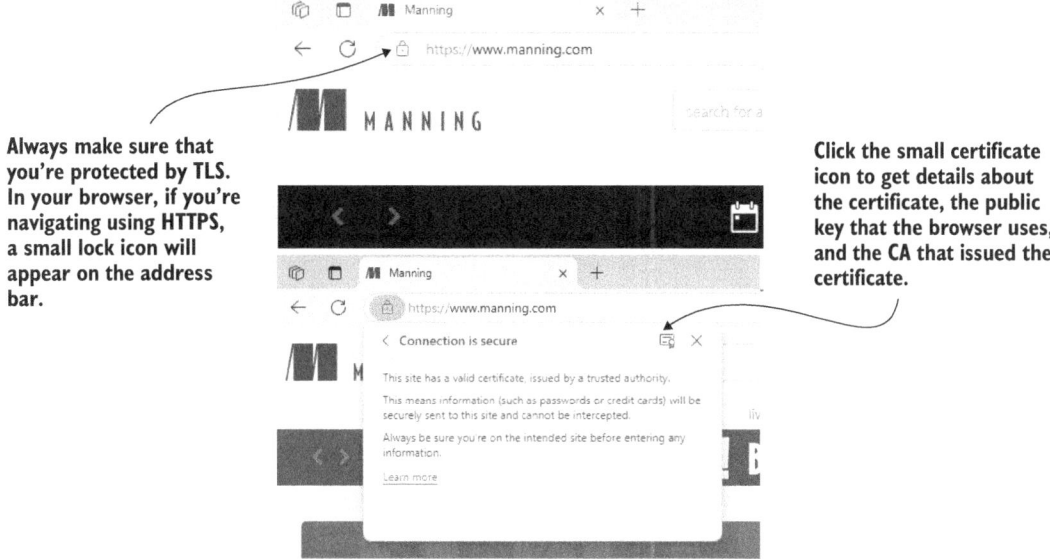

Always make sure that you're protected by TLS. In your browser, if you're navigating using HTTPS, a small lock icon will appear on the address bar.

Click the small certificate icon to get details about the certificate, the public key that the browser uses, and the CA that issued the certificate.

Figure 10.11 Browsers indicate a secure TLS connection with a padlock icon next to the URL. Clicking the icon reveals certificate details, such as the issuing CA, the site's public key, and verification that your connection is encrypted and secure.

You can click the padlock icon in your browser's address bar to view the certificate details. Most people never do, but it's one of the most important pieces of online security working quietly behind the scenes.

10.2.4 Exercises

3 What are the three main threats TLS defends against?
4 What is a MITM attack?
5 How does TLS detect tampering?
6 How do browsers know they're talking to the real website?
7 What happens if a certificate is expired or fake?

10.3 TLS in practice

At this point, you understand what TLS is and why it matters. Now it's time to bring TLS down to earth, into the real systems you're building and running every day. How would you apply TLS at ACME, Inc., for example, to enhance the system's security? This section covers the following topics:

- How to enable TLS on your public-facing services
- How to secure internal service communication with mTLS
- Real-world configuration in Spring Boot and Kubernetes

Let's start with ACME's customer-facing web app, exposed through a domain like `https://app.acme.com`. This app is built with Spring Boot and runs in Kubernetes behind an ingress controller (figure 10.12).

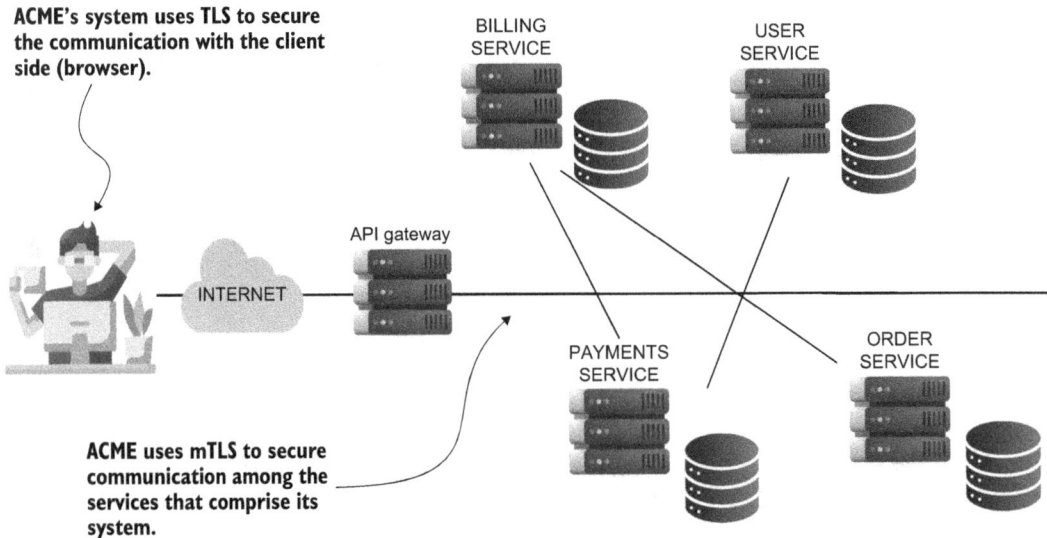

Figure 10.12   ACME uses TLS to secure communication between users and the system via an API gateway. For internal service-to-service communication, such as between billing, payment, order, and user services, mTLS is used to ensure encryption and mutual authentication within the system.

Your users must trust that they're really talking to acme.com, and their credentials and personal data must be encrypted. That's where TLS comes in.

When users connect to your app over https://, their browser starts a secure TLS connection. That means all the data they send, such as login details or form submissions, is encrypted. But where should that encrypted connection end? Where should the data be decrypted so your app can read it?

In Spring Boot, you can terminate TLS directly inside the application. Your app needs its own TLS certificate and private key configured to accept secure connections, usually on port 8443. This approach works but has downsides. Now you have to manage certificates for every app individually, ensure that the certificates are renewed before they expire, and handle TLS configuration in every project. It also complicates your infrastructure, especially in Kubernetes, because traffic must stay encrypted in the pod.

A much better, more common approach, especially in large systems like ACME's, is to terminate TLS at the ingress level. Ingress is the entry point into your Kubernetes cluster. It's like the front door. When a user connects to `https://app.acme.com`, the ingress controller (such as NGINX or Traefik) decrypts the data there, checks the certificate, and forwards the unencrypted request to your Spring Boot app inside the cluster.

DEFINITION *Ingress* is a service orchestrator (Kubernetes) component that acts as the entry point for external traffic into your cluster. It routes incoming HTTP or HTTPS requests to the right service inside the cluster and often handles things like TLS termination, load balancing, and URL path routing.

NOTE On large systems, it's much more common, and often recommended, to terminate TLS at the ingress level rather than inside each application.

Two of the most common ingress controllers are NGINX (https://nginx.org/) and Traefik (https://traefik.io/). NGINX is one of the most well-known web servers in the world. It's reliable, powerful, and has been around for a long time. When used as an Ingress controller, NGINX can handle things like routing requests to the right service, redirecting from HTTP to HTTPS, and even applying rules such as rate limits or timeouts. It works well and is used by many large companies, but it can require more manual configuration.

Traefik is newer and built with Kubernetes in mind. It's easy to set up and automatically detects your services and routes without needing a lot of extra configuration. Traefik also has built-in support for automatically requesting and renewing TLS certificates using Let's Encrypt. It even comes with a nice dashboard to monitor traffic and status.

Both tools are excellent. NGINX is a solid choice if you want fine control and don't mind writing a bit more YAML. If you prefer something more dynamic and easier to manage, Traefik may be a better fit, especially for fast-moving environments like ACME's.

A setup using an ingress is simpler and more scalable. You have to manage certificates in only one place. Tools like `cert-manager` can even renew and install certificates automatically. Your Spring Boot apps don't need to worry about TLS; they run on plain old HTTP, which keeps the app code and configuration clean.

Think of a secure building: the ingress is the front desk with security. When a visitor gets past the front desk, they can walk through the building. But if you want to protect sensitive rooms deeper inside, you can add more checks, which is where mTLS comes in for internal service communication). The following listing shows a sample configuration for the ingress with NGINX.

Listing 10.1 Configuring TLS in Kubernetes with NGINX ingress

```
apiVersion: networking.k8s.io/v1
kind: Ingress
metadata:
  name: acme-app
  annotations:
    cert-manager.io/cluster-issuer: letsencrypt-prod    ◁─┐ Tells cert-manager to
                                                            use the Let's Encrypt
                                                            production issuer to
                                                            request a certificate
                                                            for this ingress
    nginx.ingress.kubernetes.io/ssl-redirect: "true"    ◁─┐ Forces all HTTP traffic
                                                            to redirect to HTTPS
                                                            automatically
spec:
  tls:
    - hosts:                          Specifies which domain this
        - app.acme.com    ◁─┐        TLS config applies to
```

```
      secretName: acme-app-tls
rules:
  - host: app.acme.com
    http:
      paths:
        - path: /
          pathType: Prefix
          backend:
            service:
              name: acme-webapp
              port:
                number: 80
```

Points to a Kubernetes secret where the TLS certificate and private key will be stored

The certificate will be requested automatically by `cert-manager`, validated via a DNS or HTTP challenge, and mounted as a secret named `acme-app-tls`. NGINX ingress takes care of serving traffic securely.

As discussed earlier, the recommended method is to use an ingress. But in some cases (such as for admin tools), you may want your Spring Boot app to terminate TLS itself. In such cases, frameworks such as Spring and its ecosystem make configuration easier. With a Spring Boot app, you have to configure the certificate with a few lines of code, as shown in the next listing.

Listing 10.2   Enabling TLS in a Spring Boot app

```
server.port=8443
server.ssl.key-store=classpath:keystore.p12
server.ssl.key-store-password=changeit
server.ssl.key-store-type=PKCS12
server.ssl.key-alias=acmeapp
```

Points to the keystore file that contains the server's private key and certificate

This is the password used to unlock the keystore. Spring Boot needs this to access the private key and certificate inside the keystore.

This specifies the format of the keystore. PKCS12 is a modern, standardized format supported by most systems and tools.

> **WARNING** In real-world apps, passwords such as the key-store password should be stored securely (e.g., using environment variables or external secrets). Make sure that the key-store file contains your private key and certificate. You can generate it with the Java key tool or use a proper CA.

To enable mTLS for a Spring Boot app, you have to configure the application not only to present its own certificate but also to require and validate a certificate from the client. This involves setting up a trust store (to validate incoming client certificates) alongside the key store (which holds the app's own identity). It adds a strong layer of authentication between services.

But in most modern deployments (especially in Kubernetes), mTLS is often handled by a service mesh such as Istio, so the Spring Boot code stays clean. Chapter 16 explores mTLS service configuration, including trust stores, certificate rotation, and service-level authentication.

TLS is a technology that does its job quietly. Whether you're securing a customer-facing app, exposing APIs, or managing dozens of services inside your cluster, getting TLS right is essential. Although tools like Spring Boot, Kubernetes Ingress, and Istio make it easier than ever to set up TLS, how you configure it still matters. A forgotten setting, an expired certificate, or a weak cipher suite can turn a locked system into an open one.

At ACME, your systems have a solid foundation now. The front door is locked (thanks to HTTPS and ingress), and internal doors can be locked when necessary (via mTLS). You've seen how to apply these patterns with real code and, more important, how to think about TLS in practice.

10.3.1 *Exercises*

8 Why use ingress controllers for TLS in Kubernetes?

9 What's the difference between NGINX and Traefik?

10 When would you still do TLS termination inside the app?

10.4   *Exercise answers*

1 Why do we need TLS on the internet?

Your data passes through a bunch of unknown systems, some of which may be spying. TLS encrypts data so no one else can read or tamper with it.

2 What is the TLS handshake?

It's the initial exchange in which two sides agree on encryption methods, share certificates, and safely agree on a shared secret using clever math.

3 What are the three main threats TLS defends against?

Eavesdropping (reading your data), tampering (changing it), and impersonation (pretending to be a trusted site)

4 What is a MITM attack?

In this type of attack, someone sits between you and the server, silently intercepting or modifying messages. TLS prevents it by encrypting everything.

5 How does TLS detect tampering?

Each message includes a cryptographic signature. If someone changes the data, the signature won't match, and the message is rejected.

6 How do browsers know that they're talking to the real website?

They check the digital certificate from the server, verifying that the issuer, expiration date, and hostname match.

7 What happens if a certificate is expired or fake?

The browser shows a big red warning and may block the connection to protect the user.

8 Why use ingress controllers for TLS in Kubernetes?

They simplify things. You manage certificates in one place instead of in each app, and traffic inside the cluster can stay unencrypted or use mTLS.

9 What's the difference between NGINX and Traefik?

NGINX provides more manual control. Traefik is more dynamic and integrates better with Kubernetes and Let's Encrypt.

10 When would you still do TLS termination inside the app?

You'd do this in standalone apps (such as internal tools) or to provide end-to-end encryption all the way into the application.

Summary

- TLS protects data as it travels across untrusted networks by encrypting it, verifying the identity of the server, and ensuring that the data hasn't been changed along the way.
- TLS solves three major problems:
  - Eavesdropping (no one else can read the message)
  - Tampering (no one can change the message without being detected)
  - Impersonation (you know you're talking to the real server)
- Before TLS, there was SSL, a now-retired, less secure version. TLS 1.3 is the modern standard, using faster and safer encryption methods such as elliptic curve cryptography.
- mTLS extends TLS by requiring both sides to prove who they are. It's often used in secure backend systems in which services must trust one another explicitly.
- TLS is typically terminated at the ingress level (e.g., using NGINX or Traefik) in Kubernetes. This simplifies certificate management and keeps service configuration clean.
- In special cases, Spring Boot apps can terminate TLS themselves using a configured key store, but this approach is more complex to scale.

Part 4

Modern authentication and identity

In Part 3, you learned how to establish trust between systems using certificates and Transport Layer Security (TLS). That gave you the foundation for secure communication. But trust at the system level isn't enough; applications also need to know who the user is and what they're allowed to do. This is where authentication and identity protocols come into play.

Part 4 is all about people and services proving who they are. We'll explore the standards and technologies that power modern authentication, from JSON-based formats like JWS, JWE, and JWT (chapter 11) to OAuth2 and OpenID Connect, which enable single sign-on (chapter 12) and advanced identity management (chapter 13). Then we show how passwordless login options such as magic links and one-time passwords (chapter 14) work before moving on to WebAuthn (chapter 15), which brings hardware tokens, biometrics, and phishing-resistant authentication into the mainstream.

Throughout this part, you'll see how ACME, Inc. applies these protocols in real scenarios: securing APIs with tokens, simplifying user logins with an identity provider, and protecting accounts with stronger authentication methods. You'll also learn about the tradeoffs, see why some flows are safe in theory but risky in practice, and find out how to implement best practices to avoid common pitfalls.

By the end of part 4, you'll have a clear mental model of modern identity systems and authentication flows. You'll understand not just the "how" but also the "why": why tokens look the way they do, why refresh tokens exist, and why PKCE matters. With these tools, you'll be ready to design authentication systems that balance security, usability, and scalability.

11

JSON Object Signing
and Encryption

This chapter covers

- Seeing what makes up the JavaScript Object Signing and Encryption (JOSE) standard
- Creating and verifying JSON Web Signature (JWS) objects
- Encrypting and decrypting JSON Web Encryption (JWE) objects
- Avoiding common JWS and JWE security pitfalls

We live in a world where data is exchanged between systems implemented in multiple programming languages by multiple teams working for multiple organizations. Systems interoperate using standard networking protocols such as HTTP in a well-defined manner and use standard data formats. REST, for example, uses JSON, SOAP uses XML, and gRPC uses protocol buffers (protobuffers). Standardized data formats for exchanging encrypted and signed data make interoperability significantly easier.

Security protocols such as X.509 digital certificates (chapters 8 and 9), OpenID Connect (OIDC) and OAuth2 (chapters 12 and 13), SAML, and TLS (chapter 10) have to exchange encrypted and signed messages. These protocols rely on standard formats to represent encrypted and signed content. OIDC uses JSON, SAML uses XML, and X.509 certificates are represented in a standardized binary data format.

If you understand the various security data formats, you can easily create and edit files in these formats. More importantly, you'll be able to understand error messages and stack traces produced by the security libraries you're coding against. Troubleshooting is simple when you understand the underlying data formats and challenging when you don't. This chapter is a friendly introduction to the widely used JOSE suite of standards, along with a basic introduction to the JSON Web Token (JWT) standard.

11.1   *The standards layer cake*

JOSE is a collection of four standards that build on one another (figure 11.1). Each standard focuses on a well-defined set of security capabilities. In this chapter, we explore the four standards that are part of the JOSE suite:

1   *JSON Web Algorithms* (https://tools.ietf.org/html/rfc7518) (JWA) defines string identifiers for commonly used cryptographic algorithms. As an example, hash-based message authentication code (HMAC), based on the SHA-256 hash function (chapter 4) is identified using the string HS256.

2   *JSON Web Key* (https://tools.ietf.org/html/rfc7517) (JWK) represents secret, public, and private keys for various cryptographic algorithms as JSON objects. The JWK standard uses the identifiers defined by JWA.

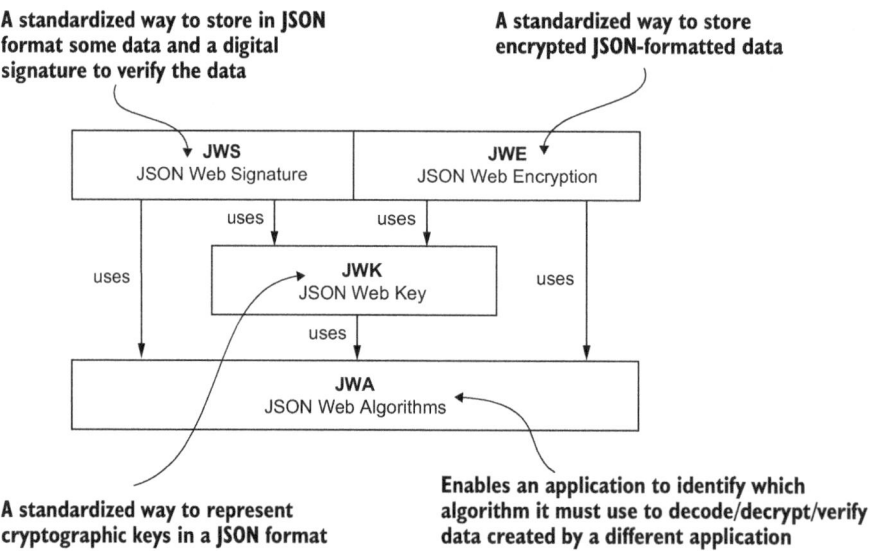

Figure 11.1   Relationships between the standards that are part of the JOSE suite. JOSE enables interoperability between applications that want to exchange encrypted or signed data using the JSON data format. JOSE standards are used extensively by popular security protocols such as OIDC for single sign-on.

3 *JWS* (https://tools.ietf.org/html/rfc7515) represents content that must be protected from tampering but doesn't have to be kept confidential. The JWS standard uses the JWA and JWK standards.

4 *JWE* (https://tools.ietf.org/html/rfc7516) represents content that must be protected from tampering and kept confidential. The JWE standard uses the JWA and JWK standards.

11.2 The problem solved by JWA

Suppose that you receive an encrypted email message and want to decrypt it so you can read it. How do you know which encryption algorithm was used to encrypt the email message? You can assume that the email message was encrypted using AES-GCM-128 because that's the algorithm you agreed to use with the person who sent you the email. The sending and receiving applications can hardcode the choice of algorithm into their implementation. This approach works when you have two applications written by the same team.

If different teams working for different companies write the applications, it's better to add metadata to the encrypted email message to indicate which encryption algorithm was used. This metadata enables the receiving application to determine the correct decryption algorithm to use when it receives the message. You can use the string `"AES-128-GCM"`, for example, to identify the encryption algorithm as Advanced Encryption Standard (AES) with a 128-bit key in Galois/Counter mode (chapter 5).

But another team might choose to use the string `"AES-GCM-128"` (notice the difference!) to indicate that the encryption algorithm is AES with 128-bit keys in Galois/Counter mode. Using standardized names for encryption algorithms enables interoperability.

JWA is an Internet Engineering Task Force (IETF) standard registry of cryptographic algorithm names and identifiers for the following:

- *Digital signatures*—Algorithms used to verify that a message truly comes from the claimed sender and hasn't been altered
- *Message Authentication Codes (MACs)*—Algorithms that ensure message integrity and authenticity by using a shared secret key
- *Key management*—Algorithms that establish, wrap, or exchange cryptographic keys securely between parties
- *Encryption*—Algorithms that protect the confidentiality of data by transforming it into unreadable form for unauthorized users

Following are a few examples of standard identifiers:

- "A256GCM" indicates AES using a 256-bit key in Galois/Counter mode.
- "A192CBC-HS512" indicates AES using a 192-bit key in cipher-block chaining mode with an HMAC based on the SHA-2 with a 512-bit output hash algorithm.
- "ES384" indicates the elliptic-curve digital signature algorithm using the NISTP-384 curve and SHA-384 hashes.

To accommodate the addition of new algorithm names, the JWA identifiers are registered with the Internet Assigned Numbers Authority (IANA). IANA is a not-for-profit organization that oversees many critical aspects of the internet, such as the IP address space, root Domain Name System (DNS) domains, and a list of media content types. You can see the full list of JWA names at https://www.iana.org/assignments/jose/jose.xhtml. You can use JWA names while debugging to identify which types of algorithms are being used.

11.2.1 Exercises

1 Why do we need standardized names for cryptographic algorithms?
2 Give two examples of JWA identifiers, and explain what they mean.
3 What organization maintains the registry of JWA identifiers?

11.3 JWK

Cryptographic algorithms take a variety of keys as inputs. AES, for example, requires a 128-, 192-, or 256-bit key. Public key encryption algorithms use private and public key pairs; the public keys are to be shared with many applications and systems. What is the data format for storing and exchanging keys?

In chapter 4, we stored HMAC keys as hex-encoded strings in the Spring Boot `application.yml` file. This approach works when you have two applications written by the same team, but it doesn't scale to multiple teams across multiple organizations.

JWK is a standard for representing keys as JSON objects. It helps represent complex keys that have multiple components. The JSON in the following listing represents an elliptic-curve public-private key pair using the NIST P-256 curve. Chapter 7 discusses elliptic-curve cryptography (ECC).

Listing 11.1   Example JWK

```
{
  "kty":"EC",
  "crv":"P-256",
  "x":"MKBCTNIcKUSDii11ySs3526iDZ8AiTo7Tu6KPAqv7D4",
  "y":"4Etl6SRW2YiLUrN5vfvVHuhp7x8PxltmWWlbbM4IFyM",
  "d":"870MB6gfuTJ4HtUnUvYMyJpr5eUZNP4Bk43bVdj3eAE",
  "use":"enc",
  "kid":"1"                    ◁─┐ The Key ID (for short KID)
}                                 uniquely identifies the key.
```

11.3.1 Exercises

4 What problem does JWK solve compared to storing keys as hex strings?
5 What does the `kid` field represent in a JWK?
6 Why is representing keys in JSON format useful in distributed systems?

11.4 JWS

Recall the ACME, Inc. refund-processing scenario we used in previous chapters. We'll reuse that scenario in this chapter to explore the JWS standard.

Customers mail shoes they don't like to ACME's warehouse. Warehouse employees verify that the returned shoes are in good condition before authorizing a credit card refund using the warehouse management app. Once a day, the warehouse management app produces a refunds.json file. The payments service uses this file to refund customers' credit cards (figure 11.2).

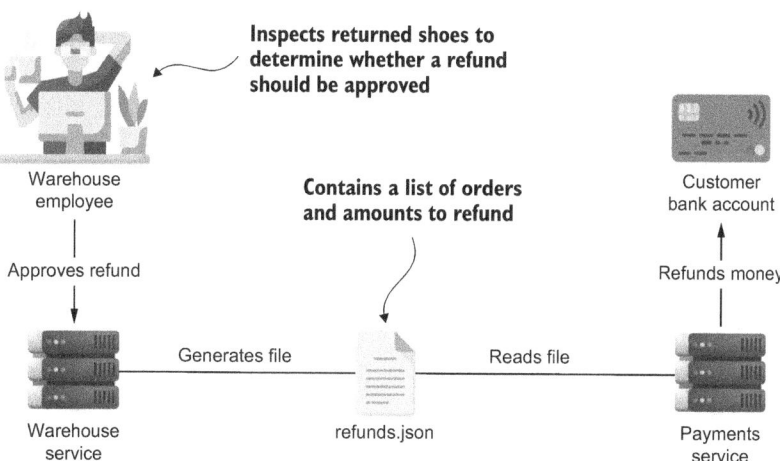

Figure 11.2 ACME's staff approves refunds using the warehouse management application. Once a day, the warehouse management application generates a refunds.json file. The payments service refunds customers' credit cards for the amounts specified in the refunds.json files.

In chapter 4, we used HMAC with SHA-256 to ensure that the refunds.json file was both authentic (created by the warehouse service) and unaltered. But the implementation creates two separate files: refunds.json.hs256 for the HMAC signature and refunds.json for the actual data.

Interoperability between services is a critical architectural design goal for the ACME software development team, as it should be for any software system. Therefore, they want to use an industry standard as the data-exchange format for the various ACME services. What industry-standard format can they use to reduce coding effort and improve portability?

JWS, defined by RFC 7515, is an IETF standard that "represents content secured with digital signatures or Message Authentication Codes (MACs) using JSON-based data structures" (https://tools.ietf.org/html/rfc7515). JWS is part of the JOSE collection of IETF standards.

11.4.1 JWS structure

A JWS object has three parts: header, payload, and signature (figure 11.3). The header is a JSON object that describes which cryptographic algorithm is used to sign the JWS object. The payload is an arbitrary sequence of bytes. The signature is a MAC or a digital signature based on public key cryptography.

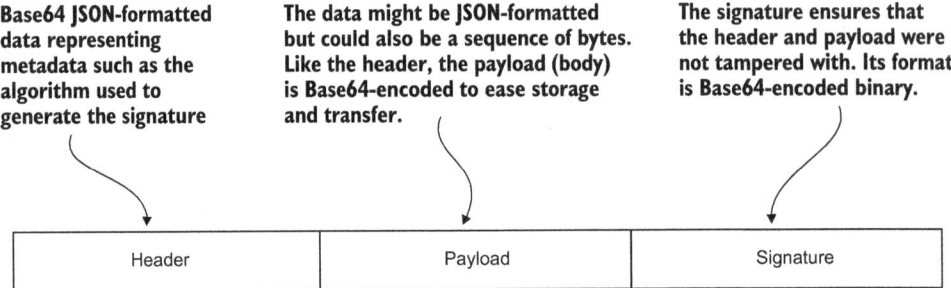

Figure 11.3   The logical structure of JWS: a JSON metadata header describing the type of signature used, a payload that can be any type of data format, and a signature used to verify that the header and payload weren't altered. A JWS payload is always readable by anyone who can access the JWS object.

Consider the following JSON payload:

```
[ {
  "orderId" : "12345",
  "amount" : 500
}, {
  "orderId" : "56789",
  "amount" : 250
} ]
```

This payload turns into JWS in the next snippet when it's signed using HMAC with SHA-256. Observe the three parts separated by dots:

eyJhbGciOiJIUzI1NiJ9.WyB7CiAgIm9yZGVySWQiIDogIjEyMzQ1IiwKICAiYW1vdW50IiA6IDUw
MAp9LCB7CiAgIm9yZGVySWQiIDogIjU2Nzg5IiwKICAiYW1vdW50IiA6IDI1MAp9IF0.wuKUe-
eeHzO7ekWMJNRC8OLOQ9EB2ZqNDRQ-DQrpuWY

JWS objects are typically exchanged between applications using HTTP header values or URL query parameters. But the HTTP and URL specifications allow only a limited set of ASCII characters in header or parameter values. Because a JWS payload can contain arbitrary binary data, it must be encoded in a way that's safe for use in HTTP headers and URL parameters.

To make JWS objects easy and safe to use as HTTP header and query parameter values, each part of the JWS object is encoded using Base64 URL encoding, and then concatenated and separated by dots. Figure 11.4 shows the process of converting the example JSON payload to JWS.

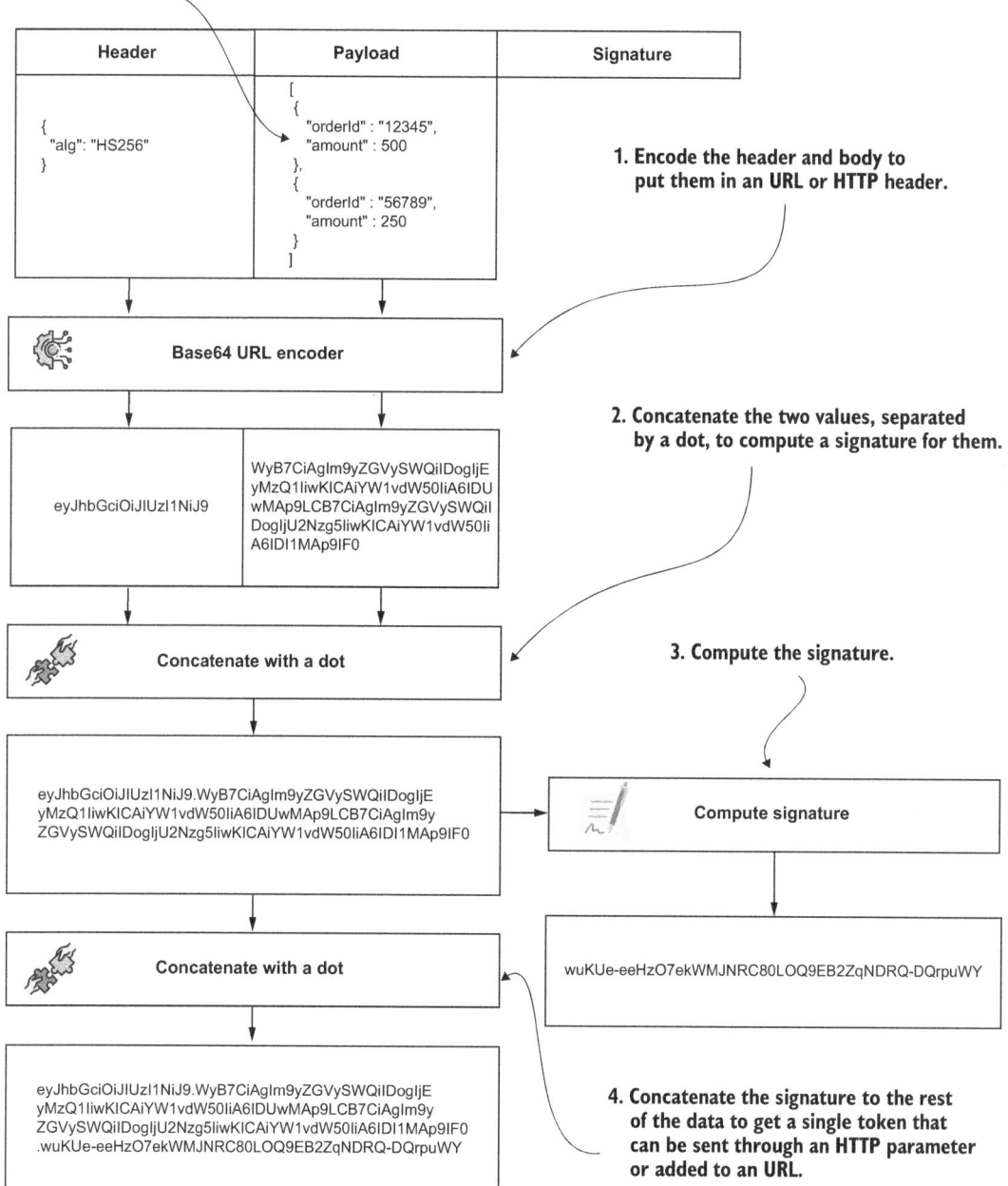

Figure 11.4   Road from data to JWS. A JWS object can be safely embedded in a URL or HTTP headers because it's represented as a Base64 URL string in which the components are separated by dots.

The header of the JWS object in figure 11.4 is `eyJhbGciOiJIUzI1NiJ9`, which decodes to the JSON object in the following snippet:

```
{
  "alg": "HS256"
}
```

The `"alg"` field in the header indicates the type of signature algorithm being used by this JWS object. The algorithm names are standardized by JWA in RFC 7518 (https://datatracker.ietf.org/doc/html/rfc7518). `HS256` is the JWA name for HMAC using SHA-256. The next snippet shows the payload component of the JWS object:

WyB7CiAgIm9yZGVySWQiIDogIjEyMzQ1IiwKICAiYW1vdW50IiA6IDUwMAp9LCB7CiAgIm9yZGVyS
WQiIDogIjU2Nzg5IiwKICAiYW1vdW50IiA6IDI1MAp9IF0

This string decodes to a list of orders to refund produced by the warehouse application:

```
[ {
  "orderId" : "12345",
  "amount" : 500
}, {
  "orderId" : "56789",
  "amount" : 250
} ]
```

The signature component `wuKUe-eeHzO7ekWMJNRC80LOQ9EB2ZqNDRQ-DQrpuWY` is the result of computing the HMAC-SHA-256 on the header and payload. This signature can be decoded to this hex string:

c2e2947be79e1f33bb7a458c24d442f342ce43d101d99a8d0d143e0d0ae9b966

> **TIP** You can use several online tools to work with JWS objects. JWT Debugger (https://jwt.io) has a nice JWT decoder that you can use to decode the components of a JWS object. CyberChef is a handy open source, browser-based tool produced by the British Government Communications Headquarters (GCHQ) for encryption, encoding, compression, and data analysis. CyberChef is available on GitHub at https://gchq.github.io/CyberChef/.

You can represent a JWS object as a JSON object with fields rather than the Base64 compact URL discussed earlier. But we don't cover the JWS JSON serialization format because it isn't used with the security protocols we discuss in the rest of the book.

Depending on the signing algorithm you use, a JWS can deliver all the goals of cryptography. The signing algorithm we use in this section doesn't support the non-repudiation goal of cryptography (table 11.1). We discussed these four objectives in part 2. JWS can provide nonrepudiating if it's used with public key cryptography, as we'll show in chapter 12.

Table 11.1 Cryptography goals and algorithms matrix

Goal	JWS-HS256
Integrity	Yes
Authentication	Yes
Confidentiality	No
Non-repudiation	No

11.4.2 Creating and verifying a JWS object

JWS is a widely supported standard with implementations available in many programming languages, including Java. One popular, user-friendly library for working with JWS and other JOSE standards is Nimbus. Nimbus is open source and commonly used in Java projects, including Spring Security, where it powers support for OIDC and OAuth2 logins. The ssfd_ch11_ex1 project provided with the book demonstrates how a JWS object can be generated in a Java app. We start by adding the Nimbus dependency to the `pom.xml` file as follows:

```
<dependency>
    <groupId>com.nimbusds</groupId>
    <artifactId>nimbus-jose-jwt</artifactId>
    <version>9.37.3</version>
</dependency>
```

The following listing shows the code that creates the JWS object explained in section 11.4.1. We use a hardcoded secret key here to make the example simpler and focus on the important capabilities. But in a real-world app, secrets should never be hardcoded or stored in properties files.

Listing 11.2 Creating a JWS object and signing it using a secret key

```
public final class JwsUtil {

  private static final byte[] HMAC_SECRET =
    Base64.getDecoder().decode(
      "VGhpc0lzQS1EZW1vLVNlY3JldC1LZXk
      ?tRm9yLUhTMjU2LUF0TGVhc3QtMzJCeXRlcyE="
    );

  public static String generateJws(
    String payloadJson) throws JOSEException {

    JWSHeader header =                                    ◁─── Configure JWS Header with
      new JWSHeader.Builder(JWSAlgorithm.HS256)                HMAC with SHA-256 for signing
        .contentType("application/json")
      .build();
```

```
JWSObject jwsObject =
    new JWSObject(header, new Payload(payloadJson));

jwsObject.sign(new MACSigner(HMAC_SECRET));

    return jwsObject.serialize();
  }

}
```

Create a JWS Object using the desired header and payload.

Sign the JWS using a secret key and HMAC-SHA-256.

Generate Base64 URL encoded representation of JWS

To create a JWS signed with HS256, you need two key components:

- *Payload*—The content you want to include in the JWS. This can be any string, such as JSON data.
- *Secret key*—A shared secret used for signing the JWS to ensure its authenticity.

The Nimbus library simplifies working with JWS by providing several useful classes:

- JWSHeader—Represents the header of the JWS. In this case, the header is configured to use the HS256 algorithm for signing.
- Payload—Represents the content of the JWS. This can be any string, such as "Hello, World!" or a JSON object.
- JWSObject—Combines the header, payload, and signature into a single object. The sign() method is used to generate the signature. In the example, the method is passed a MACSigner, which is configured with the secret key to compute the HMAC-SHA256 signature.

When an application receives a JWS token, verifying the signature is essential to ensure that the token hasn't been tampered with. Verifying the JWS token with the Nimbus library is straightforward.

Listing 11.3   Verifying a JWS object using Nimbus

```
public final class JwsUtil {

  private static final byte[] HMAC_SECRET =
    Base64.getDecoder().decode(
      "VGhpc0lzQS1EZW1vLVNlY3JldC1LZXXktR
      ?m9yLUhTMjU2LUF0TGVhc3QtMzJCZXXRlcyE="
  );

  public static boolean verifyJws(String compactJws) {
    try {
      JWSObject parsed = JWSObject.parse(compactJws);
      return parsed.verify(new MACVerifier(HMAC_SECRET));
    } catch (ParseException | JOSEException e) {
      return false;
    }
  }
}
```

Configure the object to be verified.

Verify the JWS.

The `JWSObject.parse()` method takes a Base64-encoded string and creates a Nimbus `JWSObject` from it. The `MACVerifier` class takes a secret key as input; the `verify()` method uses it to check that the computed HMAC of the JWS matches the JWS signature component.

> **WARNING** The JWS specification includes a potential vulnerability: the `"alg"` field in the header can be set to `none`, effectively bypassing signature validation. This means a hacker could intercept a JWS, change the `"alg"` field to `none`, modify the payload, and then forward the tampered request. Because `alg:none` is technically a valid option under the specification, some JWS libraries might mistakenly accept the unsigned JWS as valid, allowing the attack to succeed.

Developers must ensure that JWS libraries are configured to reject `alg:none` as a valid option. Unfortunately, many developers fail to do so, resulting in numerous real-world vulnerabilities over the years even though the problem is well known.

In October 2020, for example, it was revealed that the United Kingdom's official National Health Service (NHS) COVID-19 contact tracing app for Android was affected by the `alg:none` vulnerability. Hackers could exploit this weakness to bypass the app's security, as described at https://mng.bz/Jw4p.

Adding `alg:none` to the JWS standard was a significant design flaw with serious consequences. This mistake led several high-profile cryptographers to criticize the JWS and JOSE standards.

Fortunately, the Nimbus MACVerifier used in the sample code in listing 11.3 throws an exception if it encounters `alg:none`, ensuring that the implementation is safe from this vulnerability. Always double-check your JWS/JWT library settings to ensure that you use them securely and avoid this known pitfall.

11.4.3 *The credit-card refund scenario with JWS*

To meet integrity and authenticity, we can use JWS:

- *Integrity*—The data hasn't been changed by someone else.
- *Authenticity*—We can trust who created the data.

JWS is an industry standard and has a simple format that's easy to use in Java. In our example, the warehouse app creates a single file called `refunds.jws` in the root folder of the project, using the code in listings 11.2 and 11.3. You can check this yourself by running the project ssfd_ch11_ex2-warehouse.

Compared with what we did with HMAC in chapter 4, the warehouse code is much simpler. With HMAC, we had to write two files:

- `refunds.json` (the actual data)
- `refunds.json.sha256` (the checksum used to verify it)

With JWS, all this is packed together in one file. The JWS header also contains useful metadata, such as which signing algorithm is used. This metadata makes it easy to change the algorithm or its settings later (to switch from SHA-256 to SHA-512, for example).

On the other side, the payments app (ssfd_ch11_ex2-payments) can open the refunds.jws file, check whether it came from the warehouse app, confirm that it wasn't changed, and then extract the original data (the payload). To fulfill the exercise, follow these steps:

1 Run the warehouse app to generate the refunds.jws file.
2 Put the refunds.jws file in the payments app's resources folder.
3 Run the payments app, and observe that the payload is extracted into a new file.
4 Change the secret, and play with the content of the refunds.jws file. Observe that the payments app checks whether the data was altered and rejects it.
5 Use JWT Debugger to decode the content of the refunds.jws file. Observe that both the header and payload can be read; they aren't encrypted.

11.4.4 Exercises

7 What are the three main parts of a JWS object?
8 How is a JWS different from the HMAC-based approach in chapter 4?
9 What vulnerability is associated with the alg:none option in JWS?
10 In the ACME refund scenario, what does JWS guarantee?

11.5 JWE

In section 11.4, we used JWS to make sure that we could detect tampering in the refunds.json file exchanged between the warehouse and payments services. In this section, we want to encrypt the contents of the refunds.json file to protect confidentiality.

Interoperability between services is a critical architecture design goal for the ACME software development team. Therefore, they want to use an industry standard as the data-exchange format for the various ACME services. JWE, defined by RFC 7516, is an IETF standard that "represents encrypted content using JSON-based data structures. The JWE cryptographic mechanisms encrypt and provide integrity protection for an arbitrary sequence of octets" (https://tools.ietf.org/html/rfc7516). (An octet is 1 byte.)

11.5.1 JWE structure

A JWE object is made up of four key components, each serving a specific purpose (figure 11.5):

- *Header*—Contains metadata about the encryption, such as the algorithm used, the type of encryption key, and any additional parameters needed to decrypt the payload. It provides instructions for processing the JWE object.
- *Optional encrypted key*—The content encryption key (CEK) that was encrypted using a public key or shared secret. It allows the intended recipient to securely obtain the CEK, which is used to decrypt the actual data (payload). In some cases, this key may be omitted if a preagreed method is used to derive it.

- *Payload ciphertext*—The actual content or message being encrypted. This could be anything from text to structured data like JSON. The payload is encrypted using a symmetric encryption algorithm such as AES.
- *Authentication tag*—A cryptographic checksum that ensures the integrity and authenticity of the JWE. It verifies that the data hasn't been tampered with during transmission or storage.

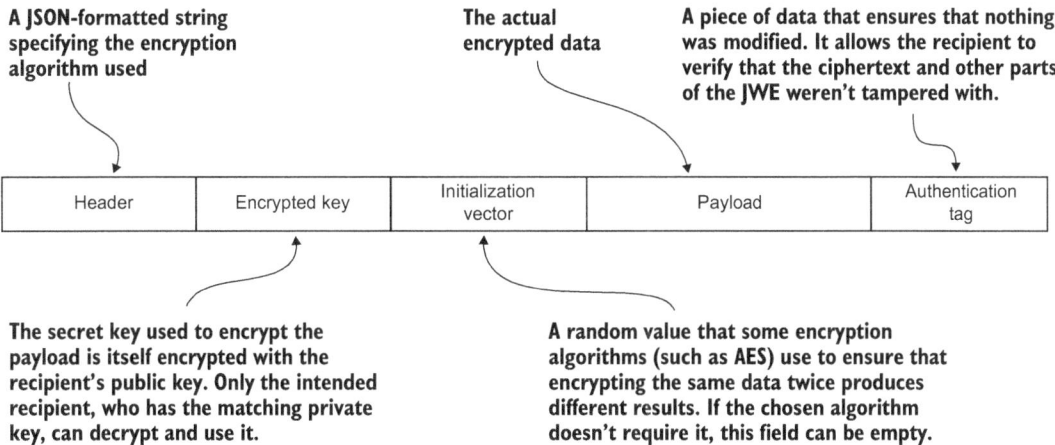

Figure 11.5 Parts of a JWE object

For this example, we use the following JSON payload:

```
[ {
  "orderId" : "12345",
  "amount" : 500
}, {
  "orderId" : "56789",
  "amount" : 250
} ]
```

This input turns into the JWE in the following snippet when it's encrypted using AES-GCM with a 256-bit key. If you need a refresher on AES, review chapter 5.

eyJlbmMiOiJBMjU2R0NNIiwiYWxnIjoiZGlyIn0.bt9LbkMg4oPbsm-l.CrF8Dq9pvvzq2
grnkI99RtwUpb5geJQ-GdGXzWO_rVunsZr1FDmdtvzYtnV_fcf7RYdf48DrYSa5rA-80b_
ujcv8BA9OVJ8WFWFmvyPykfAGPxiDTAuK1lR3p9CZ8Myot8DYj59UbF30-uLtmlUmCq6S
.5vd0ehw4cKTq7iyxXqEvtQ

Like a JWS object, a JWE object can be passed between applications in HTTP headers and URL query parameters, so it uses only characters that are legal in URL and HTTP header values. Each part of the JWE object is encoded as a Base64 string separated by a period. The JWE object shown earlier has the initialization vector and authenticated tag in bold so you can easily spot the various components that make up a JWE. Put that value in JWT Debugger. You won't be able to see the content of this object because it's encrypted.

This example JWE is encrypted with AES-GCM using a 256-bit key. It doesn't use the optional encrypted key component, which is why there are two periods before the boldface initialization vector. The following snippet describes the JWE header:

```
eyJlbmMiOiJBMjU2R0NNIiwiYWxnIjoiZGlyIn0
```

This header decodes to the following JSON object:

```
{
  "enc": "A256GCM",
  "alg": "dir"
}
```

The combination of the `enc` and `alg` fields provides enough detail for an application to decrypt this JWE. This JWE object has no encrypted key, so there's no content between the second and third dots. The initialization vector is `bt9LbkMg4oPbsm-l`. This initialization vector corresponds to the random sequence of bytes given by the hex string `6edf4b6e4320e283dbb26fa5`. The ciphertext is given by the following Base64-encoded string:

```
CrF8Dq9pvvzq2grnkI99RtwUpb5geJQ-
GdGXzWO_rVunsZr1FDmdtvzYtnV_fcf7RYdf48DrYSa5rA-
80b_ujcv8BA9OVJ8WFWFmvyPykfAGPxiDTAuK1lR3p9CZ8Myot8DYj59UbF30-uLtmlUmCq6S
```

The plaintext version of the JWE payload ciphertext is the `refunds.json` content we've been using since chapter 4:

```
[ {
  "orderId" : "5555555555554444",
  "amount" : 500
}, {
  "orderId" : "4012888888881881",
  "amount" : 250
} ]
```

The authentication tag is given by the string `5vd0ehw4cKTq7iyxXqEvtQ`, which decodes to a set of bytes given by the hex string `"e6f7747a1c3870a4eaee2cb15ea12fb5"`.

A JWE object can be represented as a JSON object with fields rather than the Base64 compact format. But we don't cover the JWE JSON serialization format because it isn't used with the various security protocols we discuss in the rest of the book.

11.5.2 Creating and verifying JWE objects

JWE is widely supported, with multiple implementations in Java and other programming languages. Therefore, it's easy to create a JWE in a Node.js application and pass it to a Spring Boot Java-based microservice that can decrypt it easily by using one of the many Java libraries that support JWE.

Nimbus is a popular, easy-to-use, open source Java library for working with the various JOSE standards. Spring Security uses Nimbus to support OIDC and OAuth2 login.

The JWS object in the preceding section was created in the following listing. We use project ssfd_ch11_ex3 to demonstrate working with JWEs using Nimbus in a Java app.

Listing 11.4 Creating a JWE object encrypted with AES-GCM

```
public String buildCompactJWE(String payload, byte[] keyBytes)
  throws Exception {
                                           Build the header where we decide also
  JWEHeader header =                  ◁─┘  the algorithms to use (AES 256 with GCM).
    new JWEHeader.Builder(JWEAlgorithm.DIR, EncryptionMethod.A256GCM)
          .contentType("application/json")
          .build();
                                           Create the full JWE object
  JWEObject jweObject =               ◁─┘  (header and payload).
    new JWEObject(header, new Payload(payload));
                                           Encrypt
  jweObject.encrypt(new DirectEncrypter(keyBytes));  ◁─┘ the data.

  return jweObject.serialize();       ◁─┐ Serialize to generate the
}                                         │ final Base64 encoded JWE.
```

Creating a JWE object with a payload encrypted with AES-GCM and a 256-bit key is easy when you use Nimbus classes to work with JWE:

- `JWEHeader` is the Java representation of a JWE header.
- `Payload` represents the cleartext payload that will be inserted into the JWE.
- `JWEObject` is a combination of a header and payload. It contains methods that encrypt, serialize, parse, and decrypt the payload.
- `DirectEncrypter` is a Nimbus object that calls the Java cryptography libraries to perform encryption. It hides the complexity of using the `javax.crypto` libraries correctly.

Notice that the code in listing 11.4 is much simpler than using the `java.crypto` library directly, as we did in part 2 of this book. We don't have to worry about generating an initialization vector or configuring the AES-GCM algorithm because those tasks are handled by the Nimbus framework when we select the `EncryptionMethod.A256GCM` configuration for the JWE encryption algorithm.

Also, we don't have to write any code to output the metadata required to decrypt the ciphertext later. Another benefit is that we don't have to document the data format for any consumer who wants to decrypt the JWE. The following listing shows the code to decrypt the JWE.

Listing 11.5 Decrypting a JWE object encrypted with AES-GCM

```
public String decryptCompactJWE(String compactJWE, byte[] keyBytes)
  throws Exception {
                                                        Parse the JWE string
  JWEObject jweObject = JWEObject.parse(compactJWE);  ◁─┘ into Java object.
```

```
    jweObject.decrypt(new DirectDecrypter(keyBytes));

    Payload payload = jweObject.getPayload();
    return payload == null ? null : payload.toString();
}
```

> ◁─┐ **Decrypt the JWE object using the private key.**
>
> ├── **Extract the clear text payload and return it.**

The JWEObject.parse() method takes a standard JWE Base64-encoded string and turns it into a Java object. The DirectDecrypter class decrypts the payload ciphertext. The next listing shows how to call the encrypt and decrypt operations in the Main class to demonstrate how they work.

Listing 11.6   Demonstrating encryption and decryption for JWE

```
public class Main {
  public static void main(String[] args) {

    try {
      ResourceReader reader = new ResourceReader();
      String json = reader.readResourceAsString("refunds.json");

      byte[] keyBytes = new byte[32];
      new SecureRandom().nextBytes(keyBytes);

      JweBuilder jweBuilder = new JweBuilder();
      String compactJWE = jweBuilder.buildCompactJWE(json, keyBytes);

      System.out.println(compactJWE);

      String decrypted =
        jweBuilder.decryptCompactJWE(compactJWE, keyBytes);

      System.out.println(decrypted);
    } catch (Exception e) {
      e.printStackTrace(System.err);
    }
  }
}
```

Annotations:
- **Reading the content of the refunds.json file**
- **Generating a random secret key (in real-world the key is read from a vault)**
- **Generating the JWE**
- **Printing the JWE in the console**
- **Decrypting the JWE**
- **Printing the decrypted content in the console**

When we talk about cryptography, we usually think about four main security goals: making sure that data isn't changed by accident or on purpose (integrity), checking who created or sent the data (authentication), keeping the content secret (confidentiality), and preventing someone from denying that they sent the data (nonrepudiation). Different algorithms help us reach these goals in different ways. Table 11.2 shows how JWS with HMAC (HS256) and JWE with direct encryption (DIR) meet these goals.

Table 11.2   Cryptography goals and algorithms matrix

Goal	JWS-HS256	JWE DIR encryption
Integrity	Yes	Yes
Authentication	Yes	Yes

Table 11.2   Cryptography goals and algorithms matrix *(continued)*

Goal	JWS-HS256	JWE DIR encryption
Confidentiality	No	Yes
Non-repudiation	No	No

11.5.3 Exercises

11   What additional cryptographic goal does JWE provide compared with JWS?

12   List the four components of a JWE object.

13   In the example, why is the encrypted key part missing?

14   What is the role of the authentication tag in JWE?

11.6 JWT

JWT (https://tools.ietf.org/html/rfc7519) is a standard for signed or encrypted security tokens used by OIDC. We'll talk a lot about the OIDC protocol and OAuth2 (the framework on which OIDC relies) in chapters 12 and 13. A JWT object can be a JWS object or a JWE object with the following requirements (figure 11.6):

- The payload must be a JSON object.
- The payload JSON can have standard fields called claims, such as sub, which is defined as the ID of the user to whom the token belongs.

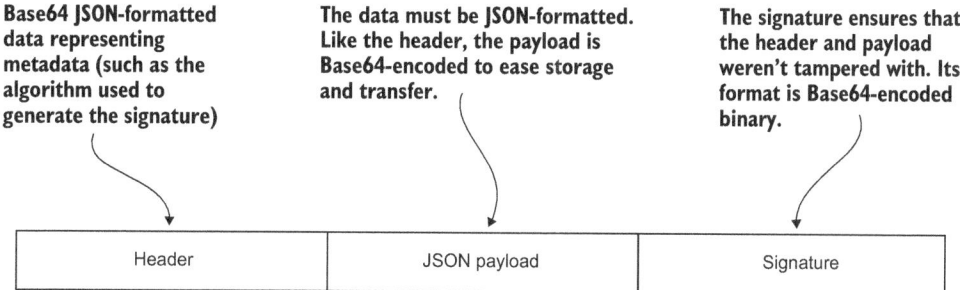

Figure 11.6   A JWT object can be a JWS object with the added restriction that the payload must be a JSON object.

The primary difference between a JWT and a JWE or JWS object is that a JWT object must have a JSON payload. JWE and JWS can have any type of data as a payload. The relationship among JWT, JWE, JWS, and JWK is illustrated in figure 11.7.

Our coverage of JWT, JWS, and JWE uses algorithms that require a secret to be shared between the producer and consumer of the JWT. In chapter 12, we'll discuss public key cryptography and see how to use JWS and JWE without the overhead of sharing a key. Computer security is a complex, challenging topic, so we'll continue breaking security into digestible topics.

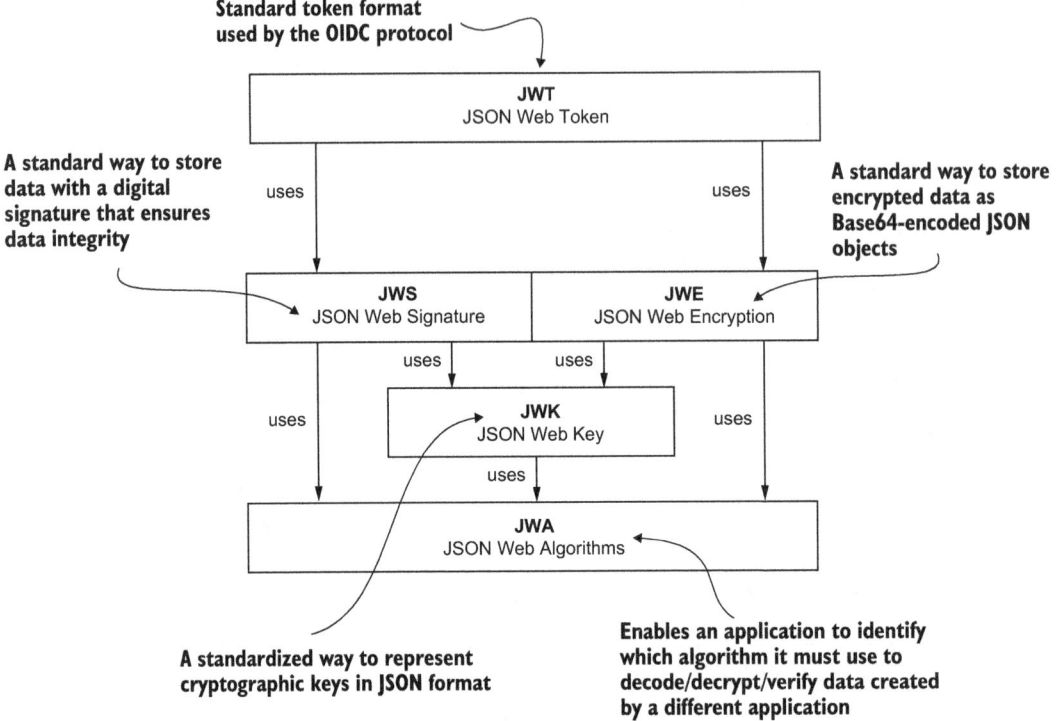

Figure 11.7   The collection of standards. JWT builds on top of the JWE and JWS standards. JWT is the token format for the OIDC standard.

Common criticisms of JWS, JWE, and JWT

The JOSE and JWT standards have come under heavy criticism from security experts. The main point of criticism is that the JWT, JWS, and JWE standards provide too many configuration options, some of which disable security features such as signature validation. This makes JWT, JWS, and JWE easy for developers to use incorrectly. Too much flexibility in a security standard leads to complex implementations that can be buggy and contain security vulnerabilities.

The JWS specification, for example, allows the alg field in the header to be set to the value none, thus bypassing signature validation. A hacker can intercept a JWS object, change the alg field to none, modify the payload, and forward the request. Because alg:none is a valid option, many JWS libraries accept the unsigned JWS as valid, thus bypassing security.

Developers must configure JWS libraries to reject none as a valid alg option. But many don't, which has led to numerous real-world vulnerabilities over the years even though the problem is well known.

11.6.1 Exercises

15 How is a JWT related to JWS and JWE?

16 What restriction does a JWT payload have compared with JWS and JWE?

17 Give an example of a standard claim in a JWT.

18 What is one major criticism of the JWT, JWS, and JWE standards?

11.7   Exercise answers

1 Why do we need standardized names for cryptographic algorithms?

Standardized names ensure interoperability between applications built by different teams and prevent confusion caused by inconsistent naming.

2 Give two examples of JWA identifiers, and explain what they mean.

Example 1: A256GCM means AES encryption with a 256-bit key in Galois/Counter mode. Example 2: ES384 means an Elliptic Curve Digital Signature Algorithm (ECDSA) using the NIST P-384 curve and SHA-384.

3 What organization maintains the registry of JWA identifiers?

IANA maintains the JWA registry.

4 What problem does JWK solve compared with storing keys as hex strings?

JWK provides a standard JSON-based way to represent complex keys, making them easier to share between applications and organizations.

5 What does the `kid` field represent in a JWK?

`kid` stands for key ID and uniquely identifies the key.

6 Why is representing keys in JSON format useful in distributed systems?

JSON is a widely supported human-readable format, which makes it easier to exchange and use keys across different platforms and languages.

7 What are the three main parts of a JWS object?

The three parts are the header (algorithm and metadata), payload (the data), and signature.

8 How is a JWS different from the HMAC-based approach in chapter 4?

JWS wraps the payload and signature into a single standardized format, making the exchange easier and more interoperable than managing separate files.

9 What vulnerability is associated with the `alg:none` option in JWS?

If `alg:none` is accepted, it bypasses signature validation, allowing attackers to tamper with the payload undetected.

10 In the ACME refund scenario, what does JWS guarantee?

JWS guarantees integrity (the data wasn't changed) and authenticity (it came from the warehouse).

11 What additional cryptographic goal does JWE provide compared with JWS?

JWE provides confidentiality by encrypting the payload.

12 List the four components of a JWE object.

The four components are the header, encrypted key (optional), ciphertext (payload), and authentication tag.

13 In the example, why is the encrypted key part missing?

The example uses `alg:dir` (direct encryption), which means that both parties already share the content encryption key, so no encrypted key is necessary.

14 What is the role of the authentication tag in JWE?

The authentication tag ensures that the encrypted data hasn't been tampered with.

15 How is JWT related to JWS and JWE?

A JWT object is either a JWS or JWE object with the added requirement that the payload must be a JSON object.

16 What restriction does a JWT payload have compared with JWS and JWE?

JWT payloads must always be JSON; JWS and JWE payloads can be any type of data.

17 Give an example of a standard claim in a JWT.

The sub claim identifies the subject (e.g., user ID) of the token.

18 What is one major criticism of the JWT, JWS, and JWE standards?

The standards are considered overly flexible, offering insecure options such as alg:none, which can lead to vulnerabilities if they're misused.

Summary

- JOSE is a suite of standards used to represent cryptographic algorithms, keys, signed content, and encrypted content as JSON objects.

- JOSE is widely used and has excellent support in many programming languages, but it has faced some criticism for unnecessary complexity in the standard that makes it easy to misuse. Watch out for the JWS `alg:none` vulnerability in any application or library you use.

- JWS is an industry-standard data format for signed data. It has a JSON metadata header, a payload that can have any format, and a signature to validate that the payload and header weren't tampered with.

- JWS supports signatures with MACs, which we cover in this chapter, and digital signatures, which we'll cover in a future chapter.

- JWE is an industry-standard data format for representing encrypted data in JSON. It supports AES and has many implementations in different programming languages.

- JWK is used to represent cryptographic keys as JSON objects.

- JWA is used to define the various algorithms used by JWS, JWE, and JWK.

- Always consult your information-security team to make sure you're using corporate-recommended configurations of common cryptographic algorithms.

- The examples in this book are optimized for educational value. They take shortcuts to make the code fit on the page and to emphasize the concepts. Don't copy and paste the sample code blindly; you must make it production-ready before you use it.

Single-sign on using OAuth2 and OpenID Connect

This chapter covers

- Defining single sign-on
- Applying OAuth2 and OpenID Connect

Suppose that over the years, Acme Inc. has experienced phenomenal growth, expanding both its business and customer base. As the company flourished, so did its number of employees and the demand for its services. Both employees and customers rely on various applications provided by the enterprise to interact with the company.

For employees, managing multiple sets of credentials for different applications throughout the workday is inconvenient and inefficient. Likewise, customers prefer the convenience of using their existing social media login credentials when accessing ACME, Inc.'s online store.

Simple applications may manage user credentials independently. But as systems expand and become more complex, strategies for handling authentication and authorization must evolve accordingly. In this chapter, we explore how large-scale systems implement authentication and authorization effectively.

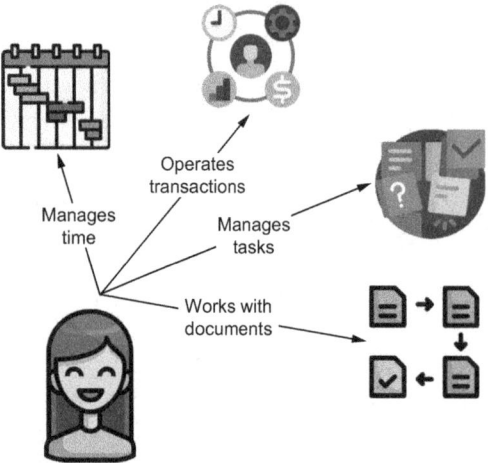

Figure 12.1   Jeanny uses multiple apps as part of her daily work routine, requiring her to authenticate in to each one individually every day.

Figure 12.1 shows Jeanny, an ACME employee. Throughout her workday, she uses several applications to manage documents, transactions, work hours, and more. She finds it inefficient to log in to each app separately and would prefer a single set of credentials so she won't have to remember multiple usernames and passwords.

Figure 12.2 shows Patrick, a typical ACME customer. Like many others, he uses multiple platforms to shop online, buy tickets, watch movies, and more. He prefers a centralized way to manage his credentials, eliminating the need to remember different usernames and passwords for each app. Because he already has a Gmail account, he'd like to use it to authenticate across all these platforms.

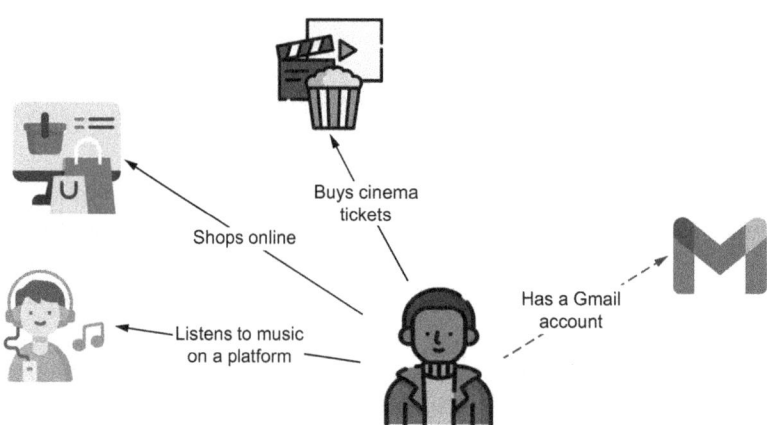

Figure 12.2   Patrick shops online, listens to music on various platforms, and purchases tickets for shows and movies, all using different apps and websites. Because he already has a Gmail account, he prefers to authenticate across these services using his Gmail credentials.

In this chapter, we'll help both Jeanny and Patrick. Section 12.1 discusses how to separate authentication responsibility in an identity provider (IdP)—an application that manages credentials and supports other apps that authenticate individuals.

After you have a solid understanding of this design, you'll dive into two of the most commonly used authentication flows: authorization code and client credentials. Then you'll apply this new approach to the ACME application.

12.1 Splitting security data-management responsibilities

In this section, we explore how to decouple authentication from the other responsibilities of an app so that multiple apps can rely on a single trusted app for authentication. This approach aligns with Jeanny's and Patrick's goals, enabling users to authenticate through a unified trusted app.

Figure 12.3 shows how to separate the authentication responsibility into another app, which we'll call the IdP. In some cases, people also refer to it as an authorization server, but to stay consistent throughout this book, we'll call it the IdP.

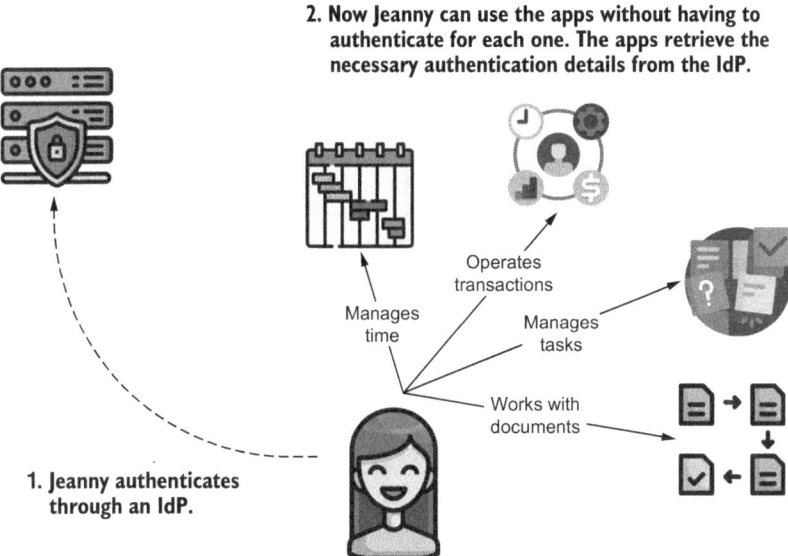

2. Now Jeanny can use the apps without having to authenticate for each one. The apps retrieve the necessary authentication details from the IdP.

Operates transactions

Manages time

Manages tasks

Works with documents

1. Jeanny authenticates through an IdP.

Figure 12.3   Before accessing an app, the IdP authenticates the user. The other apps rely on it to provide the details required to authorize the user for the specific features they offer.

Figure 12.3 shows the two steps that the user follows to authenticate and access either app:

1 Authenticates through the IdP, where authentication capabilities are centralized.
2 Access either app already authenticated by the IdP.

We'll address Patrick's concerns similarly. In his case, Gmail serves as the IdP. The app he uses must offer multiple authentication options. Typically, apps allow authentication via various social media platforms or email services, such as Facebook, X, Google, and LinkedIn (figure 12.4).

1. Patrick authenticates through Gmail.

Listens to music on a platform

Shops online

Buys cinema tickets

2. Now Patrick can use his favorite online services. These services will identify him through Gmail, which is his IdP.

Figure 12.4 **Authenticating using a known social media account. Patrick uses his Google credentials to sign in to multiple apps. In this case, Google acts as the IdP. The other apps he uses are designed to let users authenticate with their Google credentials. Generally, apps offer multiple authentication options, including social media platforms and email services.**

But how does one app know that another app has authenticated a user properly, and how does it retrieve the necessary details about that user? Because we've separated the authentication responsibility into a different app, we also need a mechanism that enables the authentication service to communicate with the other apps that rely on it.

Let's start by discussing the most common approach to implementing this authentication design: using tokens and cryptographic keys. You may want to review chapter 11, which covers JOSE standards and asymmetric key encryption, because the following discussion builds directly on those concepts.

After we cover the most common approach, we'll provide details on other variations of this design that work slightly differently. We'll compare these methods to show when to apply them in real-world scenarios.

For now, we'll focus on tokens and keys. Figure 12.5 illustrates the three steps that occur when Jeanny wants to use a feature in her time-management application for her daily tasks. Because she's just starting her workday, she hasn't had a chance to authenticate. Her time-management app redirects her to the company's IdP, which handles authentication for all the common apps that employees use. The following things happen:

1 Jeanny uses her credentials to authenticate with the IdP.

2 The IdP provides a token that plays the role of an access card.

3 The app uses the token (access card) to prove to the time-management app that she has authenticated, providing all the details the app needs for authorization.

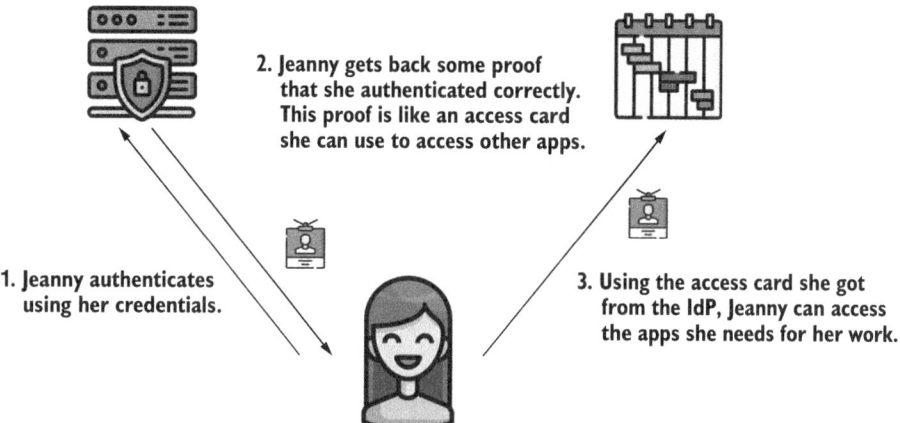

2. Jeanny gets back some proof that she authenticated correctly. This proof is like an access card she can use to access other apps.

1. Jeanny authenticates using her credentials.

3. Using the access card she got from the IdP, Jeanny can access the apps she needs for her work.

Figure 12.5   The user authenticates with the IdP, which issues a token. This token serves as proof of the user's identity and successful authentication.

We can imagine the questions running through your mind:

- How long can the token be used?
- How does the time-management app verify that the token is valid?
- Can someone steal the token and misuse it?

Don't worry; we've got you covered. We'll build on what we've discussed so far, and by the end of the chapter, we'll have answered all these questions.

12.1.1 Exercises

1 What is single sign-on (SSO)?

2 What is an IdP?

3 Why do we separate authentication into its own app?

12.2 Using authentication flows

This section further explores authentication to fill in the gaps and give you a complete understanding of this design. It covers OAuth 2, OpenID Connect (OIDC), and grant types to give you a clear picture of how one app can rely on another to authenticate its users.

To keep things simple, think of OAuth 2 as a set of guidelines (more formally, a specification) for implementing authentication and authorization. You can find the full specification at https://datatracker.ietf.org/doc/html/rfc6749. OIDC is a protocol built on top of OAuth 2; the details are outlined at https://mng.bz/wZG7. Let's walk through the essential details.

Section 12.1 covers IdPs and the separation of authentication from an app's other responsibilities. The OAuth 2 specification introduces the resource server—a fancy term for your app's backend, which handles all the business logic and identifies the user to apply the appropriate security restrictions through authorization.

The client is the app that users interact with directly. It could be a web page running in your browser that connects to a backend (resource server) to handle data, or it could be a mobile app running on your iOS or Android device.

These four main actors interact to define the authentication flow:

- *User*—Person who uses the application
- *Client*—Application used directly by the user, such as a page in a web browser or a mobile application
- *IdP*—Server responsible for authentication and management of user and client details
- *Resource server*—Backend application whose resources (usually endpoints) are consumed by the client

12.2.1 *The authorization code grant type*

This section discusses the most commonly used OAuth 2 authentication flow: the authorization code grant type. A grant type is a sequence of steps that allows a client app to access backend data on behalf of a user or independently when no user is involved. Section 12.2.3 covers the client credentials grant type, which allows an app to authenticate without user involvement. We'll also discuss tokens in detail and show how they're used as access cards.

Figure 12.6 shows the steps involved in the authorization code grant type. The figure shows the four main OAuth 2 actors: user, client, IdP, and resource server. Suppose that Jeanny wants to view her shopping list on the ACME website. She attempts to access her account, but because she hasn't authenticated yet, she has to verify her identity first.

Let's examine the steps in figure 12.6 to see what happens there:

1 The user (Jeanny) wants to access data from the backend, so she asks the client (the app she's using) to display her shopping list. To retrieve the shopping list from the backend, the client needs to know who the user is and prove to the backend that the user has verified their identity.

2 Because Jeanny hasn't authenticated yet, the client redirects her to the IdP login page in a browser. The dotted arrows in the figure represent these redirects.

3 Facing the IdP's login page, Jeanny fills in her credentials and logs in. We'll assume that she entered her username and password correctly.

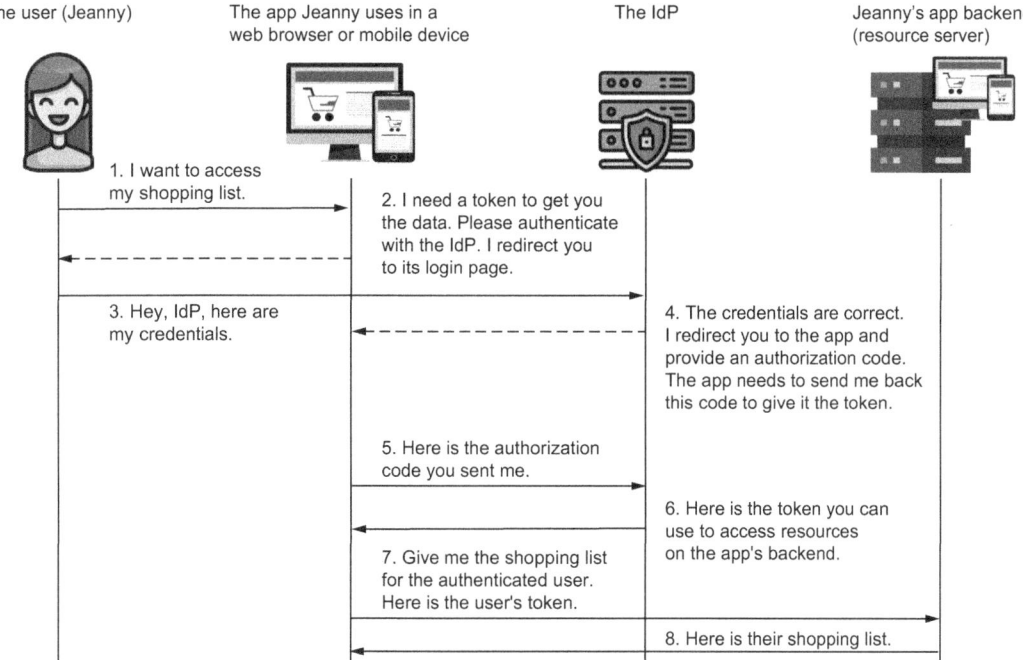

Figure 12.6   The authorization code grant type. The user verifies their identity to access and work with data managed by the app's backend.

4   After Jeanny enters her credentials correctly, the IdP authenticates her. Then the IdP generates a unique, one-time-use code called an authorization code (hence the name of this grant type). The client can use this code to retrieve an access token—the access card it needs to prove to the resource server that Jeanny has authenticated. The IdP redirects back to the client, providing the authorization code during the redirect (dotted arrow in the figure).

5   The client sends the authorization code back to the IdP and asks for the access token.

6   The IdP responds with an access token.

7   The client uses the access token to send requests to the backend (the resource server).

8   The backend responds to the client's requests.

Great! The client receives the access token and uses it to send requests to the resource server. But how does the resource server know that the token is authentic and that no one has tampered with or replaced it?

Let's revisit the concepts covered in chapters 6 and 7. The most common approach today is to sign the token using a cryptographic public-private key pair. As you'll recall, the private key is used to sign the data, and only the entity authorized to sign it has this private key (hence the term private). Then anyone who has the corresponding public key can validate that the data hasn't been tampered with.

In this case, the IdP is the authorized entity responsible for generating access tokens. It signs the tokens it creates and makes its public keys available so that anyone can validate the tokens it issued.

Figure 12.7 explains this process, which corresponds to steps 7 and 8 in figure 12.6. The client sends a request to the resource server, including an access token to prove that the user has authenticated. The resource server must verify that the access token is valid. To do this, it requests the public key from the IdP to validate the token's signature. The IdP provides the public key, and the resource server uses it to confirm the token's authenticity before responding to the client.

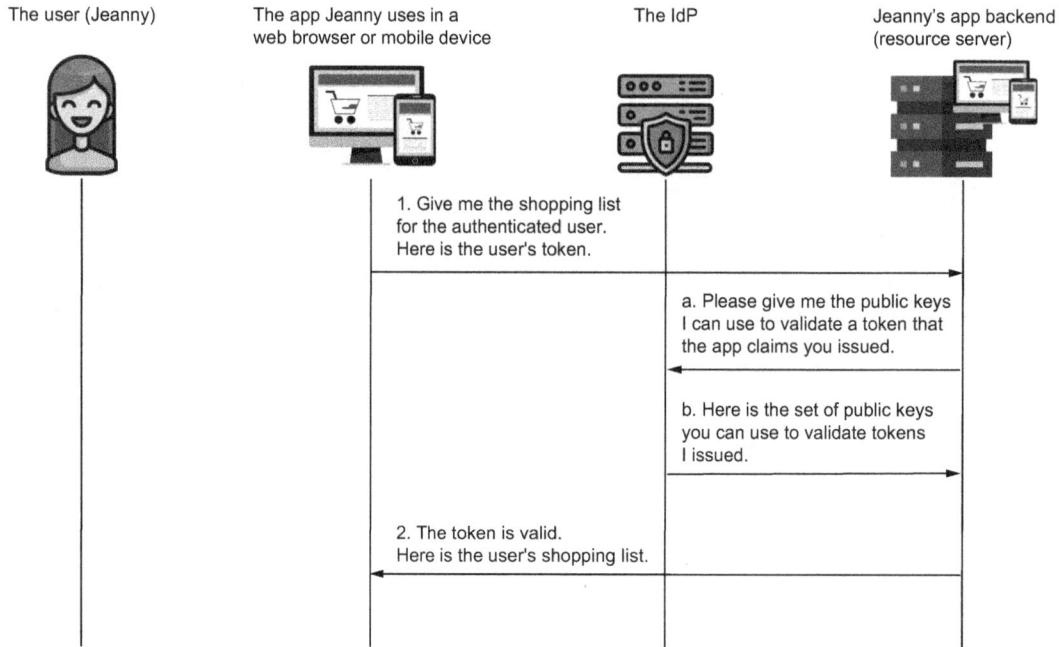

Figure 12.7   Verifying the authenticity of a signed token. When the resource server receives a signed token, it uses a public key to validate the token. The resource server obtains this public key from the IdP, allowing it to verify that the token is valid.

You may have noticed that we used the plural form keys in figure 12.7. Typically, an IdP maintains multiple key pairs and randomly selects one each time it signs a token. This approach enhances security. If one of the private keys were compromised, it wouldn't affect all the access tokens the IdP has generated.

When the IdP generates a new access token, it also stores a unique identifier for the key pair used to sign the token. The resource server uses this identifier to determine which public key it needs to validate the token.

The implicit grant type legacy

The authorization code grant type is challenging for almost everyone when they first encounter it. If you found it difficult and had to review the figures and steps multiple times, you're human.

But like many others, when you start to understand the flow better, a question might come to mind: Why doesn't the IdP provide the access token directly? Why complicate the process by sending an authorization code and then requiring it to be sent back in exchange for the actual access token?

The following figure illustrates the implicit grant type. Notice in step 4 that the redirect provides the access token directly rather than an authorization code. Compare this figure with figure 12.6 to see the differences.

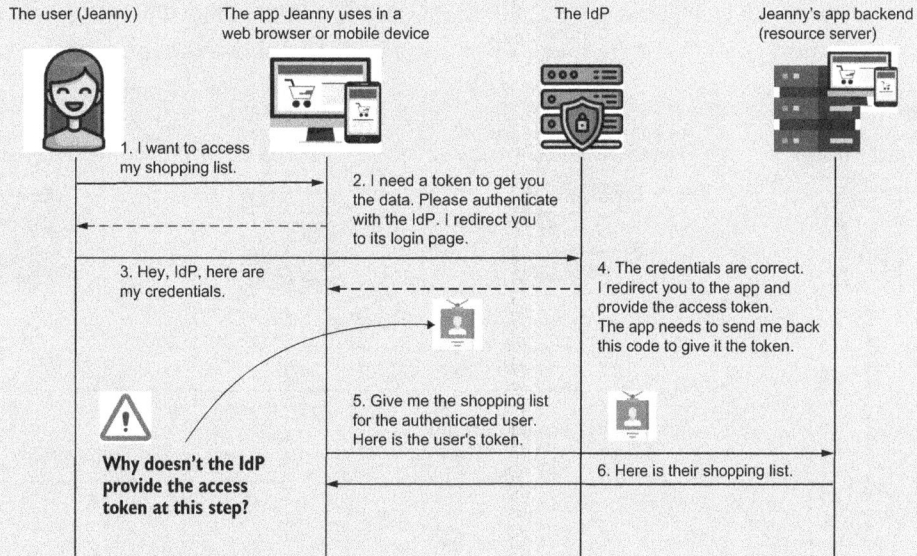

The implicit grant type. After the user authenticates, the IdP redirects back to the client and directly provides an access token. This flow is simpler but more vulnerable to access-token leakage.

If you think of this as an improvement in the flow, excellent: you've discovered the implicit grant type. Unfortunately, this grant type, as it's considered vulnerable and has been deprecated. But what makes this flow vulnerable, and why does the additional authorization code step solve the issues?

The key point to remember is that step 4 involves a redirect in the browser. Because of the redirect, the token in the implicit flow is passed through the URL. Keep in mind that the token acts as an access card and shouldn't be shared. This approach has several problematic aspects:

(continued)

1   The URL can be easily forwarded to a different site.
2   The URL might be stored in the browser history, making the token available this way to browser plugins as well.
3   The URL might be exposed in logs together with the access token.

All these issues make the authentication flow vulnerable—a risk we refer to as access-token exposure. Our goal is to eliminate this vulnerability. By using the authorization code, the IdP sends the token back in an HTTP response, not through a redirect, thereby addressing the problems outlined in this sidebar.

A second approach to validating an access token is token introspection. In this method, the resource server directly queries the IdP to verify the token. The resource server sends the token to the IdP and asks whether it's valid. The IdP responds by confirming or denying the token's validity. Figure 12.8 shows the introspection approach.

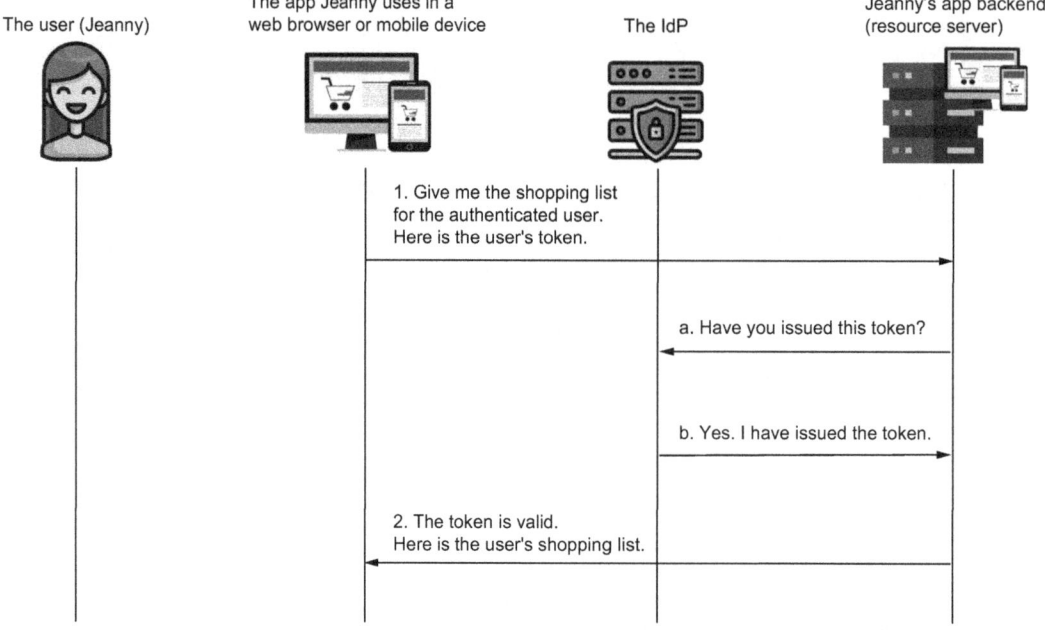

Figure 12.8   Token introspection. When a token isn't cryptographically signed, the resource server must query the IdP directly to validate the token. This process is known as token introspection.

Although introspection may seem simpler from a logical standpoint (just ask the entity that generated the token whether it's valid), it has a few disadvantages:

- The apps become highly coupled with the IdP. If the IdP is down, the apps can't validate tokens.

- Frequent queries to the IdP put additional load on it, requiring more resources and potentially higher scaling.
- Apps exchange access tokens more frequently, increasing the risk of exposure.
- Because each validation requires a new HTTP request, introspection is a slow approach.

12.2.2 What are the tokens?

Our entire discussion in this chapter has focused on how to obtain access tokens—the essential access cards a client needs to access the resources exposed by the resource server. But what are these tokens?

In this section, we dive into access tokens and cover everything you need to know about this crucial component of the OAuth 2/OIDC design. First, we explore how apps use JSON Web Tokens (JWTs) as access tokens. We also discuss scenarios in which other token formats might be used.

We covered JWTs in chapter 11, which discussed the JSON Object Signing and Encryption (JOSE) standard. The next code snippet should remind you of the shape of a signed JWT:

```
eyJhbGciOiJIUzI1NiIsImtpZCI6IjBjN2E5NDdmLWFhYjAtNDFhNS04NWYwLWZiODk4NDM2ZTEzO
SIsInR5cCI6IkpXVCJ9.eyJzdWIiOiIxMjM0NTY3ODkwIiwibmFtZSI6IkpvaG4gRG9lIiwiaWF0I
joxNTE2MjM5MDIyfQ.HqHyNVpW1J1KsN5ECyGflbsYC0wHdjmL1290f8B_wwI
```

A JWT consists of three parts. The first two parts are JSON-formatted data that has been Base64-encoded. The third part is a cryptographic signature, which allows us to verify whether the token has been tampered with and is still valid

The first part, known as the header, typically contains metadata about the token, such as the algorithm used for the cryptographic signature, the key ID, and the token type. The following code snippet shows an example JWT header in JSON format before it has been Base64-encoded:

```
{
  "alg": "HS256",
  "kid": "0c7a947f-aab0-41a5-85f0-fb898436e139",
  "typ": "JWT"
}
```

The next code snippet shows the second part of the JWT, also known as the body or payload. This part typically stores data essential to the authentication process, such as the authenticated user's username, the user's roles, the identifier of the client application that requested the token, and the token's expiration time.

```
{
  "sub": "1234567890",
  "name": "John Doe",
  "iat": 1516239022
}
```

When the system uses JWTs as access tokens, the app's backend has only to verify the token's signature and use the data within the token for authorization. This makes JWTs convenient for the purpose. Access tokens typically expire after a short period—usually an hour or less. This short lifespan makes it difficult for a stolen token to be misused.

In most cases, applications use tokens in the form of JWTs. Although the OAuth 2 specification doesn't mandate a specific token format, the OIDC protocol, which is built on top of OAuth 2, mandates the use of JWTs. Consequently, because most implementations today depend on OIDC, they also employ JWTs.

But some applications that rely solely on the OAuth 2 specification may use tokens in various formats. Generally, tokens are classified as opaque or nonopaque. Non-opaque tokens contain some form of readable information; opaque tokens don't. JWTs are nonopaque tokens because they store data in their header and body. The only way to validate opaque tokens is to use introspection (refer to figure 12.8).

12.2.3 *The client credentials grant type*

In real-world systems, applications often have to communicate with one another. In many instances, these applications must trust the messages they exchange. For this reason, authentication is also used when applications interact. OAuth 2 includes an authentication flow specifically for such scenarios. The client credentials grant type (which we discuss in this section and in more detail in chapter 16) provides a method for services to authenticate one another.

Unlike the authorization code grant type, the client credentials grant type doesn't involve a user. This grant type is used when one application has to authenticate against another without user involvement, such as when two services exchange requests (figure 12.9).

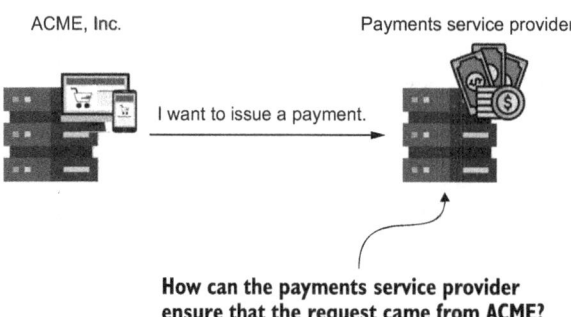

ACME, Inc.

Payments service provider

I want to issue a payment.

How can the payments service provider
ensure that the request came from ACME?

Figure 12.9   Suppose that ACME has to issue payments. In this scenario, the app must communicate with a specialized service known as a payment service provider. This provider must verify that the requests are indeed coming from ACME and that the data wasn't altered during transmission.

You'll find the client credentials grant type significantly less complex than the authorization code grant type. In this flow (figure 12.10), the client, such as the ACME service, authenticates directly with the IdP by using its client credentials. Upon successful authentication, the client receives an access token, which it can use to send requests to the resource server. In this example, the resource server is the payment service provider that ACME uses to issue payments. The IdP in this scenario is an authorization server trusted by the payment service provider,

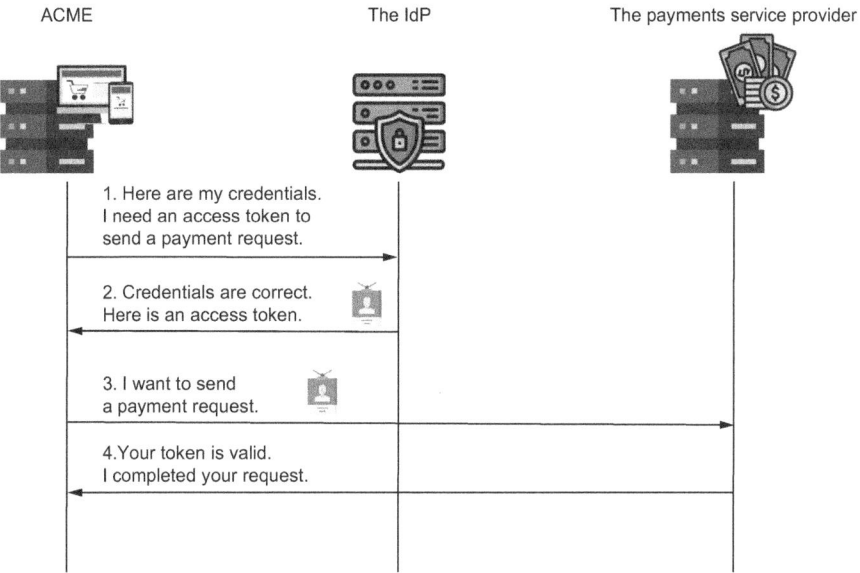

ACME   The IdP   The payments service provider

1. Here are my credentials.
I need an access token to
send a payment request.

2. Credentials are correct.
Here is an access token.

3. I want to send
a payment request.

4. Your token is valid.
I completed your request.

Figure 12.10   ACME authenticates against an IdP and obtains a token. The app uses this token to send requests to another service, which authorizes them.

12.2.4 Exercises

4   What are the four main actors in OAuth2 and OIDC?

5   What is the authorization code grant type?

6   Why not send the token directly in the redirect?

7   What is token introspection?

8   What is an access token?

9   What's the difference between opaque and nonopaque tokens?

12.3 Applying OIDC to ACME

Let's apply the concepts covered in this chapter to our ACME example. We want to ensure that the endpoints our app exposes are protected and require user authentication through an IdP that we provide. For this task, we'll use the Spring authorization server for the IdP implementation and Spring Security to manage endpoint authorization within the app.

Although this book focuses more on security principles than on specific framework implementation details, it doesn't delve deeply into the Spring authorization server or Spring Security. If you're interested in learning more about these frameworks, an excellent starting point is *Spring Security in Action, Second Edition,* by Laurențiu Spilcă (Manning, 2024).

Listing 12.1 demonstrates the IdP configuration. We include a simplified IdP to clarify the necessary configuration and its overall purpose. As shown in this concise YAML file, the IdP requires at least the following:

- *User credentials*—The IdP authenticates the users, so it has to manage their credentials.
- *Client credentials*—The IdP must be able to authenticate and differentiate between the applications it serves as clients. As discussed earlier in this chapter, an IdP might serve multiple apps. The IdP has to recognize and authenticate these apps, which is why the apps (clients) also need their own credentials.

Besides providing the client credentials, you can specify various configurations for each client. This IdP configuration, for example, determines the grant types that the IdP allows for these clients, the redirect URIs that it accepts for the authorization code grant type, and the scopes that the client may request.

Listing 12.1   The authorization code configuration

```
server:
  port: 9000

spring:
  security:
    user:
      name: user                    The definition of a user. The minimum
      password: password            details needed are the user credentials.
    oauth2:
      authorizationserver:          Begins the definition
        client:                     of a client
          oidc-client:
            registration:
              client-id: "oidc-client"        The client credentials needed
              client-secret: "{noop}secret"   for the client authentication
              client-authentication-methods:  The way in which the client needs
                - "client_secret_basic"        to send the credentials to the IdP
              authorization-grant-types:      The grant types the IdP
                - "authorization_code"        supports for this client
              redirect-uris:
                - http://127.0.0.1:8080/login/oauth2/code    The redirect URIs the
              scopes:                                         IdP supports for
                - "openid"       The scopes a client can request    redirection after an
                                                                    user authentication
```

Let's start by setting up this IdP and running some tests. (The IdP implementation is in the acme_identity_provider project.) We'll execute the authorization code grant type ourselves to better understand how it works. Here are the steps we'll follow:

1 Access the OIDC configuration URL to retrieve details about the IdP configuration. This information includes the endpoints that the IdP exposes for client app authorization and access-token issuance.

2 Use a browser to simulate the client's redirection to the IdP, as depicted in point 2 of figure 12.6, which shows the authorization code grant type process.

3 Log in using user credentials to obtain an authorization code, corresponding to point 3 in figure 12.6.

4 Use cURL to send a request to the token endpoint to acquire an access token.

Let's start with step 1 and the IdP's OpenID configuration URL. By default, the OpenID Configuration is available on the /.well-known/openid-configuration path. For our purposes, the server is hosted on localhost on port 9000. The following code snippet shows the full URL:

```
http://localhost:9000/.well-known/openid-configuration
```

You can enter the address in a web browser or use a tool like cURL to send a request. The following snippet is part of the response from the OIDC configuration endpoint. We've truncated this response to highlight the essential details: the authorize endpoint and the token endpoint. These details are crucial for subsequent steps.

```
{
  "issuer": "http://localhost:9000",
  "authorization_endpoint": "http://localhost:9000/oauth2/authorize",     ◁
  "device_authorization_endpoint":
  ➥"http://localhost:9000/oauth2/device_authorization",
  "token_endpoint": "http://localhost:9000/oauth2/token",     ◁
  ...
}
```

> The authorize endpoint. We'll use this endpoint to get an authorization code.

> The token endpoint. We'll use this endpoint to get an access token.

The next step is using the authorization endpoint obtained from the OIDC configuration to retrieve an authorization code. This simulates the process in which the client application redirects the user to the IdP's login page. During this step, the client application must include several essential parameters that allow the IdP to understand the following:

- The grant type the client expects to use
- The identity of the client requesting the authentication
- The URL to which the IdP should redirect the user after a successful authentication
- The scope for which the client is sending the request

The following snippet provides an example of the full request. The response_type parameter is set to code, indicating that the client requests the authorization code flow. The client identifies itself using the client_id parameter. The redirect_uri parameter specifies the URI where the client expects the IdP to redirect the user after successful authentication. The `scope` parameter defines the requested scope, which in this case is `openid`. This request ensures that the client can initiate the authentication flow properly with the required parameters.

```
http://localhost:9000/oauth2/authorize?response_type=code&client_id=oidc-
client&redirect_uri=http://127.0.0.1:8080/login/oauth2/code&scope=openid
```

After the user successfully authenticates, the IdP redirects the user to the Uniform Resource Identifier (URI) specified by the client. Along with the redirection, the IdP provides a unique authorization code that can be used only once. The following snippet illustrates an example of the URI to which the IdP redirects the user. This code is exchanged for an access token in the next step of the authorization process.

```
http://127.0.0.1:8080/login/oauth2/code?code=d8jhmY2i1...
```

In the next step, the app uses the authorization code provided by the IdP to obtain an access token. This step can also be simulated. To act as the client app and retrieve an access token, you must send a request to the access-token endpoint. Similar to the way we retrieved the authorization endpoint, we obtain the access-token endpoint from the IdP's OIDC configuration.

To obtain an access token using the token endpoint, we need to send a `POST` request with the following parameters:

- The `grant_type` parameter is set to `authorization_code`, which informs the IdP that we're using the authorization code grant type. This allows the IdP to expect an authorization code value in the request.
- The `code` parameter holds the authorization code sent by the IdP in the preceding step when redirecting the user back to the client.
- The `redirect_uri` contains the URI to which the IdP sent the authorization code during the redirect.
- The `client_id` identifies the client requesting the access token. This value must match the client for which the authorization code was initially issued.

By providing these parameters, the client can exchange the authorization code for an access token. The next snippet shows the access-token request. You can use cURL or a similar tool to send it. The request uses HTTP Basic authentication by default, with the client credentials (client ID and secret).

> **NOTE** In this example, the authorization code value is truncated for brevity. When you send your request, be sure to include the full authorization code value.

```
curl --location 'http://localhost:9000/oauth2/token' \
--header 'Content-Type: application/x-www-form-urlencoded' \
--header 'Authorization: Basic b2lkYy1jbGllbnQ6c2VjcmV0' \
--data-urlencode 'grant_type=authorization_code' \
```

```
--data-urlencode 'code= d8jhmY2i1…\
--data-urlencode 'redirect_uri=http://127.0.0.1:8080/login/oauth2/code' \
--data-urlencode 'client_id=oidc-client'
```

The following snippet shows the response to the access-token request. The tokens you receive are always in JWT format when you use the OIDC protocol. With OIDC you also receive two distinct tokens:

- An access token, which the app uses for authorization purposes
- An ID token, which contains details about the authenticated user that the resource server may need

These tokens play separate but complementary roles in managing authentication and authorization within the OIDC protocol.

```
{
    "access_token": "eyJraWQiOiJiMzIyODUzNS…",
    "scope": "openid",
    "id_token": "eyJraWQiOiJiMzIyODU…",
    "token_type": "Bearer",
    "expires_in": 299
}
```

In the preceding snippet, the tokens are truncated for brevity. In the next listing, you'll find the Base64-decoded version of the access token. The header includes the key ID (`kid`), which the resource server uses to identify the key required to validate the token. In addition, the token body contains important details about both the user and the client. This decoded information shows how the token is structured and what data it carries for the authorization process.

Listing 12.2 The Base64-decoded access token

```
{
  "kid": "b3228535-0e94-4c8a-8ee9-38cded00323a",    ⟵  Beginning of the
  "alg": "RS256"                                          token's header
}
                                                       The key ID the client uses to
                                                       identify the public key it can
                                                       use to validate the token

                           The token's
                    ⟵   ┘  body start
{
  "sub": "user",                                          ⟵  The user who
  "aud": "oidc-client",      ⟵  ┐ The client to whom the      authenticated
  "nbf": 1727537173,            │ IdP issues the token
  "scope": [
    "openid"
  ],
  "iss": "http://localhost:9000",
  "exp": 1727537473,
  "iat": 1727537173,
  "jti": "15e1912f-57e6-4974-8660-7e240076bc7b"
}
```

12.4   *Exercise answers*

1   What is single sign-on (SSO)?

SSO allows users to log in once and access multiple apps without logging in again—one login, many apps.

2   What is an IdP?

An IdP is a special app that handles authentication for other apps. It checks who you are and issues a token as proof.

3   Why do we separate authentication into its own app?

It makes things more secure and easier to manage, and it allows many apps to reuse the same login logic.

4   What are the four main actors in OAuth2 and OIDC?

The four main actors are the user (you), the client (the app), the IdP, and the resource server (backend that serves data).

5   What is the authorization code grant type?

This grant type is a flow in which the client gets an access token through a secure exchange that uses an authorization code and redirects.

6   Why not send the token directly in the redirect?

Doing that would be unsafe. The token could leak in the browser history or logs. The extra step with the code prevents this problem.

7   What is token introspection?

In token introspection, the backend checks with the IdP to see whether a token is still valid. It's a slow but useful technique when you can't use JWTs.

8   What is an access token?

An access token is a digital pass that lets an app talk to a backend on your behalf. It proves that you're logged in.

9   What's the difference between opaque and nonopaque tokens?

Opaque tokens don't contain data; nonopaque tokens are readable and can be validated without asking the IdP.

Summary

- SSO simplifies user authentication by allowing employees and customers to use a single set of credentials for multiple applications.
- OAuth2 and OIDC are protocols used to implement SSO by separating authentication responsibilities into an IdP.
- Among the authentication flows that the OAuth 2 specification describes, the most used ones are
  - The authorization code grant type is the most common and is used when user interaction is required.
  - The client credentials grant type is used when one application needs to authenticate another without user involvement.

- Using OAuth 2/OIDC implies multiple actors in the authentication flow:
  - The user (e.g., employee or customer)
  - The client (app or service used)
  - The IdP (also known as authorization server; a service offering authentication capabilities to multiple clients)
  - The resource server (app backend that handles data and authorization)
- Tokens are central to OAuth2 and OIDC:
  - Access tokens are used for authorization.
  - ID tokens contain user information.
- JWTs are commonly used for token formatting and include a header (metadata), a payload (user/client details), and a signature for validation.
- Token validation involves cryptographic methods or token introspection, ensuring secure communication between applications.

13

Deepening security with OpenID Connect

This chapter covers

- Boosting security in the authorization code flow
- Simplifying user logins and maintaining sessions with refresh tokens
- Enhancing user identity management
- Implementing multitenancy

As ACME, Inc. grew rapidly, it realized that it needed a better, safer way for users to log in. That's when it decided to set up single sign-on (SSO), which lets users access multiple apps with one login. To do this right, the company had to separate the job of checking who a user is (authentication) from the app that handles the user's data (the backend). This setup makes things safer and easier to manage.

ACME couldn't just make things up as it went along, of course; it needed a solid, trusted system as a guide. That's how it found OAuth 2 and OpenID Connect (OIDC). OAuth 2 is a framework that lets apps get permission as access certain user data without passwords. OIDC builds on OAuth 2 by adding a way to confirm who the user is. Think of OAuth 2 as the pizza crust and OIDC as the delicious cheese and toppings. Who wants plain crust anyway?

In chapter 12, we talked about how OAuth 2 and OIDC work. We covered the way that tokens, such as access tokens and ID tokens, help apps talk to one another securely. We also explained the different ways (called *grant types*) that apps can ask for these tokens. Knowing these steps is key to setting up secure, smooth logins.

In this chapter, we dive deeper into how ACME can use advanced tools such as Proof Key for Code Exchange (PKCE) to make the authorization process more secure, especially for public clients. We also explore how refresh tokens can keep users logged in without asking them to sign in again and again. Then we unpack how OIDC adds an identity layer on top of OAuth 2, providing even more benefits, including user profile information and stronger security measures. With these tools in place, ACME can confidently scale its systems while keeping user accounts safe and the login experience smooth.

13.1   Augmenting the authorization code flow with PKCE

A client must obtain a valid access token to access resources protected by a backend application. This token is acquired through a specific authorization flow: a grant type. In chapter 12, we explored one of the most widely used grant types: the authorization code flow. This grant type is particularly suitable when the client has to access resources on behalf of a user, providing an added layer of security by involving user authentication. Figure 13.1 is a reminder of how this authorization flow operates.

Let's revisit the steps illustrated in figure 13.1. Jeanny, our user, wants to view her shopping list in the ACME shopping app (step 1). Because Jeanny's shopping list contains private information that belongs exclusively to her, the client app must obtain explicit permission to access this data on her behalf. To achieve this, the client redirects Jeanny to authenticate with a trusted authorization server, ensuring that only authorized access to her personal information is granted (step 2).

Jeanny enters her credentials to authenticate with the authorization server (step 3). Upon successful authentication, the authorization server redirects her to the client application, delivering a unique authorization code (step 4). The client app uses this authorization code to securely request and obtain an access token (steps 5 and 6), which grants it permission to access Jeanny's protected data (steps 7 and 8).

You may wonder what would happen if someone somehow got their hands on the authorization code. Fair question. Although it's undoubtedly tricky to get this code, we can't pretend that it's impossible; nothing is foolproof. Typically, because the authorization code is sent directly from the client to the authorization server, the request must also be authenticated using the client's credentials. These credentials are essentially a username and password that the client app uses to prove its identity to the authorization server.

To succeed, an attacker would have to pull off a double heist: intercept the authorization code and get the client credentials to request the access token. Sounds like a tall order, right? Well, here's the catch: client credentials aren't guarded like crown jewels. They're stored within the client app, making them vulnerable if the app isn't well secured, as is likely with a public client. So although this scenario is tough to pull off, it's not a mission impossible (cue the suspenseful music).

This is where PKCE comes to the rescue. With a small tweak to the authorization flow, we can strengthen security significantly. Let's take a moment to analyze the root of the problem. The vulnerability arises between steps 4 and 5 in the flow shown in figure 13.1.

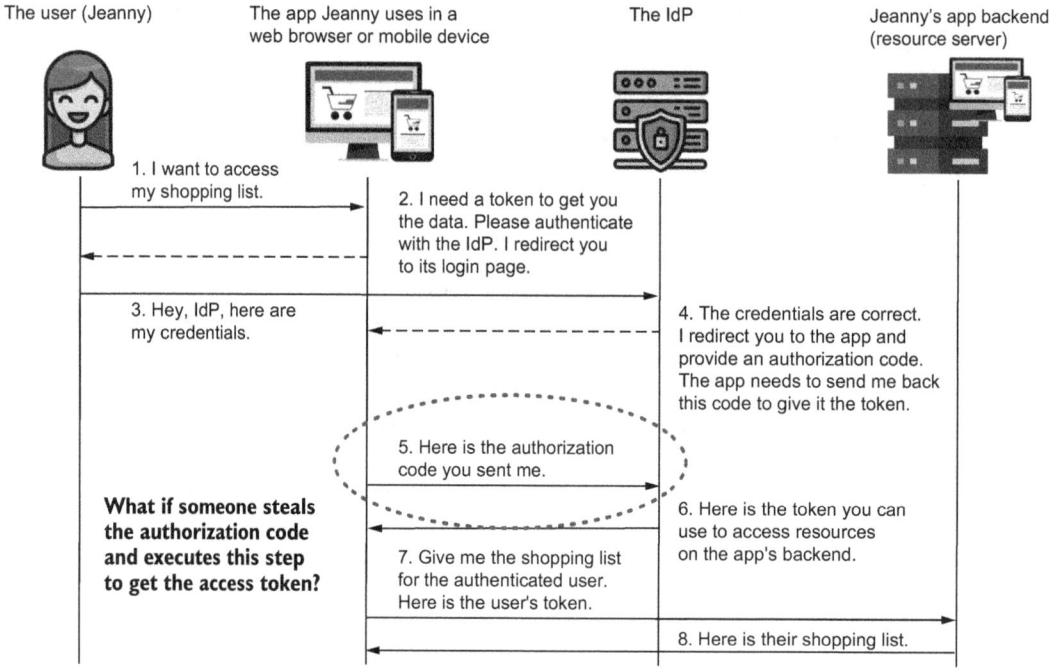

Figure 13.1 The authorization code flow. The client application requests access to resources protected by a backend application (resource server) on behalf of a user. To initiate this process, the client redirects the user to authenticate with a trusted authorization server. Upon successful authentication, the client receives an authorization code, which it exchanges for an access token. With a valid access token, the client can securely access the protected resources hosted by the backend application.

After the user successfully authenticates in step 4, an attacker could intercept the authorization code and use it to impersonate the legitimate client. Then the attacker would have unauthorized access to the user's sensitive resources. Jeanny definitely wouldn't be thrilled about someone snooping through her private shopping list.

Figure 13.2 illustrates the enhancements made in the authorization code flow. To strengthen security, the client performs an additional task before redirecting the user for authentication: it generates a data pair known as the code challenge and the code verifier. This process is straightforward and involves two key steps:

1 Generate the code verifier. The client creates a random piece of data—typically, a byte array—that is Base64-encoded for easier representation and transmission. This random value is called the *code verifier*. At its core, it's simply a unique, unpredictable string.

2 Create the code challenge. The client applies a cryptographic hash function (commonly, SHA-256) to the code verifier to produce the code challenge. (If you need a quick refresher on how hash functions work, see chapter 4.)

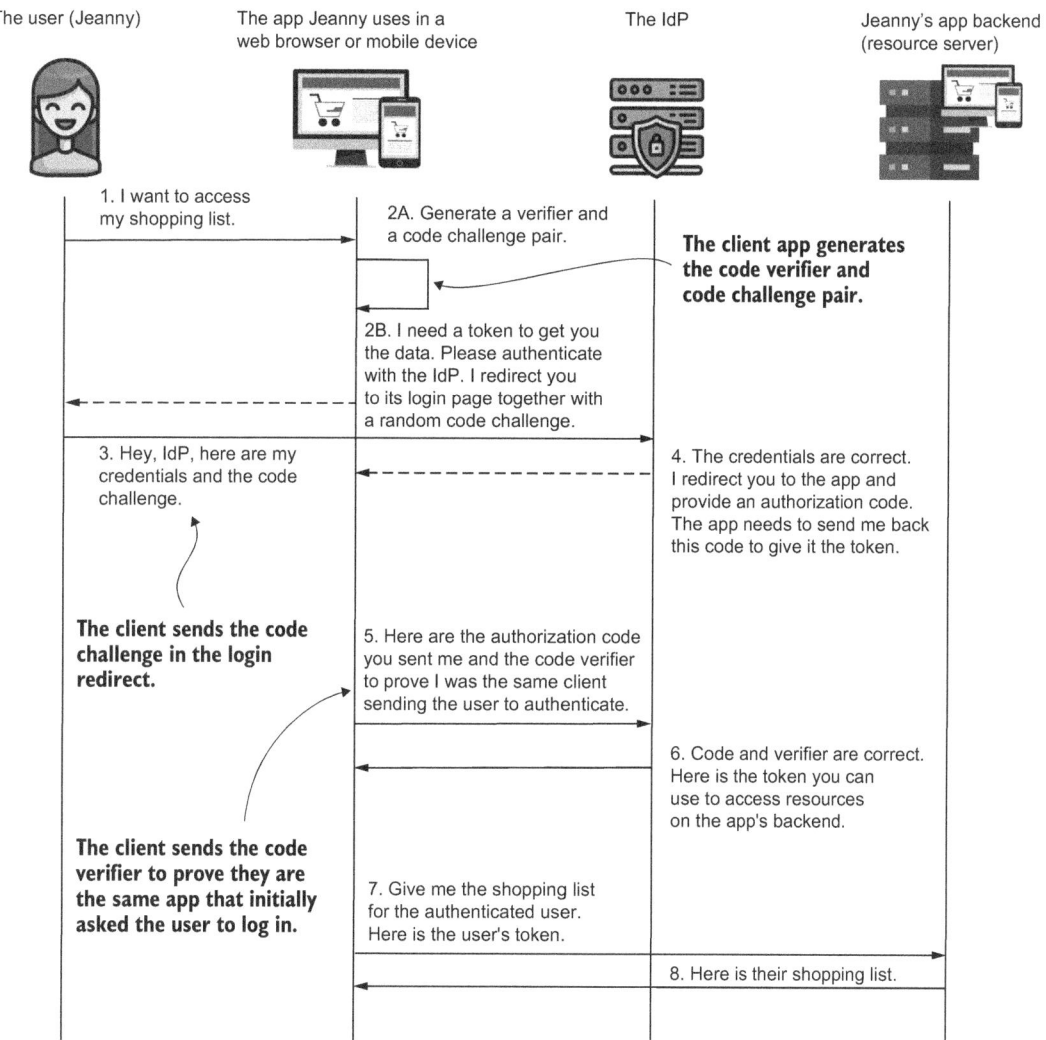

Figure 13.2 PKCE flow. Before initiating the authentication process, the client generates a unique random pair of values: a code challenge and a code verifier. The client uses this pair throughout the authorization flow to enhance security, ensuring that no unauthorized party can intercept or misuse the authentication process by impersonating the user.

In figure 13.2, the generation of the code challenge and code verifier is depicted as step 2A. The crucial part is that the code challenge (the hashed version of the verifier) is sent to the authorization server as part of the user's login redirect (step 3).

The authorization server links the authentication session to that specific code challenge when the user successfully logs in. This association ensures that only the client that possesses the correct code verifier can exchange the authorization code for an access token.

When the client application requests an access token, it must provide the authorization code and the correct code verifier (step 5). Without the valid code verifier, the authorization server will refuse to issue an access token, effectively blocking unauthorized access.

It's important to remember that the code verifier is never transmitted over the network. Only the client application knows this secret value, making it impossible for attackers to intercept or reuse it. Also, the verifier is valid only for the current session. Each new authorization flow generates a fresh, random verifier and challenge, ensuring that every session is uniquely protected.

Can an attacker guess the code verifier from the code challenge (sent during the login redirect)? The answer is a solid no. The code challenge is generated using a cryptographic hash function applied to the code verifier. Cryptographic hash functions are designed to be one-way functions, meaning that it's practically impossible to reverse the process and retrieve the original input from the output. In this case, even if an attacker intercepts the code challenge, they won't be able to derive the code verifier from it.

This property of the hash function ensures that the code challenge alone is useless to any hacker who attempts to exploit the flow. The verifier remains secret and secure, protecting the authorization process from interception and tampering (figure 13.3).

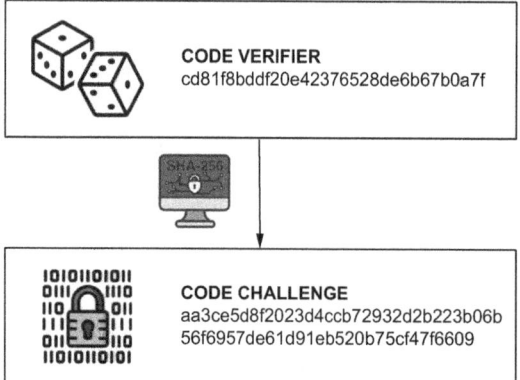

Figure 13.3 Relationship between code verifier and code challenge. The code verifier is a securely generated random value. The code challenge is derived by applying a cryptographic hash function (often, SHA-256) to the code verifier. This one-way transformation strengthens the security of the authorization process by ensuring that the verifier can't be reverse-engineered from the challenge.

PKCE is a highly effective enhancement to the authorization code flow in many scenarios, particularly for public clients, third-party integrations, browser-based applications, and even Internet of Things (IoT) devices. These environments often lack secure storage for client secrets, making them more vulnerable to attacks such as authorization code interception.

Like any security measure, however, PKCE can become unnecessary or even overengineered if it's used in contexts with little to no added value. In private or highly controlled environments, where the risk of attacks on the authorization code flow is minimal, implementing PKCE may not justify the extra complexity.

Also, PKCE is specifically designed to prevent user impersonation by securing user-driven authorization flows. In machine-to-machine (M2M) communication, in which no user is involved and systems exchange credentials securely, PKCE offers little benefit. In such cases, using the client credentials flow with properly managed secrets is more appropriate.

Let's wrap up this section with some key best practices because security is no place for shortcuts:

- Always use PKCE with public clients (such as mobile apps, single-page apps, and IoT devices) to prevent authorization code interception. Without it, you're practically leaving the front door wide open.
- Never disable PKCE where it's supported; seriously, don't do it. OAuth 2.1 now requires PKCE for all authorization code flows, so skipping it is like driving without a seat belt.
- Use SHA-256 for the code challenge instead of the plain method (S256 over plain) for stronger security. Hashing with SHA-256 is like using a steel vault; the plain method is like hiding your keys under the doormat.

Always follow best practices, and keep your apps locked down tighter than a jar of pickles.

13.1.1 Exercises

1 What is PKCE, and why is it important?
2 How does PKCE work?
3 Why is the code challenge secure?
4 When should you use PKCE?

13.2 Using refresh tokens to simplify authentication

Tokens are like keys to the kingdom, unlocking access to resources protected by the backend. But as discussed in chapter 12, leaving those keys valid forever isn't the brightest idea. That's why access tokens are designed to expire after a short period—typically, minutes—to minimize security risks.

But here's the catch: do you really want to force users to log in every 20 minutes? Put yourself in their shoes. After the third login prompt, you'd probably be ready to toss your phone out the window.

How do you strike a balance between keeping tokens secure and keeping users happy? The answer is simple and friendly: use refresh tokens. This section explores how refresh tokens let you maintain security without driving users up the wall.

Figure 13.4 illustrates the refresh-token flow. To use this flow, a client must register with the authorization server to receive refresh tokens. After registration, the client will receive a refresh token alongside every access token it obtains.

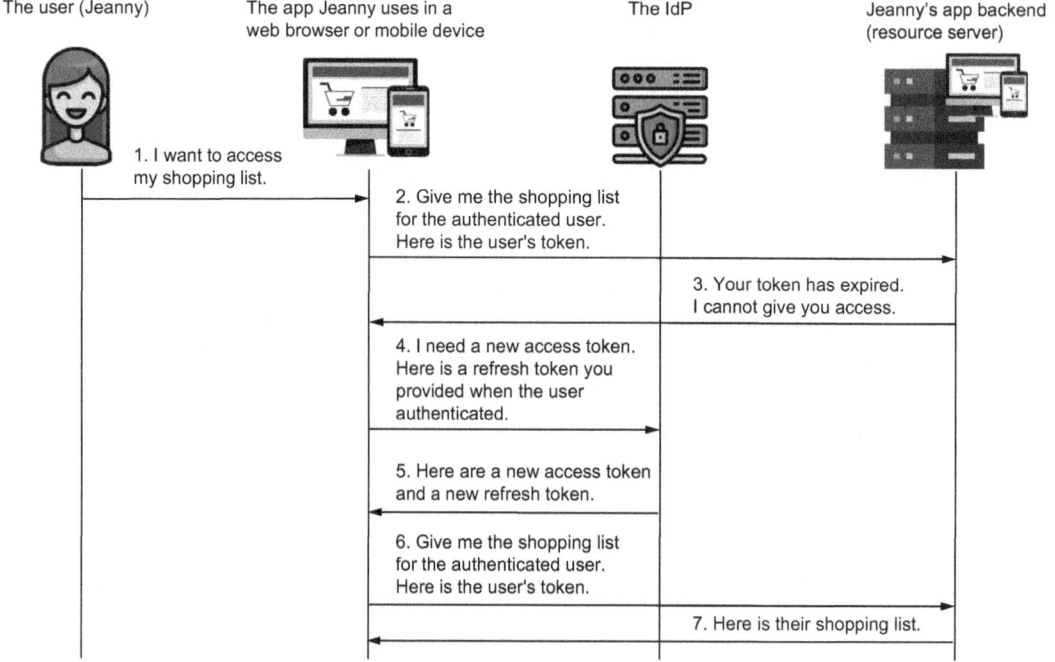

Figure 13.4   The refresh-token flow. When a client is registered to use refresh tokens, it receives both an access token and a refresh token from the authorization server. The client can use the refresh token to seamlessly request a new access token without requiring additional user interaction. This approach maintains security while providing a smooth, uninterrupted user experience.

If you read chapter 12, which demonstrates how to send a request to the /token end-point to obtain an access token, you may recall the structure of the response. The response closely resembles the following example:

```
{
    "access_token": "eyJraWQiOiJiMzIyODUzNS…",
    "scope": "openid",
    "token_type": "Bearer",
    "expires_in": 299
}
```

If the client is registered to receive refresh tokens, the response will be slightly different, as shown in the following snippet. In addition to the access token, the response includes a refresh token, enabling the client to obtain new access tokens without requiring further user authentication. This means that when a user authenticates for the first time using the authorization code flow (with or without PKCE), the client receives both an access token and a refresh token. The refresh token allows the client to request new access tokens without requiring the user to log in again, keeping the experience smooth.

```
{
    "access_token": "eyJraWQiOiJiMzIyODUzNS…",
    "refresh_token": "eaJqaEEiOiKYMzIyODUzPL…",
    "scope": "openid",
    "token_type": "Bearer",
    "expires_in": 299
}
```

> The authorization server provides a refresh token along with the access token.

As shown in figure 13.4, Jeanny is back in the ACME app, ready to check out her carefully curated shopping list. She's authenticated, spent some time browsing through products, and added some fantastic items to her cart, some of them even 40% off! (Who can resist a good sale?) Now she's ready to review her list and proceed to checkout.

But wait—when the client app tries to use the access token, the authorization server rejects it because it's expired. Clearly, Jeanny was on a serious shopping spree.

Asking Jeanny to log in again would kill the vibe. No one wants to type passwords when they're in checkout mode! So instead of disrupting Jeanny's smooth shopping experience, the client app uses the refresh token it received during her first authentication.

The app sends a request to the /token endpoint, this time using the refresh token to ask for a new access token. Because the refresh token is still valid, the authorization server responds with a new access token and a new refresh token. With the new access token in hand, the client app seamlessly retrieves Jeanny's shopping list with no password prompts or interruptions. Jeanny stays happy, and her discount deals stay safe.

We know what you're thinking: this approach might weaken security a little too much. If someone steals a refresh token, could they generate new access tokens endlessly and gain indefinite access?

Although refresh tokens offer significant advantages (as discussed in this section), handling them with care is crucial. Losing one could lead to serious security risks because refresh tokens are typically longer-lived than access tokens.

Don't worry, both OAuth 2.0 and OIDC provide robust mechanisms to secure refresh tokens and minimize potential threats. These mechanisms include secure storage, token binding, refresh token rotation, and prompt revocation strategies designed to make stealing and misusing refresh tokens difficult.

First, we have to consider the type of client we're securing. If the client is confidential, like an internal ACME app used exclusively by the company's employees, the app can store refresh tokens securely because it typically operates in a controlled, secure environment (e.g., backend servers or corporate networks). In this case, managing tokens is much more straightforward.

But extra precautions are necessary if the client is a public application, such as the ACME shopping app that Jeanny uses. Public clients (such as mobile apps and single-page web apps) are more vulnerable because they can't store secrets securely.

In these situations, we strongly recommend pairing refresh tokens with PKCE. This combination adds a critical layer of security by ensuring that only the legitimate client who obtained the refresh token can use it to request new access tokens.

Another crucial point to emphasize is that all communication among the client app, the authorization server, and the resource server must occur over a secure transmission using TLS/SSL (see chapter 11 for a refresher). This encryption ensures that sensitive data—including access tokens, refresh tokens, and user credentials—can't be intercepted or tampered with during transmission. Think of encryption as adding another solid brick to the security wall, making it even harder for attackers to find a way in.

Here are a few additional best practices for managing refresh tokens to keep your app secure and resilient against attacks:

- Minimize scopes. Issue refresh tokens with limited scopes to restrict the level of access they provide. This way, even if a refresh token is compromised, the damage is contained to specific, less-sensitive resources.
- Implement token rotation. Enable refresh-token rotation, in which a new refresh token is issued every time the old one is used and the previous token is invalidated immediately. This makes it much harder for attackers to reuse stolen tokens because the tokens become invalid after a single use.
- Set expiration and enable revocation. Configure refresh tokens with expiration times and allow the authorization server to revoke them if suspicious activity is detected. This reduces the risk of long-term misuse and gives you better control of token life cycles.

13.2.1 Exercises

5   What are refresh tokens for?

6   Why not make access tokens last longer?

7   How do you protect refresh tokens?

13.3 *Supporting identity management with OIDC*

We've explored the fundamentals of how OAuth 2.0 and OIDC function. Now let's dive into why OIDC decided to crash the OAuth 2.0 party and bring its own snacks to make things better. The most important capabilities are

- *Identity layer and ID token*—OIDC adds an identity layer with the ID token, providing a secure and standardized way to authenticate users.
- *The UserInfo endpoint*—OIDC introduces the UserInfo endpoint, which makes it easy for applications to retrieve additional user profile information.
- *Protection against replay attacks and cross-site request forgery (CSRF)*—OIDC strengthens security by using parameters such as nonce and state to prevent replay and CSRF attacks.

- *Session management and logout*—OIDC standardizes session management and logout processes, enabling seamless user sign-in and sign-out experiences across applications.

13.3.1 *The identity layer and ID token*

OAuth 2.0 is a fantastic authorization framework. It hands out access tokens like VIP passes, letting apps access user data without exposing passwords. It's great for saying "Yes, this app can look at your photos" but not so great at answering the question "Who are you, really?"

That's where OIDC steps in. Think of OAuth 2.0 as a bouncer who checks whether you're allowed into the club (figure 13.5). OIDC is the ID scanner that says, "Ah, you're Alex, born July 5th, and here's your loyalty card."

Figure 13.5 OAuth 2.0 is like a bouncer at a club. It checks whether you're allowed to enter but has no idea whether you're a VIP member.

OAuth 2.0 wasn't built for authentication; it's all about authorization. Sure, developers tried bending it to handle authentication, but the process was like using a fork to eat soup. It kind of worked but spilled a lot of data in the process. OIDC was created to fill this gap, officially adding a secure, standardized way to verify who a user is.

Why was OIDC needed? OAuth 2.0 was never meant to answer the question "Who's there?" It handled only "What can they do?" OIDC gives applications both the door keys and the guest list, making authentication smoother, safer, and much less awkward.

Technically speaking, OIDC enhances OAuth 2.0 by introducing an additional token alongside the access token. This new token is the ID token, and its primary purpose is authentication. Whereas the access token grants permission to access resources, the ID token provides a standardized way to identify who is requesting access. It contains user-specific details—such as the user's ID, email, and other profile information—offering a reliable method for verifying the requester's identity.

The response in the following snippet includes the ID token included. The authorization server issues this token when the client sends a request to the /token endpoint. But the ID token is present only if the authorization server supports and enables the OIDC protocol because the ID token is specific to OIDC and isn't part of the standard OAuth 2.0 specification. In short, OAuth 2.0 says "Here's your access pass," and OIDC adds "By the way, here's proof of who you are."

```
{
    "access_token": "eyJraWQiOiJiMzIyODUzNS…",
    "refresh_token": "eaJqaEEiOiKYMzIyODUzPL…",
    "scope": "openid",
    "id_token": "eyJraWQiOiJiMzIyODU…",       ◁─┐ ID Token stores the details
    "token_type": "Bearer",                         │ related to the user identity.
    "expires_in": 299
}
```

Speaking of tokens, chapter 12 explained that access tokens can come in different formats. These days, the most common format is JSON Web Token (JWT) because it's compact, self-contained, and easy to verify. Still, in certain scenarios, you may need to use opaque tokens—those mysterious tokens that contain no readable information (as discussed in chapter 12). Opaque tokens require the resource server to check with the authorization server to determine what the token represents.

But here's an important distinction: the ID token in OIDC is always a JWT. Why? Its main purpose is to carry information about the user, such as identity and authentication details. To fulfill this role, the ID token must be nonopaque, meaning that it has to contain readable, verifiable claims. Today, the most efficient standardized format for packaging this kind of information securely is JWT.

13.3.2 *The UserInfo endpoint*

Another key enhancement that OIDC brings to OAuth 2.0 is a standardized endpoint for retrieving user details: UserInfo. This endpoint lets client applications securely fetch additional user profile information (such as name, email, and profile picture) directly from the authorization server. It complements the ID token by providing dynamic or extensive user data that may not be included in the ID token itself.

The UserInfo endpoint is vital to the identity layer that OIDC adds to OAuth 2.0. It works hand in hand with the ID token and OIDC's authentication mechanisms to provide a complete, secure identity solution.

13.3.3 *Protection against replay and CSRF attacks*

OIDC enhances security by introducing built-in mechanisms to defend against common web vulnerabilities such as replay and CSRF attacks. A replay attack happens when a hacker intercepts a valid piece of data, such as a payment request, and resends it to trick the system into performing the same action again.

Suppose that you make an online purchase, and your payment request is sent to the store's server to process the transaction. If an attacker intercepts that payment request, they could resend it multiple times, causing the store to charge your account again and again for the same order (figure 13.6). Without proper security checks in place, the system might treat these repeated requests as legitimate and continue processing unauthorized payments.

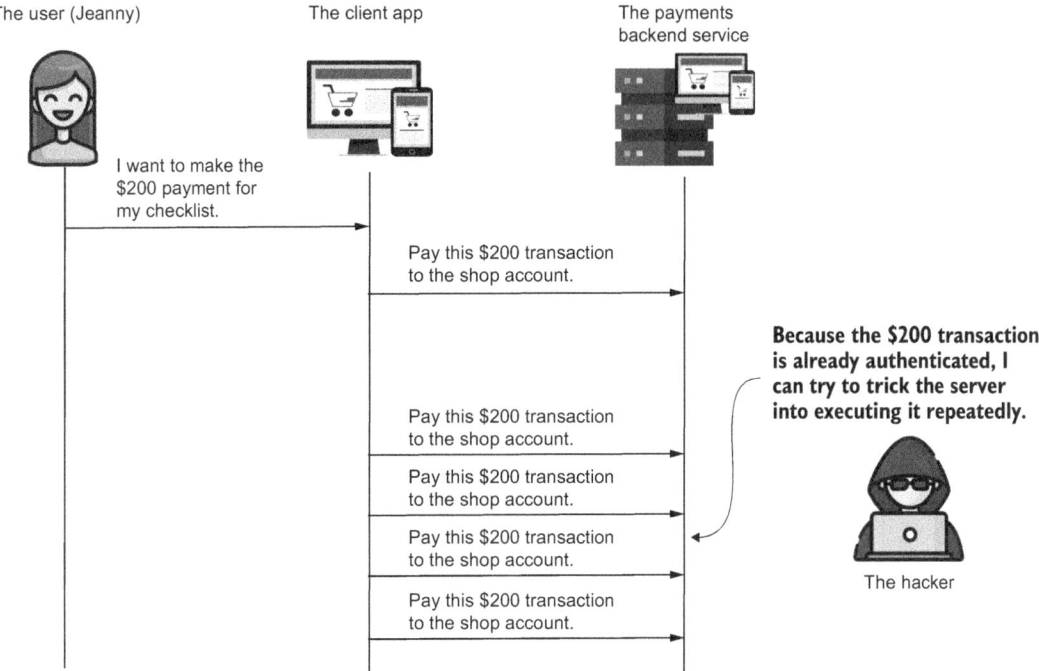

Figure 13.6   A replay attack. An attacker intercepts and maliciously resends a previously valid request to trigger unauthorized actions or changes within the system.

If the system doesn't properly validate the integrity of the request, an attacker could modify it before replaying it. In a payment system, if the transaction data isn't securely signed or encrypted, a hacker could intercept the payment request and change the recipient's account details before resending it. This would trick the system into sending the money to the attacker's account instead of the intended recipient's (figure 13.7).

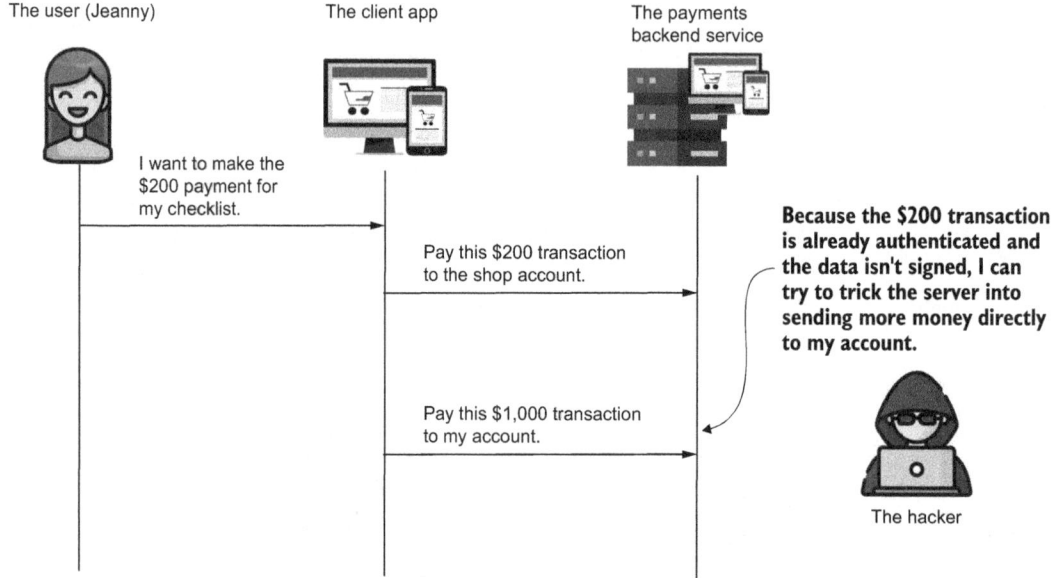

Figure 13.7   A replay attack with data tampering. If cryptographic signing isn't used, a hacker can intercept and modify a transaction. In this case, the attacker increases the transaction amount and redirects the payment to their own account instead of the legitimate shop's account.

Well-designed systems prevent this type of attack by taking the following actions:

- Digitally signing sensitive data to prevent tampering
- Encrypting the request so that it can't be read or altered in transit
- Using nonces and timestamps to make each request unique and valid for a limited time

A *nonce* (number used once) is a unique, random value generated by the client and included in the authentication request. With OIDC, when the ID token is returned, it must contain the same nonce value. This value ties the token to the original request and prevents replay attacks by making each authentication response valid only once, as shown in figure 13.8. If the nonce doesn't match, the response is rejected, effectively blocking the malicious reuse of authentication data.

The state parameter is another random value sent with the authentication request and returned unchanged by the authorization server. Its primary role is to prevent CSRF attacks by linking the request to the user's session. A CSRF attack occurs when a malicious website tricks a user's browser into performing unintended actions on a trusted site where the user is already authenticated (figure 13.9).

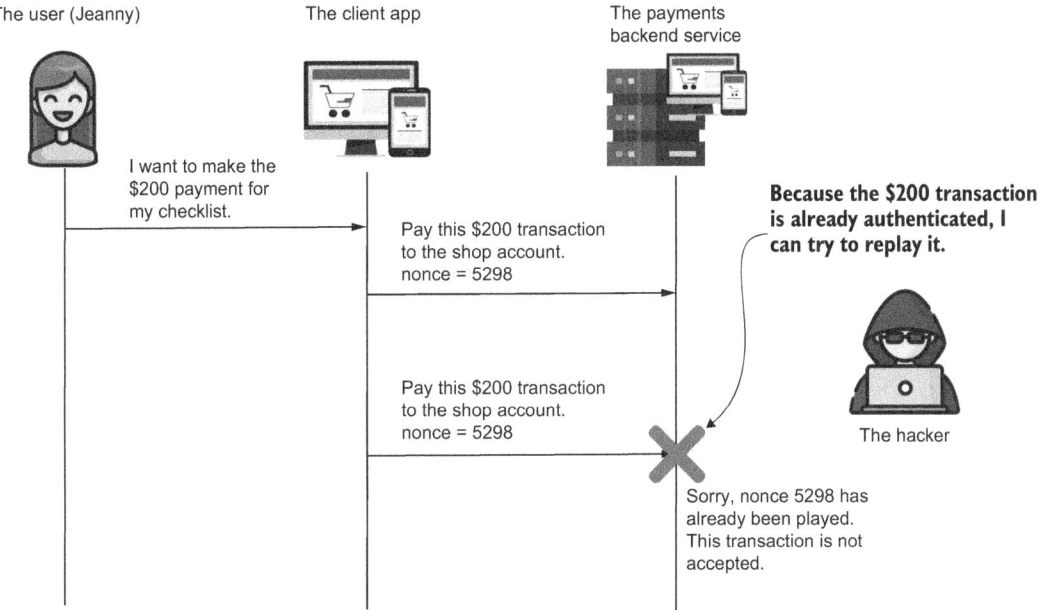

Figure 13.8 Using a nonce with a properly signed transaction prevents hackers from replaying or modifying the request, ensuring the transaction is secure and unique.

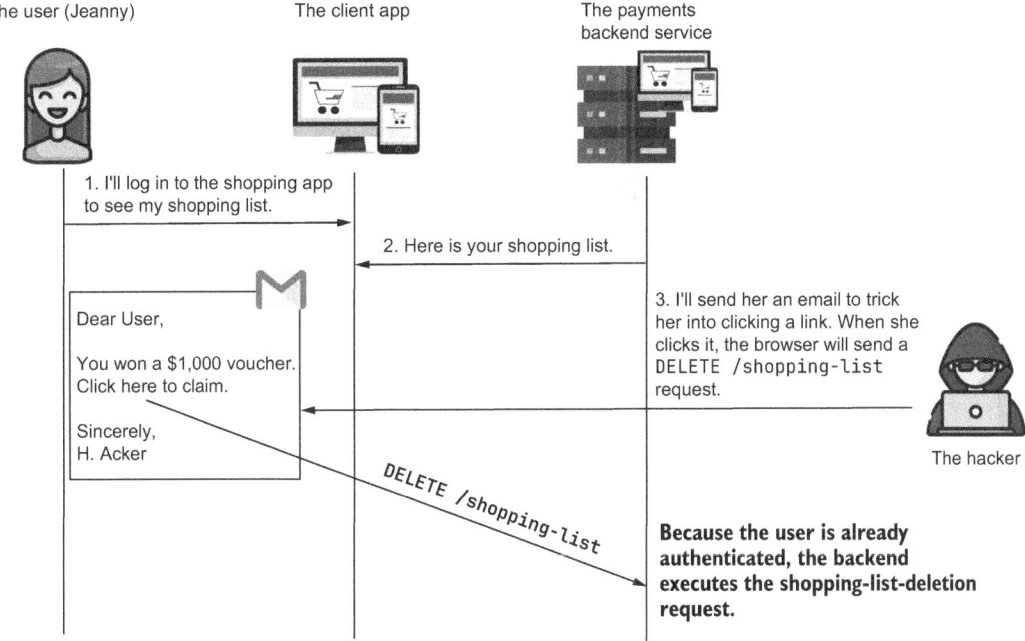

Figure 13.9 In a CSRF attack, an attacker tricks a logged-in user into unknowingly sending a malicious request to a trusted website. Because the user is already authenticated, the server treats the request as legitimate and executes unauthorized actions, potentially leading to unintended changes or data exposure.

If a user is logged into their bank account, for example, an attacker could exploit CSRF to initiate unauthorized transactions without the user's consent. By verifying the state parameter, OIDC ensures that each authentication request is legitimate and originates from the correct client session, blocking such malicious attempts (figure 13.10).

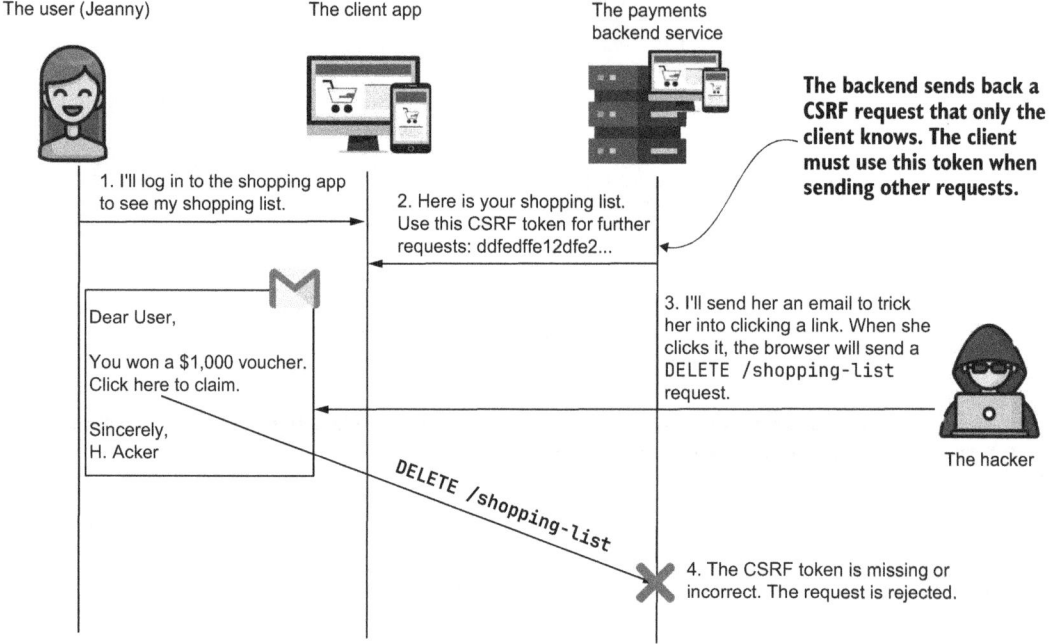

Figure 13.10   CSRF tokens. The server issues a unique, random token to the client, which must be included in all subsequent requests. If the token is missing, invalid, or incorrect, the server rejects the request. Because the attacker doesn't know this token, they can't craft a valid request, preventing them from tricking the user into executing unauthorized actions.

13.3.4 Session management and logout

OIDC introduces standardized session management and logout mechanisms, making it easier for applications to handle user sessions securely and consistently across multiple services. This is a significant improvement over OAuth 2.0, which leaves session handling up to developers, often resulting in fragmented, insecure implementations. Session management ensures that user sessions are properly maintained and synchronized between the client application and the identity provider (IdP).

Suppose that a user is logged in to several apps through the same IdP:

- Email service
- ACME's online storage service
- ACME's project management tool

Without session management, logging out of the project management tool wouldn't affect the other two apps. The user would still be logged in to their email and storage.

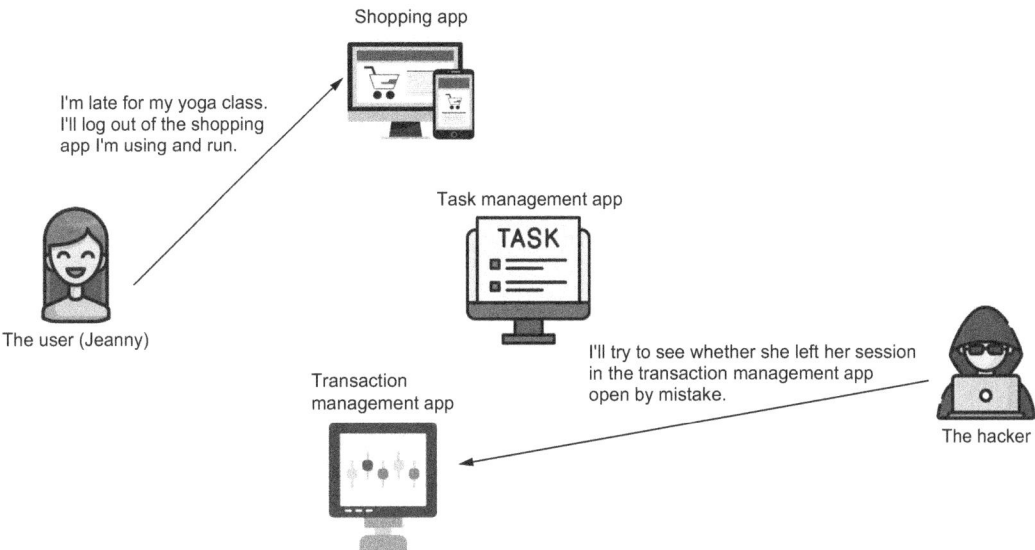

Shopping app

I'm late for my yoga class. I'll log out of the shopping app I'm using and run.

The user (Jeanny)

Task management app

TASK

I'll try to see whether she left her session in the transaction management app open by mistake.

Transaction management app

The hacker

Figure 13.11   Without centralized session management, users may unintentionally leave multiple sessions open across different devices or applications, increasing the risk of unauthorized access and security breaches.

With OIDC's session management and logout, logging out of the project management tool triggers a logout request to the IdP, which also logs the user out of the email and storage apps. Also, if the user's session expires with the IdP, all connected applications recognize this expiration and automatically sign the user out. This consistent session handling improves security by preventing forgotten active sessions and enhances the user experience with seamless login and logout across apps.

OIDC provides ways to check whether a user is still logged in or their session has expired:

- *Session* state *parameter*—OIDC introduces a session `state` parameter that tracks the user's login state. The client can silently check with the authorization server to see whether the user is still authenticated without disrupting the user experience. If the session has expired, the client can prompt the user to log in again.
- Silent authentication (`prompt=none`)—OIDC allows the client to send a request with `prompt=none`, which checks the user's session in the background. If the session is still active, the user remains logged in; if not, the client can initiate a login flow.

OIDC also standardizes how applications handle user logout, addressing the problem of logging out across multiple connected applications:

- *RP-Initiated logout*—The relying party (RP), or client application, can trigger a logout by redirecting the user to the identity provider's logout endpoint. This ends the session at the IdP level and may redirect the user to the application or to another page after logout.
- *Single logout (SLO)*—OIDC supports SLO, in which logging out from one application automatically logs out the user from all connected applications. This prevents situations in which users think they've logged out but other services remain active.

13.3.5 *Exercises*

8   What does OIDC add to OAuth 2?

9   What is the ID token?

10   Why is the ID token always a JWT?

11   What is the UserInfo endpoint for?

13.4   *Using multitenancy*

Multitenancy in the context of OIDC is like a massive apartment building in which each tenant (client, organization, or application) has its own private space, keys, and decor but the whole building uses the same security system, elevators, and utilities. In technical terms, it means designing authentication and identity management systems that can serve multiple tenants securely and efficiently from a single IdP. Each tenant operates independently, with its own users, roles, and settings, while relying on the same underlying authentication infrastructure. So tenants get the freedom to paint their walls whatever color they want, but the building makes sure that the locks work, the alarms are set, and no one sneaks into anyone else's apartment.

For an enterprise, implementing multitenancy with OIDC is highly beneficial in several scenarios, especially if the organization delivers services or manages systems for multiple clients, departments, or business units. Here's where and why organizations would use it:

- *Software as a Service (SaaS) platforms*—If your enterprise offers a SaaS product to multiple companies or customers, multitenancy allows you to serve all clients through a single platform while keeping their data, users, and access controls separate.
- *Large enterprises with multiple business units*—If your company manages IT services for multiple clients, multitenancy lets you provide secure, tailored authentication for each client from a unified system.
- *Customer and partner portals*—Enterprises often have different portals for customers, vendors, and partners. Multitenancy provides separate authentication and access control for each group.

Let's revisit our ACME scenario to make things clearer. As ACME grew into a leading enterprise, it rapidly expanded into an online retail giant, selling everything from high-tech gadgets to stylish home decor. But as the business scaled, ACME encountered a significant challenge. Managing suppliers, handling logistics, and tracking inventory became increasingly complex—not just for ACME but also for many other online retailers.

Recognizing this industrywide pain point, ACME decided to turn its operational expertise into a business opportunity. It launched ACME Commerce Cloud, a powerful SaaS platform designed to help e-commerce businesses streamline inventory management, supplier coordination, and order processing. ACME offers this platform to a variety of online retailers, each with unique security requirements and authentication systems.

Let's explore how ACME uses OIDC multitenancy to serve these diverse clients securely and efficiently. Among ACME's clients are the following three tenants:

- *Trendy Threads*—A fashion e-commerce startup that uses Google Workspace for all its internal operations, including employee accounts.
- *MegaMart Online*—A large online retailer that sells everything from groceries to electronics. Given its size and the sensitivity of customer data, it uses Microsoft Azure Active Directory (Azure AD) for secure authentication and enforces strict security policies such as multifactor authentication (MFA).
- *CozyHome Decor*—A small online store selling handcrafted home-decor items. The owner doesn't have a dedicated IT team and prefers a simple, built-in authentication system.

As you can see, all three tenants have distinct business models and security requirements—a common scenario in the real world, where each organization follows its own business strategies and IT policies. Trendy Threads wants its employees to log in to ACME Commerce Cloud using their existing Google accounts to keep things simple and seamless. MegaMart Online prioritizes security and compliance, insisting on managing authentication through Azure AD to meet industry regulations and enforce strict access controls. CozyHome Decor seeks an easy-to-use login system managed entirely by ACME Commerce Cloud, eliminating the need for technical expertise. By implementing OIDC multitenancy, ACME Commerce Cloud caters to these diverse needs.

One point of interest is flexible authentication, which involves dynamic routing of login requests to different identity providers (Google Workspace, Azure AD, or ACME's native system). ACME Commerce Cloud routes login requests from Trendy Threads to Google Workspace (`https://idp.acmecommercecloud.com/trendythreads/authorize`), whereas MegaMart employees are redirected to Azure AD for login (`https://idp.acmecommercecloud.com/megamart/authorize`).

Each tenant also prioritizes a specific customer experience, requiring personalized and branded login pages tailored to their identity. Employees of Trendy Threads see a login page featuring their company's logo and brand colors, creating a seamless and familiar experience. Similarly, MegaMart's login page is fully customized with their branding, and critical security policies like MFA are automatically enforced. Meanwhile, CozyHome Decor employees access a clean, ACME-branded login page with simple email/password login options and optional social logins for added flexibility.

The three tenants will likely implement different authorization strategies, defining unique roles, privileges, and access controls based on their business needs. These roles and permissions may be named and structured differently across tenants. ACME Commerce Cloud can handle this situation by embedding tenant-specific claims in the issued tokens. The following code snippet shows how the user-info response might look for a user from MegaMart:

```
{
    "sub": "user567",                    |  The tenant ID identifies the
    "tenant_id": "megamart",      ⊲──┘   company to whom the user belongs.
    "role": "inventory_manager",
    "permissions": ["view_reports", "manage_suppliers"]
}
```

ACME must also manage session handling carefully to ensure security and a smooth user experience. If Emma from Trendy Threads logs out, her action shouldn't should affect John from MegaMart. Each tenant's session must remain fully isolated to prevent cross-tenant interference. Fortunately, the OIDC protocol offers robust solutions for managing these challenges when implementing multitenancy,

Here are some key concepts you should understand and remember about multitenancy with OIDC:

- *Tenant isolation*—Each tenant should have isolated identity data, configurations, and security policies. This prevents one tenant from accessing or interfering with another tenant's data.
- *Dynamic client registration*—OIDC supports dynamic client registration, allowing tenants to register their own client applications with the IdP. This makes scaling across tenants easier without manual intervention.
- *Tenant-specific endpoints*—Authentication requests and token exchanges can be routed through tenant-specific endpoints. For tenant1, the app would use https://idp.example.com/tenant1/authorize, and for tenant2, the app would use https://idp.example.com/tenant2/authorize as the authorization endpoint. This keeps each tenant's authentication flow separate.
- *Custom branding and user experience*—The IdP can serve customized login pages, branding, and user flows for each tenant. OIDC enables this by allowing tenant-specific configuration for the login UI, consent screens, and user journeys.
- *Tenant-aware claims and scopes*—OIDC allows the inclusion of tenant-specific claims in the ID token or responses from the UserInfo endpoint. This helps client applications distinguish between users from different tenants.
- *Role-based access control (RBAC) per tenant*—Each tenant can define its own roles and permissions. The IdP can include these roles in the ID token or access token, enabling tenant-specific authorization.
- *Isolated session management*—OIDC can manage user sessions separately for each tenant, ensuring that a logout from one tenant's app doesn't affect sessions in another tenant's environment.

13.4.1 Exercises

12 What is multitenancy in identity systems?

13 How does OIDC help with multitenancy?

14 Can different tenants use different login methods?

15 How do you prevent users from mixing between tenants?

13.5 Exercise answers

1 What is PKCE, and why is it important?

PKCE protects public clients, such as mobile or web apps, from attackers who might steal an authorization code and use it to get access.

2 How does PKCE work?

Before authentication, the client app generates a random secret (the code verifier) and sends a hashed version of it (the code challenge) with the request. Later, it must present the original secret to get the token.

3 Why is the code challenge secure?

The challenge is made using a cryptographic hash function like SHA-256, so reverting it to the original secret is nearly impossible.

4 When should you use PKCE?

Always use it with public clients that can't store secrets safely, such as single-page apps, mobile apps, or IoT devices.

5 What are refresh tokens for?

Refresh tokens let apps get new access tokens without asking the user to log in again, keeping sessions smooth and secure.

6 Why not make access tokens last longer?

Long-lived tokens are risky if stolen. Short-lived tokens reduce that risk, and refresh tokens help maintain usability.

7 How do you protect refresh tokens?

Store them securely, rotate them after use, set expiration times, and revoke them when you detect suspicious activity.

8 What does OIDC add to OAuth 2?

OIDC adds authentication. It asks "Who is the user?", whereas OAuth 2 asks "What can they access?

9 What is the ID token?

The ID token a special token that contains user identity information (email, name, and so on) and proves who logged in.

10 Why is the ID token always a JWT?

It must contain readable claims. JWTs are perfect for packaging identity data in a secure, standard way.

11 What is the UserInfo endpoint for?

It gives you extra user profile data in case you need more than is in the ID token.

12 What is multitenancy in identity systems?

Multitenancy means that one identity system can serve multiple clients or organizations, keeping each tenant's users and data separate.

13 How does OIDC help with multitenancy?

It supports tenant-specific endpoints, claims, branding, and roles so that each client gets a custom experience.

14 Can different tenants use different login methods?

Yes. One tenant can use Google, another can use Azure AD, and still another can use your native system. OIDC handles the routing.

15 How do you prevent users from mixing between tenants?

Use tenant-specific login URLs, and issue tokens with tenant-specific claims (such as tenant_id).

Summary

- PKCE strengthens the authorization code flow by preventing authorization code interception, especially for public clients such as mobile and web apps.
- Refresh tokens allow applications to maintain user sessions without repeatedly prompting for login, balancing security (by limiting access-token lifespan) with user experience (by reducing interruptions).
- OIDC's identity layer introduces the ID tokens, securely providing user identity information alongside access tokens, enabling applications to authenticate users safely and reliably.
- The UserInfo endpoint allows applications to retrieve additional user profile information in a standardized, secure manner, complementing ID Tokens.
- OIDC enhances security against replay and CSRF attacks by using security parameters such as nonce and state, ensuring that requests are legitimate and unique.
- Session management and logout are standardized in OIDC, allowing consistent user session handling and SLO across multiple connected applications, improving both security and user experience.
- Multitenancy with OIDC enables ACME Commerce Cloud to securely serve multiple tenants with distinct authentication flows, custom branding, isolated sessions, and tenant-specific roles and permissions—all from a single IdP.
- Best practices include always using PKCE with public clients, securely storing refresh tokens, enabling refresh-token rotation, and enforcing secure communication with TLS/SSL.

14

Passwordless login: Using magic links and one-time passwords

This chapter covers

- Using magic links
- Using one-time passwords for authentication
- Protecting your apps from passwordless-authentication vulnerabilities

You're trying to log in to your favorite app, but you can't remember your password. Was it your dog's name plus your birth year? No, wait—that was your banking account. Maybe it's P@ssw0rd123? No—you changed it last month. After five failed attempts and a CAPTCHA test that makes you question your ability to recognize traffic lights, you finally give up and click Forgot Password. And just like that, passwords have once again defeated you.

But relax—passwordless authentication is here to rescue you from the endless cycle of password resets and security questions like "What was the name of your childhood best friend's second cousin's goldfish?"

In this chapter, we explore the magic (literally) of magic links. Think of them as the portkeys of authentication, instantly transporting you to your account. Next, we dive into the thrilling world of one-time passwords (OTPs), the digital equivalent of casting the Alohomora spell to unlock your login.

The passwordless adventure doesn't end here. Chapter 15 unveils the high-tech sorcery that is WebAuthn, in which your face, fingerprint, or a tiny security key acts like a personal wand, proving that you—and only you—are the true master of your account.

14.1 The real magic of magic-links authentication

Alice was on a mission. She had found the perfect pair of shoes on ACME.com, and nothing would stop her from buying them. She eagerly navigated to the login page, but something was off. Instead of the usual Username and Password fields, there was one lonely box asking for her email address.

"Wait a minute," Alice muttered, double-checking her screen. "Where's the Password field? Did ACME forget it? Have I been hacked? Is this some sort of trap?"

She hesitated, feeling the ghost of a thousand forgotten passwords haunting her. Then curiosity won. She typed her email address and clicked Log In. Within seconds, a new email arrived: "Click this link to log in to your ACME account!"

No password. No security questions. Just one click.

Alice stared at the email and then back at her screen. Was this sorcery? A trick? Had ACME secretly hired wizards to make her life easier?

She clicked the link. Boom. She was in. And just like that, Alice realized that passwords were things of the past.

Let's dive into the implementation of magic-links authentication. Following are the key steps that make it work securely and efficiently (figure 14.1):

1 The user requests a login link by entering their email address on the login page. This triggers the authentication process.

2 The app generates a secure, time-limited magic link. A unique, cryptographically signed token is created and added to the link, ensuring that the link is valid for only a short period and can't be easily forged or reused.

3 The app sends the magic link via email, ensuring that it's tamperproof, properly formatted, and set to expire after a short duration (usually, a few minutes).

4 The user clicks the link, expressing their intention to enter the application.

5 When the user clicks the link, the app validates the token and checks it for expiration. Then it establishes a secure session, granting the user access without requiring a password.

The magic-links authentication process begins when the user enters their email address on the login page. Then the system checks whether the email address exists in the database. If it's a valid, registered address, the process moves forward to generate a secure login link. But if the system doesn't find the address, it doesn't reveal this fact directly. Instead, it returns a generic message like "If an account exists, we've sent a login link." This message prevents attackers from using the login page to guess which

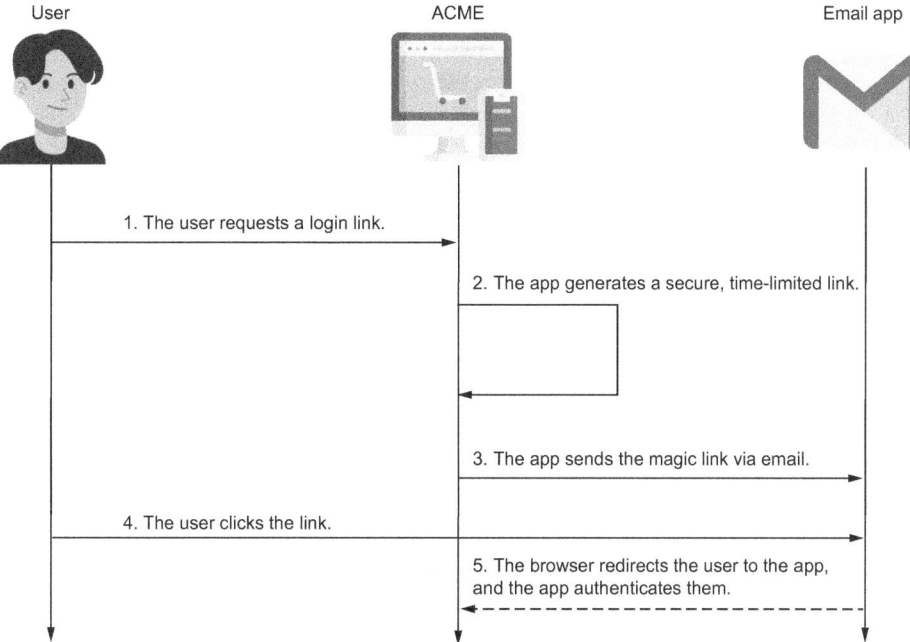

Figure 14.1   Authenticating through magic links. At the user's request, the app generates a unique link and sends it to the user by email. The user clicks the link to authenticate.

emails are registered. This small but crucial detail helps protect user privacy and minimizes the risk of email enumeration attacks.

An *email enumeration attack* occurs when an attacker systematically tests whether specific email addresses (or usernames) exist on a system by observing how the application responds to login, signup, or password-reset attempts. If the system provides different responses based on whether an account exists, the attacker can confirm valid accounts and use this information for further attacks, such as brute-force logins, phishing, and credential stuffing.

> **NOTE**   One of the most critical security principles in credential-based authentication is never disclosing whether an account exists. Messages like "The password is incorrect" may seem harmless, but they can unintentionally confirm that an attacker has found a valid username or email. This information leakage gives hackers one more piece of the puzzle, making it easier to target specific accounts, attempt credential stuffing, or launch password-reset attacks. Instead, always use generic error messages like "Invalid credentials" or "If an account exists, we've sent a login link" to avoid assisting attackers unintentionally.

You may wonder why this is so important. What can attackers do with just a username or an email? Well, they can do quite a lot, and none of it is good. When hackers confirm that an email exists, they can target high-value accounts like corporate email accounts or admin users, making them prime victims for advanced attacks. If you've ever reused a password (and let's be honest—most people have), they can try credential stuffing, plugging your email and old passwords into different websites, hoping to get lucky. If they find a match, they're in. Another thing they can do is perform targeted phishing. If they know you have a Spotify account, they can send a more realistic fake email, tricking you into clicking a malicious link.

Now let's take the examples a step further. What if attackers combine email enumeration with magic links? When they know that an email is valid, they can send convincing fake emails pretending to be from your app, saying things like "Here's your secure login link for ACME, Inc.! Click to sign in." If the email looks real enough—maybe even spoofing the sender address—there's a good chance that the user will click the fraudulent link without thinking twice. Instead of logging in, they unknowingly hand over their authentication token or get redirected to a fake login page that steals their credentials (figure 14.2).

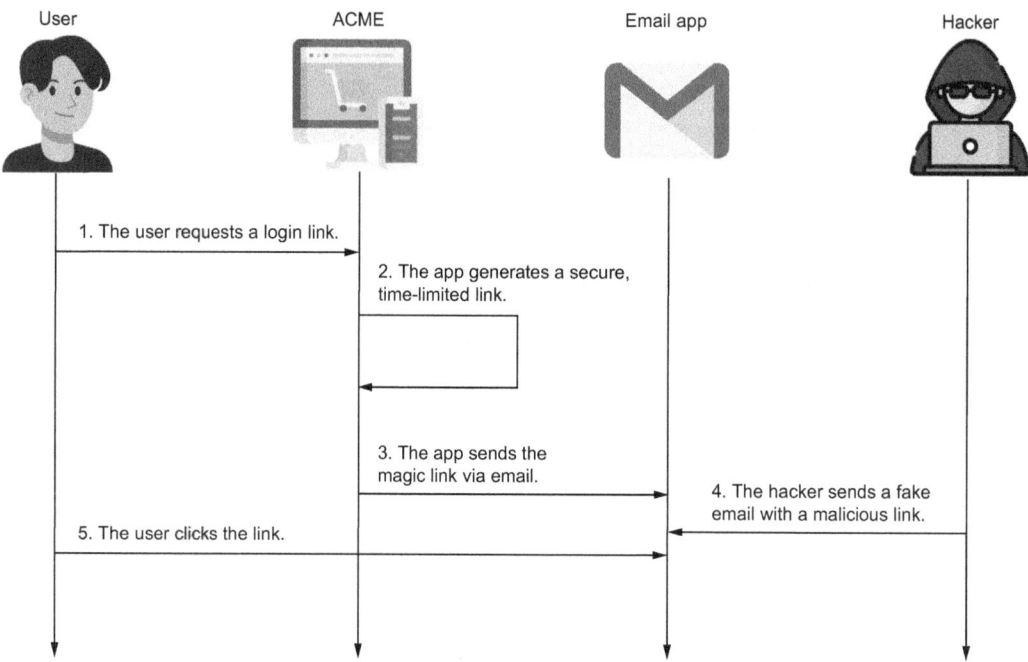

Figure 14.2   A malicious individual might send a fake but realistic-looking email between steps 3 and 4 of the process. An inattentive user could be fooled into clicking the wrong link.

Because magic links eliminate the need for passwords, users might let their guard down, thinking "It's secure because I don't have to type anything." In reality, if an attacker tricks you into using a fake magic link, they can intercept your login request and gain access to your account without needing your password. This is why email security, link verification, and proper domain checks are just as crucial as authentication. Also, *multifactor authentication (MFA)* is usually an excellent addition to an app's authentication process. (We discuss MFA in section 14.2.) After all, even the most secure system can't protect users if they're tricked into handing over the keys themselves.

Security is a lot like an alarm system: it doesn't matter how expensive or high-tech it is if it's poorly installed or not used correctly (figure 14.3). You could have the best locks, motion sensors, and surveillance cameras, but if you leave a window open, an intruder can walk right in. The same goes for authentication. Even if magic links or other security measures are designed to be safe, they can be exploited if users make careless errors like clicking a fake login link in a phishing email.

As discussed in previous chapters, security isn't just about having the right tools; it's also about implementing them properly and ensuring that users don't unknowingly bypass them. Even the most advanced system is only as strong as its weakest link, and if that link is human error or a poorly configured setting, attackers will find a way in.

Figure 14.3   Security is only as strong as its weakest link. You can have the best defenses, but if you leave the key under the rug . . . well, good luck!

When the user requests a magic link, the system must generate a secure, one-time-use token to verify their identity. This token acts like a temporary digital key, allowing users to log in without a password. To ensure security, the token must be cryptographically signed, typically using JSON Web Token (JWT) or hash-based message authentication code (HMAC) encryption so that it can't be easily forged or manipulated.

You might want to take a break and revisit chapter 11, which explored JSON Object Signing and Encryption (JOSE) and the fundamentals of JWT. Understanding how JWTs work and how they're signed, verified, and securely transmitted will help you grasp the mechanics behind magic links. You'll see why they're both powerful and potentially risky if they're not implemented correctly.

The token should include essential claims such as the user's email or ID, an expiration timestamp (e.g., 10 minutes), and a nonce (a random value that prevents replay attacks, ensuring that the token can't be reused maliciously. (Chapter 13 discusses nonces.)

```
{
  "email": "user@example.com",
  "exp": 1715179200,
  "nonce": "random-string-here"
}
```

Without storing the token, the system can't invalidate it after it's used. This means that if an attacker intercepts or obtains the magic link before the user clicks it, they may be able to reuse it.

With database storage, the system can mark the token as used immediately after the first successful login. If someone tries to use the same token again, the system rejects it. If a user reports suspicious activity, the system can immediately revoke the magic link by deleting or invalidating the token in the database.

Attackers can brute-force generation of magic links by repeatedly requesting links for different emails. If the system doesn't store tokens, it won't be able to detect excessive login attempts from the same IP or email address; neither can it limit how often a user can request a magic link. The system can throttle requests and prevent abuse by keeping a record of issued tokens.

Another best practice is auditing and security monitoring for generated magic links. The system can trigger an alert if multiple tokens are generated for the same email within a short period, for example. At the same time, if a magic link is used from an unexpected location or device, the system can require additional verification.

After the magic link token is generated, the system constructs a secure login URL containing the token:

```
https://acmeinc.com/auth/magic?token=eyJhbGciOiJIUzI1NiIsInR5cCI6IkpXVCJ9
.eyJ1c2VySWQiOiIxMjM0NTYifQ.SflKxwRJSMeKKF2QT4fwpMeJf36POk6yJV_adQssw5c
```

This link is emailed to the user (step 3), but several security precautions must be taken to prevent misuse:

- First, the link should expire quickly—typically, within 5 to 15 minutes—to minimize the risk of unauthorized access if intercepted.

- Second, the email should include clear branding and familiar design elements so users recognize it as a legitimate communication from your app, reducing the risk of phishing attacks.
- Last, the link should never be included in plaintext within the email body; it should exist only within the clickable link to prevent accidental exposure or leaks.

If the link (or attached token) appears as plaintext in the email, the user might accidentally copy and share it, such as by pasting it in a public chat. Some email clients preview text content before the user opens the email. If the token appears in the email body, it might be cached or exposed in notifications, increasing the risk of unauthorized access. If someone else gets access to the token, they can use it to log in as the user without needing their email or password.

Moreover, many email services and security tools automatically scan, log, or archive email contents. If the token is in plaintext, it might be stored or indexed in logs, where an attacker or a malicious insider could retrieve it later.

When the user clicks the magic link (step 4), they're redirected to your application, and the system extracts the authentication token from the URL and begins the validation process. First, it checks the token's signature (if JWT or HMAC is used) to ensure that it hasn't been tampered with. Then it checks whether the token has expired, rejecting tokens that are no longer valid. If the system stores the tokens, it also ensures that the token hasn't already been used to prevent replay attacks.

If all checks pass, the user is logged in, either by creating a session or issuing a new authentication token (such as a fresh JWT or session ID). For added security, the system can invalidate the magic link after first use, ensuring that an attacker can't reuse it. Finally, the user is redirected to their dashboard or the page they originally intended to visit, completing the passwordless authentication flow smoothly and securely.

Table 14.1 summarizes the best practices for using magic links.

Table 14.1 Best practices for implementing magic links

Best practice	Why?
Use short-lived tokens (5–15 minutes expiration).	Minimizes the window for attackers to use a stolen or leaked token
Store tokens in a database or cache.	Prevents token reuse, enables manual revocation, and allows tracking of authentication attempts
Invalidate used tokens after use.	Stops replay attacks by ensuring that a token can be used only once
Use cryptographically signed tokens.	Ensures that tokens can't be forged or manipulated, adding security against tampering
Never send tokens in plaintext within email.	Prevents accidental exposure if the email is forwarded or intercepted

Table 14.1   Best practices for implementing magic links *(continued)*

Best practice	Why?
Ensure that magic links include clear identity.	Reduces phishing risks by making emails easily recognizable as legitimate
Limit how often a user can request a magic link.	Protects against automated attacks that try to flood the system with requests
Check token validity (signature, expiration, and uniqueness).	Prevents expired, tampered, or duplicate tokens from being used for authentication
Warn users about suspicious activity.	Detects and notifies users of potential unauthorized login attempts
Allow fallback authentication.	Provides a way for users to access their accounts if the magic-link email is delayed or blocked

There you have it: passwordless authentication through magic links, a system so smooth that it feels like you waved a wand and logged in. There'll be no more forgetting passwords, no more resetting them every time you take a vacation, and definitely no more shouting "I swear I used the right one!" at your screen.

But as with all magic tricks, there's a catch: if you don't secure the system properly, someone else might pull the rabbit out of the hat. Expired tokens, phishing attacks, and email leaks can turn your sleek login experience into a hacker's best friend. So although magic links make life easier, they're only as good as the security practices behind them.

Now, if only we could magic away those "Verify you're not a robot" CAPTCHAs, we'd truly be in the future—or do CAPTCHAs put us in the future? Who knows?

14.1.1 *Exercises*

1 How does magic-link authentication work?
2 Why should the app not reveal whether an email exists?
3 What are the security risks of magic links?
4 Why store magic-link tokens in a database?
5 Why shouldn't the link appear in plaintext in an email?

14.2 *Authentication through OTPs*

OTPs are those little six-digit codes that always seem to arrive at the worst possible moment. You're trying to log in, feeling confident, when suddenly your screen displays a message like this one: "We've sent a code to your phone. Please enter it below."

And just like that, the waiting game begins. You check your phone. Nothing. You stare at it, willing the SMS to appear. Still nothing. Maybe your signal dropped? Maybe your carrier is taking a lunch break? You try resending the code, and just as you do, the first one arrives. Great. But wait, which code is the right one now? You take a guess, and of course, "Invalid OTP. Request a new one."

Welcome to the chaotic world of OTPs. Sure, they can be frustrating, but they're also among the most widely used security measures, helping prevent unauthorized access even if someone has your password. In this section, we explore how OTPs work, when they're useful, and what security risks they pose if they're not implemented correctly. Keep your phone nearby (ideally, with signal), and let's dive in.

Despite their occasional inconvenience and delayed arrivals, OTPs provide several key security advantages in authentication. Here's why they remain one of the most widely used methods for protecting user accounts:

- *They're time-sensitive and single-use.* Unlike traditional passwords, OTPs expire quickly (usually, within 30 seconds to a few minutes) and can be used only once. Even if an attacker intercepts an OTP, it will likely be useless by the time they try to use it.
- *They work without a persistent secret.* Unlike passwords, which users store, reuse, or write on sticky notes, OTPs don't require users to remember anything. As a result, there's nothing static for attackers to steal.
- *They can be delivered in multiple ways.* Users can receive OTPs via SMS, email, or authentication apps (such as Google Authenticator, Authy, and Microsoft Authenticator). This makes them versatile and easy to deploy across platforms.
- *They don't require users to create or remember another password.* Let's face it: people are terrible at remembering passwords. OTPs eliminate this problem by acting as a temporary login key, reducing the need for users to create and store complex passwords.

Let's analyze the steps for OTP authentication (figure 14.4):

1. The user requests an OTP for authentication by entering their email address or phone number. The system checks whether the provided contact is registered to prevent enumeration attacks.
2. The app generates a secure, random, time-limited OTP (usually six to eight digits).
3. The app sends the OTP to the user via SMS, email, or an authenticator app.
4. The user enters the OTP for authentication. The system verifies the OTP for correctness, expiration, and single use. If it's valid, the user is authenticated.

When a user wants to log in with an OTP, they start by entering their email address or phone number on the login page. The system checks whether the provided information is registered before generating an OTP and sending it to the user, allowing them to proceed with authentication.

After the system verifies the user's email or phone number, it generates a random numeric code, usually six to eight digits long. To ensure security, this OTP must be cryptographically random, making it impossible to predict or guess. Then the system assigns an expiration time—typically, 30 seconds to a few minutes—to prevent attackers from using an old OTP to gain access. For validation, the OTP is stored temporarily, preferably in a hashed format, ensuring that it remains secure and can't be retrieved easily.

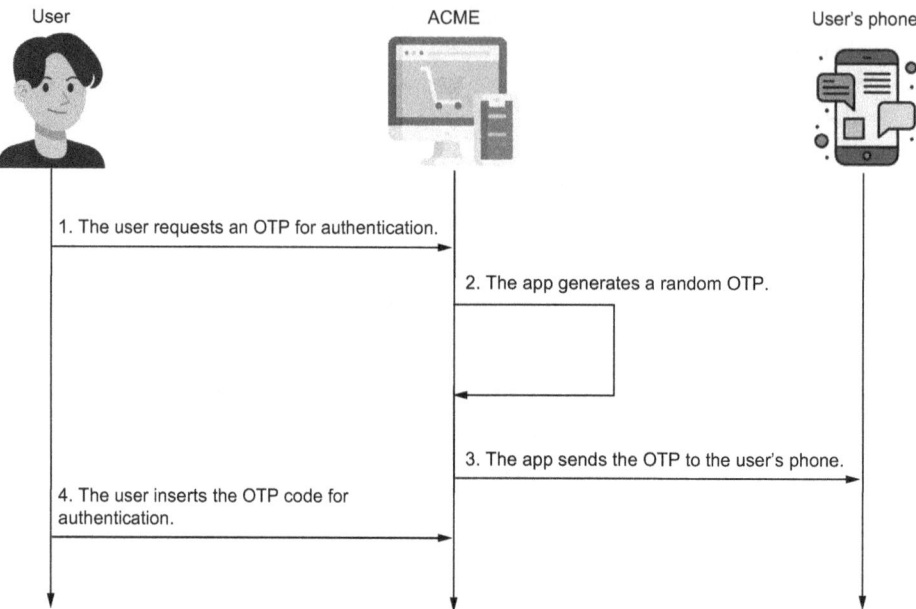

Figure 14.4   The OTP authentication process. The app generates a random OTP and sends it to the user. The user uses the received OTP to authenticate.

Unlike magic links (section 14.1), which contain a self-contained token such as a signed JWT embedded in the link, OTPs require user interaction. The user must receive, read, and manually enter the code. Although magic links simplify authentication with a single click, OTPs introduce an extra step but provide flexibility because they can be delivered through multiple channels, such as SMS, email, or authenticator apps.

After receiving the OTP via email or SMS, the user enters it on the login page. The system validates the OTP, checking whether it's correct and still within its expiration window. If the OTP is incorrect, the login attempt is rejected, and if it has expired, the user is prompted to request a new one. Because OTPs are designed for one-time use, they're removed from the database after validation to prevent reuse. If the OTP is valid and matches the one generated, the system authenticates the user, grants access, and establishes a session by creating a session ID or issuing a new authentication token, such as a JWT.

A key best practice for securing OTP authentication is implementing rate limiting to prevent brute-force attacks. Users should be restricted to a reasonable number of OTP requests, such as no more than five attempts per minute, to stop attackers from flooding the system with guesses. Also, the system should monitor login attempts for suspicious behavior, such as multiple failed OTP entries or repeated requests from different locations, and flag unusual patterns for review. These measures help prevent abuse while ensuring a secure, controlled authentication process.

OTPs and MFA

You may have encountered the OTP concept in other contexts, such as MFA. In high-risk scenarios, such as logging in to sensitive accounts, consider requiring OTPs as part of the MFA process, alongside a primary password or another authentication factor such as biometrics or security keys.

MFA is a security mechanism that requires users to provide two or more independent factors to verify their identity. Instead of relying solely on a password, MFA ensures that even if one factor is compromised, an attacker still can't gain access. These authentication factors typically fall into three categories:

- *Something you know*—A password, PIN, or security question
- *Something you have*—A smartphone, security token, or OTP
- *Something you are*—Biometrics such as a fingerprint, a face scan, or voice recognition

By combining multiple factors, MFA significantly reduces the risk of unauthorized access, making it much harder for attackers to compromise accounts even if they obtain a user's password.

Although OTPs can be used as a standalone authentication method, they're often implemented as one factor in an MFA setup. A typical MFA process works like this:

1 The user enters their username and password (something they know).
2 The system verifies the credentials and then prompts for an OTP (something they have).
3 The user retrieves the OTP from SMS, email, or an authenticator app and then enters it on the login page.
4 If both the password and OTP are correct, authentication is granted.

By requiring an OTP in addition to a password, the system ensures that even if an attacker steals the password (e.g., through phishing or credential stuffing), they still can't log in without access to the user's OTP device.

Magic links and OTPs may look similar. In the end, both aim to make authentication more secure and convenient by eliminating the need for passwords. But although they have a common goal, they work differently and have unique strengths and weaknesses. Table 14.2 compares the two techniques.

Table 14.2 Comparing OTPs and magic links

Feature	OTPs	Magic links
How it works	User receives a temporary code (via SMS, email, or an app) and enters it manually.	User receives a unique link via email, clicks it, and is logged in automatically.
User effort	User is required to enter a code manually.	Just click a link; no typing is required.

Table 14.2   Comparing OTPs and magic links *(continued)*

Feature	OTPs	Magic links
Security risks	SMS OTPs can be intercepted (in SIM swapping or SS7 attacks, for example). Phishing attacks can trick users into entering OTPs on fake sites. Brute-force attacks are possible without rate limiting.	If an attacker gains access to a user's email, they can log in easily. Phishing emails can mimic real magic links. If links don't expire after first use, they can be reused.
Speed and user experience	Both can be slow if the OTP is delayed or expires too quickly.	Speed is faster because entry is a single click (but it depends on email delivery speed).
Dependency	Dependency relies on SMS, email, or an authenticator app.	Dependency relies entirely on email security and availability.
MFA	Can be used as a second factor in MFA	Usually a single-factor authentication method
Phishing resistance	Users may be tricked into entering OTPs on fake sites.	Users may be tricked into clicking fake login links.
Best for	Securing accounts with MFA. Apps that support TOTP (Google Authenticator, Authy). Users with unreliable email access.	Passwordless login experiences. Users who struggle with passwords. Websites where authentication must be quick and seamless.

Table 14.3 summarizes best practices for using OTPs.

Table 14.3   Best practices for using OTPs

Best practice	Why?
Use short-lived OTPs (30 seconds to 5 minutes).	Reduces the window of opportunity for attackers to reuse or intercept an OTP
Generate OTPs using a cryptographically secure method.	Ensures that OTPs can't be guessed or predicted, making brute-force attacks ineffective
Limit OTP requests to prevent brute-force attacks.	Prevents automated attacks from flooding the system with OTP requests
Use OTPs only once and invalidate them after use.	Prevents replay attacks, in which an attacker tries to reuse a stolen OTP
Encourage the use of app-based OTPs over SMS/email.	Secures better than SMS, which is vulnerable to SIM swapping and SS7 attacks
Monitor login attempts for suspicious behavior.	Detects potential attacks, such as multiple failed OTP entries from different locations
Provide fallback authentication methods.	Allows users to log in securely if they don't receive an OTP (e.g., backup codes or alternative authentication methods)
Implement rate limiting on OTP entry attempts.	Stops attackers from attempting multiple OTP guesses by locking out excessive attempts

To conclude our discussion of OTPs, it's important to recognize that although they enhance security better than static passwords, they still have vulnerabilities, such as phishing and man-in-the-middle attacks. Chapter 15 covers WebAuthn, an even more secure, phishing-resistant authentication method. We'll discuss how it enables passwordless authentication by using public key cryptography and biometric or hardware-based authenticators.

14.2.1 Exercises

6 What makes OTPs more secure than passwords?

7 What are OTP security risks?

8 How do OTPs fit into MFA?

14.3 Exercise answers

1 How does magic-link authentication work?

The user enters their email address, gets a login link by email, and clicks it to log in. No password is required.

2 Why should the app not reveal whether an email exists?

If it does, attackers can find out who's registered and target them. Always use generic messages like "If your email exists . . ."

3 What are the security risks of magic links?

Phishing attacks can trick users with fake emails. If links aren't short-lived or invalidated after use, attackers might reuse them.

4 Why store magic-link tokens in a database?

To detect replay, limit how often a user can request one, and let the system invalidate the tokens after they're used.

5 Why shouldn't the link appear in plaintext in the email?

It could be leaked, cached, or seen by others. Always hide it behind a proper clickable button.

6 What makes OTPs more secure than passwords?

They expire quickly, are used only once, and don't have to be remembered. There's nothing to reuse or guess later.

7 What are OTP security risks?

If sent by SMS, they can be intercepted (e.g., via SIM swapping). If rate limiting is missing, attackers can guess them.

8 How do OTPs fit into MFA?

They're often the "something you have" part, combined with a password or biometric to boost account protection.

Summary

- Passwordless authentication improves security and convenience by eliminating weak or reused passwords. This chapter explored magic links, OTPs, biometric authentication, and hardware security keys as alternatives. Each method has advantages and risks.

- Magic links allow users to log in via a one-time link sent to their email address. They're vulnerable to phishing and email compromise. Using short-lived, cryptographically signed tokens and preventing email enumeration helps mitigate risks.

- OTPs provide temporary numeric codes via SMS, email, or authenticator apps. They're susceptible to SIM-swapping, phishing, and brute-force attacks. Using an app-based OTP such as Google Authenticator or Authy and limiting OTP requests will increase security.

- Passwordless authentication reduces phishing, credential leaks, and login friction, but no single method fits all use cases. Choosing the right approach depends on security needs, usability, and risk factors.

- Proper implementation is key. Even the most secure authentication method can be exploited if it's configured poorly. Following best practices and encryption standards and handling authentication data securely ensures a stronger, safer login experience.

Passwordless login: WebAuthn and hardware authentication

This chapter covers
- Using biometric authentication
- Using hardware keys for authentication
- Protecting your apps from passwordless-authentication vulnerabilities

Imagine this: You're trying to log in, but instead of typing a password and playing the "forgot password" game, you look at your phone, tap a key, or scan your finger, and you're in. There are no passwords to forget, no Short Message Service (SMS) codes to wait for, and no hacker guessing your childhood pet's name (RIP Fluffy).

But how do these futuristic authentication methods work? Are they as secure as they sound? What happens if you shave your beard or lose your security key? In this section, we'll explore the magic behind biometric authentication and hardware security keys, discussing their strengths, their potential weaknesses, and their prospects for being the future of secure login.

Biometric authentication and *hardware security keys* are passwordless-authentication methods that verify a user's identity in a highly secure and convenient way. Instead of relying on something you know (such as a password), they rely on something you are (biometrics) or something you have (a physical security key).

One of the most widely adopted standards enabling passwordless authentication is *WebAuthn* (Web Authentication), developed by the FIDO Alliance and standardized by the World Wide Web Consortium (W3C). WebAuthn allows websites and applications to authenticate users using public key cryptography instead of traditional credentials. It supports authentication through biometrics (such as fingerprints or facial recognition) and security keys (such as FIDO2-compliant hardware tokens or built-in authenticators on modern devices).

As you'll see in this chapter, WebAuthn enhances security by eliminating the risks associated with passwords, such as phishing, credential stuffing, and brute-force attacks. Because authentication is tied to a specific device and involves cryptographic key pairs, attackers can't reuse stolen credentials elsewhere. Also, WebAuthn is supported by major web browsers and operating systems, making it a scalable, user-friendly solution for passwordless authentication. This chapter covers the essentials, but if you're curious about the details, you can find the official WebAuthn documentation at https://www.w3.org/TR/webauthn/.

15.1 Biometric authentication

A core part of WebAuthn is biometric authentication, which uses unique biological traits to verify identity. Because biometric data is stored securely on the user's device and never transmitted, it significantly reduces the risk of credential theft. Also, WebAuthn ensures that each authentication is bound to a specific device, preventing attackers from using stolen credentials elsewhere. Common biometric authentication types include

- *Fingerprint scanning*—Used on smartphones, laptops, and security systems.
- *Facial recognition*—Unlocks devices and accounts with a quick face scan.
- *Iris or retina scanning*—Used in high-security environments for precise identification. Iris scanning analyzes the colored ring of the eye; retina scanning maps blood vessels at the back of the eye and is more intrusive.
- *Voice recognition*—Identifies users based on speech patterns.
- *Palm-vein scanning*—Used in high-security systems for contactless identity verification based on vein patterns.

15.1.1 Fingerprint scanning (most common)

Fingerprint scanning is one of the most widely used biometric authentication methods, used in smartphones, laptops, and smart cards. It uses fingerprint sensors to capture and compare unique fingerprint patterns, ensuring quick, reliable authentication. Its biggest advantages are speed, widespread adoption, and strong security. Still, it has weaknesses: high-quality fingerprint replicas can trick the system, and sensor wear over time may lead to false rejections or reduced accuracy. Despite these challenges, fingerprint scanning remains a trusted, efficient method of biometric authentication.

15.1.2   Facial recognition (rapidly growing)

Facial recognition has become a popular biometric authentication method, widely used in smartphones (Face ID), laptops (Windows Hello), and security systems. It uses infrared depth sensors or AI-based 2D/3D mapping to scan and verify a user's face. Its key advantages include speed and hands-free authentication, making it both convenient and seamless. But its security depends on the technology used: systems without 3D depth sensors can be vulnerable to photo or video spoofing, making them less reliable in high-security environments. Nevertheless, facial recognition continues to grow because it's a fast, user-friendly authentication method.

15.1.3   Iris or retina scanning (highly secure)

Iris scanning is a highly secure biometric authentication method, commonly used in high-security environments and on select smartphones. It works by analyzing the unique patterns in a person's iris, making it extremely difficult to spoof, even more so than fingerprint or facial recognition. Also, it remains effective even if a user's fingerprint is damaged or unreadable. But its adoption is limited because it requires specialized hardware and is generally slower than other biometric methods. Despite these drawbacks, iris scanning is one of the most secure biometric authentication technologies available.

15.1.4   Voice recognition (moderately secure)

Voice recognition is a convenient biometric authentication method, commonly used in banking call centers and voice assistants like Siri and Google Assistant. It analyzes a user's unique voice characteristics to verify their identity. The greatest advantages of voice recognition are that it's hands-free and highly accessible, making it useful for users who have disabilities or prefer a simple authentication experience. But it also has significant security risks: it can be spoofed using voice recordings or AI-generated voices, making it less secure than fingerprint or facial recognition in high-risk scenarios.

15.1.5   Palm-vein recognition (high security, less common)

Palm-vein recognition is a highly secure biometric authentication method, used primarily in ATMs, secure facilities, and health-care authentication systems. It works by scanning the unique vein patterns inside the palm with infrared sensors, making it nearly impossible to replicate or spoof. This method offers exceptional security because vein patterns are internal and not as easily accessible as fingerprints and facial features. But its adoption is limited due to the need for specialized hardware, and it isn't as widely available as other biometric methods. Still, palm vein recognition remains an excellent choice for high-security applications.

Biometric authentication is fast and user-friendly but comes with concerns such as privacy risks and false rejections (e.g., your phone doesn't recognize you before coffee). Integrating biometric authentication into an app involves securely verifying a user's identity using a device's built-in biometric sensors (such as fingerprint readers or face scanners). The essential steps for enabling biometric authentication are

1   *User enrollment.* The user registers their fingerprint, face, or other biometric data on their device.

2   *Request authentication.* The user attempts to log in to the app. Instead of a password, the app prompts for biometric authentication (e.g., fingerprint scan or face recognition).

3   *Verify the user.* The device checks the user's biometric input against the previously stored biometric data. If it matches, the system generates a cryptographic authentication token that confirms the user's identity. With a valid token, the app grants access by logging the user in or allowing sensitive actions (such as approving a payment).

Implementing biometric authentication follows a simple process involving enrollment, authentication, and verification (figure 15.1). Although it provides a fast, secure way to log in, it has vulnerabilities.

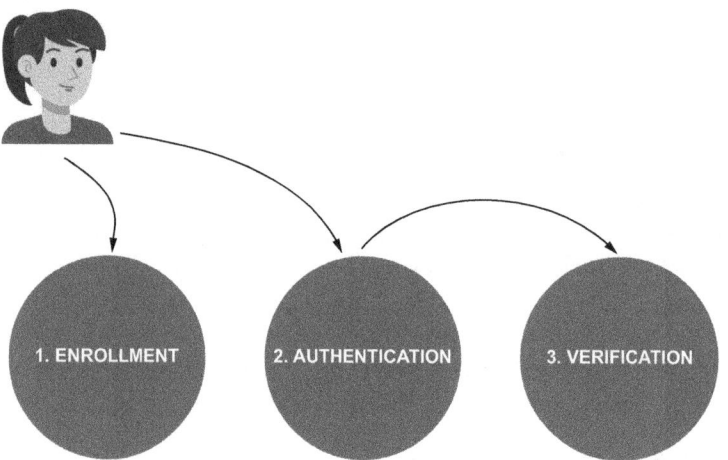

Figure 15.1 Biometric authenticatation is a three-step process. First, a user registers their data. Then the user tries to authenticate and be verified by the system.

Problems may appear from the start, with user enrollment. First, you should understand how the process works. When a user sets up biometric authentication, they register their fingerprint, face, iris, or voice on their device. The system captures the unique features and stores them securely in a trusted execution environment (TEE), such as Apple's Secure Enclave, Android's TEE, or a hardware-backed trusted platform module (TPM). Instead of saving raw biometric data, the system converts it to a mathematical template, creating a hashed representation of the biometric pattern.

Think of biometric authentication as making a unique key for a lock. Instead of storing the shape of the key, the system creates a blueprint that describes its key pattern in a way that only the lock can understand.

Or suppose that you press your fingerprint into soft wax to create a seal. Instead of keeping the wax, you take a picture of it and store only the measurements of the ridges and curves. Later, when you try to unlock a door, you press your real fingerprint into another wax mold. The system doesn't compare the fingerprint; instead, it checks whether the new measurements match the stored ones. If they do, you're granted access.

This is exactly how biometric authentication works. The system doesn't store your actual fingerprint, face, or iris; instead, it converts those features into a mathematical representation (a template). When you try to log in, the system checks for a close resemblance, not an identical match.

Now let's review some vulnerabilities that can arise with this approach. David is a seasoned hacker. He pulled off password leaks before, but this time, he's after something even more valuable: biometric templates. He knows that unlike passwords, biometric data can't be changed. If he could steal that data, victims would be vulnerable forever.

One day, David found that a company was storing biometric templates in an unsecured database. Jackpot! Instead of finding encrypted tokens, he found raw biometric templates—mathematical representations of users' fingerprints and facial features. With this data, he didn't need to trick users into handing over passwords; he could generate fake biometric scans that matched the stolen templates, giving him access to their accounts as though he were them.

The worst part was that users couldn't reset their faces or fingerprints as they could their passwords. Once stolen, their biometric data was permanently compromised. David knew that if companies didn't store templates securely inside hardware-protected areas, attackers like him would have a gold mine of unchangeable identities to exploit.

Even if template stealing didn't work, David had other ways to exploit user registration for biometric data. Imagine an application that didn't properly verify the user before letting them register a fingerprint or face scan; it simply trusted whatever was submitted.

Using deepfake technology (which is no longer difficult to acquire), David created an ultrarealistic AI-generated face that mimicked the real user's biometric patterns. Then, he enrolled the fake face in an account, essentially registering himself as an authorized user. From then on, whenever he wanted access, he didn't have to hack anything; he used his fake biometric profile, and the system treated him like a legitimate user.

The beauty of this trick is that the actual user would never know. Even if they later tried to log in, the system wouldn't alert them that an extra face or fingerprint had been registered. David had created a permanent backdoor, bypassing passwords, one-time passwords (OTPs), and even multifactor authentication (MFA).

If companies didn't enforce strict identity verification before allowing biometric enrollment, attackers like David could register fake or stolen biometric data, granting them undetectable, long-term access to high-value accounts. But user registration isn't the only part that could be vulnerable if the developers didn't implement security properly. The authentication process itself might have its own flaws.

One method to exploit is a replay attack, in which a hacker captures and replays biometric authentication data to trick the system into granting access (figure 15.2). Another serious threat is a man-in-the-middle (MITM) attack, in which biometric data can be intercepted if it's transmitted unencrypted over a network, allowing an attacker to spoof authentication remotely.

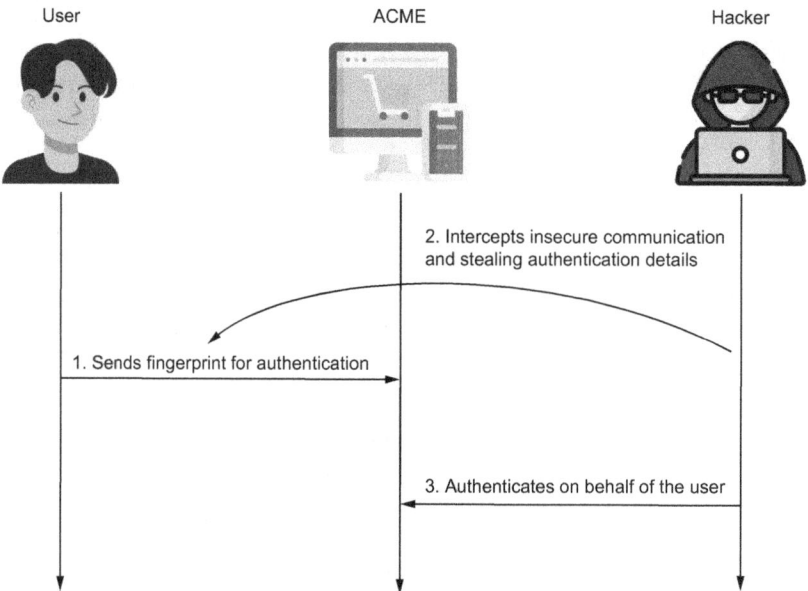

Figure 15.2 Improperly secured transmission and storage of biometric authentication data can expose it to hackers, who might exploit it in replay attacks.

But not all attacks require hacking. Phishing via social engineering can be just as dangerous. A well-crafted message like "Please scan your fingerprint to confirm this transaction" can trick users into authenticating a malicious request without realizing it. These vulnerabilities show why biometric authentication must be properly implemented with encryption, antireplay protections, and strong user awareness.

Biometric systems are designed to recognize unique physical traits, but attackers have found ways to fool the technology. Spoofing attacks involve using high-quality fake fingerprints, 3D face masks, or AI-generated voices to trick biometric sensors into granting access. A similar method, presentation attacks, relies on showing the system a photo, video, or fingerprint mold—a common weakness in poorly secured facial recognition systems that lack liveness detection. But even if the biometric scan is secure, attackers can bypass authentication by stealing security tokens. If malware or session hijacking allows an attacker to capture the cryptographic token generated after successful biometric authentication, they can impersonate the user without using their fingerprint or face scan.

If you've ever watched a spy movie, you've probably seen a scene in which the bad guys cut off someone's finger to bypass a fingerprint scanner or plucked out an eyeball to fool an iris scanner. Classic Hollywood hacking, right? Fortunately, real-life biometric security isn't that easy to break. Modern systems use liveness detection to check for things like blood flow, muscle movement, and blinking to ensure that the biometric input is attached to a living person. (Sorry, bad guys.)

But although finger-snatching villains may not be a real-world threat, biometric authentication has weaknesses. Spoofing attacks, stolen biometric templates, and deepfake-generated faces can create vulnerabilities if the system isn't designed with proper security measures. Unlike passwords, faces and fingerprints can't be changed if they're compromised, so companies that implement biometrics must get everything right the first time.

Biometric authentication is incredibly powerful, offering both security and convenience. But as in spy movies, the real danger isn't always in the technology itself; it's in how well (or poorly) it's implemented. You may never need to worry that someone will steal your eyeball, but you should definitely worry about weak encryption, poor anti-spoofing measures, and bad implementation.

15.1.6 Exercises

1 How does biometric authentication work?
2 What is stored during biometric registration?
3 What are spoofing and presentation attacks?
4 Why is storing biometric templates insecurely a problem?

15.2 Authenticating using hardware keys

Alice had struggled with every frustrating login method imaginable: passwords she could never remember, OTPs that expired too soon, and magic links that always ended up in spam. But today, her boss handed her a tiny USB-like device and said, "This is your new login method. Keep it safe."

Alice examined the device skeptically. That little thing? It didn't have a screen, a password, or even a blinking light. How was it supposed to keep her accounts secure? But when she plugged it into her laptop and tapped the button, she was in without passwords or codes.

The experience reminded her of Lara Croft unlocking an ancient tomb with a mystical key, but instead of opening a chamber filled with priceless artifacts, Alice accessed her email. This little device was her "Triangle of Light," the key that granted instant access while keeping digital treasure (a.k.a. her data) locked away from intruders. Phishing and stolen passwords were no use against this solid, hackerproof authentication method.

How does this real-world digital relic work, and what would happen if Alice lost it? (Let's be real; she probably will lose it. She can't even keep a pair of glasses for more than a couple of months.)

Think of a hardware security key as a supersmart, uncopiable key that fits only your digital locks. Instead of typing passwords or waiting for a one-time code, you simply plug in (or tap) your key, which proves to the system that you're really you without exposing any secret information that hackers could steal. Here's how the process works:

1 *You try to log in.* You go to your email, bank, or any account that supports hardware keys. Instead of asking for a password, the system asks you to prove that you're the owner of the account.

2 *Your hardware key responds.* You plug in or tap your key (via USB, NFC, or Bluetooth). The key doesn't send a stored password; it uses a unique cryptographic handshake to prove that it's legitimate.

3 *The system verifies the key.* Your account checks the key's response, confirming that it's yours, not a fake or part of a hacking attempt.

When a user registers a hardware security key with an online service, the device generates a unique key pair:

- *Private key (stored securely on the device)*—This key never leaves the security key and is used to sign authentication requests.

- *Public key (stored by the application that requires it for authentication)*—This key is registered with the website or app and is used to verify authentication attempts.

NOTE   The private key is never exposed or transmitted, making it impossible for attackers to steal or reuse it.

When a user tries to log in using a hardware key, the process follows a challenge-response model, ensuring that no sensitive data is sent over the network (figure 15.3):

1 *The website sends a challenge.* Instead of asking for a password, the website generates a random challenge (nonce) and sends it to the security key.

2 *The security key signs the challenge.* The key digitally signs the challenge using its private key and returns the signed response to the website.

3 *The website verifies the signature.* The server checks the response against the registered public key. If it matches, authentication is successful.

Another important feature is that hardware security keys use an origin/domain binding technique, meaning that they work only on the site on which they're registered. If you register your key with `https://securebank.com`, it will sign only authentication requests for that domain. If the phishing site `https://fakebank.com` tries to authenticate, the security key won't sign the request, preventing credential theft. This makes hardware keys immune to phishing attacks, unlike passwords and OTPs.

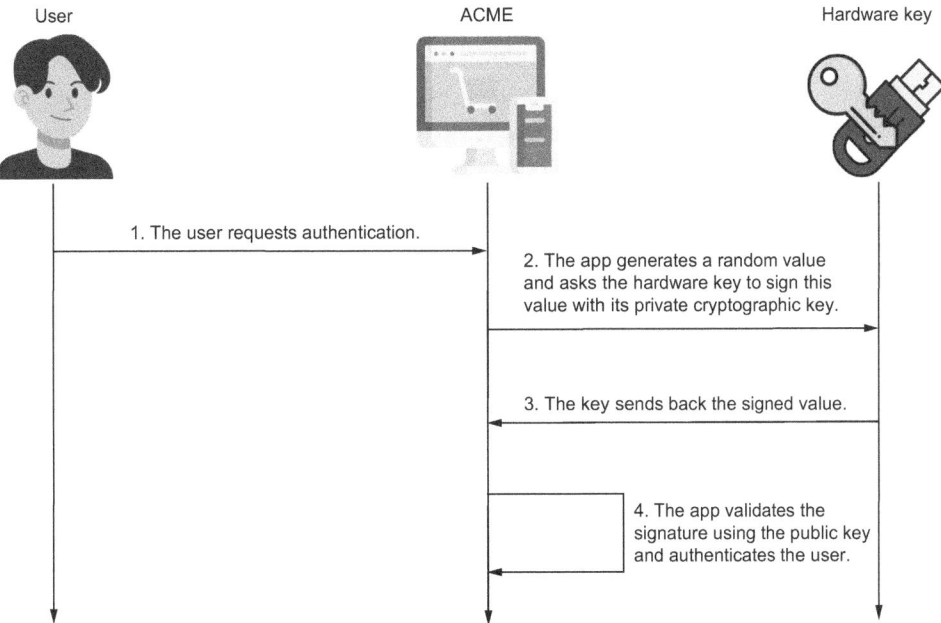

Figure 15.3 The authentication process using a hardware key. The app generates a random value and asks the key to sign it with its private key. The app verifies the signature using its public key. The public key from the pair must already be configured at the app level. This configuration happens during the registration step.

After everything we've covered, one thing is clear: hardware security keys are like digital vault keys that hackers can't steal, phish, or guess. Unlike passwords that get leaked, OTPs that arrive too late, and biometrics that can't be changed after they're compromised, these tiny devices offer rock-solid security with a simple tap. Sure, they may seem old-school compared with facial recognition and magic links, but hardware keys outperform them all in keeping hackers out. No phishing attack, MITM interception, or sneaky deepfake can trick a security key into authenticating on the wrong website.

No system is perfect, of course. Losing a hardware key can be a hassle, and not every website supports hardware keys yet. But as more services embrace passwordless authentication, hardware keys may prove to be the gold standard of security.

15.2.1 Exercises

5 What is a hardware security key?

6 How does a hardware key prevent phishing?

7 What is the attestation object in WebAuthn?

8 Why are hardware keys considered more secure than biometrics?

9 What happens if you lose your hardware key?

15.3   *Implementing WebAuthn authentication*

Sections 15.1 and 15.2 dissected WebAuthn definitions, exploring the advantages and disadvantages of various approaches. Now it's time to delve into the code and review the practical aspects of implementation. This section works through a simple example to demonstrate how to implement authentication with WebAuthn.

We'll begin with the registration process. To do this, we'll create a basic web page using plain JavaScript, allowing users to set their authentication credentials. We'll also develop a demo backend to support this functionality.

The second step is authentication. We'll implement another simple web page using plain JavaScript, where users will be prompted to authenticate.

The following listing illustrates the first step in creating a simple registration web page. The page contains only a basic button that, when clicked, triggers a simple JavaScript function. This function, which we'll develop in the upcoming listings, is responsible for gathering the necessary registration details.

Listing 15.1   Preparing the JavaScript registration function

```html
<!DOCTYPE html>
<html lang="en">
<head>
    <meta charset="UTF-8">
    <meta name="viewport" content="width=device-width, initial-scale=1.0">
    <title>WebAuthn Registration</title>
</head>
<body>
    <h2>WebAuthn Registration</h2>
    <button onclick="registerWebAuthn()">      ⟵  Creating a button that we'll
      Register WebAuthn Credential                    use in this demo to trigger
    </button>                                          the registration event

    <script>
        async function registerWebAuthn() {    ⟵  The function called
          // to implement                             when clicking the
        }                                             registration button
    </script>
</body>
</html>
```

The next listing begins implementing the JavaScript registration function. We start by checking whether the current system supports WebAuthn hardware-based authentication for registration. Because the web page runs in a browser, this check can be performed easily with standard JavaScript, as shown in the listing.

Listing 15.2   Checking whether the browser supports WebAuthn

```javascript
async function registerWebAuthn() {          │  Verifying if the browser supports
  if (!window.PublicKeyCredential) {      ⟵  │  WebAuthn authentication
    console.error("WebAuthn is not supported in this browser.");
```

```
        return;
    }

    // to continue implementation
}
```

The next listing adds the logic for retrieving the public key credentials. These credentials must be stored on the server side because they're essential for verifying responses from the hardware authentication device. The retrieval process is performed only if the system supports hardware authentication; otherwise, an error message appears on the console, and the registration process halts.

> **NOTE** This simplified approach is intended for learning purposes, allowing you to focus solely on the core steps. Naturally, a more polished user experience, with proper error handling and user feedback, would be necessary in a real-world application.

Listing 15.3 Requesting public key credentials for registration

```
async function registerWebAuthn() {
    if (!window.PublicKeyCredential) {
        console.error("WebAuthn is not supported in this browser.");
        return;
    }

    const publicKeyCredentialCreationOptions = {          The challenge
        challenge: new Uint8Array(32),                    value           The app
        rp: { name: "My WebAuthn App" },                                  name
        user: {
            id: new Uint8Array(16),
            name: "user@example.com",           The user details
            displayName: "User Example"
        },
        pubKeyCredParams: [{ type: "public-key", alg: -7 }],
        authenticatorSelection: { authenticatorAttachment: "platform" },
        timeout: 60000,                                         The timeout for accepting
        attestation: "direct"                                   the registration
    };

    // to continue implementation
}
```

The following listing completes the process by creating the public key using the previously retrieved details. If the operation is successful, the key's essential components—such as the credential ID, key type, algorithm, and raw public key—are printed to the console. Otherwise, an error message is logged.

> **NOTE** In a real-world application, this public key object would be sent to the server, typically as part of a JSON payload via an HTTPS POST request. The server stores the credential ID and associated public key, which it later uses to

verify signed authentication responses during login attempts. For demonstration purposes, we simply log the key details to the console to confirm that the frontend portion of the WebAuthn registration flow works as expected.

Listing 15.4   Requesting creation of the public key

```
async function registerWebAuthn() {
  if (!window.PublicKeyCredential) {
    console.error("WebAuthn is not supported in this browser.");
    return;
  }

const publicKeyCredentialCreationOptions = {
    challenge: new Uint8Array(32),
    rp: { name: "My WebAuthn App" },
    user: {
      id: new Uint8Array(16),
      name: "user@example.com",
      displayName: "User Example"
    },
    pubKeyCredParams: [{ type: "public-key", alg: -7 }],
    authenticatorSelection: { authenticatorAttachment: "platform" },
    timeout: 60000, // Timeout in milliseconds
    attestation: "direct"
};

  try {
    const credential = await navigator.credentials
      .create({
      publicKey: publicKeyCredentialCreationOptions
    });

    if (!credential) {
      console.error("Credential creation failed.");
      return;
    }

    const attestationObject =
      btoa(String.fromCharCode(...new
        Uint8Array(credential.response.attestationObject)));
    const clientDataJSON =
      btoa(String.fromCharCode(...new
        Uint8Array(credential.response.clientDataJSON)));
    const credentialId =
      btoa(String.fromCharCode(...new
        Uint8Array(credential.rawId)));

    console.log("WebAuthn Registration Data:");
    console.log("Attestation Object:", attestationObject);
    console.log("Client Data JSON:", clientDataJSON);
    console.log("Credential ID:", credentialId);
  } catch (error) {
```

Creating the public credentials (public key)

If the public key creation failed, the app displayed a console message and stops the process.

If the public key creation succeeded, we display the details in the console.

```
      console.error("WebAuthn registration failed:", error);
    }

}
```

Now it's time to run the page. Because it's an HTML file, your first instinct may be to double-click it and let the browser do its thing. Unfortunately, WebAuthn isn't that easygoing; it insists on running in a secure context. Simply opening the file directly won't work.

But you don't have to buy a domain or spin up some heavy enterprise server to impress WebAuthn. Fortunately, localhost is considered a real domain for security purposes, so any local web server will do the trick, even the small-but-mighty kind.

Because this book uses Java for examples, we'll stick with the tools Java offers. Starting with Java 21, the Java Development Kit (JDK) includes a handy little HTTP server that you can launch from the command line:

```
jwebserver --port 8000
```

If you use the preceding command, the web-page file must be located in the current working directory (.) from which you started the web server. Alternatively, you can specify a different folder by using the `--directory` option, like this:

```
jwebserver --port 8000 --directory /path/to/your/files
```

Figure 15.4 shows the `jwebserver` command being used for a Java 21 installation.

```
Windows PowerShell
Copyright (C) Microsoft Corporation. All rights reserved.

Install the latest PowerShell for new features and improvements! https://aka.ms/PSWindows

PS C:\Users\lspilca\.jdks\azul-21\bin> ./jwebserver --port 8000
Binding to loopback by default. For all interfaces use "-b 0.0.0.0" or "-b ::".
Serving C:\Users\lspilca\.jdks\azul-21\bin and subdirectories on 127.0.0.1 port 8000
URL http://127.0.0.1:8000/
```

Figure 15.4 Running a local web server using the jwebserver command from the JDK. The server is started in the bin directory of the JDK installation, binding to 127.0.0.1 on port 8000. This allows the HTML page to be served over a secure context (localhost), which is required for WebAuthn functionality.

Accessing the page on localhost and port 8000 displays the page. Click the button to initiate the registration process, as shown in figure 15.5.

The prompt shown during WebAuthn registration can vary depending on the device, browser, and available authentication method. In this example, the system prompts for a PIN because it's using Windows Hello as the platform authenticator, and the current configuration relies on verification based on a personal identification number (PIN).

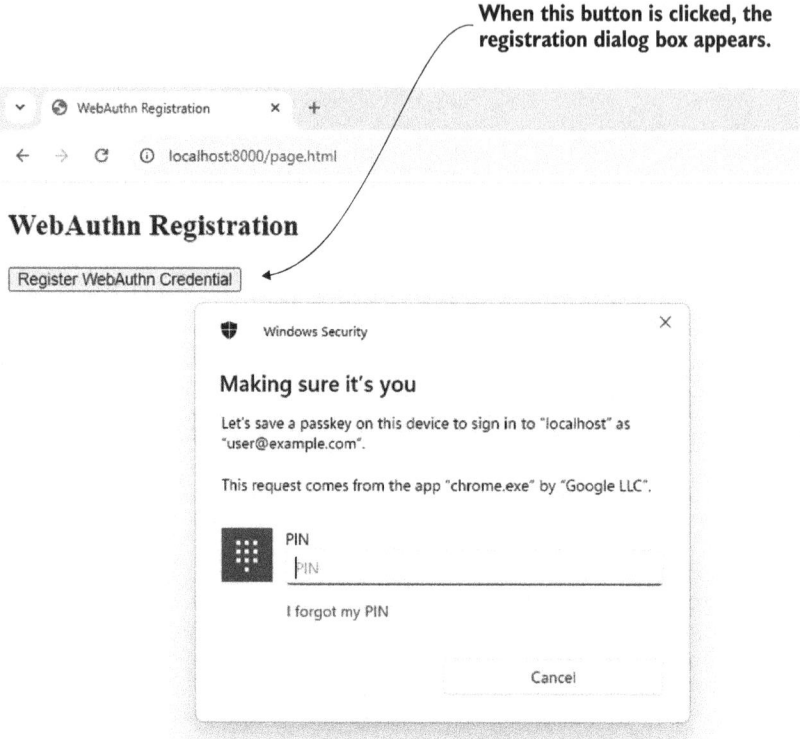

Figure 15.5   When the Register WebAuthn Credential button is clicked, the browser initiates the WebAuthn registration process. The system prompts the user with a Windows Security dialog box to confirm their identity and save a passkey for the specified domain (localhost in this case), using platform authentication.

Windows Hello supports several user verification methods, including PINs, fingerprints, and facial recognition. If the device has biometric hardware (such as a fingerprint sensor) and is configured, the system may prompt the user to authenticate using that method instead of a PIN, ensuring that only the legitimate user can register a passkey on the device.

On other platforms, the experience differs. macOS users, for example, may be prompted to use Touch ID, and Android users may see a native biometric prompt for fingerprint or facial recognition. If the user is registering with an external security key (such as a YubiKey), the browser may prompt them to insert or tap the device and then, if required, enter a PIN associated with that hardware key.

In short, although the underlying WebAuthn process remains the same, the user experience is platform-dependent. Each system chooses the most appropriate verification method based on its configuration and available hardware. Figure 15.6 shows the output in the browser's developer console, confirming the completion of the front-end portion of the WebAuthn registration process.

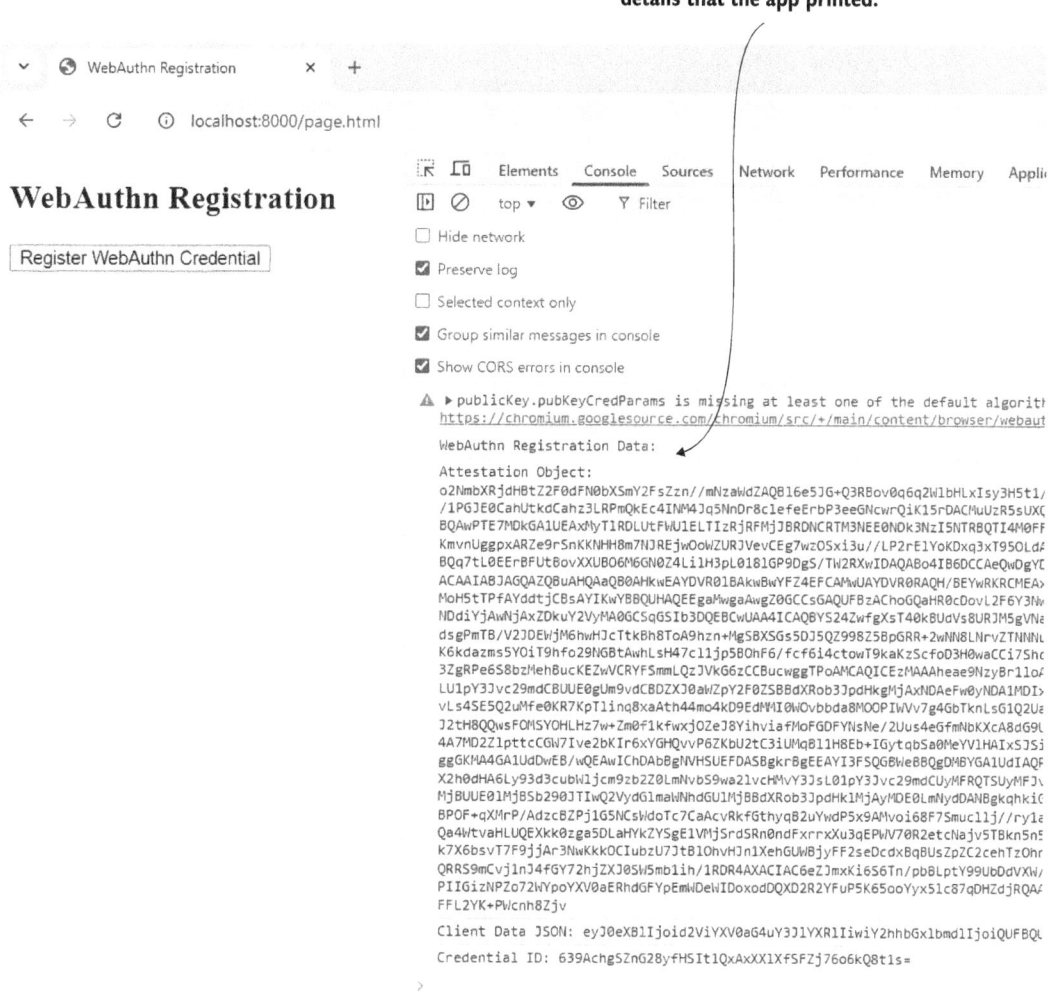

Figure 15.6   **Output in the browser's developer console after triggering the WebAuthn registration process. The console displays the attestation object and client data in Base64-encoded form, representing the public key credential generated by the browser.**

The next listing illustrates the backend component responsible for handling the WebAuthn registration request. In this stage of the flow, the backend's role is relatively simple: it receives the credential data from the frontend and stores it, associating it with a specific user account. This data typically includes values such as the credential ID, public key, and (optionally) client data.

NOTE   The example shown here uses a placeholder response and doesn't persist the data. In a real-world application, you'd store these details in a database, linked to a user record. If the user is already logged in or identified during the registration flow, you could associate the credential with their email address or username: email/username -> [credentialId, publicKey, algorithm]. This stored data will be used later to validate authentication attempts, ensuring that only users with a valid credential can sign in successfully.

Listing 15.5   Storing the registration details associated with an account

```
@RestController
@RequestMapping("/api/webauthn")
public class WebAuthnController {

  @PostMapping("/register")
  public String register(@RequestBody RegistrationRequest request) {

    return "Registration successful";         Store the details and associate
  }                                            them with an account
}
```

Now let's talk about authentication, which implies three steps:

1 The backend generates a challenge (random value).
2 The client signs the backend's challenge and sends the signed value to the backend.
3 The backend verifies the signature using the public key stored during registration.

We'll assume that registration has already taken place because the system needs to know the user and have a public key registered for the user's hardware device to allow them to authenticate. The backend has to provide two endpoints:

- An endpoint to present the challenge to the client (step 1)
- An endpoint to validate the data sent by the client (step 3)

NOTE   As in the preceding example, we've intentionally kept things as simple as possible to help you digest the explanation more easily. Including a full, production-ready implementation in a book would be impractical, but the code and concepts presented here should give you a solid foundation to build on.

TIP   When you're ready to implement this approach in a real-world scenario, a good understanding of your chosen framework is essential. If you're working with Spring and want a refresher, we highly recommend *Spring in Action, Sixth Edition,* by Craig Walls (Manning, 2022) and *Spring Security in Action, Second Edition,* by Laurențiu Spilcă (Manning, 2024). Both are excellent resources for deepening your knowledge.

The next listing presents a simplified implementation of the endpoint that gives the client a challenge for authentication. The application identifies the user based on the provided username and generates a secure, random challenge. Then it stores an association between the user ID and the challenge in a temporary store.

Listing 15.6 The challenge endpoint

```
@PostMapping("/authenticate/challenge")
public Map<String, Object> getAuthenticationChallenge(
  @RequestBody Map<String, String> request) {
    String username = request.get("username");

        String storedCredentialId = getUser(username);     ⊲─┐

        byte[] challenge = new byte[32];            ⊲─┐
    new SecureRandom().nextBytes(challenge);

        store.put(storedCredentialId, challenge);      ⊲─

    Map<String, Object> allowCredential
    ⇒ = new HashMap<>();                   ⊲─
    allowCredential.put("type", "public-key");
    allowCredential.put("id", storedCredentialId);

    var encChallange = Base64.getEncoder()
    ⇒ .encodeToString(challenge);            ⊲─

    Map<String, Object> response = new HashMap<>();   ⊲─┐
    response.put("challenge", encChallange );
    response.put("allowCredentials", List.of(allowCredential));

    return response;
}
```

Getting user details from the database. We assume the getUser() method exists and correctly gets the details from a persistent storage.

Generating a secure, random challenge

Storing the username and challenge association to use it later for authentication

Preparing the credentials ID to be returned along with the challenge

Encoding the challenge to send it as a string value in the response

Preparing the full response and returning it

NOTE When implementing this in a real-world scenario, pay close attention to how and where this association is stored. If your application must be horizontally scalable, running across multiple instances, storing this data in memory (e.g., using a map) is unsuitable. Instead, consider using a shared storage mechanism such as a database or a distributed cache (e.g., Redis) to ensure consistency and availability across nodes.

The application prepares the response and returns the challenge to the client. In addition to the challenge itself, notice that we included the previously stored credential ID in the response. We did this by populating the allowCredentials field, which explicitly tells the client which credentials are permitted for authentication.

Providing allowCredentials is highly recommended when you already know the user's identity (after they enter a username or email address, for example). By doing so, you're instructing the browser to limit the authentication options to a specific credential or set of credentials registered for that user. This not only improves performance but also enhances security and the user experience by eliminating unnecessary prompts and confusion.

If you omit the `allowCredentials` field, the browser assumes that you're logging in without a username and may prompt the user to select a credential from any passkey or security key available on their device. This situation can have unintended consequences. If a user has multiple credentials registered with different services or identities, for example, they may accidentally try to authenticate with the wrong one, causing the authentication to fail or produce misleading errors.

Beyond verifying the signature, the server can and should enforce several additional rules to strengthen the security of the authentication process:

- *Challenge timeout*—The server should associate each challenge with a limited time window—typically, a few minutes—during which the user must complete authentication. This prevents an attacker from capturing and reusing an old challenge later. When the timeout expires, the server should reject any authentication attempt using that challenge. Implementing this mechanism reduces the risk of replay attacks and unauthorized use of stale challenges.
- *Relying party ID enforcement*—The server should verify that the authentication data's relying party ID (`rpId`) matches the expected domain (such as example.com). This ensures that the client is genuinely interacting with your server and not tricked into authenticating against a malicious domain. Enforcing the correct `rpId` protects against phishing and MITM attacks, in which a rogue site attempts to hijack the authentication process.

The next listing demonstrates a basic implementation of the authentication logic. You see how the server receives the authentication details from the client. The most essential elements are the credential ID and the signature generated by the authenticator for the previously issued random challenge. The backend uses the public key, which was stored during registration, to verify the signature cryptographically. If the verification is successful and the signature matches the challenge, the authentication is considered successful, and the user is granted access.

NOTE   This example is intentionally simplified to help you understand the key steps in the process. In a production-grade application, especially if you're using Spring, this logic should be properly integrated into the authentication mechanism using Spring Security's standard design patterns. If you need a refresher, see *Spring Security in Action, Second Edition*.

Listing 15.7   The authentication endpoint

```
@PostMapping("/authenticate")
public String authenticate(
  @RequestBody AuthenticationResponse response) {        Getting the
                                                          authentication details
  String credentialId = response.getId();            ←── from the request body
  byte[] signature = Base64.getDecoder()
    .decode(response.getResponse().getSignature());
  byte[] authenticatorData = Base64.getDecoder()
```

```
    .decode(response.getResponse().getAuthenticatorData());
byte[] clientDataJSON = Base64.getDecoder()
    .decode(response.getResponse().getClientDataJSON());

byte[] storedPublicKey                          Getting the public key
    = getRegiteredPublicKey(credentialId);      and the original challenge
byte[] originalChallenge                        the server stored
    = store.get(credentialId);

var succss = verifySignatureAndAuthenticate(    ◁──  Verifying the signature using
    storedPublicKey,                                 the registered public key and
    orginalChallenge,                                the original challenge
    signature);

if (success) return "Authentication successful";
else throw new UnsuccesfulAuthenticationException();
}
```

NOTE Signature verification may be challenging to implement on your own. Implementing it yourself could also lead to errors, which in turn could introduce vulnerabilities. We recommend that you use a known library for this capability, such as WebAuthn4J (https://github.com/webauthn4j/ webauthn4j) for Java apps.

There you have it: the core steps of WebAuthn authentication from both the frontend and backend sides. Although we've kept things simple to help you grasp the essentials, now you have all the key pieces you need to move toward a secure, passwordless login flow.

In a real application, of course, you'd want to tighten things: use proper cryptographic verification, secure your challenge storage, and integrate cleanly with your authentication framework. But for now, you've earned the right to say "Yeah, I know how WebAuthn works." Just don't try it in production with an in-memory map and a prayer.

Take a deep breath. You just tackled a modern authentication flow that combines cryptography, browser APIs, and backend logic.

15.3.1 Exercises

10   What are the main steps of registration in WebAuthn?

11   Why does WebAuthn require localhost or HTTPS?

12   What's the role of the challenge during authentication?

13   Why is it important to verify the challenge and origin?

14   Create a basic WebAuthn registration and authentication demo, using JavaScript and a simple backend:

Part A: WebAuthn registration (frontend)
   Requirements:
   ▪ A simple HTML page with a Register Credential button

- JavaScript code that
  - Checks WebAuthn support
  - Generates a credential using `navigator.credentials.create()`
  - Logs or displays credential ID and client data JSON

Bonus: Convert the data to Base64 and show it as a simulated payload to send to the backend.

Part B: Simulate the backend

- Use Spring Boot or a minimal Java HTTP server to
  - Accept `POST` requests at `/api/webauthn/register`
  - Log and associate credentials with users in memory (e.g., `Map<String, Web-AuthnCredential>`)

Part C: Simulate authentication

Implement the following:

- A challenge generator (32-byte random value)
- A frontend that
  - Requests this challenge from the backend
  - Signs it using `navigator.credentials.get()`
  - Sends the response back to the backend for verification

15.4   *Exercise answers*

1 How does biometric authentication work?

It verifies identity using traits such as your fingerprint, face, or voice. These traits are scanned and matched with data stored securely on your device.

2 What is stored during biometric registration?

Instead of the actual face or fingerprint, a math-based template of the biometric data is stored in a secure chip such as the TPM or Secure Enclave.

3 What are spoofing and presentation attacks?

Spoofing tricks sensors using fake fingerprints or 3D masks. Presentation attacks use photos, videos, or AI-generated data to fool systems.

4 Why is storing biometric templates insecurely a problem?

Unlike passwords, biometrics can't be changed. If they're stolen, attackers can impersonate users forever.

5 What is a hardware security key?

It's a physical device that stores a private key and uses it to prove your identity during login without sending the key over the network.

6 How does a hardware key prevent phishing?

It's tied to the original website (origin binding), so it won't respond to a fake site even if the two sites look identical.

7 What is the attestation object in WebAuthn?

It's data that the browser sends during registration to prove that a real, trusted device created the key pair.

8 Why are hardware keys considered more secure than biometrics?

Hardware keys use cryptography, never expose secrets, and can't be faked or copied, as biometric traits might be.

9 What happens if you lose your hardware key?

You're locked out unless you registered a backup key. That's why having a backup is best practice.

10 What are the main steps of registration in WebAuthn?

The browser checks support, creates a key pair, and sends the public key to the backend. The private key stays safely on the device.

11 Why does WebAuthn require localhost or HTTPS?

Secure context is mandatory because it protects the key and data against interception during registration and login.

12 What's the role of the challenge during authentication?

The challenge is a random string sent by the server. The device signs it with its private key to prove that it's the same device.

13 Why is it important to verify the challenge and origin?

Verification prevents replay and phishing attacks. Only the original challenge from the right domain should be accepted.

14 Create a basic WebAuthn registration and authentication demo, using JavaScript and a simple backend.

URL to solution: https://mng.bz/qRaK

Summary

- Passwordless authentication improves security and convenience by eliminating weak or reused passwords.
- Spoofing attacks (such as deepfakes and fake fingerprints) and stolen biometric templates pose risks, such as unauthorized access to sensitive accounts, MFA bypass, and long-term identity compromise
- Storing biometric data in secure hardware (such as TPM and Secure Enclave) and implementing antispoofing measures improve security.
- Hardware security keys provide the strongest authentication by using public key cryptography.
- Hardware security keys eliminate phishing risks but require physical possession, making backup keys necessary.
- Using FIDO2/WebAuthn and enforcing domain binding ensures maximum security.

- Passwordless authentication reduces phishing, credential leaks and login friction.
- No single method fits all use cases. Choosing the right approach depends on security needs, usability, and risk factors.
- Proper implementation is key. Even the most secure authentication method can be exploited if it's configured poorly.
- Following best practices, encryption standards, and secure handling of authentication data ensures a stronger, safer login experience.

Part 5

Securing service-to-service call chains

We've reached the final part of this book. So far, you've learned to use cryptography, build trust with certificates and Transport Layer Security (TLS) and authenticate users with modern identity protocols. But securing applications doesn't stop at users. In large systems, the real challenge is keeping the services honest, proving who they are and making sure that they can do only what they're allowed to do.

In this part, we'll look at service identity (chapter 16), the foundation for secure service-to-service communication in a zero-trust world. Then we'll turn to authorization at scale (chapter 17), exploring RBAC, ABAC, and ReBAC, and showing you how to choose the right model for your architecture without drowning in complexity.

This closing part ties everything together. By the end, you'll have the tools to secure not only users but also the services and workflows that make up modern cloud-native systems. It's a fitting way to conclude our journey from understanding the math behind cryptography all the way to building systems that stay secure at scale.

16

Implementing service identity

This chapter covers

- Understanding what service identity is
- Enforcing service-to-service authorization directly within the application code
- Exploring infrastructure-level approaches to delegating identity enforcement
- Choosing between application and infrastructure-level strategies

If you've ever tried to figure out why one service is refusing to talk to another, only to discover that the reason was that the caller was impersonating someone else, you already understand why service identity matters. In a world in which machines talk to machines more than people talk to people, knowing who's calling isn't just a nice-to-have feature.

The days when we could trust everything inside the perimeter are gone. The perimeter itself is gone. Services are multiplying, and every call in your system should be treated with suspicion. Service identity brings order to chaos. It's the badge each service wears to say, "Yes, it's really me, and here's the cryptographic proof."

16.1 What service identity is

Service identity is the mechanism that allows systems to determine which service (app) it is. Just as user identity helps us determine who a human is, service identity does that for apps in a system. Without a reliable way to identify services, authorization, auditing, and secure communication become guesswork.

If you can't prove who's making a request, granting access is a gamble, and every decision could be a security breach in disguise. Without a strong service identity, you accept anonymous API calls and hope that they're from a friend. Hackers love optimism.

> **DEFINITION**   *Service identity* is a unique, verifiable identity assigned to a service instance or application component.

Here's a story about a seasoned hacker named Alexey who found a breach: an exposed debug pod inside a company's Kubernetes cluster. It had no password, no protection, as though someone had left the back door wide open. This should never happen, but it does, and that's why the zero-trust principle is essential.

> **DEFINITION**   *Zero trust* is a security principle that means never trusting anything automatically, whether it comes from inside or outside your system. Instead, everything must be verified: every user, every device, and every service request.

Once he was inside, the hacker began to explore. Many services were talking to one another, such as the order, billing, and user services. These services trusted one another because they were inside the same network. No one checked who was sending the requests (figure 16.1).

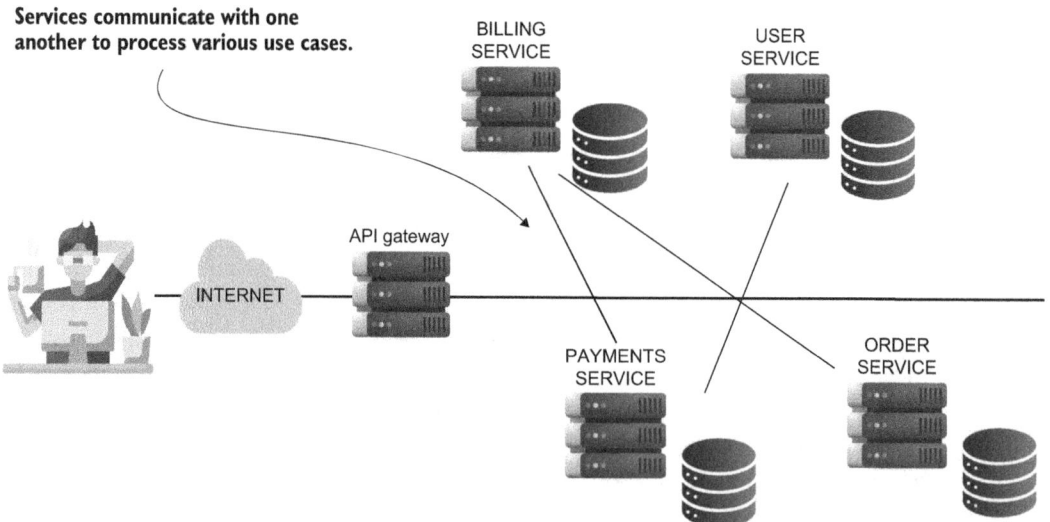

Figure 16.1   In a system, multiple services communicate to solve various use cases. If the communication isn't secure, attackers may exploit vulnerabilities and alter or steal data.

Alexey focused on the billing service; which accepted requests from the order service to process invoices. But instead of checking for a digital signature or certificate, it simply looked at a header:

```
X-Service-Name: order-service
```

"That's it? No secret key, no certificate, nothing to prove who's sending the request? Perfect," Alexey thought. So he created his own service (figure 16.2). Then he started sending fake requests to the billing service, adding the header that claimed to be from the order service. The trick worked. The billing service couldn't tell the difference. It accepted fake requests, processed fake invoices, and even leaked real billing data. Alexey quietly kept going, generating fake transactions, modifying amounts, and collecting information because the system had no reliable way to check service identity.

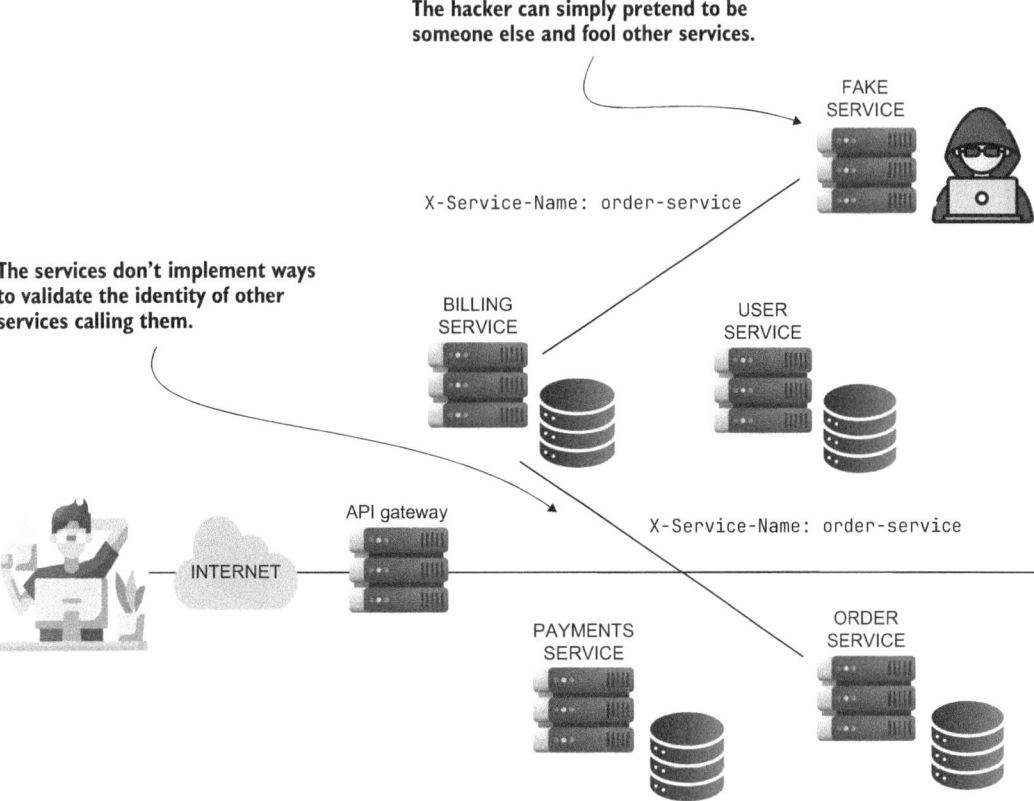

Figure 16.2   Services that trust incoming messages without verifying the sender's identity are vulnerable. If an attacker gains access, they can impersonate trusted services and send messages to manipulate or extract data from the system.

This kind of attack is possible only when services can't prove who they are. Let's look at the building blocks that help prevent this situation. We'll look at the key components that make systems' service communications more secure:

- *Identity*—Typically encoded in certificates, tokens, or metadata
- *Authentication*—Verifying the identity (e.g., using mutual TLS [mTLS], JSON Web Tokens [JWTs], or signatures)
- *Trust anchors*—Who vouches for this identity? (e.g., a certificate authority [CA] or token issuer)
- *Scope of identity*—What the identity is assigned to and how specific it is

Every service in a system needs a way to say, "This is who I am." That's what we call *identity*. Just as people carry passports or ID cards, services have something that proves who they are. This identity is usually in the form of a certificate, a token (such as a signed JWT), or trusted metadata provided by the system (such as a Kubernetes service account). Identity is unique to each service and helps other parts of the system recognize it. Without this kind of identity, any service could claim to be anything, and that's when bad things can happen.

When a service says, "This is who I am" (identity), the next step is authentication: checking whether that's true. Authentication is how a system ensures that the service owns the identity it claims. The process is usually done with tools such as mTLS, with both services presenting and verifying certificates, or with JWT tokens, with the token being signed by a trusted party. Authentication is like checking the hologram and signature on a passport. You're not just reading the name; you're also proving that the document isn't fake.

But who decides which identities are real? That's where trust anchors come in. A *trust anchor* is a system or authority that everyone agrees to trust. It could be a CA that signs service certificates or a token issuer that creates signed JWTs. If a service shows a certificate signed by a trusted CA, others will believe it. If it uses a token from a known and trusted source, that's accepted too. It's like a friend you trust saying, "Yes, this person is who they say they are." Without trust anchors, services wouldn't know who to believe

Finally, we have to consider the *scope of identity*—how specific a service's identity is. Sometimes, all copies of a service have the same identity, much as every driver at a delivery service wears the same badge. That's a wide scope. At other times, each service instance or container gets its own unique identity, which is like each driver having a personal badge with their name and time of access. That's a narrow scope. Using a narrow scope makes your system more secure because it lets you control access more precisely and see exactly who did what. The more dynamic your system is, the more useful it is to have a smaller, more specific scope for each service identity.

Now that you understand what service identity is and why it matters, the next step is learning to use it to control access between services. Section 16.2 looks at ways to implement service authorization directly in application code, verifying who's calling and deciding what they're allowed to do. Section 16.3 explores how to push that responsibility down into the infrastructure, using tools such as service meshes and gateways to enforce security without changing application logic. Both approaches have strengths; knowing when to use each one is key to building secure, maintainable systems.

16.1.1 Exercises

1 What is service identity, and why does it matter?
2 What's the difference between identity and authentication?
3 What is a trust anchor?
4 Why does zero trust apply here?

16.2 Implementing service authorization at the application level

When a service knows who is calling (through authentication), the next question is whether the caller is allowed to do what they're trying to do. That's where authorization comes in. "At the application level" means that the service itself makes the decision through code or middleware. It checks the caller's identity and applies rules like "Can `order-service` call `/process-invoice` on `billing-service`?" If the answer is yes, the request goes through; if not, it gets blocked in the application (figure 16.3).

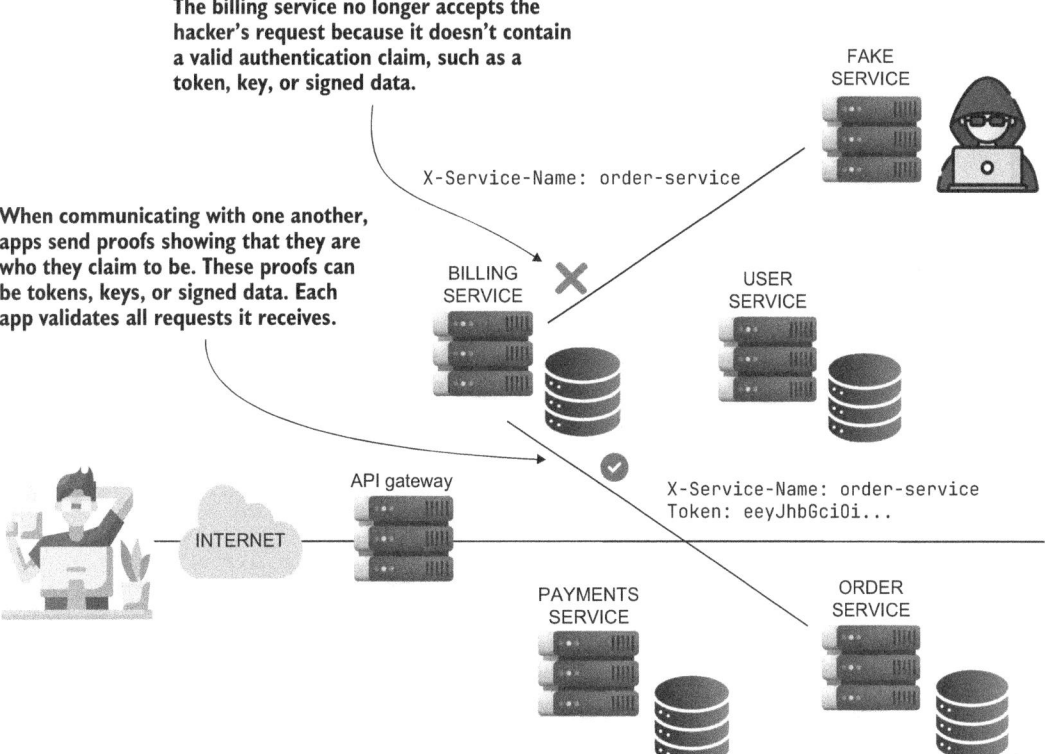

The billing service no longer accepts the hacker's request because it doesn't contain a valid authentication claim, such as a token, key, or signed data.

When communicating with one another, apps send proofs showing that they are who they claim to be. These proofs can be tokens, keys, or signed data. Each app validates all requests it receives.

FAKE SERVICE

X-Service-Name: order-service

BILLING SERVICE

USER SERVICE

API gateway

INTERNET

X-Service-Name: order-service
Token: eeyJhbGciOi...

PAYMENTS SERVICE

ORDER SERVICE

Figure 16.3   Each application includes logic to validate incoming requests. Every request should contain a token, key, or other proof that identifies the sender as a trusted counterpart. If the request lacks valid proof, the service rejects it.

This approach gives you fine-grained control because you can build logic directly around your business needs. But it also means that every service has to play by the rules. If one service forgets the rules or gets lazy, you might end up with gaps in your defenses. With application-level authorization, each service is responsible for checking who is making a request and whether that request should be allowed. This approach gives you fine-grained control because you can write logic that is specific to your business. A service can say, "Only the `order-service` is allowed to create invoices" or "Only users with the role manager can approve refunds over $1,000."

This flexibility is powerful, especially when the decision depends on something that only the application knows, such as user roles, order history, or product inventory. You can tailor the rules to fit your needs and enforce them directly inside the part of the code that handles the request.

But there's a downside: because each service is in charge of enforcing its rules, you must trust every team to get it right. One service might perform proper checks while another might skip a step or apply weaker rules. Errors can lead to inconsistent policies across the system and create security holes that attackers can exploit.

The following steps describe service authorization at the app level (figure 16.4):

1 The caller (another service) sends a request along with a token or credential that proves who it is.
2 The receiving service (the app itself) validates that token, checking whether it's real and unexpired.
3 The service (the app itself) checks a set of authorization rules based on the caller's identity.
4 If everything checks out, the request is processed; if not, it's denied.

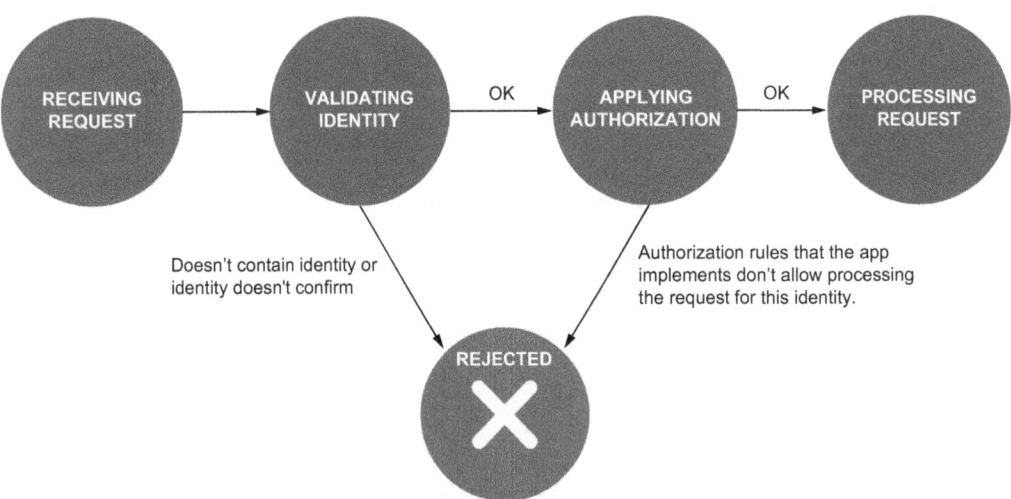

Figure 16.4 **Steps the app follows to validate a request**

What tools can you use to implement service authorization at the application level? Most systems identify and verify callers by relying on a few common patterns, each of which has tradeoffs in terms of security, complexity, and flexibility:

1   *The OAuth2 client credentials grant type*—A service authenticates with an authorization server to obtain a token, which it uses to prove its identity when calling other services.

2   *API keys*—A simple static token is included in requests to identify the caller. This token is often easy to use but less secure and harder to manage at scale.

3   *Custom authorization logic*—Application-specific rules written in code to decide whether a request is allowed, offering flexibility but requiring careful and consistent implementation.

16.2.1 Using the OAuth2 client credentials grant type

One of the most robust approaches is the OAuth 2 client credentials flow. Chapters 12 and 13 discussed OAuth 2 and OpenID Connect (OIDC), focusing on authorization flows that involve a user, such as the authorization code grant type. But OAuth 2 also defines userless authorization flows for service authentication. Services use OAuth 2 client credentials to authenticate to one another.

In this model, a service (such as `order-service`) authenticates with an identity provider (IdP), such as Keycloak or Auth0, and gets a token—usually, a JWT. This token is attached to any outgoing requests to another service (such as `billing-service`). The receiving service validates the token and reads its identity information (figure 16.5).

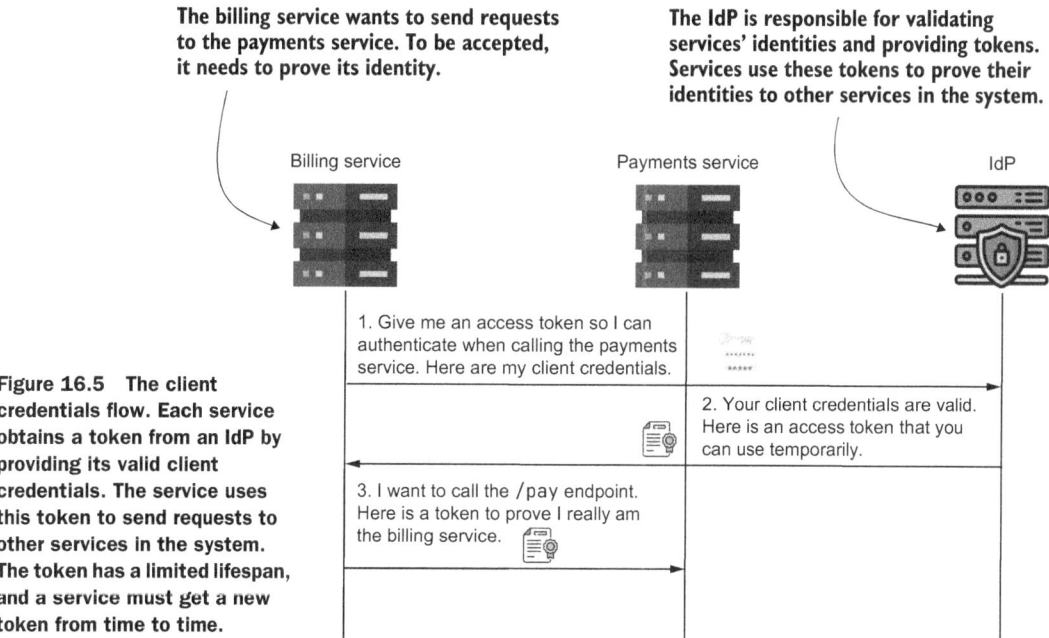

The billing service wants to send requests to the payments service. To be accepted, it needs to prove its identity.

The IdP is responsible for validating services' identities and providing tokens. Services use these tokens to prove their identities to other services in the system.

Billing service   Payments service   IdP

1. Give me an access token so I can authenticate when calling the payments service. Here are my client credentials.

2. Your client credentials are valid. Here is an access token that you can use temporarily.

3. I want to call the /pay endpoint. Here is a token to prove I really am the billing service.

Figure 16.5   The client credentials flow. Each service obtains a token from an IdP by providing its valid client credentials. The service uses this token to send requests to other services in the system. The token has a limited lifespan, and a service must get a new token from time to time.

Usually, implementing OAuth 2 flows is straightforward. Frameworks such as Spring Security provide out-of-the-box configurations that let you develop these flows with minimal effort and offer excellent flexibility for customization. The following listing shows a Spring Security configuration for a service that uses the OAuth2 client credentials grant type.

Listing 16.1   Using Spring Security to configure the client credentials grant type

```
spring:
  security:
    oauth2:
      client:
        registration:
          my-client:                            The client
            client-id: your-client-id        ◁┘ identifier        The client secret
            client-secret: your-client-secret            ◁┘ (password)
            authorization-grant-type: client_credentials
            scope: read,write                    ◁┐ The scopes it
        provider:                                 │ wants to access
          my-provider:                                        The authorization
            token-uri: https://auth-server.com/oauth2/token   ◁┘ server address
```

The grant type the app wants to use

This book focuses on best practices rather than going deeply into frameworks such as Spring Security. But if your intention is to learn Spring Security more deeply, we recommend *Spring Security in Action, Second Edition,* by Laurențiu Spilcă (Manning, 2024).

16.2.2 Using API keys

API keys are among the simplest ways to identify and authorize a service. An API key is a unique string, such as a password, that one service includes in its request to another service. If the receiving service recognizes the key, it accepts the request; if not, it rejects the request.

   This approach is easy to implement. Many internal systems or hobby projects start with API keys because they don't require complex setup: just generate a key, put it in your app's configuration, and check for it in incoming requests (figure 16.6). The order service could send a request to the billing service with a custom header like this:

```
X-API-KEY: abc123-secure-token
```

The next listing shows a simple code example that implements the logic for validating the API key.

Listing 16.2   Validating the API key

```
@PostMapping("/process")
public ResponseEntity<String> processRequest(
  @RequestHeader("X-API-KEY") String apiKey) {
                                                       Validating
                                                    ◁┘ the API key
    if (!"abc123-secure-token".equals(apiKey)) {
```

```
    return ResponseEntity
      .status(HttpStatus.UNAUTHORIZED)
      .body("Invalid API Key");
  }

  // continue logic

  return ResponseEntity.ok("Invoice processed");
}
```

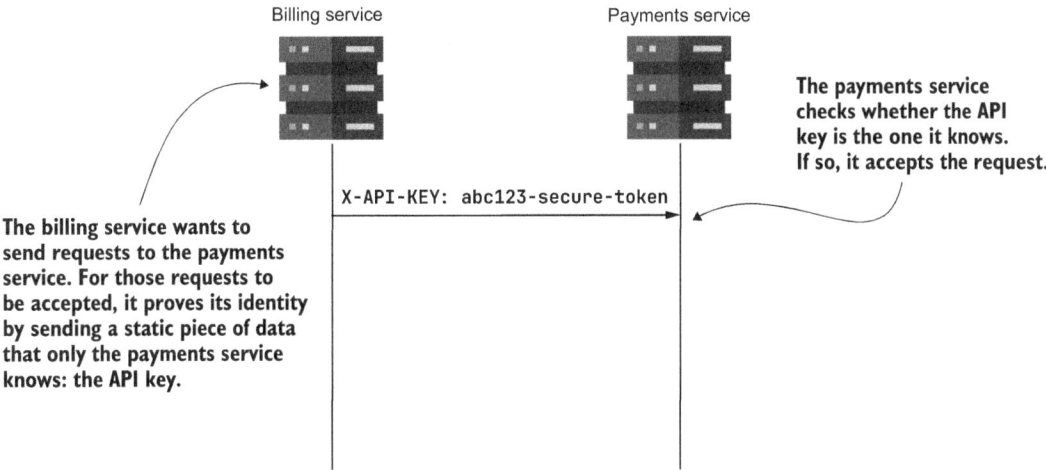

Billing service

Payments service

The payments service checks whether the API key is the one it knows. If so, it accepts the request.

X-API-KEY: abc123-secure-token

The billing service wants to send requests to the payments service. For those requests to be accepted, it proves its identity by sending a static piece of data that only the payments service knows: the API key.

Figure 16.6   The API key authentication approach is simple. Both sides know a secret that they use to prove who they are when sending requests.

NOTE   In listing 16.2, the logic appears in the controller to make it straightforward to understand. In a real-world implementation, such logic should be extracted into an aspect or handled with an alternative approach that prevents code duplication.

Even though they're easy to use, API keys have important weaknesses. The biggest problem is that they can be easily leaked (e.g., in logs, in GitHub repos, in error messages, or inside container images). If someone gets hold of a valid API key, they can impersonate the service and access everything that the key allows.

Another problem is that API keys are static. Unless you rotate them manually (a task that's often forgotten), they remain valid forever. Also, because they're simple strings, they don't carry any information; they don't say who made the request, when, or why. You can't limit them to specific actions unless you write a lot of custom logic.

Also, headers like X-API-KEY can be spoofed if you're not using HTTPS or mTLS. If your internal network is breached or misconfigured, another service (or attacker) can simply send a fake request with the same header and trick your service into accepting it. Remember how hacker Alexey proceeded at the beginning of this chapter.

API keys can be acceptable in tightly controlled environments, such as internal tools that aren't exposed to the internet and in which traffic is already protected by encryption (such as mTLS). They're also handy for temporary setups, demos, or simple systems with few moving parts.

But for production systems, especially in microservices or multitenant architectures, API keys should be replaced with more secure options such as JWTs, OAuth2, and mutual TLS, which make identity harder to fake and secure management easier to do.

16.2.3 *Using custom authorization logic*

Sometimes, standard tools such as OAuth2 and JWTs don't fit your use case, or you need tighter control of how services prove who they are but want to avoid using less-secure approaches such as API keys. That's where custom authorization logic comes in. To make things more secure, you can use asymmetric keys (chapter 7).

Here's how asymmetric keys work. The calling service (say, the inventory service) has a private key that only it knows. Before it sends a request to another service (such as the product service), it takes some important parts of the request—the path, a timestamp, or even the request body—and creates a digital signature using that private key. That signature is added to the request as a header.

When the product service receives the request, it doesn't trust the service name blindly. Instead, it uses the public key (which is safe to share) to verify that the signature is valid. If the signature checks out, the request is accepted (figure 16.7). Otherwise, the request is rejected because it might have been forged or tampered with.

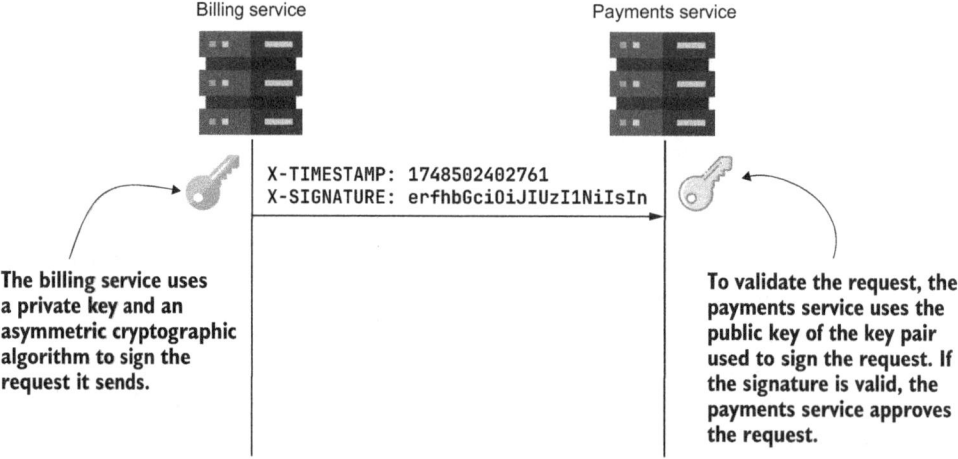

Figure 16.7   Key pairs and asymmetric cryptographic algorithms can be used to sign requests made by services to improve security. In this approach, the service signs the request with a private key. The service receiving the request can validate the signature using the public key and decide whether to approve or reject the request.

This method adds a good layer of safety: even if someone sees the request, they can't copy or fake it without the private key. The next listing shows a simple Java implementation that creates such a signature.

Listing 16.3 Signing a request

```java
public class RequestSigner {

    private final PrivateKey privateKey;

    public RequestSigner(PrivateKey privateKey) {
        this.privateKey = privateKey;
    }

    public String signRequest(String path,
      String timestamp) throws Exception {
        String message = path + "|" + timestamp;

        Signature signature = Signature.getInstance("SHA256withRSA");
        signature.initSign(privateKey);
        signature.update(message.getBytes(StandardCharsets.UTF_8));

        byte[] signedBytes = signature.sign();
        return Base64.getEncoder().encodeToString(signedBytes);
    }
}
```

In simple terms, to use the RequestSigner implementation, a service augments each request by adding the signature to an HTTP header. The next code snippet shows that code. Most likely, an app would decouple this, probably into an aspect in the case of a Spring app, so that it doesn't have to be repeated for each endpoint implementation.

```java
String path = "/adjust-stock";
String timestamp = Instant.now().toString();

String signature = signer.signRequest(path, timestamp);

HttpHeaders headers = new HttpHeaders();
headers.add("X-Timestamp", timestamp);
headers.add("X-Signature", signature);
headers.add("X-Service-Name", "inventory-service");
```

When a request includes a signature, the receiving service has only to validate it to confirm that the request came from the expected application and hasn't been tampered with. This step ensures both authenticity and integrity. The following listing shows a straightforward implementation of a utility that verifies the signature on an incoming request.

Listing 16.4 Validating a request

```java
public class RequestVerifier {

    private final PublicKey publicKey;
```

```
public RequestVerifier(PublicKey publicKey) {
    this.publicKey = publicKey;
}

public boolean verifyRequest(String path,
  String timestamp,
  String receivedSignature) throws Exception {
    String message = path + "|" + timestamp;

    Signature verifier = Signature.getInstance("SHA256withRSA");

    verifier.initVerify(publicKey);
    verifier.update(message.getBytes());
    byte[] signatureBytes =
      Base64.getDecoder().decode(receivedSignature);

    return verifier.verify(signatureBytes);
    }
}
```

Remember that keys must be stored securely, not hardcoded within the app, source code, or container. One of the biggest security mistakes is hardcoding private or public keys directly in your source code or configuration files. If your code is ever pushed to a public repository or shared within a company, those keys may be exposed. Instead, store sensitive keys in a secure vault such as HashiCorp Vault, Amazon Web Services (AWS) Secrets Manager, Microsoft Azure Key Vault, or even environment-specific secret stores such as Kubernetes Secrets (with encryption enabled). These tools protect your keys and give you options including automatic rotation, access logging, and fine-grained permissions. By keeping keys outside the application code, you reduce the risk of accidental leaks and simplify key management over time.

Another thing to think about when using this approach is replay attacks. Just verifying a signature isn't enough. If an attacker gets hold of a signed request, they could try to resend that same request later—even hours or days after it was originally sent. To prevent this kind of attack, include a timestamp when signing the request, as shown in our example, and validate it on the receiving side. A common practice is to allow a time window (such as plus or minus 5 minutes from the server clock). If the timestamp is too old or too far in the future, reject the request. This ensures that even if someone sees a signed request, they can't reuse it outside that time window, which adds a strong layer of protection.

Also, you may want to add more data for authorization. By default, you might sign only the URL path and timestamp, but that leaves some room for tampering. To make your request signature more robust, include additional fields such as the HTTP method (such as GET or POST), query parameters, and even a hash of the request body. Signing the full string "POST|/adjust-stock|timestamp|SHA256(body)", for example, ensures that even tiny changes in the body or method will result in an invalid signature. This helps protect against man-in-the-middle (MITM) modifications or subtle replay attempts, making your authorization mechanism much harder to bypass.

Custom authorization logic gives you full control and flexibility, but it also places the burden of security on each service. As systems grow, security can become harder to manage and easier to get wrong. Section 16.3 focuses on infrastructure-level authorization, in which security is enforced by the platform itself with tools such as service meshes, API gateways, and workload identity. This approach can simplify enforcement, improve consistency, and reduce the risk of human error.

16.2.4   Exercises

5 How does application-level service authorization work?

6 What is the OAuth2 client credentials flow used for?

7 Why are API keys risky?

8 How does custom request signing work?

9 What is a replay attack, and how do you stop one?

16.3   Implementing service authorization at the infrastructure level

So far in this chapter, we've looked at how services can take responsibility for authorization, such as validating tokens, checking headers, and making decisions in application code. Those approaches work well, but as systems grow, it becomes harder to ensure that every team follows the same rules and every service is secure in the same way.

At this point, infrastructure-level authorization comes into play. Instead of burdening each service, we move the responsibility to the platform by using tools such as service meshes and API gateways. These components act like security guards at the gates, checking who's calling and what they're allowed to do before the request reaches your application logic.

This approach provides centralized policy enforcement and stronger identity guarantees, and it creates less room for human error. In this section, we'll look at how this approach works in practice, when to use it, and what tools you can rely on to make it both secure and scalable

Most large systems use one or two approaches to apply infrastructure-level service authorization. You can use these approaches together when your system needs extra strength:

- *Service mesh with mTLS (e.g., Istio and Linkerd)*—A service mesh transparently secures service-to-service communication by encrypting traffic and verifying service identity using mTLS.
- *API gateways with identity enforcement (e.g., Kong and Apigee)*—API gateways serve as entry points that authenticate requests, validate tokens, and enforce access control before traffic reaches backend services.

A *service mesh* is an infrastructure layer designed to manage, observe, and secure communication between services in a distributed system. It takes over responsibilities that traditionally lived in application code—such as service discovery, traffic routing, retries, timeouts, encryption, and access control—and moves them into a dedicated network layer. This is typically achieved using lightweight sidecar proxies deployed alongside each service, which intercept and manage all incoming and outgoing traffic (figure 16.8).

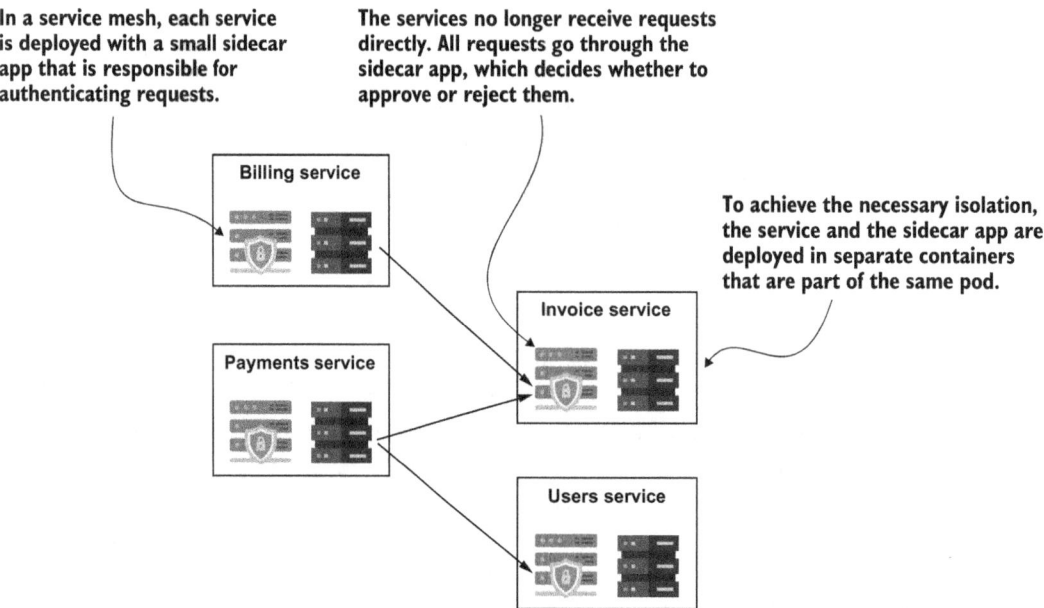

Figure 16.8   In a service mesh, each service is deployed together with a sidecar app. The sidecar app validates requests going to the app it protects.

Suppose that every service in your system has a tiny security guard (called a sidecar proxy) standing next to it, as shown in figure 16.9. When a service wants to talk to another service, it doesn't talk to that service directly. Instead, it tells its guard, "Please send this message." The receiving service has its own guard, who asks, "Who are you? Do you have the right badge? Is your message signed?" Only then does the message go through.

These guards handle tasks like the following:

- Encrypting traffic between services (using mTLS)
- Verifying service identity (using certificates)
- Applying access rules (such as "Only service A can talk to service B")

Service meshes such as Istio, Linkerd, and Consul Connect make this happen automatically. You don't need to write the security logic into your app; the mesh does it for you consistently across all services

**The sidecar app intercepts
any request going toward
the service app.**

**The two apps are always
deployed together and can
be scaled together if necessary.**

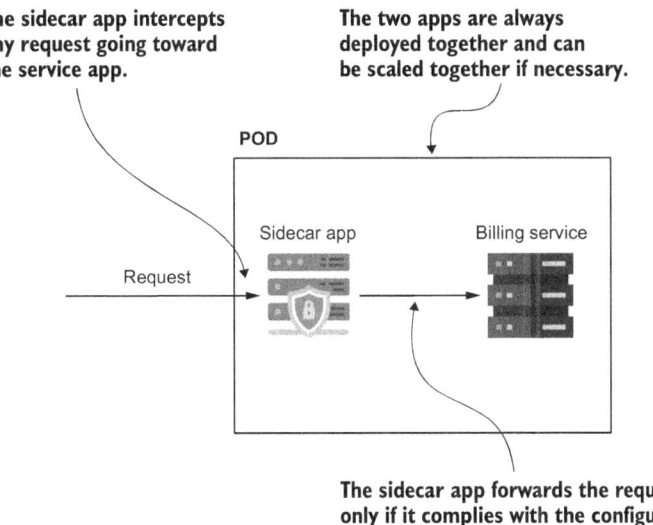

**The sidecar app forwards the request
only if it complies with the configured
authorization rules.**

**Figure 16.9 The anatomy of a pod. The two apps—the sidecar app, which takes
care of authorization, and the service—are always deployed together and can be
scaled only together. The sidecar app intercepts all requests and decides whether
to forward the request to the service based on the configured authorization rules.**

When you use infrastructure-level authorization, such as with a service mesh, security decisions happen outside the application code. The mesh sits between services, handling tasks such as encryption, service identity, and access rules. One big advantage is that you don't need to write or maintain this logic in your own code. Everything happens automatically. The mesh applies the same rules across all services, which results in fewer mistakes and more consistent behavior. It also encrypts all traffic between services and checks (usually with mTLS) that each service is who it claims to be. This makes it easier for security teams to manage policies from one place without involving every developer.

Still, this approach isn't perfect. Setting up a service mesh can be complex. It adds extra pieces to your infrastructure and requires learning new tools and concepts. You also need more computing resources because every service runs with a sidecar proxy. Although the mesh is good at enforcing general rules (such as "Only service A can talk to service B"), it doesn't know anything about your business logic. It can't decide, for example, whether to allow a user to cancel an order or to approve a refund. Such logic still has to live in your application.

On the other hand, with application-level authorization, your service handles the decision-making itself, which enables you to make detailed choices based on the content of the request, the user's role, or other internal rules. This approach gives you flexibility, and you can build exactly the access control your application needs. Developers are in full control, and changes can be made quickly right in the code.

But this flexibility has a cost: every service has to implement its own authorization logic, and if one service forgets to check something, it can create a big security hole. Also, it's harder to track what rules are in place because the logic is spread across services and codebases. Often, teams repeatedly write the same code, such as checking tokens or validating headers, which adds to the maintenance burden.

Infrastructure-level authorization is great for consistency, simplicity, and strong baseline security, especially in large systems. Application-level authorization is better when you need detailed, business-aware decisions that depend on the content or purpose of the request. Many teams use both approaches together, letting the infrastructure enforce basic identity and access while the app adds finer rules on top.

If you want to build a secure, reliable system, using infrastructure-level and application-level authorization together is one of the smartest choices you can make (figure 16.10). These two layers solve different problems, and combined, they give you much stronger protection than either alone.

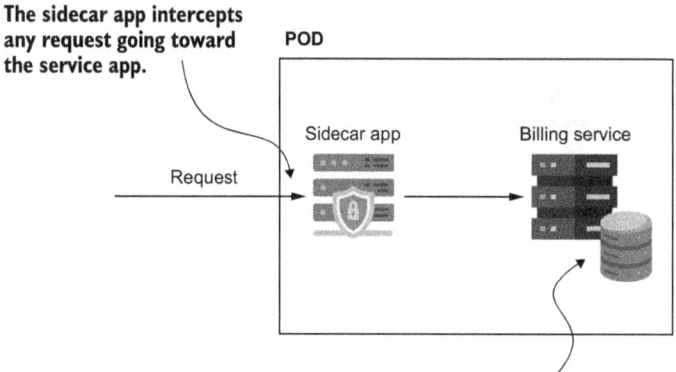

The sidecar app intercepts any request going toward the service app.

POD

Sidecar app

Billing service

Request

The service app can still apply certain authorization rules, so it may reject a request even if the sidecar app approved it. A service app usually has more context (such as access to a database) than the sidecar app and may apply different business-specific rules.

Figure 16.10   Infrastructure authorization is often combined with app-level authorization. In some cases, authorization rules are more specific to the business context and have to be defined in the service with access to the needed data.

The infrastructure layer, such as a service mesh or API gateway, is great for handling the basics. It ensures that only trusted services can talk to one another, traffic is encrypted, and every request comes from a known source. This approach can stop attackers or unauthorized services before they reach your code. It's like having a security guard at the door who checks IDs before letting anyone into the building

But when a request gets past the front door, you still need to check what the request is trying to do, which is the role of the application layer. Your application can look at the request in more detail, checking the user's role, validating tokens, and applying business-specific rules. It can decide, for example, whether a user is allowed to cancel an order or a certain service has permission to update data—something the infrastructure layer simply can't see or understand.

Another common approach is applying authorization at the API gateway (figure 16.11). An API gateway is like the front door of your system—the first thing a request hits before reaching any of your internal services. Think of it as a smart doorman for your system: it checks who's coming in, what they're allowed to do, and where they should be sent.

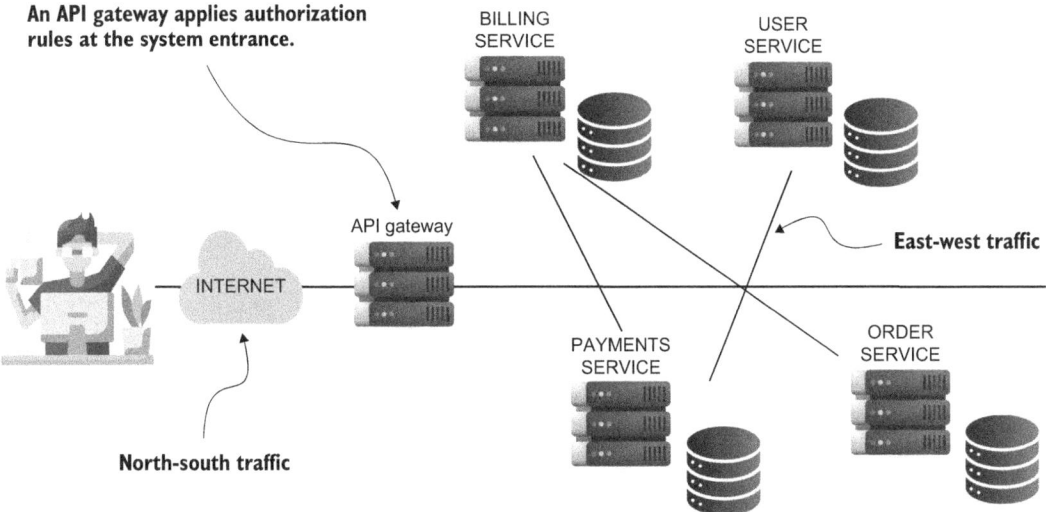

Figure 16.11   An API gateway is designed to guard the system entrance. Besides handling security, it sometimes has other responsibilities, such as observability (tracking the requests that go in and out) and service discovery (finding out which service a request is addressed to).

When we talk about identity enforcement at the API gateway, we mean that the gateway is responsible for authenticating and authorizing requests before they go any further. This task involves the following:

- Checking who made the request (identity)
- Validating tokens (such as JWTs or OAuth2 access tokens)
- Applying policies (such as rate limits, scopes, or IP restrictions)

A gateway like Kong, Apigee, or AWS API Gateway can be set up to allow only requests that include a valid token from a trusted identity provider. If the token is missing or invalid, the request is blocked immediately and never reaches your services.

This approach is powerful because it centralizes security in one place. You don't have to add token validation logic to every microservice; the gateway handles it for you consistently and efficiently. It also keeps your services cleaner and focused on business logic, not authentication code.

API gateways also help with north-south traffic (requests coming from outside your system, such as browsers or mobile apps). They're secure barriers between the public world and your internal architecture. You can combine them with service meshes to protect east-west traffic (traffic between internal services).

> **DEFINITION**   *North-south traffic* represents communication from external systems. *East-west traffic* refers to internal communication between services.

An API gateway is the first thing a request hits when it enters your system from the outside, such as requests coming from a browser, a mobile app, or a third-party client. It sits at the edge of your system and acts like a gatekeeper. It checks who's making the request, whether they're allowed in, and where the request should go.

By contrast, a service mesh works inside your system. It manages how your own services talk to one another. It can secure communication between your order and billing services. The mesh adds a small helper (a sidecar proxy) next to each service. Sidecar proxies handle security, routing, and monitoring without changing your app's code. The service mesh makes sure that every internal request is secure, encrypted, and coming from a verified service.

Although both API gateways and service meshes enforce authorization, they do so in different places and for different purposes. The API gateway protects the system from outside traffic. It validates tokens such as JWTs, applies rate limits, and blocks unauthorized access at the door. The service mesh focuses on internal trust, making sure that even inside the system, only approved services can talk to one another and that all traffic is encrypted using mTLS.

In many systems, you'll find both tools working together. The API gateway handles requests from users or clients and forwards them safely inside. Then, the service mesh takes over to control and protect traffic between services. Used together, these tools form a strong security model: the gateway keeps intruders out, and the mesh makes sure that everyone inside behaves.

16.3.1 Exercises

10 What does a service mesh do for security?

11 How do sidecars in a mesh help?

12 What's the role of an API gateway?

13 How do service meshes and API gateways work together?

14 What are the pros and cons of moving authorization to the infrastructure?

16.4   Exercise answers

1 What is service identity, and why does it matter?

Service identity is how an app proves who it is to other services. Without it, any service could pretend to be another, making your system easy to trick.

2 What's the difference between identity and authentication?

Identity says, "This is who I am," and authentication checks whether that's true. Both are required to trust a request.

3 What is a trust anchor?

A trust anchor is someone (or something) that everyone trusts to vouch for identities, such as a CA or token issuer.

4 Why does zero trust apply here?

Even services inside your system shouldn't be trusted automatically. Every request must prove who it's from.

5 How does application-level service authorization work?

The app checks who is calling and whether that service is allowed to do the requested action, usually by verifying tokens or API keys.

6 What is the OAuth2 client credentials flow used for?

It lets one service get a token from an IdP securely and use it to authenticate to another service, without user involvement.

7 Why are API keys risky?

They're static strings. If they're leaked, anyone can use them. API keys are easy to spoof, hard to rotate, and carry no useful info.

8 How does custom request signing work?

A service signs its request with a private key, and the receiving service uses the public key to verify the signature. It's safer but takes more work.

9 What is a replay attack, and how do you stop one?

In a replay attack, an attacker reuses a valid signed request to trick your system. You prevent it by including a timestamp and rejecting old or reused requests.

10 What does a service mesh do for security?

It encrypts service-to-service traffic using mTLS and checks service identity before forwarding the request, all outside your app code.

11 How do sidecars in a mesh help?

They sit next to each service and handle encryption, authentication, and authorization rules consistently and transparently.

12 What is the role of an API gateway?

It's the first line of defense for incoming (external) requests. It checks tokens, enforces policies, and blocks unauthorized traffic before it reaches your system.

13 How do service meshes and API gateways work together?

The gateway filters and secures traffic from outside the system (north-south), and the mesh secures traffic inside the system (east-west).

14 What are the pros and cons of moving authorization to the infrastructure?

This approach provides strong consistency and fewer human errors but can be complex to set up and doesn't handle detailed business rules, which remain the app's responsibility.

Summary

- Service identity is the foundation for securing service-to-service communication.
- At the application level, services validate tokens, API keys, or signed messages to decide whether a request should be allowed.
- Application-level authorization provides flexibility and fine-grained control, but it requires every service to implement authorization correctly, which can lead to inconsistencies and security gaps.
- Infrastructure-level approaches such as service meshes and API gateways move the responsibility outside the app, providing consistent enforcement, automatic mTLS, and centralized policy management.
- Service meshes secure internal traffic (east-west), and gateways focus on external requests (north-south).
- Modern systems often combine both approaches: infrastructure handles identity and baseline access, and the app enforces business-specific rules.
- A mixed model (which includes both application- and infrastructure-level configurations) for implementing service authorization improves security, reduces human error, and supports zero-trust architectures.
- No single solution fits all systems. Choosing between application- and infrastructure-level authorization depends on system complexity, security needs, and team responsibilities.
  - System complexity refers to the number of services, the communication patterns among them, and the diversity of technologies in use. Simple systems might get away with centralized gateways or API keys; distributed microservices often require more fine-grained, decentralized enforcement at the application level.
  - Security needs vary based on the sensitivity of the data and the threat model. Systems that deal with financial transactions, personal data, or regulated workloads may require multilayered authorization (e.g., both infrastructure- and application-level) to ensure defense in depth.
  - Team responsibilities influence where enforcement is best placed. If a platform team manages shared infrastructure, but app teams own service logic, it's often more maintainable to delegate coarse-grained rules to the infrastructure layer and keep fine-grained policies within the applications.

Taming authorization: RBAC, ABAC, and ReBAC

This chapter covers

- Comparing RBAC, ABAC, and ReBAC
- Identifying when a system needs more than roles to make access decisions
- Designing authorization layers that scale

You've locked the front door. Great! But now comes the real question: who gets to open the fridge?

Welcome to the wild world of authorization, the part of security that decides not just who you are but also what you're allowed to do. Most systems today aren't just one app or one database; they're a sprawling jungle of services, APIs, functions, dashboards, admin panels, and probably three forgotten Lambda functions you deployed last year and can't find now. Each of these services has to decide the following:

- Should I allow this request?
- Can this user see this document?
- Should I trust this service call?

Authorization models answer those questions. In this chapter, we walk through authorization models with real-world examples, explain where they shine and break, and look at how authorization plays out in monoliths, microservices, and clouds. We discuss how companies enforce who can do what, as well as the tools and patterns that keep the logic sane.

17.1 Core authorization models

Before we start throwing around tokens, graphs, and policy engines, let's ask a simple question: how do systems decide who's allowed to do what? This section explores the three main strategies used to answer that question (figure 17.1):

- *Role-based access control (RBAC)*—If you have the right badge, you get in.
- *Attribute-based access control (ABAC)*—You get in if your badge, department, and clearance match the rules.
- *Relationship-based access control (ReBAC)*—You get in if you know the right people.

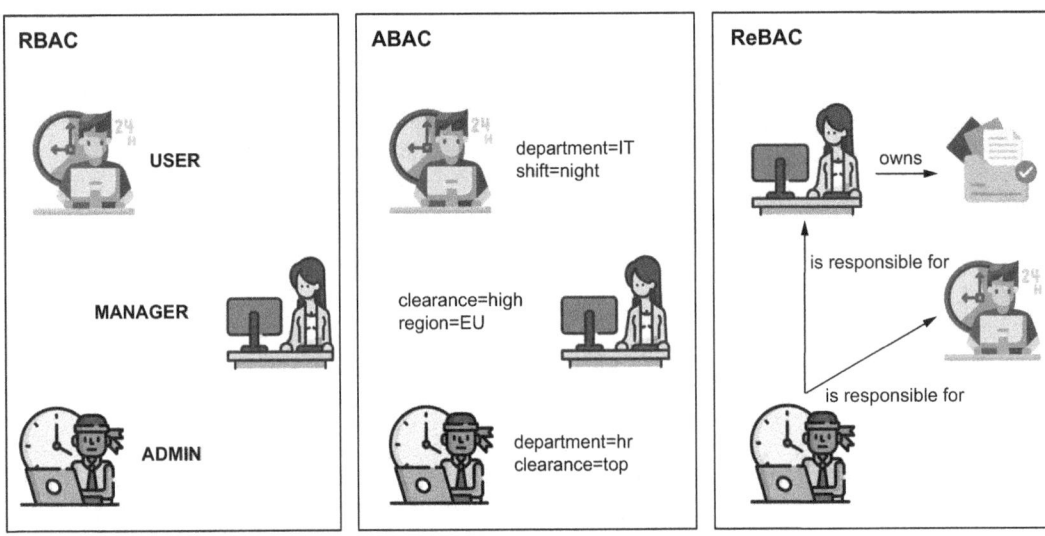

Figure 17.1   Comparing RBAC, ABAC, and ReBAC. RBAC grants access based on predefined roles such as user, manager, and administrator. ABAC adds flexibility by using user and resource attributes such as department, shift, and clearance level to make decisions. ReBAC focuses on relationships among entities, such as who owns a resource or who is responsible for whom, making it ideal for collaborative and delegated access scenarios.

Each model solves the same problem: *controlling access.* But each one does that in its own way. Understanding these models helps you choose the right tool for your system's complexity, growth stage, and security needs.

17.1.1 *RBAC*

RBAC is the simplest and by far the most common authorization model in use today. It works this way: every user is assigned one or more roles, and each role comes with a set of permissions. When someone tries to access a resource, the system asks, "Does this user have a role that allows this action?" If so, they're in; if not, they're denied access.

DEFINITION   A *role* (figure 17.2) is a named collection of permissions that represents a set of responsibilities or access rights within a system. Instead of assigning individual permissions to each user, you assign them a role, such as admin or editor. This role comes bundled with the actions the user or service is allowed to perform.

DEFINITION   A *permission* is a specific action or operation that a user or service is allowed to perform (e.g. "read report," "edit profile," or "delete invoice"). Permissions are the building blocks of access control, and roles are typically made up of multiple permissions.

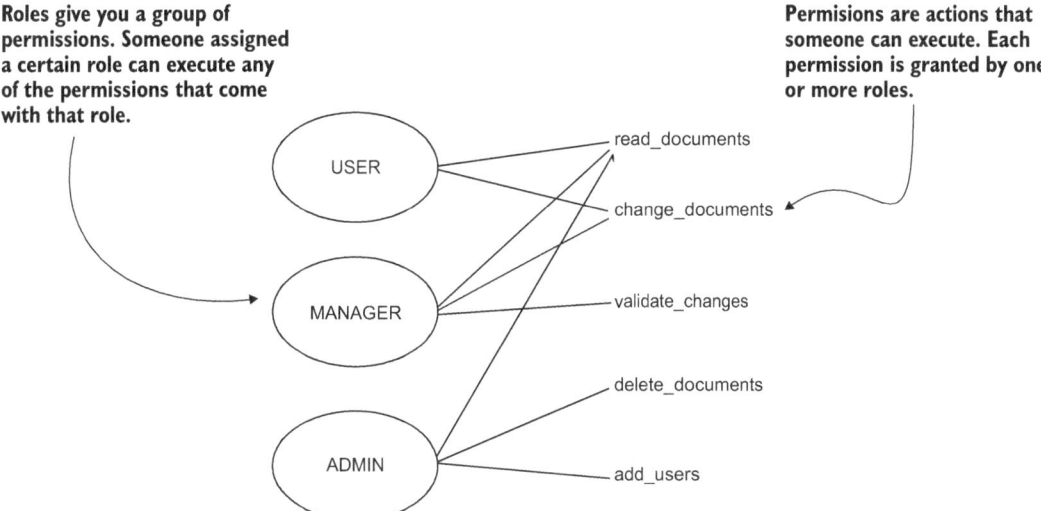

Roles give you a group of permissions. Someone assigned a certain role can execute any of the permissions that come with that role.

Permissions are actions that someone can execute. Each permission is granted by one or more roles.

USER

MANAGER

ADMIN

read_documents

change_documents

validate_changes

delete_documents

add_users

Figure 17.2   Roles and their associated permissions in RBAC. Each role represents a bundle of permissions. A user assigned to a role automatically inherits all the permissions granted by that role. This structure simplifies access control but can become difficult to manage as permission needs grow more specific.

Roles act like security badges for apps:

- If you're wearing an admin badge, you can go everywhere.
- If you're wearing a standard badge, you can look, but not touch.
- If you're an intern, you can go to the kitchen. Maybe.

Suppose that we're implement a human-resources system for ACME, Inc. The following employee roles employees are based on which actions employees are allowed to perform:

- *Employee*—Can view their own profile
- *Manager*—Can view and edit reports for their team
- *Admin*—Can access everything

In a token, the access rule might appear as a claim. The next snippet shows the JSON defining the body of a JSON Web Token (JWT):

```
{
  "sub": "alice",              ◁—┤ Username
  "roles": ["manager"]                    ◁—┤ Roles for authorization
}
```

RBAC is popular mainly because it's easy to understand. Most people have a basic sense of what a role is. In real life, we all have roles: teacher, manager, team lead, intern, and so on. Each role has a set of responsibilities. Systems work the same way: you assign someone a role, and that role tells the system what that person is allowed to do.

Another reason why RBAC is so widely used is that it's supported almost everywhere. Whether you're working in a web framework or a cloud platform or designing access in a spreadsheet, you'll find built-in support for roles.

Also, RBAC is fast and simple to implement. At the technical level, checking a role means comparing words such as admin and editor with a list. There's no need to build a complex rules engine or learn a new language.

The following listing shows a simple example of applying an authorization rule. Frameworks such as Spring Security make authorization straightforward by eliminating all the boilerplate code. A simple annotation of the method tells the framework who can call that method.

Listing 17.1   Applying an authorization rule on roles with Spring Security

```
@RestController
@RequestMapping("/admin")
public class AdminController {
                                              Only requests with the ADMIN role are
  @PreAuthorize("hasRole('ADMIN')")     ◁—┘  authorized to call this controller methods
  @GetMapping("/dashboard")
  public ResponseEntity<String> getAdminDashboard() {
    return ResponseEntity.ok("Welcome to the admin dashboard.");
  }
}
```

All this makes RBAC a great choice when you're starting to secure access to your application. You can make progress quickly and cover a lot of ground simply by assigning people roles that reflect what they're supposed to do.

Like most simple solutions, of course, RBAC struggles as your system and organization grow. At first, you may have two basic roles: user and admin. That's easy. But soon, someone asks, "Can we have an admin who can manage invoices but not users?"

You create a new role: invoice_admin. Then another request comes in: "What about someone who manages invoices and contracts but nothing else?"

Now you're adding invoice_contract_admin. The work doesn't stop there. This problem is called *role explosion.* You end up with so many roles that no one can track what all of them mean. Your system becomes harder to manage, and people start assigning roles to make things work without understanding what access they're giving.

DEFINITION   *Role explosion* occurs when a system accumulates too many narrowly defined roles in an attempt to cover increasingly specific access needs. Instead of reusing a few well-scoped roles, teams keep creating new ones, such as invoice_admin, contract_approver, and regional_editor_eu. Eventually, the list becomes impossible to manage, hard to audit, and subject to inconsistencies.

Even worse, RBAC isn't great when access decisions depend on context. You can't easily answer questions like these:

- Can this manager edit this specific employee's profile?
- Can this user see only data from their own region?

For more precise control, you need something more flexible: ABAC. RBAC can still take you far, however, if your roles are well designed and your team avoids creating new ones whenever someone has a slightly different job.

17.1.2   ABAC

ABAC takes authorization one step further by using attributes (figure 17.3) to make decisions. Instead of asking, "Does this user have the right role?", ABAC asks, "Do the attributes of the user, the resource, and the environment match the rules?"

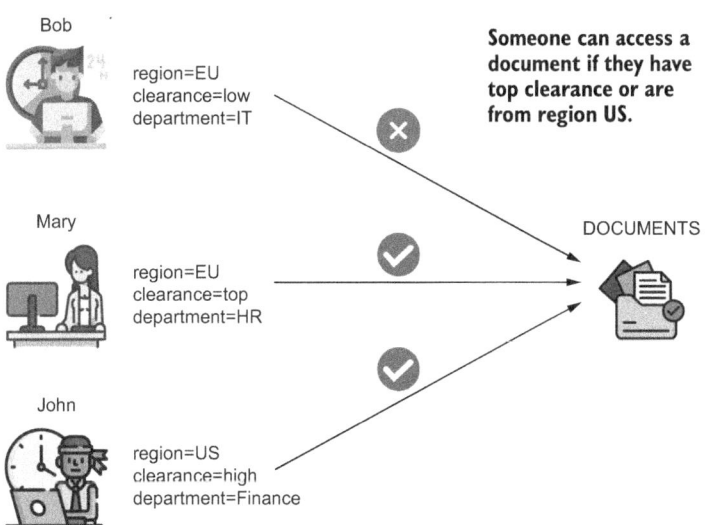

Bob

region=EU
clearance=low
department=IT

Someone can access a
document if they have
top clearance or are
from region US.

Mary

region=EU
clearance=top
department=HR

DOCUMENTS

John

region=US
clearance=high
department=Finance

Figure 17.3   ABAC rule based on multiple user attributes. In this example, access to documents is granted if a user has a clearance level of top or belongs to the US region. Mary meets the clearance requirement, and John meets the region condition, so both are granted access. Bob, who has neither top clearance nor US region, is denied. This figure illustrates how ABAC evaluates access dynamically based on attribute values rather than fixed roles.

DEFINITION   An *attribute* is a piece of information about a user, resource, or environment—perhaps the user's department, a document's owner, or the time of a request. Attributes are used to define and evaluate access rules in systems that support ABAC.

In plain terms, an attribute is information. A user might have attributes like `department =finance`, `clearance=high`, and `region=EU`. A resource, such as a document or invoice, might have attributes like `owner_id=1234`, `sensitivity=confidential`, and `created _at=2023-01-01`. The environment might include attributes such as the time of day, the requester's IP address, and whether the request is coming from a mobile device.

With ABAC, you create rules that say things like this: A user can access a report only if their department matches the report's department and their clearance level is high enough.

This makes ABAC much more flexible than RBAC. Instead of assigning access through predefined roles, you can describe the exact conditions under which access should be granted.

The biggest benefit of ABAC is its flexibility. You're no longer limited to predefined roles. You can create fine-grained rules that change depending on who the user is, what they're trying to access, and the situation that led to the request. It's especially powerful in environments such as the following, where access depends on real-time context or sensitive data boundaries:

- Users in the finance department can access invoices marked with `region=EU`.
- Operators with `clearanceLevel=HIGH` can download encrypted backups.
- Access is denied if the request is made outside working hours.

ABAC is also helpful for enforcing the least-privilege principle, a security principle that says users should have the minimum access they need and no more. With ABAC, it's easier to grant access only when the attributes truly match than to hand out broad roles just in case.

But the power of ABAC comes with a price: complexity. Writing attribute-based rules can get confusing, especially when you're dealing with many user types, resource types, and business scenarios. You may start with a few clear rules, but over time, the policy set can grow into a maze of conditions that no one wants to touch.

Also, attributes must be accurate and available. If your system relies on `user.region` but that value is missing or inconsistent, your policies may behave unpredictably or block access when they shouldn't.

NOTE   Attributes are only as useful as they are accurate and available. If your system relies on an attribute such as `user.region` but the value is missing, outdated, or inconsistent, access decisions can go wrong.

Because ABAC decisions are often based on live data, performance can become a concern. Evaluating a rule that compares 10 attributes may be slower than a simple role check. Still, ABAC is often the only reasonable choice for systems that need rich, context-aware decisions, especially in regulated industries or multitenant environments.

17.1.3 ReBAC

ReBAC makes access decisions based on relationships among entities such as people, resources, groups, and projects. Instead of checking a user's role or matching a set of attributes, ReBAC asks, "What is the relationship between this user and the thing they're trying to access?"

> **DEFINITION** An *entity* is any object in the system that can participate in access control—users, groups, documents, projects, teams, or any other resource you want to protect.

> **DEFINITION** A *relationship* is a connection between two entities that describes how they are linked, such as Alice is a member of Team X or Document Y is owned by Project Z. These relationships are used to decide whether access should be allowed.

This model works especially well when access depends on who owns what, who is part of what, or who has been granted access by someone else. Imagine a document-sharing app like Google Docs. A user shouldn't be able to access a document just because they're a viewer in general. They should be able to see it only if at least one of the following applies:

- They own the document.
- The document has been shared with them.
- They're part of a team that owns the document.

In ReBAC, relationships such as ownership, membership, and sharing are modeled explicitly. A policy might say any of the following:

- Allow access if the user has a viewer relationship to the document.
- Doctors can view medical records only for patients in their care.
- Employees can approve transactions only if they didn't initiate them.

ReBAC shines when access isn't determined by job titles or static rules but by how people and resources are connected, especially in systems with

- Collaborative features (e.g., shared files, boards, and tasks)
- Multitenant platforms (e.g., Software as a Service [SaaS] apps in which each customer sees only their own data)
- Organizational hierarchies (e.g., managers can access reports for their direct reports)

This model lets you support powerful use cases such as delegation (Alice can approve on Bob's behalf"), project-based access (everyone on Project X can see these dashboards), or dynamic sharing (only people I explicitly invited can see this).

Many modern systems already have these relationships in their databases but don't always use them for access control. ReBAC turns those connections into part of the security model. But ReBAC also has challenges:

- *It requires you to build and maintain a graph of relationships.* In many systems, you don't have this graph by default. You have to know who is connected to what and how those connections are structured and stored. That requirement could introduce extra complexity to your data model and access control logic.
- *Performance can be a concern.* Answering the question "Is user A related to resource B through some path?" often means querying a relationship graph or policy engine. This query can be slower than a simple role or attribute check, especially as your system grows.
- *Reasoning about access can be harder.* It's not always obvious why someone has access, especially when relationships are indirect or inherited (e.g., Alice is on a team that's part of a group that owns the folder).

Still, for systems that need fine-grained, context-aware access and especially those that allow users to share, collaborate, or delegate, ReBAC may be the best fit. Table 17.1 summarizes the essential characteristics of these models, which we've discussed throughout this section.

Table 17.1   A summary of the three models

	RBAC	ABAC	ReBAC
What access depends on	User's role	Attributes of user, resource, and environment	Relationships among entities
Typical use case	Small apps and admin panels	Regulated systems and dynamic conditions	Collaboration tools and multitenant systems
Risk as system grows	Role explosion	Attribute sprawl/policy complexity	Relationship- graph complexity
Performance	Fast (simple role checks)	Depends on attribute access and evaluation	May require graph traversal or relationship lookups

17.1.4   Exercises

1   What are the main differences among RBAC, ABAC, and ReBAC?
2   Why does RBAC struggle in large systems?
3   When would you choose ABAC over RBAC?

17.2   *Authorization in real-world architectures*

At ACME, things were simple at first. The app was a monolith, and the backend team added a quick check: only users with the admin role could access the settings page.

Then came the mobile app, the reporting service, and the microservices. Soon, authorization wasn't happening in only one place; it had to be enforced across five services, each written by a different team. Some services checked roles from the JWT; others pulled user info from the database. One service simply trusted what the previous service said.

One day, a user without the right permissions accessed confidential audit logs through a chain of three services, none of which rechecked the user's access. Nobody noticed until a customer filed a complaint.

After that, ACME's teams sat down to rework their authorization model. They had to decide where checks should live, how to share identity information across services, and how to log who accessed what. The work wasn't glamorous, but it turned out to be essential.

So far in this chapter, we've talked about authorization and the models you can use to decide who gets access to what. But in the real world, things aren't so neat. It's one thing to define access rules; it's another to figure out where those rules should live and how they should be enforced across a system that spans apps, APIs, cloud functions, and maybe a few mystery services running under someone's desk.

17.2.1 *Authorization within monoliths*

In a monolithic application, the business logic, data access, and user interactions typically live in the same codebase, often in the same process. That makes authorization relatively easy to manage: you usually have access to all the data and user context you need, and you can enforce rules where the action happens.

Monoliths support all three models: RBAC, ABAC, and ReBAC. Usually, they're easier to implement in monoliths than in distributed systems because everything is already in one place.

- RBAC is the most common starting point. Most frameworks (including Spring Security, Django, and ASP.NET) support simple role checks out of the box, making it easy to check `user.hasRole("ADMIN")` or use an annotation like `@Pre-Authorize("hasRole('MANAGER')")`.
- ABAC becomes useful when roles aren't enough, such as when you want to restrict access based on the user's department, region, or project. Because the monolith has access to both user and resource data, evaluating attributes is straightforward. You might load both the user and the invoice and then check whether `user.department == invoice.department`.
- ReBAC can also be implemented inside a monolith, especially if your domain already includes hierarchical relationships (users, teams, and projects). Because all your data is local, you can load the necessary relationships directly from the database and check things like whether the user is related to the document through a chain of ownership or membership.

In nonmodular monoliths, authorization logic often ends up scattered across controllers, services, or helper classes. This works at small scale but becomes a maintenance headache as the system grows. A developer might add a permission check in one place but forget it in another.

> **DEFINITION** A *nonmodular monolith* is a single codebase in which all application parts are tightly coupled, often sharing data structures, services, and logic without clear separation. Changes in one part of the system can easily affect others, and code tends to grow tangled over time.

You can do better with modular monoliths. If each module—such as Users, Invoices, Reports, and Teams—has clearly defined boundaries and owns its own data and business logic, you can localize authorization rules within the module that knows the context best. The Invoices module can contain all the rules about who can create, view, or approve invoices without needing to rely on other parts of the system. This improves encapsulation, meaning that each module becomes responsible for protecting its own domain objects and making the system easier to maintain and audit. It also avoids the trap of having one giant security service that tries to know everything about everything (the God Object antipattern). Instead, each module becomes the gatekeeper for its own resources, enforcing access rules based on the data and relationships it manages. It also makes testing easier: you can unit-test authorization rules as part of the module's normal logic without simulating the entire application state.

> **DEFINITION** A *modular monolith* is still a single application but is organized into well-defined, independent modules, each responsible for a specific domain or feature. These modules communicate through clean interfaces, making the system easier to maintain, test, and reason about even as it grows.

Best of all, this modular approach helps teams reason more clearly about access control. If someone asks, "Who can edit an invoice?", you know that the answer lies in the Invoices module, not scattered across controllers, utility classes, or some forgotten `SecurityUtils` file.

> **BEST PRACTICE** Avoid sprinkling authorization checks randomly across the code. Instead, centralize them inside clearly named methods or decorators that act as gatekeepers. Create a method like `canEditInvoice(user, invoice)` and use it consistently throughout your codebase.

One benefit of doing authorization in a monolith is that you can easily add logging, tracing, or even audit events every time an access decision is made. Because you're not dealing with cross-service communication, you can see and control the full flow of data and decisions.

> **TIP** Consider logging failed access attempts with enough detail to help troubleshoot without leaking sensitive information. This is often the first sign of a misconfigured role, expired session, or attempted attack. For details on the subject, you can find an extended discussion of logging in Java apps in *Troubleshooting Java, Second Edition*, by Laurențiu Spilcă (Manning, 2025).

17.2.2 Service-oriented authorization

As systems grow beyond a single codebase and evolve into service-oriented architectures (SOAs) or microservices, authorization becomes more complex and more important. Now, instead of a single application making decisions in one place, multiple services must decide independently whether a request should be allowed.

In these architectures, services often communicate over the network using REST, gRPC, messaging queues, or event streams. Each service might be developed by a different team, deployed independently, and scaled separately. That means you can't assume that a request reaching a service is safe just because it passed some check upstream. Every service has to take responsibility for its own authorization:

- *RBAC* often relies on roles embedded in tokens (e.g., in a JWT). Each service checks roles locally, but the logic can drift over time. One service might treat the manager role as powerful while another barely uses it. This leads to inconsistent access unless role semantics are well-defined and shared.
- *ABAC* works well when identity tokens carry rich claims (such as `department`, `region`, or `clearance_level`). Each service can evaluate these claims against the resources it owns. Again, everyone has to agree on the meaning of these attributes and where to source them.
- *ReBAC* in service-oriented systems usually means maintaining a central relationship store, such as a graph that services can query or defer to when making access decisions. You can do this by calling an authorization service (such as OpenFGA or a custom engine) or by embedding relationship data in the request context.

TIP When going distributed, always assume that your service is operating in an untrusted environment. A frontend or upstream service might say that the user doesn't have access, but you shouldn't necessarily believe it. Validate everything.

RBAC in service-oriented systems often relies on roles embedded directly in identity tokens, most commonly in a JWT issued by an authentication server. These tokens might include `"roles": ["user", "manager"]`, which each service uses to determine access:

```
{
  "sub": "1234",
  "name": "Alice Smith",
  "roles": ["admin", "manager"],        ⊲──┤ RBAC roles
}
```

At first, this seems straightforward. Each service reads the token, checks whether the user has the right role, and proceeds accordingly. But over time, role interpretation tends to drift. One service might consider the manager role to be someone who can view and edit team data; another service might treat it as a read-only role for summary reports. Still another might not recognize the manager role.

This drift happens because roles are only labels. Without a shared definition, such as a documented, agreed-upon meaning for each role, teams start making their own assumptions, leading to inconsistent access control across services. A user with the same token might be allowed to edit data in one place and denied access in another simply because each service interprets the role differently.

On a logistics platform, the dispatcher role was meant to allow viewing shipment routes. But one service also allowed dispatchers to cancel deliveries because the dev team assumed that it needed full control. The fact that one service also allowed dispatchers to cancel the service wasn't a bug; it was a misunderstanding of the role. To prevent this situation, do the following:

- Define role semantics centrally, and document them well.
- Encourage teams to refer to a shared access-control specification or contract.
- Avoid using role names alone as the source of truth for permissions. Tie roles to well-defined capabilities or scopes, or combine them with ABAC rules for extra precision.

ABAC works well in SOAs when identity tokens, such as JWTs, carry rich claims, such as `department`, `region`, `project_id`, or `clearance_level`. These attributes give services the context they need to make more fine-grained decisions than simply checking roles. A document service can allow access only if `user.department == document.department`, and a reporting API might allow users to fetch data only for the region they belong to.

Each service can evaluate these claims locally, using the attributes directly from the token, without making extra calls to a user directory or central service. This makes ABAC performant and scalable, especially when paired with caching or stateless authorization logic.

But as with RBAC, there's a catch: attribute definitions must be consistent across the system. If one service treats region as a country code (e.g., `FR`) and another as a continent (e.g., `Europe`), and a third expects it to be a data-center name, your access rules will break in unpredictable ways (figure 17.4).

There's also the question of where authorization data comes from and who's responsible for keeping it correct and consistent. This includes things like roles (e.g., admin or manager), attributes (e.g., `department=HR`, `region=EU`, or `clearance=high`), or relationships (e.g., Alice owns document X).

In many systems, this data is expected to come from identity provider (IdP) ls such as Keycloak, Auth0, Microsoft Azure Active Directory (AD), and Okta. These tools often support storing basic roles and user attributes and can include them in the tokens they issue (such as in a JWT). That works well when you need only a few fixed fields and the user's data doesn't change often. But IdPs don't always have all the context required for fine-grained authorization decisions.

Keycloak may know that someone is a manager, but it probably doesn't know which projects they're assigned to. It might include `department=HR` but not the fact that they're a reviewer for Document 42. It definitely doesn't track things like dynamic relationships among users and resources, such as which customers a sales representative currently handles.

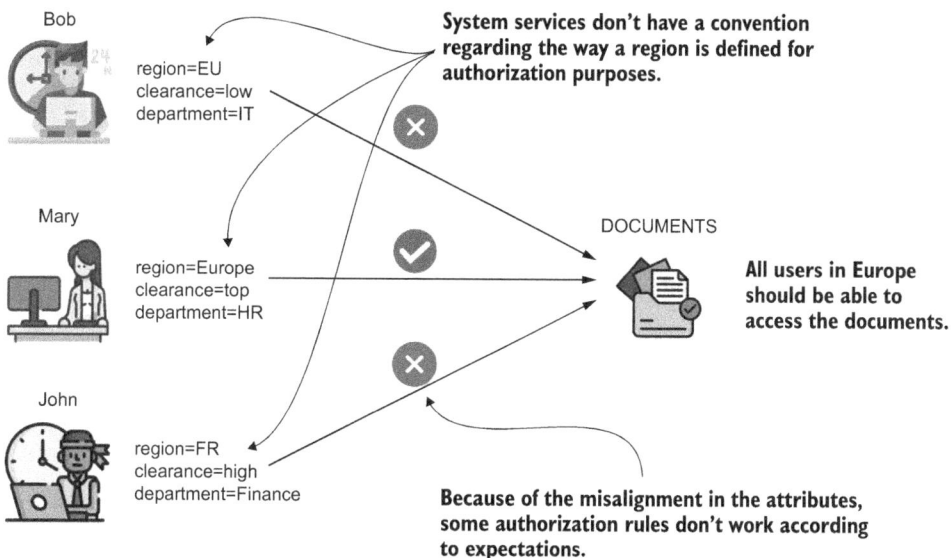

Figure 17.4 Attribute inconsistency leads to broken authorization. In this example, all users are meant to access documents if they're from Europe. But inconsistent attribute values such as EU, Europe, and FR cause authorization failures.

In more complex systems, this kind of dynamic or domain-specific data is managed elsewhere. Usually, it's managed in a dedicated user profile service, business domain system, or centralized authorization service. These systems can be queried in real time or can inject data into tokens when necessary.

Another common option is to use an API gateway or authentication middleware that enriches the request with additional claims or attributes by calling internal services. This can be useful for attaching context-specific claims ("ip_address", "geo_region", "locale", and so on) just in time, but it also adds complexity and coupling between components. Figure 17.5 shows these system components.

For simple systems, having the IdP (e.g., Keycloak) store and inject roles and a few core attributes is usually enough. For larger systems, especially those with multitenant setups, fine-grained access rules, or fast-changing data, it's better to split responsibilities. Let the IdP handle authentication and base-level identity, and use a dedicated service (such as OpenFGA, OPA, or a custom authorization API) to manage fine-grained permissions, attributes, and relationships. This separation keeps your tokens clean, your data sources reliable, and your security logic easier to test, change, and understand.

> **TIP** To make ABAC work in a distributed system, teams must agree on a shared attribute vocabulary: a list of well-defined, consistent attributes, their allowed values, and their sources. Treat this vocabulary like an API contract; access control remains predictable and secure if everyone uses it correctly.

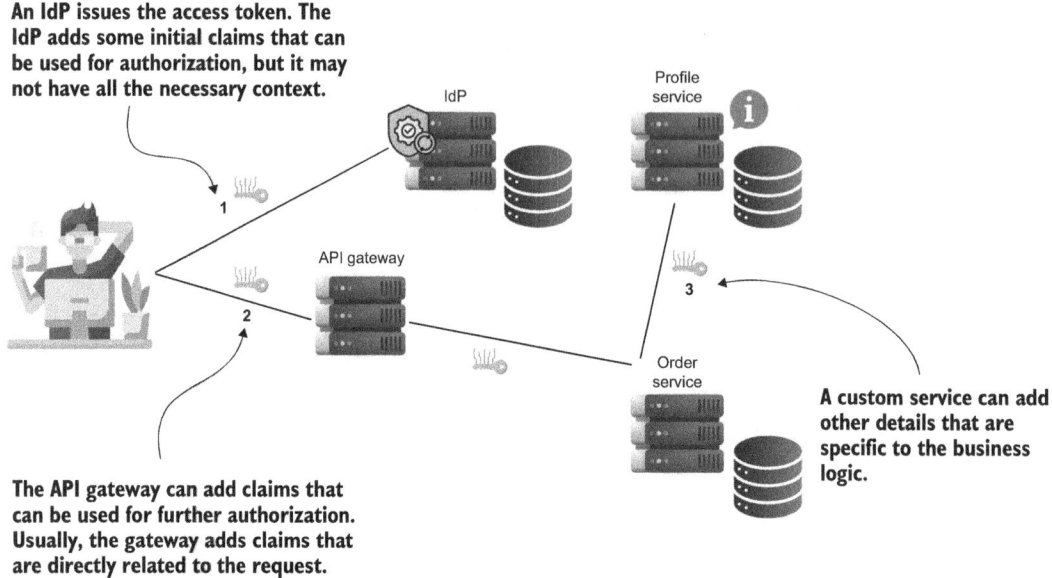

An IdP issues the access token. The IdP adds some initial claims that can be used for authorization, but it may not have all the necessary context.

The API gateway can add claims that can be used for further authorization. Usually, the gateway adds claims that are directly related to the request.

A custom service can add other details that are specific to the business logic.

Figure 17.5   Enriching authorization claims across system layers. The IdP issues a token with basic claims, such as roles or user ID. The API Gateway can enhance the token with request-specific claims, such as active project IDs or request origin. Finally, backend services (such as the order service) might fetch additional business-specific data, such as user preferences, access scope, and customer assignments, from a profile service or a custom authorization component. This layered enrichment ensures that services receive the right context to make fine-grained authorization decisions.

ReBAC in service-oriented systems usually requires a central relationship store (figure 17.6). This central store tracks how users, resources, and groups are connected. Think of it as a graph database in which nodes represent entities (users, teams, projects, and documents) and edges represent relationships (owns, member_of, or shared_with).

In a distributed setup, no single service can afford to know the entire relationship graph. Instead, services query this central store when they have to decide whether access should be allowed. A service might ask the following:

- Is user 123 a collaborator on document 456?
- Does this user belong to a team that owns this project?

This job isn't easy to implement, particularly in a microservices architecture. Implementing ReBAC in a microservices architecture can be tricky because each service owns a piece of the puzzle. The UserService knows who a user is, the TeamService knows who's on which team, and the DocumentService knows who owns each document. But access decisions in ReBAC often rely on relationships that span these services, such as whether Alice can view this document because she's part of a team that owns the project that owns the document. No single service alone has all the information required to answer that question.

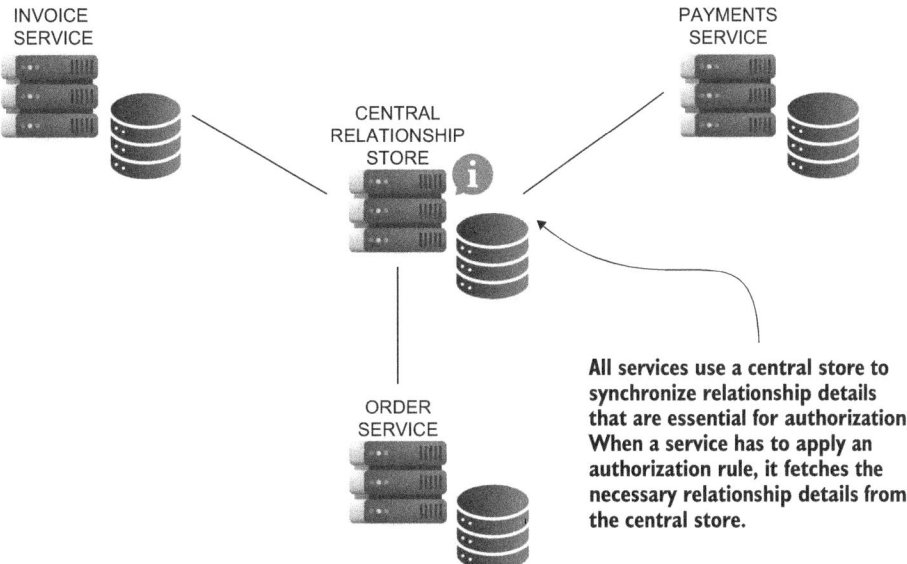

Figure 17.6 Using a central relationship store for ReBAC in a microservices architecture. Each service syncs its relationship data (such as ownerships, memberships, and associations) to a central relationship store. When a service needs to authorize a request, it queries the store to evaluate whether a valid relationship exists between the user and the resource in question.

To solve this problem, most real-world ReBAC implementations use a central relationship store—a dedicated service, often a graph database or specialized authorization engine, that keeps track of how users, resources, and groups are connected.

But the relationship store doesn't automatically know everything. Each microservice must push its own relationship data to this central store. The TeamService has to publish team memberships, the ProjectService has to report ownership, and so on. This adds complexity: if services forget to sync their data or if the data becomes stale or inconsistent, access checks may fail or behave incorrectly.

A good way to simplify such an implementation is to use a dedicated authorization service (such as OpenFGA [https://openfga.dev/], Authzed [https://authzed.com/], or a custom ReBAC engine) that evaluates the relationships and returns a yes or no (figure 17.7). The policy itself may be defined using a simple DSL (like OpenFGA's, presented in listing 17.2) or a graph-aware language.

Listing 17.2 The OpenFGA DSL

```
model
  schema 1.1

type user            ←──┘ Defines an
                          entity user

type organization        ←──┘ Defines an
                               entity oganization
```

```
relations
  define member: [user]
```

The organization
has users.

```
type document
  relations
    define owner: [user]
    define org: [organization]
```

Defines an entity document.
It has an owner of type user
and an organization.

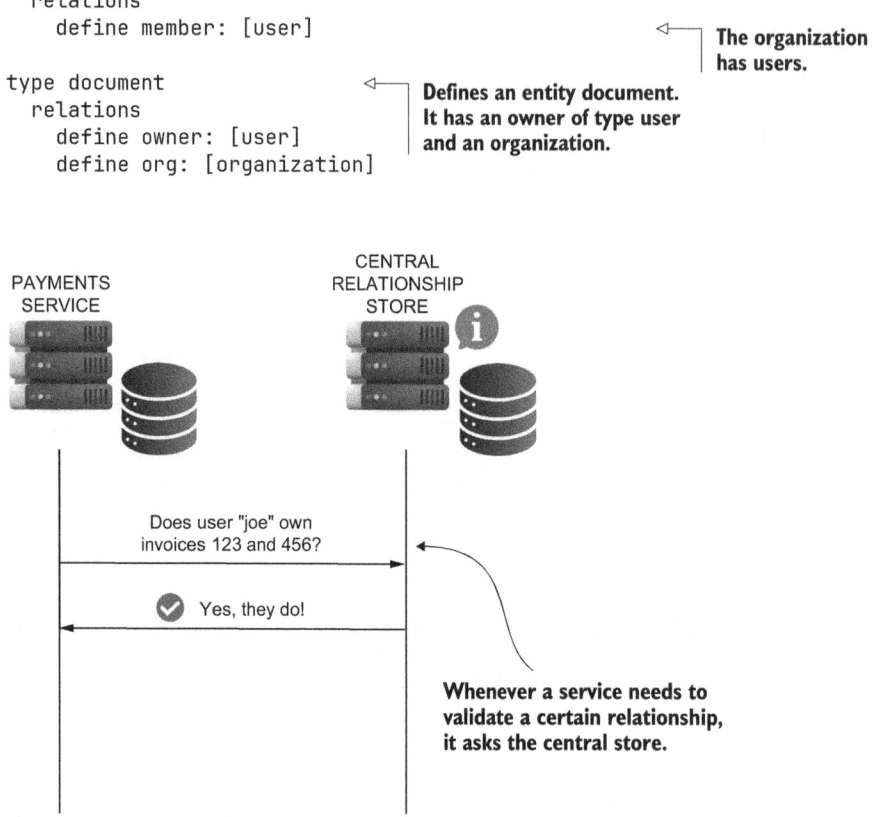

Figure 17.7   A service querying the central relationship store to evaluate access. In a ReBAC-enabled architecture, services don't store or compute relationship logic locally. Instead, when the payments service has to verify whether user "joe" owns specific invoices, it sends a query to the central relationship store. The store evaluates the relationship graph and returns the answer.

On the plus side, a centralized store makes authorization consistent, auditable, and easier to reason about. Any service can query the relationship store to ask, "Does user X have a relationship Y to resource Z?", without having to reimplement the logic or fetch data from multiple services. This keeps business logic out of microservices and in a centralized place where it's easier to manage. It also enables complex access patterns such as delegation, group-based access, and shared ownership.

But this approach isn't free of tradeoffs. The biggest downside is that it adds a dependency between your services and the ReBAC store. If this dependency goes down or becomes a bottleneck, access decisions across your system may be delayed or blocked (figure 17.8). You also must ensure that data synchronization is reliable and secure, ideally by using events or background jobs to keep the relationship store up to date. In addition, the ReBAC engine needs to scale independently, especially if many services are making access checks in parallel.

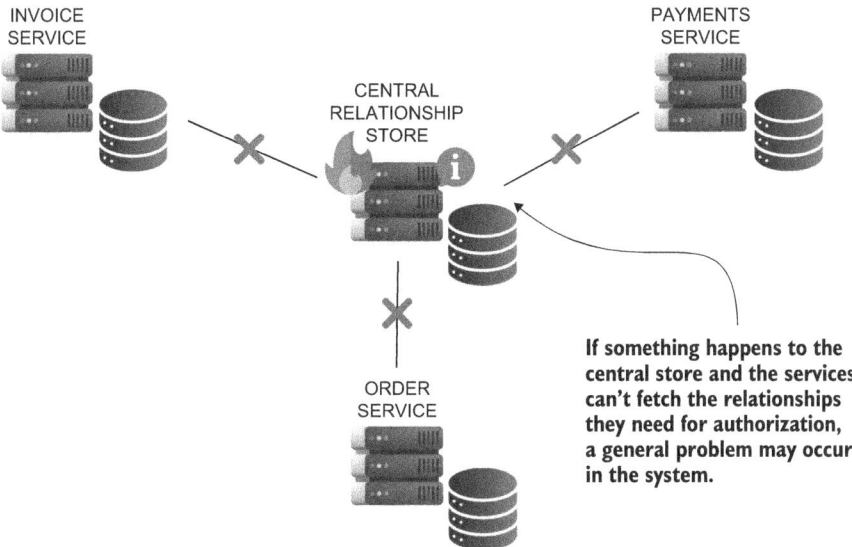

Figure 17.8   Central relationship store as a single point of failure. If the central relationship store becomes unavailable, services that rely on it for authorization can't validate user-resource relationships. This dependency introduces a potential single point of failure: even if business services are fully operational, access checks may fail, blocking critical functionality across the system. High-availability strategies or fallbacks are essential to mitigate this risk.

In some cases, systems embed relationship data directly in the request context. An upstream service might enrich a JWT with `project_ids` or `resource_links` the user is connected to. This works well for performance, but it comes with risks, especially if those relationships are stale, incomplete, or forged. When implementing ReBAC in a distributed system, one approach is to embed relationship data (such as `"projectIds": [42, 51]`) directly in the user's identity token (such as a JWT) or in the request context (see the next snippet). This means that the service doesn't have to look up relationships at runtime. The app checks what's already there.

```
{
  "sub": "user-123",
  "name": "Alice Johnson",
  "roles": ["user"],
  "project_ids": [42, 51, 88],         | Embedded relationships
  "teams": ["team-finance", "team-europe"],
  "exp": 1717603200
}
```

That approach can be fast because you're skipping database or graph lookups. But it introduces some real risks:

- *Stale relationships*—The relationships embedded in the token may no longer reflect the current reality. Alice was part of Project 42 yesterday, but she was removed today. If her token says that she belongs to Project 42, she can still access its resources until the token expires or is reissued.

- *Incomplete relationships*—The data in the token might be simplified or truncated to reduce token size or complexity. Maybe the system includes only a user's direct project memberships in the token, not the ones they inherited through team or organization relationships. As a result, some permissions may not be enforced correctly.

- *Forged relationships*—An attacker could forge or tamper with the data if a service blindly trusts the relationship data without validating the token signature or its source. A compromised frontend could send a fake token claiming that the user belongs to a high-privilege group, and if no signature verification happens, the backend could wrongly grant access.

Some of these risks may be acceptable in high-trust environments, but in general, on-demand queries to a trusted relationship store offer stronger guarantees.

> **TIP** Design your system so services that can easily ask whether the user is connected to this resource in a valid way without having to know the full graph. Delegate that logic to a central service, and treat it as part of your critical security infrastructure.

ReBAC provides powerful flexibility, especially in systems with sharing, delegation, or nested teams, but it also introduces architectural complexity. Getting it right means investing in a reliable, queryable source of truth for relationships and making sure that every service knows how to use it.

17.2.3 Exercises

4 Why is authorization easier in monoliths?

5 What's the benefit of using modular monoliths for access control?

6 Why should every service check access on its own?

7 What happens if services interpret roles or attributes differently?

8 Why do microservices use a central relationship store in ReBAC?

9 What's a big risk of using a central relationship store?

10 What's the problem with putting relationship data directly in tokens?

17.3 Exercise answers

1 What are the main differences among RBAC, ABAC, and ReBAC?

RBAC gives access based on a user's role, such as admin or editor. It's simple: if you have the role, you get access. ABAC goes further by checking user and resource details, such as department, region, or time of request, making it more flexible. ReBAC is about connections between entities. It looks at relationships such as "Alice is part of Project X" or "This file is shared with Bob" and uses them to decide access.

2 Why does RBAC struggle in large systems?

In large systems, you often need more precise control than basic roles can provide. Over time, teams start creating very specific roles, such as invoice_approver_eu or contract_editor_fr, to handle small differences in access. This leads to role explosion: too many roles, unclear naming, and a system that becomes hard to manage or audit. It becomes difficult to know who has what access and why.

3 When would you choose ABAC over RBAC?

You'd choose ABAC when access decisions depend on more than just a person's role. If a user should access a file only if they're from the same department or region, RBAC can't handle that situation easily. ABAC allows you to write rules like "user.department == document.department", making it ideal when you need more dynamic, context-aware decisions based on user or resource attributes.

4 Why is authorization easier in monoliths?

Authorization is easier in monoliths because all the parts of the system (like user info, business logic, and resources) live in the same codebase and usually the same process. You have all the data you need at your fingertips, and you can make access decisions without worrying about networking, consistency across services, and how to share identity data. It's much simpler than doing the same in a distributed system.

5 What's the benefit of modular monoliths for access control?

Modular monoliths simplify access control (RBAC/ABAC) by keeping all authorization logic in one deployable unit while separating concerns by module. This allows consistent policy enforcement, easier auditing, and shared context for identity and permissions without the complexity of distributed services.

6 Why should every service check access on its own?

In a microservices system, a request might pass through multiple services before it reaches the one that holds the resource. If each service trusts the ones before it to do the authorization, a mistake in one place could let unauthorized access through. That's why every service needs to validate access independently. It's the only way to ensure consistent, secure enforcement in a system where you can't fully trust upstream checks.

7 What happens if services interpret roles or attributes differently?

If services don't agree on what roles or attributes mean, they may apply different access rules for the same user. One service might treat the manager role as having full edit rights; another sees it as view-only. This inconsistency leads to confusion and security problems. Users may be overprivileged in one service and underprivileged in another. Shared definitions and standards are key to preventing this problem.

8 Why do microservices use a central relationship store in ReBAC?

In ReBAC, access decisions depend on relationships between users and resources, such as ownership, membership, and delegation. But in microservices, no single service has all that relationship data. Each service pushes its own piece (such as "Bob is a member of Team A") to a central relationship store. This store holds the full picture and lets services query it to make access decisions based on the complete relationship graph.

9 What's a big risk of using a central relationship store?

The biggest risk is that it becomes a single point of failure. If the relationship store goes down or slows down, services that depend on it can't make access decisions. Even if the rest of the app is healthy, you could end up blocking users from doing anything. To prevent this problem, you need high availability, caching, or fallback mechanisms.

10 What's the problem with putting relationship data directly in tokens?

Adding relationship data like project IDs to the token makes authorization faster, but it comes with dangers. That data might be outdated (if someone was removed from a project after the token was issued), incomplete (missing indirect relationships), or even forged (if the token isn't verified correctly). Although it improves speed, you trade accuracy and security unless you handle it carefully.

Summary

- RBAC assigns access based on roles, making it easy to implement and widely supported, but it can lead to role explosion in larger systems.
- ABAC adds flexibility by evaluating user, resource, and environment attributes, enabling context-aware decisions but requiring consistent attribute definitions and data quality.
- ReBAC uses relationships among entities to determine access, allowing fine-grained permissions in collaborative or multitenant systems but requiring a relationship graph or central store.
- Monoliths simplify authorization logic, making it easier to implement and test all three models locally. Authorization model implementation is even easier and more efficient when the monoliths are designed modularly.
- In distributed systems, all services must agree on what roles, attributes, and relationships mean. If they don't, access rules become inconsistent, and security gaps can appear.
- Service-oriented systems demand that each service enforce its own rules, making identity propagation and the consistent interpretation of roles and attributes essential.
- Cloud-native and serverless architectures offload part of the authorization logic to IAM policies, which combine app-level decisions with infrastructure-enforced rules.
- In distributed environments, consistency and trust are key.
- Choosing among RBAC, ABAC, and ReBAC depends on the system's complexity and access patterns. In many systems, a hybrid approach provides the best balance.

appendix
Installation and setup

You can run all the sample applications and their dependencies on your laptop. This appendix tells you what you need to set up your laptop/workstation to run all the examples as you read the book. This book assumes that you have access to a Windows, Linux, or macOS machine configured to run the following:

- Java 21 Development Kit
- Your favorite Java IDE capable of working with maven projects (such as IntelliJ IDEA or Eclipse IDE)

A.1 Setting up the Java development environment

The sample applications are plain Maven projects or are based on Spring Boot 3.x and Java 21 (with Maven as the build tool). Spring Boot is compatible with Java 8, but we chose to use Java 21 because it was a more recent long-term-supported release of Java at the time of writing.

A.1.1 Set up Java 21

The book samples have been tested with OpenJDK, distributed by the Adopt-OpenJDK project. You can download and install AdoptOpenJDK 21 at https://adoptium.net/. Other distributions of Java 21 should be 100% compatible with AdoptOpenJDK. Feel free to use them if you have them on your machine.

A.1.2 Set up the Java IDE

The sample projects use Apache Maven as the build system. You can compile the code and run it from the command line, or you can import it into your favorite IDE as a Maven project. The samples have been tested with Eclipse and IntelliJ IDEA. We recommend that you use the most recent stable release of Eclipse or IntelliJ IDEA to work with the code.

A.2   *Obtaining the code samples*

You can find the code samples for the book at https://mng.bz/7Q9x. There is a repository of samples for each chapter.

index